e computer industry

ucture, economics, perspectives

Gérard Dréan
gdrean@sfr,fr

About the English edition

This book is a case study in industrial economics, using the computing industry as a base. It attempts to use economic theory and management theory to explain and to some extent predict the evolution of industry structures, taking advantage of the spectacular changes that were taking place in the computer industry in the 90's.

It was originally written in French and published in printed form in 1996, based on research done in 1994/1995 and on the statistics available at that time. I immediately translated it into English, but the French publisher could not find an English-language counterpart. I therefore made it available on Scribd, where it was read and downloaded a respectable number of times, but in my view nowhere near the number of potentially interested readers in the English-speaking world.

Relative to the French version, the only substantial changes concern chapter 4 (The structure of the industry), which includes analysis of new figures that were not available at the time when the original version was completed, Incorporating those findings led to a restructuring of the chapter, and some extensions to chapter 5 (Structure and performance).

The French version is now out of print and the publisher has renounced the rights. New publishing techniques, including print on demand, now allow to make a book available in printed form with a minimal investment and at a moderate price. I have therefore decided to issue the English version as an independent publisher.

The world has changed since the book was written, most notably computers and the computing industry. There have been giant advances in microelectronics and in their applications to all walks of life. Many firms and products have disappeared, and many new have emerged. Many concepts and catch-phrases are now obsolete; new ones are now popular. The industry continues to change at a hectic pace. Also, the easily accessible industry statistics that I used have been discontinued. Updating the book to 2013 would involve a complete rewrite and extensive additional research.

But I happen to believe that the approach and concepts that I put forward in 1996 are still valid and worth publishing in their original state, as an exercise in combining economics and management theory and testing the applicability of the resulting approach to an actual case.

In implementing that approach, I quickly found that those theories, as I was able to understand them at the time, were lacking in explanatory power when applied to reality, which led me to suggest novel approaches and concepts extending the theoretical corpus.

Continuing my exploration of the available literature, I found new applicable references, most of them outside of the mainstream of economics and particularly in the so-called "Austrian" tradition, which offers a unique approach to the economics of production and a much higher degree of realism. Those insights proved to be useful complements to my original analysis, but I did not find anything which would have invalidated the analysis.

So I do believe that the concepts that I put forward in 1996 are still valid and worth publishing. At any rate, the factual part, i. e. the history and the industry statistics in the period 1950-1995, may still be of interest as far as it goes.

Concerning the analytical approach and the conclusions, I leave it to the reader to evaluate which are obsolete and which are still valid today. Concerning the predictions that I ventured at that time, it turns out that they did materialize to a large extent, which gives some credibility to the approach and tools that supported them. I certainly overestimated the impact of some factors and underestimated others, for instance the development of the PDA concept with the mobile phone, GPS and the like, or that of open source software and very high-speed communications. The most conspicuous absence is of course the Internet. But by and large, the structure of the industry has evolved as foreseen.

Be that as it may, I urge the reader to constantly keep in mind that the book was actually written in 1995, using data available at that time, relying on the technologies of the time and on whatever literature I was able to lay my hands on. In the context of this book, "today" must always be understood as "in 1995".

Finally, I have to apologize for the awkward English throughout this book, which would require been reviewed by a native English speaker

Table of contents

Introduction

The origins of this book. Myths and preconceived ideas. A model of industry. In search of laws. Structure of the book. Perspectives.

This book is intended for those with a need or a desire to understand how the computer industry operates, be they actors in that industry or users of its outputs, or simply wondering about its potential impacts on society and on daily life. I wish that it will also be read by people interested in the development and operation of industrial structures in general, hoping that they can find in my approach and in my propositions some useful elements for analyzing other fields of economic activity.

The main subject of this book is the analysis of those major forces and mechanisms which account for the evolution of the computer industry, in order to propose a guide for understanding the events that make the news, as well as a rational perspective of its evolution. The goal is to reveal the order hidden behind the current chaotic appearance. In the light of a few basic economic and technological phenomena, this book attempts to explain the current and forthcoming mutations in this industry, the foreseeable evolution of its products and its interactions with the rest of the economy.

This book is not another presentation of data-processing products and techniques. However, by analyzing supplier strategies and the dynamics which they obey, it sheds some light on the rationale used by suppliers when converting the potential of technologies into specific products. Through the constraints that it imposes and the opportunities that it presents, the industrial structure determines the offerings of the various players. Products and services available in the marketplace can be thought of as instruments of competition between productive firms, resulting at least as much from their motivations and preferences as from the supposedly impersonal effects of technology evolution or market demand.

In the same manner, this book does not address any questions related to the applications of information technology or its influence on economy or society at large. However, by helping to anticipate the evolution of computer products and services, it can provide useful perspectives on the evolution of their applications and more generally of their impact on other industries and on our environment.

This book also differs from most books in the field of economics. It does not attempt to establish new laws of a scientific nature for general application in a wide area, but it satisfies itself with using tools developed by other authors in order to understand the reality of a particular subset of the economy. However, it may claim some originality in attempting to use in a coordinated fashion disciplines which are usually considered as separate.

Compared to other books of industrial economics, its subject, namely one particular industry, is limited enough for theoretical considerations to remain always confronted with the experience of the business professional. At the same time, that subject is comprehensive enough to allow moving beyond a pure factual mono-graph and to support the beginnings of some conceptual developments. It is quite possible that the same approach and the same concepts could prove useful in the analysis of other complex industries, and perhaps could form a starting point for more general contributions to research into industry structures.

Some facts about enterprises

As is the case for all books, the starting point of this one is my personal experience, and more precisely three beliefs acquired during my professional life. The first one is that firms differ from each other not only by their output and their performance, but also by their motivations, their mode of operation and the alter-native courses of action available to them. Second, the conviction that any firm cannot be successful in any endeavor. Finally, the observation that the above two facts are not recognized by a vast majority of observers and commentators, although they contribute strongly to explaining the realities of industry.

In 1981, I left IBM, still at the height of its power, to take over executive responsibilities in a large computer services company. Although I fully expected to have to adjust to a different way of doing business, I was going be surprised by the magnitude and duration of the cultural shock. I was leaving a world structured by a highly sophisticated management system and a unifying company culture, where decisions were collectively thought over until they reached overriding acceptance, and where conflicts were explicitly articulated and resolved for the greater benefit of the enterprise. I had to enter a world of quick decisions, relying more on the intuition of managers than on any kind of staff work, since whatever limited staff existed was overloaded by daily housekeeping chores, and unavailable and ill-pre-pared for any significant prospective analysis.

Instead of a concert where each one played his or her specific part with con-fidence, but where the coherence of the whole was only visible from higher levels, I discovered companies where profit responsibility was delegated and claimed down to the lowest levels. In that fragmented structure, strategic decisions as well as oper-ational ones were largely decentralized, and management systems were relatively simple and informal. Different operating units would adopt distinctive behaviors and methods, giving rise to conflicts between different culture groups and to fre-quent disagreement at the executive level on matters of strategy, organization and management systems.

It took a little time and some humility to accept that such differences are not accidental deviations which need to be brought back in line rapidly, but reflect gen-uine and basic differences between activities of different natures. Attempting to suppress them by imposing a single set of values and systems, for instance those which had accounted for the success of the industry leader, would be not only an impossible task, but a destructive one as well. Success in different forms of activities demands different organizations, cultures, styles and management systems.

A couple of years later, those differences turned into critical issues when I had to restructure the business in response to market evolution. That confirmed one of my earlier experiences related to the unbundling of software and services. By sticking to its traditional culture and organization when tackling those markets, IBM was headed for failure, even though it was only perpetuating those methods which had made its success up to that point in time. Activities which are different enough to demand different organizational and management philosophies have a very hard time coexisting within the same enterprise.

Later again, I had to face related problems during negotiations with the French authorities on the opening of telecommunication services to third parties. At that time, France Télécom and some dour nationalists were convinced that IBM had a grand plan to dominate the world's communication networks, and therefore advocated a very restrictive policy, which happened to be contrary to the interests of service companies which I was representing. Now one could as well believe, as I did, that IBM's best interest was not to engage into a competition with the large public operators, and that it did not have the required capabilities anyhow. Either its management subscribed to that latter opinion and would stay away from large-scale communications services, or by following those who advocated an aggressive communications strategy, it would eventually fail and waste a lot of resources and energy. Whichever happened, restrictive measures were useless.

In the case just described, failure to understand the fundamental differences between sectors of activity caused each party to project its own motivations and intentions onto the others, for whom they could actually be irrelevant or even eccentric. Most people tend to believe that others share their goals and motivations, and that a firm which has succeeded in one area will automatically be able to succeed in any other area. In reality, the rules of the game and the success factors vary so much from sector of activity to sector of activity, that enterprises must behave very differently in order to succeed in the various areas.

The information industry is a heterogeneous one, where firms of different nature coexist and are governed by different systems of economic and competitive forces. It is a very fundamental mistake to regard the information industry as a homogeneous sector where the same criteria of success would be valid for all players. Nobody in his right mind would want to study the transportation industry as a whole, without separating the cab driver from General Motors or Air France, and assuming that all players have the same problems, the same objectives and the same criteria for success. By the same token, it is impossible to make any sensible and relevant statement about the computer industry without understanding its diversity and its structuring.

Myths and preconceived ideas

One consequence of the heterogeneity of industry is a mutual lack of understanding between players, which extends naturally to the industry watchers. The press frequently produces erroneous analysis and predictions, which are nevertheless copied and repeated, producing a body of "industry fiction" literature, which is most often rather far-fetched. At the root of those errors of judgment and hazardous forecasts lies a lack of understanding of the motivations of enterprises, and of the constraints imposed on them by the laws of economics and of competition.

Once upon a time, the information industry was a model of growth, profitability, commercial dynamism, management practices, etc.... One company called IBM dominated it with its market share, which oscillated between 50% and 70 % depending on the year, the methods of evaluation and the prejudice of the commentators.

Such domination, and the progressive invasion of society by information technologies, nurtured anxieties and predictions. It was accepted as a reasonable forecast that IBM would dominate the world if nothing was undertaken to prevent it from doing so, and that only national administrations had enough power to do that. According to augurs, IBM would exploit remote computing technologies in order to wrap the planet into a network which would displace both the computer centers of enterprises and the major telecommunications operators, and thus establish IBM's domination over the entire world. That vision supported the prediction of an upcoming «battle of the giants» between IBM and AT&T, and called for states and telecommunications operators to engage into a full-scale crusade. The favorite myth in the industry-fiction literature was that of Big Brother.

Everybody knows what happened to the dominance of IBM and to the computing energy distribution services. The rise of minicomputers and later of microcomputers enabled users to acquire their own computers instead of resorting to shared resources, and has resulted in eliminating "computing energy distribution" from the market between 1975 and 1983. IBM posted impressive losses in 1991, 1992 and 1993, is continuing to cut down on staff, and now accounts for little more than 30% of the information industry market. The great battle between IBM and AT&T did not happen, and nobody expects it any more.

Today, the information industry is in a crisis. Firms which once were the most prosperous are now going through gloomy times, while newcomers such as Intel or Microsoft display an impressive health. A world of clear competition has given way to an entanglement of alliances, where cooperation and competition coexist between the same enterprises, and where one can no longer tell the friend from the foe. Innovation and the creation of standards have escaped the large equipment manufacturers, who seem to be fighting rearguard battles rather than contributing to progress. The current genre of industry-fiction is now disaster scenarios.

But myths are hard to kill. Although the time-sharing market vanished in the seventies without any hope of return, many were still predicting its birth in the late eighties under the name of "Value Added Services", with an enthusiasm typical of neophytes. That particular myth survives until our days in the form of the announced impending marriage between data-processing and telecommunications, even though teleprocessing has been in existence for over 35 years, and telecommunications are lagging a little more each year behind the performance of computing systems.

Those ideas which are most in fashion today rest on a hardly more valid base than the myths of the seventies and of the eighties. People moan over the poor shape of the computer industry, forgetting that it gives birth to an avalanche of increasingly effective products at plummeting prices, which is the best sign of an exemplary strength. Some announce the collapse of the equipment business, although it accounts for almost two-thirds of the total market and always exhibits sufficient growth to attract new entrants. Some declare that "in order to be profitable, firms must subcontract manufacturing", but to whom if everybody implements that same strategy? Some predict that the only way for manufacturers to survive will be to provide services instead of products, arguing that "services alone are profitable". Even ignoring the fact that there is no factual evidence to support the latter statement, what equipment would then services relate to?

In their quest for answers, most commentators continue to rely solely upon technology considerations and satisfy themselves with conventional wisdom, preconceived ideas or oversimplified sketches when it comes to economic mechanics and business dynamics. But for anything to happen in the business world, it is not sufficient that technology makes it possible. Some player in the industry must find his own interest in making that event happen and must have the capability to do so. Evolution of the industry is not an abstract process, but a consequence of the undertakings of actual suppliers attempting to exploit the potential of technology in the pursuit of their business objectives.

The approach used in this book

The primary ambition of the present book is to contribute to a better understanding of the information industry, by looking at it in the light of those laws which govern all enterprises.

Many industry watchers and commentators are trying to achieve that same goal by extrapolating the major trends that can identified from an overall bird's eye view of the industry. Past predictions based on that approach have repeatedly been proven wrong, and therefore I believe that it is mandatory to dig below the surface in order to understand the essential driving forces of the industry and to take apart its inner mechanisms.

In doing that, it is essential to recognize the heterogeneity and complexity of the information industry. It produces a large array of products and services of various natures, and makes room for a large variety of suppliers offering them in different selections or combinations. Every single product or service involves a certain type of production process, which in turn determines the specific economics of producing and marketing it. Conversely, every product and service is offered by a number of different firms, which compete against each other in an arena defined as the marketplace for that item. In each of those sectors, the combination of market structure and production economics result in a specific form of competitive rivalry, and therefore in a specific set of rules of the game and success factors.

The industry can thus be segmented into a number of sectors obeying different sets of economical and competitive rules, resulting in different structural configurations in each sector, for instance in terms of market share and profitability. These differences call for different types of strategy and competitive behavior according to the applicable rules of the game in each sector.

The specific nature of a firm's output not only dictates the form and the economics of its production machinery, but it also has a profound influence on the organization and culture of the entire enterprise, which can be called its personality. The nature of a firm's output is closely related to some of its fundamental characteristics, in the same way as the anatomy, the physiology and even the psychology of a sports champion relate to the discipline which he or she practices. A weight lifter is not built like a marathon runner, and a marathon champion will most probably not be very brilliant at weight lifting. He will even decline at marathon if he does starts training for weight lifting. Winning weapons and strategies in one arena are not necessarily winners and can even be losers in other areas. The exact same practices which account for the success of such and such equipment manufacturer can lead a services company to failure, and vice versa.

The enterprises involved are not always aware of that tight relationship between their offerings and their personality, but competition is there to sort out those who do understand that reality from those who don't. In each sector, successful firms emerge as those with a structure and a culture better adapted to the specific requirements of the sector. An industry sector is characterized not only by the nature of its products, but also by a certain type of enterprise and a certain form of the rules of the competitive game.

For each firm, the possibility of succeeding in a new sector is conditioned by its existing structure and culture. Any attempt to enter an area of production too remote from the present personality will most often result in both a failure in the new area and a regress in the traditional area. Each acquired specialization thus tends to perpetuate itself, and consequently the organization of the industry into sectors, which are as many different arenas where different players play different games using different weapons and different strategies.

Yet products and services from different sectors must eventually be assembled into systems, either at the next level of production or at the user site. All sectors interact in some way, and their borderlines are subject to permanent challenge. Although most players in the information industry operate in very few sectors, some are active in many, either by strategic choice or by historical tradition. It is important to examine how events taking place in one arena are affected by what happens in others, how a player must organize in order to play in several arenas and what are the odds for success.

Observation of the industry from inside thus leads to propose a pragmatic model which resembles by many aspects that of natural evolution in biology. Enterprises, which are different from each other and offer different combinations of products and services, are competing in the market. To succeed, they adopt specific

behaviors which translate in particular into their offerings, and which are determined by factors specific to each firm (its personality). The market reacts to those
behaviors, and those reactions determine the evolution of each firm, its place in
industry and its future behavior.

In search of the laws of industry

At this pragmatic stage of my reflection, I had to turn to theory in order to
validate the above model and to complement it by specifying the laws applicable to
market operations, to the mechanisms of industry structuring and of decision-making in the enterprise, etc.... This analysis would hopefully form a solid basis for
understanding the behavior of industrial actors, as dictated by their roles, their
interests and their constraints, and finally for proposing a coherent and rational
view of the industry and of the computing offerings, as well as of their evolution.

This work had no theoretical ambition. Starting with an industry about which
I notice a lot of incomprehension and interrogations, its purpose was simply to take
apart and explain its mechanisms with the help of available conceptual tools. My
objective was not to establish new economic laws, but to search existing theories for
elements that would provide some explanation to what can be observed in reality.

Three main considerations have guided my exploration of the literature. First,
the central subject of this book, which is the behavior of enterprises. This behavior
has two sides: upstream, it results from internal decisions made in the enterprise,
the study of which relates to the theory of organizations and decision-making;
downstream, it sets off interactions with the market, the study of which relates to
microeconomics. In other words, the conceptual bases called for by the present
book straddle economics and organizational theory.

Aside from providing the major concepts and fundamental economic mechanisms used in our analysis, classical and neoclassical economics are of little help
here, since their basic paradigms—perfect competition and the general equilibrium
—ignore the very notions of enterprise, product differentiation and competition.
Only around 1975 did the new discipline called industrial economics focus on
studying the productive system and the strategies of its components. Up to this
point in time, that area of research has produced a significant number of contributions addressing many specific points, but very few genuine works of synthesis
which could qualify as a general theory of industrial structures. Even those few
books of synthesis acknowledge significant gaps, some of which relate to features
which can be considered as major specific features of the computer industry.

On the other side, the literature on organizations and decision-making most
often stops at the border of the enterprise and seldom tackles the reciprocal influence between internal choices and the working of the market. More generally, the
separation of those two disciplines is an essential weakness when considering the
subject of this book. Economic theory uses too schematic a view of the firm, and
organizational theory has too little concern for the market environment.

A second orientation criterion in exploring the literature relates to my basic
assumption that enterprises are different from each other and obey differentiated

models of behavior. When trying to explain those differences, there is obviously little to expect from theories which rely precisely on the opposite assumption. An important part of industrial economics considers enterprises as "black boxes" which conform to one stylized model of behavior identical for all, for example profit maximization. Similarly, most books on organization consider more or less implicitly than the rules of organization do not depend on the activity of the firm. One had to wait for the "contingency" theories introduced in 1950 and synthesized for the first time by Lawrence and Lorsch (1968) to recognize that "the required type of organization varies with the nature of goods or services provided, the means used and the economic environment at a given point in time".

The third selection criterion relates to my personal experience, which is that of an actor in the business and not that of a scholar. Among those theoretical developments which purport to describe decision-making in the enterprise, a large number (if not most...) do not resemble even remotely the manner in which such decisions are actually taken. In particular, I have never seen mathematical formalization and reasoning used in real world management decisions. I do not believe it reasonable to believe that business managers would unconsciously perform reasonings of a mathematical nature, in the same way that planets move on elliptic paths without knowing what an ellipse is. On the contrary, I tend to believe that any description of decision-making in the enterprise that demands this type of formalism has probably little relation with reality, if any.

Some may deem convenient to represent in mathematical form behaviors where mathematics play no part, but such convenience only holds for a small community of economists and certainly not for the majority of the public intended for the present book. In addition, mathematical formalization is only possible at the expense of assumptions which introduce gaps between reality and its representation. Worse still in my view, one thus disguises under an appearance of rigor and accuracy an area dominated in reality by uncertainty, approximation, intuition and gut reactions. Resorting to mathematical formalism when describing the behavior of decision makers in an enterprise is useless at best, misleading at worst.

I have therefore resolved to use the density of mathematics in a contribution as a (negative...) indicator of its relevance to the present work, and to consider as prohibitive the appearance of any symbol other than the four operations of arithmetic. Of course, I have abided by the same discipline in my own writing, which makes the present book totally exempt of mathematics.

In total, those successive filters have let surprisingly few conceptual contributions pass through as applicable to my purpose, and have of course favored rather recent and pragmatic works, and presented in literary form. Therefore, while taking advantage of certain contributions from economic theory, I have made significant use of Michael Porter's work on competitive strategies in order to specify the forms and outcomes of inter-firm competition. Similarly, my analysis of the behavior of enterprises in strongly indebted to the works of Lawrence and Lorsch on organizations, and more generally to the behavioral concepts introduced by March and Simon.

Unfortunately, my exploration of the theoretical literature has not always resulted in discovering a satisfactory explanation for every phenomenon observed in reality. It has been necessary therefore to exceed somehow my initial objective and to take the risk of suggesting novel conceptual approaches where appropriate.

Structure of the book

This book is organized in four parts,

In part one, we will carry out a preliminary survey of the terrain which we want to cover, by devoting the first three chapters to the past evolution of the structure and practices in the computer industry. We will see how the market has segmented and how the different games and their particular rules have developed. Then in Chapter 4 we will examine the actual structure of the industry at the beginning of the nineties, and in Chapter 5 the recent performance of enterprises.

Those observations, like all discussions that follow, look at the information industry on a global planetary scale, deliberately ignoring possible differences between countries or groups of countries. The vast majority of enterprises which make up the industry do indeed operate at the global level, and national borderlines do not really define separate markets. By the same token, national industrial policies implemented by some countries are regarded here as happenings of secondary importance, which should not obscure the more fundamental economic mechanisms.

The information industry appears as populated on one hand by a few general-purpose enterprises offering a wide range of products and services, and on the other hand by a multitude of specialist companies. We will begin by analyzing the functioning of the latter category, distributing them for the sake of convenience into four categories: components, equipment, software packages and services.

Part two combines an introduction to the key concepts and tools used for industry analysis with a study of the hardware-related sectors. Using the actual cases provided by the first two sectors to introduce the basic concepts of this book makes it possible to keep to a minimum the preliminary conceptual refreshers which might otherwise be tedious.

Chapter 6 is mostly concerned with economics. It summarizes the main mechanisms of competition and of the formation of sector structures, applying them to the four major areas identified earlier. The sector of electronic components (Chapter 7) will serve as the archetype of a concentrated sector and provide the base for describing the mechanics of monopolistic competition, which tends to result in coexistence between a small handful of suppliers with very unequal market shares. The equipment sector (Chapter 8) will serve as the model of a fragmented sector dominated by a niche-based competition, making room for many diversified strategies, and resulting in the coexistence of a large number of suppliers of similar size. Together with those basic concepts, we will introduce the specific dynamics and perspectives of each sector.

Chapter 9 complements that analysis by discussing the differences in organization, management systems and corporate cultures associated with the various
forms of production economics and competitive dynamics.

In part three, the concepts of concentration and fragmentation, and of enterprise differentiation, are applied to the analysis of software and services.

It will first be necessary to clarify what exactly is covered under the categories
of "software" and "services", which are too often lumped together into a so-called
sector of "immaterial" offerings. As we will see in Chapter 10, software includes a
wide array of activities ranging from packaged software to custom development
services, and the economics of producing software packages are in every respect
much more similar to that of industrial products than to most services. Bundling
software packages together with services into one single sector called "software and
services" makes no more sense than would the study of a sub-sector of the transportation industry including "fuels and taxis".

The packaged software industry will be the subject of Chapter 11. Using the
concepts of concentration and fragmentation introduced in chapters 6 to 9, we will
show that this industry can be analyzed as a complex of sub-sectors of a more or
less concentrated nature, each one subject to its own competitive dynamics, and at
the same time interacting with the other sub-sectors. We will address separately in
Chapter 12 the specific case of operating systems, including a discussion of the
economics of standardization and the place of the UNIX system.

In Chapter 13, we will analyze services, which are generally discussed as a
homogeneous sector, but actually form a complex of largely unrelated sectors
obeying diverse sets of economic rules. In those sectors, differences in the rules of
the game imply different supplier behaviors depending on the actual nature of services offered. Moreover, suppliers must adjust continually to a changing demand,
facing tough issues in an activity where sensitivity to individual motivations and corporate culture is unusually high.

The final part of this book brings together the conclusions of the previous
chapters into an overall picture of the industry.

Chapter 14 summarizes the trends identified in the four areas analyzed above,
ans describes their effects on the entire industry. Forces driving the explosion of
the information industry into specialist sectors are described, together with the perspective of the structure of the PC world overtaking the whole data-processing
industry, as well as the critical problems which that explosion creates for generalist
firms.

In Chapter 15, we review the opposite forces which can operate towards
restructuring of the industry on a new basis. It addresses the problems facing the
users as result of the explosion of the industry, the ways in which Data Processing
Managers may cope and how the supply side can organize to address those issues.
Integration services will appear as playing a critical role, which will lead us to consider the idea that products might vanish behind services. We will also discuss how
players mitigate their specialization by weaving alliances of various kinds. We will

assess the industrial significance of such alliances and their likely impact on indus-trial structures.

Finally, we will sketch in Chapter 16 an overall scenario for the evolution of the information industry, looking in particular at the interaction between the infor-mation industry and other industries including telecommunications. How is each sector affected by its increasing proximity to activities thus far unrelated to data processing? What is the place of the data processing industry in the information industries? How is the structure of other industries changed by the invasion of computer technology? Can we derive from economic theory longer-term perspec-tives for the data-processing industry?

When closing this book, I wish that the reader has gained a better under-standing of the hidden mechanisms which command the evolution of the com-puter industry, and can better interpret an avalanche of news and events often hard to decode. May that improved understanding assist him not only in satisfying a legitimate curiosity, but also to better assume his professional responsibilities as a data processing executive or user, as an executive with one of the many players in the industry, or as a commentator, a teacher, a policymaker or any other opinion leader.

I also hope that, even with its embryonic contributions, this book may enjoy the attention of a part of the economic research community, and may contribute to the advancement of knowledge even outside of the information industry which was its origin and its testing ground.

Part one - Facts and figures

*Let us make quite sure of the facts before worrying about the
cause.*
Fontenelle

The future states of the computer industry will result from the effect of natural forces starting from its current state, which can itself be explained by the past
effects of those same forces. A historical examination of the evolution of the different products and services that constitute data-processing, of their modes of supply by the various players in the industry, of the postures and strategies of the different suppliers, will enable us to identify the major currents which run through the
industry. Many books begin by stating and developing theories, and then attempt to
seek out cases where those theories might be applicable. On the contrary, we will
take care to delineate the facts before searching for theories that might explain
them. In short, we want to survey the ground thoroughly before we start digging.

We will divide the forty-plus years of history of the computer industry into
three chapters covering respectively its birth (1951-1968), the teenage crises (1968-
1980) and the emergence of a different data-processing industry (1975-1993), That
breakdown is related to the central subject of this book, the structure of the industry itself. Indeed, in years 1969 to 1975, a series of events have challenged the existing structure, and their developments have had repercussions up to the beginning
of the eighties. The end of that period saw the emergence of the microcomputer
industry, which differs from traditional data-processing at least as much by its original structure as by the technologies it uses.

In this historical overview, we will often mention IBM. Not doing so would
be surprising, since that company alone accounted for about two-thirds of the
entire computer industry until 1985 at least. But that dominance means much more
than just market share. Throughout that period, its actions have had an effect on
the entire industry, and the actions of other players have been to a large extent
decided upon with respect to IBM. In that sense, IBM has been, more than a competitor, an essential element of the environment of the other players.

It also turns out that IBM has traditionally been a very rational player, spending a lot of effort in systematically organized strategic thinking. That reflection is
not carried out exclusively by some specialized departments, but involves the totality of management as well as groups of operational experts. Thereby, it relies not
only on thorough studies, but also on the large variety of trends and opinions constantly present in the company, which is by its sheer size a form of microcosm.
Contrary to an oversimplifying image, IBM has always been a breeding ground for

change and change-makers, which has been kept alive by management more or less willingly. On many occasions, it has demonstrated its capability to give a chance to mavericks and to take the initiative of major changes.

Even if the objective of many decisions was only to resolve internal problems, as we will see, those same decisions have affected all sectors of the industry because of IBM's dominant position. The announcement of System/360 in 1964, the unbundling decision in 1969/70, the announcement of the Personal Computer in 1981 or, conversely, the demise of the Future Systems project in 1975 have thus become historical landmarks for the entire industry. The following abbreviated historical summary will accordingly be structured around those events.

Chapter 1 - Birth of the industry (1951-1968)

Unit-record begets data-processing. "Free" software and services. Prices, profits, progress
«battle of the giants» between IBM and AT&T, and called for states and
telecommunications operators to engage into a full-scale crusade. and proliferation.
The IBM/360, a forerunner of open systems. Technological limits and integration. Standards
and the fragmentation of hardware. Boxes or systems? A concentrated sector.

The beginnings (1951-1963)

As an industry, data-processing was born in 1951 when the Univac 1 was introduced on the market by the Remington-Rand Corporation. Before that date, there existed on one hand a unit-record machine industry, and on the other hand experiments in the implementation of stored program calculators, which were going to give birth to computers but were not the subject of an industrial activity properly speaking[1].

Unit-record equipment relied on the utilization of punched cards and included different specialized machines, mostly mechanical although some had made use of electronic devices starting in 1946. Those machines were marketed by a few manufacturers, among which IBM, Remington Rand, Burroughs and NCR in the USA, Bull or ICT in Europe.

During and after World War II, several experimental calculators were built by Universities or research centers. As part of those developments, the idea of the stored program emerged and electronic technology became the foundation of data-processing. If one accepts that the distinctive characteristic of a computer, compared to a simple calculator, is to be controlled by a program stored in memory, the first implementation of a real computer dates from 1948, with the SSEC built by IBM.

It should come as no surprise that the IBM and Remington Rand companies, which participated in those pioneering developments, were also the first to perceive the commercial potential of that new technology. Remington Rand introduced its Univac computer on the market in 1951. IBM followed, after much hesitation[2], with

---

1   For a good coverage of the period from the origins to year 1963, see René Moreau "Ainsi naquit l'informatique" (Dunod - 1981)

2   For a detailed history of the development of the first IBM computers, see the excellent book by Charles Bashe, Lyle Johnson, John Palmer and Emerson Pugh, "IBM'S Early Computers" (The MIT Press, 1986). This book offers a fascinating account of the marketing and technological tradeoffs, as well as conflicts of opinion and personal and

the 701 in 1952, the 702 and 650 in 1953. Those two companies were rapidly imitated by other punched cards equipment manufacturers, and soon all unit-record
equipment manufacturers (Burroughs and NCR in the USA, Bull in France and
ICT in the United Kingdom) had started a computer department. Very rapidly,
those firms were joined by large electricity or electronics companies such as General Electric, RCA, Honeywell, Westinghouse or Bendix. Later on, new firms were
created, which started in the computer field by specializing on particular markets,
like Control Data in 1957 or Digital Equipment in 1962.

Early business practices

At the outset, data-processing was therefore a secondary activity of unit-
record firms and large electronics companies. Business practices that accompanied
market introduction of the first computers were naturally those of unit-record: the
manufacturer provided the hardware, and the user had total responsibility for
implementation, with more or less significant assistance from the manufacturer.

The operations of unit-record equipment were manual and relied on implementing a specific procedure for each application. Defining those procedures was
the responsibility of users, but was generally supported by a significant amount of
assistance provided by the manufacturer at no additional charge. That approach carried over to computers, but for the latter the assistance of manufacturers was all the
more important because the technique was new. To meet that diversified and growing demand, IBM structured its customer assistance activities by creating the systems engineering organization in 1962.

On the contrary, the software offering was initially almost non-existent. The
very first computers of IBM and Remington Rand were provided "bare". According to the scientific tradition, which had presided over their development, users
developed the required software and exchanged it among themselves, ranging from
assemblers and mathematical routines up to the most complex pieces of code. The
only original contribution from IBM before 1960 is the Fortran language and associated compilers, which come with scientific computers since 1957. Faced with a
growing need for general software, IBM formalized its program development organization and methods in 61 (Bald Peak Conference), by applying new management
disciplines derived from those already in usage for hardware.

Starting in years 1961-1962, each announcement of a new piece of hardware
will include that of a more or less sophisticated operating system, in every case specific to that machine and to its anticipated field of application. But the contractual
and commercial offering continues to rely exclusively on hardware. Only hardware
and its maintenance are subject to billing. Software, training and implementation
assistance are provided "free". In reality, the cost of those services is obviously
taken into account in the pricing of hardware. It is the responsibility of the local
sales organization to negotiate with each customer the supply of those services,

---

organizational struggles, that have underpinned product development and organization
changes in IBM since its entry into automatic computing until 1962.

since nothing specifies what software (free) each customer is entitled to order, nor what nature and what volume of (free) technical assistance it is entitled to receive.

In the period 1956-1964, data-processing enjoys a spectacular development, even though it is only implemented in a limited number of large organizations. Pioneers experiment with new areas and new forms of usage such as remote computing, non-numerical information processing, process control or various flavors of "artificial intelligence". In all those areas, the first operational implementations appear around 1960, quite often as ambitious projects. It is hardly an exaggeration to say that all fields of applications and all forms of usage of data-processing known today have been experimented as early as that period.

That blossoming of applications is matched by a very rapid technological progress, which translates into a proliferation of equipment introduced on the market at a quick pace. In that period, each piece of hardware is generally replaced by a more effective successor less than two years after its original introduction. Since that period is that of the discovery of data-processing, each successive piece of hardware incorporates new concepts and new functions which make it different its predecessors. The overall design of each computer reflects the technological bottle-necks of the moment, so that each advance in such key areas as circuits or memory technologies, or in peripheral areas such as magnetic tapes, is the opportunity to get rid of a global limitation, and often translates into the introduction of a new computer presenting areas of incompatibility with its predecessors.

According to customs acquired with unit-record, those machines are offered mainly on a rental basis, which satisfies the interests of users considering the extremely rapid evolution. Hardware remains thus most often the property of the manufacturer, its maintenance being therefore the responsibility of the latter and being covered by the rental price. That mode of billing, and the importance of technical assistance provided to customers, allow manufacturers to appear primarily as suppliers of services. The slogan of manufacturers "we supply services, not machinery" dates back to the fifties and has not been invented in 1970 with the introduction of billable services, nor in 1992 with the creation of consulting and support Divisions.

Early competitive dynamics

The emerging computer industry is thus made of generalist players, each of which offers its own computer architecture, or even several for the largest, provides the full complement of elements required for each customer and integrates them into operational systems.

The free nature of software and services provided by manufacturers leaves no place for independent providers, except in a marginal manner for software or sufficiently differentiated services. Anyway, the diversity and rapid evolution of hardware gives manufacturers a decisive advantage in the supply of all services linked to hardware, be that maintenance, training or technical assistance. The existence of a separate maintenance price is only an administrative provision intended for the few customers which purchase hardware and does not foster a third-party maintenance offering. Moreover, the predominance of rental precludes the existence of independent maintenance services and that of financial services such as leasing. Conversely, that approach exposes the supplier to the permanent risk of replacement of its equipment by a competitor if the customer is dissatisfied or if a more cost-effective successor appears.

The only form of services charged by manufacturers is the "Service Bureau", which consists in processing customer work on the equipment of the service provider. It allows the sharing of computers and skills, and addresses mainly small customers, as well as occasional projects or projects requiring unique skills. That activity is a straightforward consequence of the acquisition of computers by the conventional unit-record Service Bureaus, which have existed for several decades. The first independent service companies will initially move into that processing activity. It must be noted that, unlike other forms of service which remain free, the Service Bureau competes with the installation of a computer on the customer's premises, and is not a complementary offering but a possible replacement.

The price of hardware is in most cases a rental price including software and services. It is called "functional" because it is based on the value of services rendered rather than on costs. There are many examples of a machine A, less powerful than machine B and therefore offered for a lower price, being built by adding to B some speed-reducing device or another limitation, which increases its cost over that of B. The more powerful machine B is therefore both more expensive for the customer and less costly for the manufacturer.

Functional pricing enables the manufacturer to pocket the totality of the difference between the usage value which the product brings to its user and the cost of manufacturing that product. It is consistent with economic theory, but it can only last in a monopolistic type of situation resulting from strong barriers to entry. Otherwise, a potential competitor could easily offer products of a comparable usage value at a lower price by giving up part of the profit.

Conversely, the prices of the dominant competitor, namely that one which enjoys the maximum overall competitive advantage, constitute a reference level for the other suppliers as well as for the market. As long as a supplier can price slightly below the dominant competitor for comparable products, it is sure to obtain some share of the market and (to the extent that its costs are reasonable) to reach profitability. That *price umbrella* effect has secured a good prosperity for the whole industry until some vendors started a price war, mainly at the end of the sixties with the arrival of "minicomputers".

High profits on hardware enable manufacturers to sustain an important Research and Development activity, resulting in an avalanche of new products. They also enable them to devote a lot of efforts to market development, by experimenting with new applications and promoting them, by educating the target population, by assisting users in implementation, etc. But of course, even if the high prices and promotional efforts of IBM also serve the other firms to a certain extent, the potential profitability of the sector can only be realized at the expense of a sustained effort, as a certain number of firms will find out painfully after entering that sector and being forced to pull out rapidly.

But that abundant and extremely rapid evolution carries the seeds of disintegration.

On one hand, from the beginning of the sixties, every machine appears as a catalog of attachable and tailorable units, each implementing different functions using different technologies. Each system includes its own range of computing units, memories, magnetic tapes, disk storage units, printers, communications controllers, … which generally cannot be used in other systems. The large manufacturers are going to attempt to organize in order to manage separately the different types of units according to their technology, while providing the possibility to assemble them into systems in a very flexible manner. For example, creating a separate magnetic tapes development organization will normally result in a single range of tape units, capable of being attached to all computing units. That will maximize both the profitability of development investments for the manufacturer and configuration flexibility for the customer. That trend will result in the announcement of System IBM/360 in 1964, which marks the beginning of standardization.

On the other hand, the diversification of applications and modes of usage, as well as their evolutionary character, will cause an explosion and a diversification of assistance and training needs. At the same time, the relative weight and the diversity of software will grow in a dramatic way. What was only ancillary services at the outset will become a major expense item for the manufacturer, as well as an often dominant competitive factor. The need to manage those activities in a rational fashion will result in the *"unbundling"* announcement by IBM in 1969, which will open up the software and services market.

System/360 and the fragmentation of hardware (1964)

An open architecture

In April 1964, IBM, which largely dominates the whole computer industry, announces System/360. That announcement is one of the major events in the history of data-processing. Not only the concepts and new standards that it defines have remained valid until this day and are still the basis of current computers, but it introduces the very notion of standards at the heart of the computer industry, when until then the only relevant standards were related to the high-level languages Fortran and Cobol. In that sense, after the effervescence of the first years, that announcement marks the beginning of a "classical era", which will be challenged only by the rise of the microcomputer phenomenon around 1980.

Prior to System/360, IBM offered at least five mutually incompatible lines of computers: a scientific computer family using 36-bit words (7040/7044, 7090/7094), a family of business computers using 6-character words (7070, 7074), several families of business computers with character addressing (1401, 1410/7010, 1440, 1460, 7080), a family of scientific personal computers (1620, 1710) and a family of communications computers (7740, 7750).

The objective of System/360 is to replace all existent computer lines with a single compatible range, meaning that any program which can be executed by one processor can be executed by any other processor with at least as much memory capacity and equivalent input-output units. Moreover, the design of the new line must be such that all future developments in data-processing, whether the evolution of technologies, the invention of new unit or new functions, or the emergence of new applications or new modes of usage, can be integrated without conflicting with the fundamental design options.

To achieve that, IBM introduces a conceptual distinction between the "architecture" and the "structure" of its machines. The "architecture" of System/360 is defined as the set of usage rules and conventions, for example the representation of information, the addressing mode, the instruction set, etc. The "structure" of each machine includes the characteristics of a particular implementation of the architecture. The 360 architecture is unique, but it is implemented in the form of different structures.

For example, in the most powerful models of the range, all instructions are recognized and executed directly by circuitry, transfers of information occur in blocks of 8 bytes[3], computing functions and input-output are handled in parallel by physically distinct units. At the opposite, in entry models many instructions are simulated by program, transfers occur byte by byte, some logically distinct functions are executed by the same unit. All models nevertheless recognize the same instruction set and can execute the same program, but with different levels of performances and cost.

Furthermore, it must be possible to attach to processing units a variety of peripherals which may differ considerably by their functions and their performance, and whose evolution must be independent from that of central units. To that end, System/360 distributes input/output functions between the processing units and input-output control units, in such a way that functions specific to a device are implemented by a control unit associated with that device. The role of central components of the system is reduced to the transmission of necessary information to the control unit. The development of a new function or a new input-output device can thus become an autonomous activity which does not require modifications to other units of the system.

The announcement of System/360 foreshadows the concept of open systems by separating the concepts of "architecture" and "implementation" and by introducing the notion of a standard interface between units. By doing that, IBM involuntarily opens the way to providers of compatible equipment.

Changing borderlines

The separation between a unique architecture and varied implementations is made possible by the introduction of "microcode", a form of software which implements functions of the architecture not directly realized by circuits[4]. A partic-

---

3   A byte is a set of 8 binary digits or bits, capable of taking 256 distinct values, and used as the smallest element of information in the 360 architecture and successor architectures. A byte can represent for instance a character in a range of 256, including lowercase and uppercase, figures, ponctuation marks and special characters.

4   in its original implementation, microprograms are strings of microoperations residing in

ular model of the range is characterized by a certain distribution of functions between hardware itself (circuitry) and a layer of software associated with that hardware, the microcode. A technological evolution, correction of a failure or addition of a new function will most often require only a modification of microcode, which can later be carried forward into hardware upon subsequent introduction of new machines.

Microcode is used in particular to implement "emulators", which allow machines of the 360 series to execute the instruction set of earlier machines efficiently. The same possibility can be offered in the form of pure software simulation, at the expense of a substantial performance loss. Using an intermediate layer, more flexible than circuitry but with direct access to the elementary functions, enables the same machine to present several different appearances (or architectures) at comparable performance levels. Microcode introduces an intermediate level between functions directly realized by circuits and those realized by programming, and tends to make the traditional distinction between hardware and software a largely irrelevant convention.

As before, the contractual relations of IBM with its customers rely exclusively on hardware. Software and services remain "free" complements. But in System/360, "hardware" is actually a mix of hardware and software (called microcode for the occasion), in proportions which vary from one model to another and also change in time for equivalent models. That continuity between hardware and software carries over to the other side of the frontier assigned to hardware, since the operating system quickly becomes an integral part of the manufacturer's offering (although still "free"). It is indeed inconceivable to operate a computer as complex as System/360 without its operating system, when it was still current practice with the previous generations. More significantly, gradual improvements of the operating system are often supported by the definition of new "machine" instructions implemented in microcode.

In summary, with System/360, the distinction between hardware and software becomes blurred and loses its business significance. It would be more relevant to consider on one hand the complex formed by the hardware and its operating system, made up of a mix of hardware and various varieties of software, controlled by the manufacturer and the details of which are irrelevant for the user, and on the other hand application software which is the business of the user. Inside the complex formed by the hardware and base software, the borderline between circuits and programs results from technical and economic tradeoffs which are valid for a particular state of technology and a particular model of the range, and must remain under the control of the manufacturer. That view, which precludes dividing the industry into hardware and software, accounts for the reluctance of IBM to separate totally the billing of software at the time of unbundling, and will have a strong influence on the "Future Systems" project in the early seventies[5]. Although that atti-

---

read-only memory. Each microoperation controls the operation of a basic functional block in hardware

5   see next chapter

tude has been blamed on IBM as an abuse of a dominant position, the validity of that vision is not to be demonstrated, since the microprocessors used today in microcomputers contain a large quantity of software.

At the technology level, IBM chooses (first among the large manufacturers) the new technology of integrated circuits for the implementation of System/360, and begins to manufacture its own componentry. Until then, computer manufacturers purchased from electronic component manufacturers the vacuum tubes and later the transistors used in the manufacture of computers. The manufacturing of components was thus external to the computer industry. However, as soon as 1956, IBM had decided to manufacture its own ferrite core memories. It discovered on that occasion that it was able to mass produce components more reliably and more cheaply than its usual suppliers, and later took a significant leadership in circuit packaging from 1959 on.

With the transition from discrete components to integrated electronics, circuit design becomes an integral part of computer design. It is therefore natural that manufacturers start to develop and use their own components technology, thus parting from the manufacturers of traditional electronic components, and covering henceforth the totality of the path from raw silicon to complete operational systems installed at the customer's with software and necessary services. System/360, opens the times of peak industrial integration of computer hardware manufacturers.

Impact on the structure of the sector

Originally, the major architectural choices which have presided over the definition of System/360 have been determined only indirectly by competitive considerations, even if the overall program obviously aimed at maintaining the competitiveness of IBM. In the end its announcement was also somewhat hurried by threats from Honeywell, General Electric and Control Data, all three of which announced very competitive new systems in 1963. The intention was more to structure the work of the different development laboratories of IBM in an optimal manner, by enabling separate management and evolution of the different components, at the same time allowing the totality of the range to benefit from those developments. In others terms, IBM's goal was to maximize economies of scale for investments in Research and Development. Simultaneously, the definition of a standard architecture allowed customers to move easily within the range and to benefit from technological progress without jeopardizing their past investments. Finally, it united all users into one single community, facilitating exchanges between them and accelerating the dissemination of innovations.

Nevertheless, that announcement was going to have deep consequences for the structure of the industry, which were probably not anticipated or were at least underestimated by those who made the decision.

As soon as the 360 architecture spreads widely and seems likely to remain stable for several years, it will constitute a *de facto* standard on the basis of which third-party enterprises will build their own offerings. Those will be either complements, meaning elements that the leader does not provide, or substitutes, meaning elements that compete with equivalent offerings from IBM.

By establishing general interconnection standards between units of a computer system, IBM opens to others entrepreneurs the possibility of offering equipment which can be attached to its own. Such devices can compete with IBM equipment as well as be complementary. Firms can thus specialize on a type of device for which they believe that they have a competitive advantage, while still taking advantage of the driving effect of the market leader.

Indeed, a competition differentiated on a niche basis gradually develops as the 360 architecture penetrates the market and demonstrates its universality and durability. First to appear are compatible attachable devices (Telex magnetic tapes in 1967, Memorex disk storage in 1968, printers, then screens), then compatible memories which can be plugged into IBM central units. Finally, in 1975, compatible central units appear (Amdahl) when the durability of the architecture has been validated by 10 years of existence and reinforced for at least an equal duration by the announcements of System/370 in 1970 and of virtual memory in 1972, both compatible extensions of the 360 architecture. Without really trying, IBM has invented open systems.

At the end of the seventies, each and every element of IBM systems is competing with several non-IBM perfectly compatible equivalent products offered by specialized enterprises, and competitive in terms of performances, reliability and price. It becomes possible to assemble an entire IBM-compatible system without buying anything from IBM. That new form of the competitive game concerns other manufacturers only in proportion with their success, since the motivation to develop a compatible machine increases as the market share of the equipment that it can complement or replace. Around that same time, a part of the market begins to believe that computer architectures will durably stabilize and turns to the purchase of equipment rather than rental. The first computer leasing companies appear, while the perspective of an active used computer market starts to materialize.

That explosion of the computer sector creates a fundamental question of strategy for the generalists, and mainly to IBM. Should they seek their competitive advantage in the architecture of the system, consistency of the components that they propose and service rendered at the system level, or on the contrary in the quality and price of each component unit taken separately? That choice between a "system strategy" and a "box strategy" has deep organization and business practices implications, and has fueled inside IBM an underground debate which dominates strategic decisions since the beginning of the seventies. The choice of a system strategy went without saying until the announcement of System/360 which was one of its highest points, together with System/370 and the SNA[6] communications architecture in 1974. The advocates of the box strategy (mainly the finance and manufacturing organizations) were then going to gradually take the upper hand over the advocates of the system strategy (mostly present in development and

---

6   Systems Network Architecture

sales), especially after IBM discontinued the "Future Systems" project[7] which represented an epitome of the system strategy.

Summary

The computer industry was born from the conversion of unit-record industry to the computer. Initially a minor activity, data-processing has taken an increasingly large place within each of the firms which compose that industry, as they introduced on the market low-range computers to replace unit-record machines for a similar price. Only in 1962 did the IBM computer revenue begin to exceed its unit-record revenue. Towards the end of the sixties, unit-record machine manufacturers have evolved into computer manufacturers, still retaining a residual unit-record activity which will soon totally disappear.

Others companies have also entered that field. At the end of the fifties, large electricity or electronics Companies such as General Electric, RCA, Honeywell and others established internal computer manufacturing activities, but most of those attempts will abort more or less rapidly. On the other hand, new firms that began in computers by specializing on particular markets, like Control Data (1957) or Digital Equipment (1962) will fare better.

The computer industry that we know today is primarily composed on one hand of the descendants of the unit-record companies of the beginning of the century, on the other hand of younger firms that never had any other activity than data-processing. In total, data-processing is the business of firms specialized in that area, and can therefore be legitimately considered as an autonomous industry. The notable exceptions are Japanese players like Fujitsu, NEC, Hitachi, Toshiba, or European players like Siemens or Olivetti, for which the computer activity is only a part of a diversified group.

Moreover, the computer industry has separated from the electronics industry in the sixties by undertaking its own manufacturing activity for computer components. Data-processing firms are therefore totally integrated vertically, meaning that they incorporate the totality of the path that leads from raw silicon to the computer; they are also integrated in terms of offerings, since their final production includes everything that their customers require to implement an operational system.

All data-processing companies of the sixties adhere to a single model, that of the integrated firm offering all elements necessary for implementation of a complete system, together with corresponding software, assistance and maintenance. Since the billing of that complex of hardware and services is based exclusively on the hardware catalog, there are practically no independent software or services offerings, except the service bureau which is already on its way to recession.

During that period, the computer industry forms a sector as defined by Porter[8]. All manufacturers offer comparable baskets of products and services, and for each user the offerings of one manufacturer (hardware, software and services)

---

7   see following chapter

can be substituted to that of anyone of its competitors. Even the Service Bureau constitutes an alternative to acquiring a computer. On the other hand, until the middle of the sixties, there are no independent sectors for software or services.

The sector exhibits all the features of a concentrated sector. The search for innovation and the marketing expenses related to market development require a high level of investments. Switching costs between competing products, that is to say costs incurred by customers for converting from one architecture to another, are high and increase together with the inventory of application programs and the number of people to be retrained.

That sector, emergent by definition, exhibits the usual characteristics of sectors in the introduction and early growth phase:
- differentiated products, no standards, frequent design changes,
- dominant Research and Development functions,
- short product life, high marketing costs, high share of qualified work,
- low price-elasticity of demand, pricing strategy based on skimming, high margins and profits,
- small number of firms in the sector.

IBM, which already enjoyed a dominant position in the sector of unit-record equipment, maintains that dominance in data-processing where its market share will reach or exceed 50% (or 70% depending on sources) in the beginning of the seventies. Competitive forces in that emerging sector, especially the importance of R&D and the large capital requirements to finance not only R&D and growth, but also the rental inventory, favors the largest firms and those with the strongest financial base. Among the small number of large hardware and service providers, IBM offers the most complete range, while most its competitors cover only a particular market segment with a more narrow range.

The System/360 announcement gives IBM a sufficient advantage over its broad-based competitors of the pre-1964 period to force most of them to withdraw (RCA, GE, Honeywell) or to merge (Univac with Burroughs, NCR with ATT, ICT with Fujitsu). But at the same time, another competition emerges, aiming specifically at those sectors where the will of IBM to offer universal and compatible products makes it vulnerable to the competition of specialized manufacturers. The end of the sixties sees the early beginnings of a disintegration of the industry according to the type of equipment and the target market.

---

8   see chapter 6.

Chapter 2 - The teenage crises (1968 - 1980)

Dominance of IBM and miscellaneous reactions. Much litigation about nothing. IBM splits in two. The rise of minicomputers. Unbundling and the fragmentation of services. Future Systems or the end of a dream. Towards maturity?

The announcement of System/360 has reinforced IBM's dominance of the computer industry, by making that system a *de facto* standard. The first successes of the 360 range, its modularity and probable long life have caused the emergence of new forms of competition such as leasing, secondhand systems and compatible equipment. At the same time, the first independent computer consulting and development companies appear. Those developments result in a growing state of tension between IBM and those new competitors, which are going to attempt to use the legal weapon to restructure the industry to their advantage. On its side, while insuring its defense, IBM engages into a series of structural reform projects which aim at shielding it from further legal attacks. In that sense, the trials, the separation of prices, the implementation of separate organizations for the lower product range and the "*Future Systems*" project are interrelated.

Those endeavors have something in common: all have essentially failed, or at least their actual results have been very remote from the hopes of their originators, whether IBM itself, its competitors or the public authorities. Let us interpret that as an indication that the intrinsic evolutionary dynamics of an industry hardly tolerate being jostled by artificial accelerations.

The time of trials (1968 - 1982)

By worsening the fears of increasing IBM dominance of the computer industry, the announcement of System/360 leads the United States Government to start a preliminary inquiry in 1964. In parallel, between 1969 and 1973, IBM will be the target of about twenty trials brought by private firms, plus in 1973 legal action from the European Community.

Control Data opens fire in December 1968 by charging IBM of having announced 360/90 prematurely with the only goal of deterring customers from ordering the Control Data 6600. That action never came to court and ended in January 73 with an amicable agreement stipulating in particular the transfer of IBM's Service Bureau activity to Control Data. It is remarkable that the substance of that agreement had so little to do with the original motivations of the complaint.

The US Department of Justice brings its own trial in January 1969. Under the pretext of challenging certain allegedly illegal practices, its real core is to combat

IBM's dominant position irrespective of its causes. It is hardly an exaggeration to say that, for many promoters of that action, the important point is not so much to find out whether IBM is guilty of unfair competition practices, but to put an end to its dominant position whatever its reasons. That action takes on a particular significance because of the nature of the plaintiff, the height of the stakes and the legal subtlety of the arguments[9].

Let us mention two crucial debates in that trial, which relate to basic issues of law and economic theory. The first one concerns the evaluation of market share. The numerator of that fraction, namely IBM's revenue, is well known, but it is more difficult to decide what its denominator should be, in other words what are the limits of the relevant market. For IBM, the market is made of the totality of equipment, software and computer services, of which it estimates its share to be approximately 30%, in a timely modest way. For its prosecutors, the relevant market must be limited to IBM-compatible equipment, of which one can easily prove that IBM holds more than 90%. It is as though the French government would bring suit to Chanel for monopolizing the sector of Chanel dresses and thereby doing wrong to imitators! More seriously, the position of the Justice Department tends to imply that the 360 standard has escaped IBM and is now become part of the public domain.

The second debate is to decide whether a dominant position is condemnable by itself and whether, for that reason, actions which are otherwise lawful for secondary players must be forbidden to IBM. In the book by DeLamarter, one of the most critical towards IBM ever published, it is striking that the only serious grievance, and practically the subject of the entire book, is that IBM establishes its prices in such a way as to make a higher profit on equipment less exposed to competition, and to accept lower margins on other equipment. Economists and businesspersons would regard that policy as a normal business decision. Does it become a crime when it is practiced by IBM? More deeply, insofar as the objective of antitrust law is to foster competition, is it legitimate to forbid one player the very competitive behavior that those laws are supposed to protect?

Between 1969 and 1971, several lawsuits are brought by leasing companies, following action by DP Financial and General. All will be dropped sooner or later when the courts begin to pass their first judgments in favor of IBM. A second round is then brought by compatible equipment manufacturers, in the wake of the Telex suit.

The Telex case is the only one where IBM was temporarily declared guilty of unfair practices, while Telex was convicted for theft of trade secrets. A first judg-

---

9   Those lawsuits, in particular the one from the US Justice Department, are the subject of many books, two of which were written by lawyers or economists who assisted the two parties in the trial.
     For prosecution: DeLamarter RT : Big Blue - IBM's use and abuse of power (Donald Mead, 1986)
     For defense: Fisher FM, McGowan JJ, Greenwood JE: Folded, Spindled and Mutilated - Economic Analysis of US vs IBM (MIT Press, Cambridge, 1983)

ment was passed along those lines in September 1973. The sentence against IBM was later canceled by a court of appeals in 1975. Meanwhile, a dozen of small firms had used the Telex precedent and brought similar actions calling for *"treble damages"*, in accordance with antitrust legislation[10]. For an ailing firm, suing an IBM company plagued by trials including one from the United States Government seemed a reasonably secure way to eventually benefit from a welcome financial transaction. The reversal of the Telex judgment in 1975 made IBM's attitude much tougher and quickly dried up that surge of lawsuits, the legal validity of which was questionable to say the least, and which should not be considered too significant simply because of their number.

The US Government trial started in May 1975 after six years of discovery, and after fourteen independent judges had concluded in favor of IBM on the same or related charges. It led to six more years of rather surrealistic debate, abounding in errors of fact and of law, inconsistencies in the plaintiff's position and procedural aberrations. It did not reach any formal conclusion until the whole case was declared *"without merit"*) in January 1982.

However questionable their motivations may be, that series of lawsuits can be viewed as a critical examination of the structure of the computer industry and of possible provisions for modifying that structure. Even if none of those actions has succeeded, they have formed together an important part of the environment in which some key decisions of the computer industry were taken between 1969 and 1975. At that later date, almost all actions had found their conclusion, consistently in favor of IBM, and the suit brought in 1969 by the US Department of Justice entered a deep sleep until it was dropped in 1982.

In 1973, while the mood was temporarily euphoric for the opponents of IBM, the European Community began its own inquiry. In December 1980, the community filed charges for abuse of a dominant position, at a time when all comparable charges had been dropped in the USA, including practically the Department of Justice complaint, which would be formally dropped one year later. Disappointed in the United States, some plaintiffs were hoping to obtain satisfaction in Europe thanks to differences between the EEC legislation and that of the USA, and by counting on a certain anti-American attitude always fashionable in Europe. The European Community action began therefore as a masquerade; it ended in buffoonery in August 1984, when the European Community dropped its charges in exchange of a commitment by IBM to publish and to update information on its SNA standard for communications, which it already published or would have published in any event as it does for all its major software products. That window-dressing commitment enabled the European Community to exit a bad dispute while keeping up appearances. It was nevertheless celebrated as a big victory against IBM, which the latter took care not to minimize. In retrospect, that whole action appears as an insignificant aberration.

What are the results of that episode of legal battles? IBM's activities have indeed been somewhat hindered during about ten years, when legal experts have

---

10   fines equal to three times the alleged damages to the plaintiff

exerted a finicky control over all decisions of organization, products and commercial practices. Similarly, separate pricing of software and services has definitely been accelerated, even though it is likely that it would have been introduced sooner or later. The combination of those two effects has enabled the emergence of many new software and service companies, as well as a gradual move of customers towards more independence. This has encouraged the multiplication of competitors, the erosion of IBM's market share and the acceleration of technical progress. Towards the end of the lawsuit period, IBM was remarking ironically that most of the firms from which the US Government and the European Community were collecting testimonies of abuse of dominant position did not exist at the time when IBM was supposed to monopolize the industry. Indeed, from a few hundreds of companies in 1964, the computer industry grew to approximately 20000 firms in 1980 and 50000 in 1992.

A study of the yearly growth rates of IBM does not show any obvious relation with the progress of the lawsuits. After two poor years in 1969 and 1970, it returned to a stable 15% or so from 1972 to 1974, started a decrease from 1975 to 1977 and oscillated between 9 and 15% from 1978 to 1982. Upon conclusion of the trials in 1982, the growth rate increased to 18%, but only to begin an inexorable decrease, which would end in negative rates in 1991 and 1992, after a few bumps between 1987 and 1990. Over that whole period, IBM's market share went from over 70% to approximately 30%, contradicting the ominous predictions that IBM's dominance would inescapably end in a monopoly situation, which could only be avoided through vigorous judicial action. In reality, at the same time as legal action failed, other natural economic forces came into play to limit the expansion of the dominant actor, and to reshape and re-balance the structure of the industry.

On the other hand, the lawsuits have had only little influence on the culture and customs of IBM. All persons that were in contact with the outside world (salespeople, purchasing personnel, managers, …) had to confirm in writing every year that they had read the "Business Conduct Guidelines" once more. All commercial actions were scrutinized by business policy departments, who chased the slightest deviations from official prices or from the delivery schedules quoted by plants. IBM employees and customers, who were the witnesses and sometimes the victims of more flexible maneuvers (to use a euphemism) of their competitors, could just not believe that those would have the guts to accuse IBM of unfair practices, and could not imagine that serious people, as governments and judicial institutions were supposed to be, could lend an ear to such accusations. Therefore, in the whole, IBM personnel never doubted that IBM would eventually prevail. That confidence eroded slightly as time showed that the action of the US Government was indeed serious, which could portend as irrational an outcome as the charges themselves. It also vacillated somewhat in the wake of the initial Telex verdict at the end of 1973.

In summary, both from the different judgments passed or the other forms of outcome of legal actions, our general conclusion is that the structure of the computer industry in the seventies was the result of the normal action of competitive economic forces, not of conspiracy or abuse of power. At the same time the action of those same forces enabled the emergence of new players, which was going to result in the explosion of the industry and the gradual decline of IBM's dominance, irrespective of legal considerations.

Unbundling (1969-1972) and the fragmentation of services

Motivations and principles

The early years of System/360 have been difficult in the software sector, due to development delays, memory requirements far in excess of estimates, and needs for high levels of customer assistance and training to alleviate problems met by users. IBM discovers that the very structure of its offer makes base software a highly critical element of the system, and begins to be strongly concerned by the growing costs of software and systems engineering assistance, which burden the pricing of equipment and jeopardize its competitiveness.

Even when the initial difficulties are overcome, towards the end of 1967, the customer needs and demands for software and assistance continue to diversify and to grow. In response to that demand, specialized companies begin to offer software and services. Those offerings, when compared with their equivalents from the manufacturer, have the disadvantage of not being free of charge, but they can be provided under clear contractual terms rather than at the discretion of the manufacturer. In addition, they provide application, organization or system design skills that manufacturers do not offer or offer sparingly.

In that same period, part of the market turns to purchasing rather than renting equipment, thus creating an opportunity for leasing companies and for an active used computer market. That perspective raises the issue of the supply of services usually related to the acquisition of a computer, when the supplier is a financial organization or a computer broker.

Finally, IBM is at that time the target of several lawsuits. Although those actions are only marginally related to software and support services, IBM probably believes that accepting sacrifices in those areas will help it to better hold its position in hardware. Accordingly, in the beginning of 1969, it initiates an internal study of separate billing for software and services ("unbundling"). That new policy is publicly announced in the USA in June of the same year as being immediately applicable to the entire product line. Nine months later, in March 1970, IBM World Trade announces that those new provisions will only be applicable in Europe to newly announced equipment for the time being, and will be extended to the whole range in July 1972, after a 15-month transition period.

In this respect, it is rather funny that critics have blamed IBM (and some still blame it) for using anti-competitive practices until 1969 through its "*bundling*" policy. In reality, until IBM took the initiative of charging separately for software and services, no manufacturer had yet offered such services on a separate basis. IBM was only following the unanimous practice of the industry, and at no time did it bundle services which had so far been offered separately. On the contrary, its unique contribution was to take the initiative of "unbundling" and to implement it in a rather strict fashion well ahead of the other vendors.

Like the announcement of System/360, that IBM initiative is intended to address internal objectives more than to respond to direct competitive pressure. Those objectives are on one hand to better control software development and customer assistance activities by matching them more closely with demand, and on the other hand to obtain an indirect advantage in a legal conflict concerning hardware. As for the announcement of System/360, the resulting decisions will nevertheless contribute to shaping the structure of the entire computer industry.

A quick review of the decisions made and of the manner in which they will be implemented will shed light on the position of IBM at that time regarding software and services, a position which will evolve only slowly thereafter.

Until then, IBM provided a basket of services (software, training, technical assistance) for a single price attached to hardware, and decided unilaterally which and how much of those services were provided to each customer. Maintenance of the equipment was either included in the rental price or covered by a separate maintenance contract for purchased equipment. No contractual provision existed for software maintenance, training and assistance, which had the advantage of being free of charge, but excluded any formal commitment or warranty concerning those elements. In addition, IBM offered processing services separately, through its affiliate the Service Bureau Corporation in the USA, through its normal commercial organization in the rest of the world.

Unbundling does not directly concern Service Bureau or hardware maintenance, but focuses on the software, technical assistance and training sectors. For each of those activities, a part remains "free", which actually means charged as part of hardware prices, and another part becomes subject to a separate charge.

Software

Software is divided in two categories. The price of equipment continues to include software "necessary for (its) operations", specifically the operating systems or SCP (Systems Control Programming). That decision reflects the assumption that the utilization of all computers requires an operating system, and on the other hand the will of IBM to retain complete control over those systems. Conversely, pieces of software that implement functions specific to an application or to a form of usage, and are not essential to general operations, become separately billable. Such programs make up the category called Programs Products.

Charging for software does not imply any modification in the organization and management systems. The sources of programs remain essentially the product development divisions for SCP's and industry competence centers (which are part of the marketing divisions) for PP's. Decisions pertaining to software can therefore be taken centrally, as for the other products. Market introduction of software follows the same rules as the other products, including definition of their price. They are the subject of formal announcements, similar to those of equipment and are listed in the same catalog. Thus, their marketing and their management conform to established procedures and do not raise particular implementation problems.

From the outset, IBM has assimilated software to hardware and has treated software packages as products. Thereafter, the field of free SCP software has been gradually reduced to the point of disappearance. Beginning in the eighties, all software packages offered by IBM carry a price tag, and one can consider in retrospect that the initial distinction between SCP and PP was only a temporary provision. In parallel, the prices of software have been gradually increased, and the combination of the two has caused a spectacular growth of the share of software in IBM's income. But software was never managed as an independent sector. IBM sells only that software which it would have developed anyhow to support the sale of its hardware. On the other hand, although IBM has remained dominant in base software, it has accumulated false starts and failures in application software (like most other hardware suppliers) to the point of having practically pulled off.

Technical assistance

For technical assistance, the distinction between a "free" part and a "fee" part raises more serious issues. Such assistance is provided essentially by Systems Engineers, who also provide technical assistance to sales people in their marketing activity. Barring an internal specialization that would be detrimental to the image and to the marketing effectiveness of IBM, the separation between fee assistance and free assistance, whatever its principle, must therefore be managed by each Systems Engineer for his or her activities.

Study groups in charge of unbundling spent considerable time attempting to define for Systems Engineering a borderline that would both be simple enough to be accepted by the lawyers and manageable, and realistic enough to avoid a marketing disaster. That internal debate will continue during several years, raising frequent heated debates, and will result in several successive changes of policy.

The rule selected for the first announcement in the USA is drastic: it states that any (free) assistance by Systems Engineering to marketing must exclusively take place on IBM premises. Any presence of Systems Engineering at a customer site is therefore deemed to be for the purpose of assisting the customer, and is therefore billable. Moreover, since in the US the new business practices are applicable immediately upon announcement, Systems Engineers are ordered to stop visiting their customers from announcement day until a fee services contract is signed with the customer by the sales representative responsible for the account.

That decision, which showed a complete ignorance of field realities on the part of its authors, causes of course an outcry not only from customers, but also from the entire IBM marketing organization. At the same time, although the cause-effect relationship cannot be proved, revenue growth slows down from over 25% per year in 1967 and 1968 to less than 5% in 1969 and 1970.

After some time, top IBM management will have to recognize their mistake and will seek ways to correct it, without appearing to repudiate the principles that it has decreed a few months earlier. The idea of the solution eventually retained is to remove part of the Systems Engineering field force from the branches and to assemble them in Centers, the activity of which will be charged by definition. All branch activity is then considered free as a matter of principle, within rather fuzzy bounds. The idea seems to be that, if Centers are able to exhibit a sufficient level of billing, that revenue will serve as an excuse for the lawyers and outside authorities to tolerate a certain level of flexibility at branch level.

But that move entails a reduction of resources directly available to field management, which is badly resented by the majority as a form of impoverishment. In the end, even if the initial blunder ends up being corrected, albeit in a clumsy way, it has nonetheless severely damaged the image of IBM and its relationships with customers, as well as, to a large extent, the confidence of IBM personnel in the company's executive management.

At the time of that unfortunate experience, no announcement has yet been made in the rest of the world and especially in Europe, other than the continuation of the study. The approach under consideration in those studies is a more flexible one. It is still based on dividing systems engineering activities into those that are for the sole benefit of IBM (for example proposal preparation and presentation), and those that are for the benefit of the customer (for example assistance in operations or program development). The former will not be billable, even if they take place on a customer site, and the latter will be charged, even if they take place on IBM premises.

Implementing that policy requires the development of a realistic catalog of all tasks performed by systems engineers, indicating for each its free or fee character according to the main beneficiary. Many difficulties arise, which are also opportunities for flexibility. For instance, activities like the preparation and following-up of the installation plan, or the selection of technical solutions, can be considered as benefiting both IBM and the customer. Classifying such activities as fee or free involves tradeoffs between legal, marketing and financial considerations. The initial position of IBM Europe is define those activities as billable, but under pressure from the USA busily attempting to correct their own prior decision, those intermediate activities end up free.

In all that launching period, the main concern of IBM is to charge for part of the technical assistance that it provides to its customers anyhow, not to develop a new services offering. The invoiced share must be sufficient to result in a more efficient control on the activities of systems engineering personnel and to satisfy legal constraints without harming the marketing of hardware. Never did IBM seriously intend to turn that technical assistance activity into a somehow autonomous profit center. Moreover, IBM applies to those services a high-price policy consistent with its compensation practices but deterrent for customers, who gradually reduce their use of IBM fee resources to tasks demanding an excellent knowledge of products and/or software. Similar policies, generally less formal, will be adopted by the other manufacturers, that in the whole are eager to preserve their flexibility and their capacity to use free assistance as an argument in support of hardware sales.

Training

In the case of training, the practicable methods required for a partial billing raise an intermediate problem between software and assistance. Like products, education courses are listed in a catalog and produced (taught) in dedicated centers. It is therefore possible to treat them as products by attaching a price to each course once and for all. The decision on the fee character is thus restricted to a central level and not left to the judgment of each individual involved, as is the case for assistance.

The fee/free principle retained by IBM is as follows: promotional and general information courses remain free and are available only to customers and prospects, while all professional and technical courses are charged and open to all students. In practice, that system translates first into a restructuring of the course catalog, so that the actual content of each course falls unambiguously into one of the two categories. Apart from those adjustments, as late as 1975, the new billing policy is basically superimposed on the existing curriculum structure, and training remains managed as part of the marketing activity.

In the wake of the oil crisis of 1973, IBM undertakes an ambitious program to cut down on central staff. Systems engineering is not involved because it is viewed as belonging to the field organization, while education departments are labeled "indirect" and are therefore under strong pressure to reduce staffs. Interestingly enough, revenue generation is not deemed to be an applicable consideration. To protect itself, and to protect IBM's interests at the same time, the education function undertakes a far-reaching program of reforms aimed at redefining its place and its mission in the overall IBM organization, and to maximize its strategic contribution to corporate objectives.

One key outcome is to define unequivocally the mission of education as being support to the marketing of hardware, with two main objectives: first, to reduce the field marketing workload through better information of customers, and second to make customers more self-sufficient in systems implementation tasks through technical training of their personnel. The number of sales and systems personnel man-years saved thanks to training of customer personnel can therefore be used as a measure of the efficiency of customer training, and indeed became a major planning parameter from that point on. One could find no better way to express that the major objective of the training activity remains to support the sales of equipment, irrespective of fee or free considerations.

Between 1976 and 1980, in order to improve its productivity and that of students, IBM replaces many of its stand-up courses with self-study, whenever the subject matter does not require frequent direct interaction between student and teacher, which is the case for almost all free technical courses. As a result, direct classroom teaching ends up being used only for brief free product presentations at one extreme, advanced fee technical courses requiring a high content of hands-on practice at the other extreme, plus occasional intermediate courses with too low an audience to justify investing in self-study. The entire teaching staff can then be devoted to high-level courses which have the three advantages of producing the highest contribution to the customer self-sufficiency objective, offering teachers the highest level of job satisfaction and justifying the highest prices and profit.

The spectacular growth of customer education revenue at the end of the seventies was only the consequence of that strategy of maximal support to hardware marketing. As soon as it is established that every customer person trained equals a measurable saving of workload and expense for IBM, it becomes desirable to train

the largest possible number of customers. Education revenue is thus a measurement and a by-product of an activity basically dedicated to hardware support. IBM
did welcome the strong financial profitability of that activity, but like customer
assistance, training was never managed towards independent financial objectives.

Organization and strategy

In the United States, the new modes of service do not raise fundamental
organizational problems, since IBM has discontinued its Service Bureau activity as
part of the settlement of the Control Data case. In Europe, on the contrary, the
relationship of the new billable activities with the Service Bureau is a hot issue. The
independent services companies that compete with IBM usually offer all those services, so that the logic of antitrust or fair competition would lead IBM to combine
all fee services including Service Bureau into a separate organization with independent profit objectives.

That issue is closely related to that of the objective of fee services: support
to sales or profit? Should IBM retain separate objectives, strategies and organizations for service bureau on one hand, customer training and assistance on the other,
or should it implement for training and assistance a business strategy independent
of hardware, by drawing them and Service Bureau together? On the contrary,
should it redirect service bureau to support sales of equipment, and possibly accept
a degradation of its growth and profit? In other words, should IBM create an organization similar to that of specialized Service Companies? If yes, what should be
the borderlines, the goals and the strategy of that new organization?

In the period from 1970 to 1974, that question is asked in an insistent fashion
on the occasion of many organizational changes, without ever receiving a clear
answer. After many vicissitudes, IBM returns by the end of the seventies to the
organization and strategy that were in place prior to the unbundling decision, meaning implicitly that, whereas the goal of Service Bureau remains profit, the objective
of all other services is still support to hardware sales. That situation will remain stable until the end of the eighties, and will not evolve in any significant manner until
1987 when the "Systems Integration" organization is created.

Initially designed as a defensive action against the explosion of software and
assistance costs, as well as a political maneuver in a legal battle against competitors
and the US Government, separate pricing has translated into the charging of activities which IBM so far performed free of charge to support its main activity of
hardware sales. Far from entering the field of services aggressively, IBM has used
billing to curtail and eventually reduce its involvement in tasks that were not essential to equipment support. It has thus created a market for those tasks that it does
not want to perform, therefore a market on which it will deliberately not be competitive.

What IBM considers as essential support to hardware has been left free of
charge, unless it could exploit a decisive competitive advantage (for example the
knowledge of hardware for technical training) to ensure the provision of service
despite the high prices imposed by its compensation and pricing practices. For that
reason, resources dedicated to services have always been managed as part of mar-

keting resources until very recently, and no truly autonomous organization, whose evolution would have been ruled by its own profitability, has been created. Services revenue has long been a by-product, not an objective.

The reason why IBM has nevertheless wished to sustain a certain level of services revenue was initially to show the reality of its fee services policy. The market and involved authorities would not have understood that, after attaching a price tag to a part of customer support, IBM ceased to provide that support (assuming that it is feasible) and only provided the free part. During the implementation of the new policy, a sufficient level of billing has been considered as sort of a necessary alibi for a flexible utilization of branch systems engineering. Moreover, some of those services, like customer training and later systems integration, are so critical to hardware revenue that IBM wants to provide them in a certain amount, revenue being a convenient measurement.

The development of that case also shows that the traditional IBM culture is deeply hostile to charging for services based directly on personnel. That reluctance relates to two basic reasons, both going back to the "basic beliefs" which decorate the office of every IBM manager ever since they were formulated by old Tom Watson back in 1914. In the IBM culture, devotion to customer service and the search of excellence preclude invoicing customers for time spent by people assigned to their support. Similarly, respect for the individual and the personnel policies that come with it preclude making the compensation of an IBM employee dependent on whether a customer accepts an invoice for the time of that employee. If IBM has always considered that its actual strength and its main objectives are in hardware, the primary reason is that hardware allows the highest possible decoupling between the revenue of the firm and the individual work of each employee. For that reason, IBM prefers selling products to selling services, among services prefers selling machine time to people time, and among personnel-based services prefers selling training to selling assistance.

Emergence of a services sector

The billing of services, although only in part, opens up new markets for independent service companies, specially in the area of applications or for tasks of a level incompatible with the prices of manufacturer assistance. A new support services sector, addressing mostly application program development and system installation and operations, is created both as a natural evolution of service bureau companies and through the appearance of new specialized firms. Until the nineties, that sector will grow rapidly by exploiting an endemic shortage of skilled personnel.

That dramatic growth of the services sector contrasts with the modesty of the packaged software sector until the eighties. General-purpose software is provided by equipment manufacturers and is too dependent on specific hardware characteristics to be developed by third parties, while application requirements are most often met by specific developments for each customer. A large part of services is therefore custom software development. Some service providers gradually develop preprogrammed frameworks or reusable modules which they present as "products" in their advertisements, but those pieces of software generally cannot be used without significant help from their author, and are only the foundations of a custom development service. The confusion or continuity that has long existed between custom development and ready-to use software explains why packaged software is often put in the same class as services, although we will see that they are two fundamentally different activities from an economic viewpoint[11].

Nevertheless, an independent software sector begins to emerge towards the end of the sixties, but only in the eighties will it develop in a dramatic fashion with microcomputers.

Concerning training, the IBM policy of concentrating on high level practical product-based courses, and of using its traditional high-price policy for training, opens up a large field to independent training companies, which IBM wishes to encourage in their development. For example, its policy precludes offering programming courses in classroom form, although the existence of such courses offered by third parties is a positive contribution to its objective of user self-sufficiency. Consequently, IBM will encourage and provide technical support to third-parties offering programming education. The strategy selected by IBM for training has thus been very favorable to independent firms, for which IBM creates a demand and establishes a high price umbrella, while only being active in very few specific segments.

Unbundling has had a serious long term impact on the entire computer industry. Let us remember that through the period 1969-1985, the IBM market accounts for a share -between 50% and 70%- of the total potential market for computer services. It has enabled the boom of independent services companies and the emergence of a packaged software industry, however timid and not distinct from computer services companies in the beginning. It has motivated users to become less dependent on a dominant manufacturer, which contributed, together with the standardization of equipment, to the disintegration of the large manufacturers' offerings and to the boom of specialized suppliers and independent integrators. In addition, by its indirect effects, unbundling has contributed to the gradual erosion of IBM's market share.

Movements at the low end

The minis and the decline of Service Bureau

The announcement of System/360 has given IBM enough of an advantage over its generalist competitors to force many of them to withdraw (RCA, GE, Honeywell) or to merge (Univac with Burroughs, NCR with ATT, ICT with Fujitsu). At the same time, however, a different breed of competition begins to target specific sectors where the universality and compatibility strategy of IBM renders it vulnerable to competition from specialized suppliers, most notably the sector of scientific computing.

---

11   see chapter 10

In that market, it is not only possible to develop more closely adapted equipment by forgoing the constraints of a universal architecture, but technical support can be limited because of a generally high user competence. Moreover, buyers are often laboratories keen on preserving their independence and with a strong tendency to break free from central staffs and from the manufacturer most related to them. By exploiting those features, and often by using aggressive business practices in sharp contrast with the civilized and somewhat highbrow manners of IBM, companies specializing in "minicomputers" start blossoming, such as Digital Equipment in 1965, Data General in 1969, Prime, Modcomp, Hewlett-Packard, and so on. Even Control Data, better known later for supercomputers, pioneered that area in 1958 with one of its early machines the Control Data 160.

The minicomputer is more a phenomenon of a marketing nature than a genuine technical breakthrough. Apart from their adaptation to a particular type of application, those machines do not implement concepts or technologies different from those of similar machines from the broad-based suppliers. From a purely technical viewpoint, the entry models of the 360 or 370 series, as well as their cousins System/38 or AS/400, deserve the label "minicomputers" just as much as their competitors from Digital Equipment or Hewlett-Packard. It is literally nonsense to wonder why "the traditional manufacturers have been absent from the beginnings of the minicomputer". The word "minicomputer" stands for a series of focused attacks by new entrants against established manufacturers, with arguments and methods of a marketing nature, but in no way a technological innovation missed by the traditional manufacturers.

Contrary to what the mini manufacturers want to make believe, the dividing line is not between reactionary mainframe manufacturers and progressive mini manufacturers. There are on one side broad-range manufacturers offering an extended line of general-purpose equipment across a large performance scale, and the other hand specialized manufacturers addressing only a selected part of the applications and performance spectrum. That same niche is also covered by generalists, possibly with specific equipment and dedicated marketing approaches. In the overlapping market segments, each camp fights the competitive battle with different arguments, but what is involved here is purely sales arguments in support of similar technical proposals, not two opposed data-processing philosophies as many were pretending.

The emergence of the minis brings along new players, but does not change the underlying competitive forces (as defined by Porter[12]) or the structure of the sector, in contrast to what will happen with microcomputers. Just like IBM, the mini manufacturers offer in their selected niche complete configurations and a full training assistance and maintenance service, tailored to their target segment. Although they compete with the broad-based manufacturers, they comply with the rules of the game established by them. The mini phenomenon is only the accidental dramatization of a general trend of data-processing, that is the constant introduction of increasingly effective equipment at lower and lower price levels.

---

12   see chapter 6

With success, Digital Equipment, the mini pioneer, will itself become a broad-based manufacturer by extending its range upwards into the performance levels of the large IBM computers, and by entering the area of business applications. Digital Equipment will become the number two in the industry by implementing the same strategy as IBM: a broad range of machines, proprietary systems software, a complete offering including all services required by users, etc. As a consequence, Digital Equipment is now faced with the same problems as IBM, after being the most effective of its challengers.

The rise of the mini will have its most important impact on services with the erosion of the Service Bureau market. The availability of low-cost powerful equipment enables users to acquire machines tailored to their own needs instead of resorting to shared facilities. As a consequence, Service Bureau gradually vanishes between 1975 and 1983 almost to a point of non-existence, resulting in the disappearance, regression or redeployment of companies that had specialized in that area. The only survivors are services that rely on highly specialized skills or data bases, or that imply by their nature the sharing of information between user firms.

The General Systems Division

IBM has always wanted to be present in the low-end computer segment, in order to establish its presence very early with as many customers as possible and then follow their evolution by capitalizing on their loyalty. For that reason, it introduced machines such as the 610 in 1957, one of the first scientific computers designed for personal use, then the 1620 in 1959, the 1440 in 1962, and more.

After 1964, while offering low-end implementations of System/360, small system designers run into the constraints of that architecture. Any general architecture includes requirements which set a lower bound on the cost of implementing it in a given state of technology, and therefore a price level below which it can not economically be offered[13]. Moreover, small systems have specific requirements which are hardly compatible with the general 360 architecture as conceived in the early sixties. One key area is user-friendliness, since small systems are most often installed and operated by a single person, generally not a data processing professional.

For that reason, the announcement of System/360 did not stop IBM from continuing to address specific needs with systems of different and mutually incompatible architectures: the 1800 for process control in 1964, its successor System/7 in 1970, the 1130 for personal scientific computing in 1965 (which featured the first personal disk operating system), System/3 for small businesses in 1969. That small systems segment, by definition not covered by the 360 architecture and its unifying effect, perpetuated the anarchic dynamics of the previous years.

Thanks to technological progress, the price of small systems continued to decrease at the same time as their functional content increased. Moreover, it quickly appeared that traditional sales approaches, based on one-on-one contacts and personalized technical support, were inadequate for a mass market where each sale is

---

13   A similar problem exists at the high-end because of the limitations of the architecture

of relatively low value. The widening of the market, together with the decline of unit prices, increasingly called for different forms of marketing and technical support.

To enable a break with tradition in that area, IBM created the General Systems Division (GSD) in 1974. That Division, which brought together development, manufacturing, marketing and support functions for small systems, reported directly to Group executive management. In each country, it included an organization totally separated from the Data Processing Division (DPD), which remained in charge of 360/370 systems. For the first time, IBM split into independent competing industrial entities, which the legal actions under way at the time were threatening to achieve. Faced with the prospect of being cut up, IBM was drawing the dotted lines...

Addressing originally those market segments which were not covered by the 360/370 line and with a mission to implement new forms of mass marketing, GSD was gradually going to set itself up as a competitor of DPD in increasingly large segments of the market. Being indeed in control of its product line and not tied to the 360/370 architecture by design, it tried to meet the growth of its customers' requirements by extending upwards the lines introduced in 1974. GSD even developed advanced and powerful systems such as System/38 in 1980, which incorporated many of the concepts of the defunct Future Systems line. At the same time, DPD continued to extend its 360/370 range downwards, mainly to meet the needs of its large customers for distributed equipment. GSD enjoyed a decisive advantage in the small enterprises through its business practices and low prices, and DPD had an advantage in the large accounts through the consistency of its range. But competition was severe enough to trigger many attempts at managing it at branch or country level, without much actual success. For customers, there were now two competing IBM companies, a situation which some found highly regrettable while others were delighted.

That situation was going to last until 1983, when IBM merged again DPD and GSD and returned to a unified marketing organization, where marketing trade-offs between competing products from relatively autonomous development divisions can be made internally. The last of the large lawsuits, that the US Justice Department, had just come to a conclusion with the removal of the charges, which their originator now declared unfounded. IBM was now presenting a single face to the market, but the new forms of marketing and the new distribution channels established by GSD remained in place. IBM had given up open internal competition, but had become used to selling its products through all available distribution channels: direct sales, agents, retailers, services companies, etc.

That exercise in internal competition has probably been beneficial to IBM, proving right those critics of the US Government who predicted that several small IBM's would be far more efficient that a single large one, and therefore more dangerous for competition. In retrospect, the 1983 merger of DPD and GSD can be considered as a step backwards in the light of the major restructuring under way since 1991.

Future Systems, the end of a dream (1971 - 1975)

In the beginning of the seventies, a project whose nature and precise contents have remained a well-kept secret developed inside IBM: the so-called Future Systems or FS project, sometimes also called AS for Advanced Systems.

The secrecy of that project is all the more remarkable that it involved in 1973/1974 close to 2000 full-time people. Exceptional care (even for IBM) had been taken to insure total confidentiality. In the best secret services tradition, the project was partitioned in such a way that the vast majority of participants could only access that small part which was strictly necessary for the execution of their particular assigned task. As a result, very few people have ever been able to visualize the project in its entirety and to fully understand its strategic implications. More than twenty later years, I feel free to mention some of its general aspects without breaking my commitment to keep it in confidence.

Besides the need to give successors to the 360 series, the deep motivation of the project is the fear that compatible central units will eventually be available on the market, in the same way as disk storage units, magnetic tapes, terminals, add-on memories, and so on. IBM traditionally spends an important share of its expenses in basic research, experimental development and general promotion of data-processing. Those costs are distributed over the costs of all products and are therefore included in their pricing base. Suppliers of compatible products get a "free ride" since they do not need to support those general costs, although they benefit largely from their effect on the market, and can therefore offer their products at lower prices. IBM is thus forced to reduce the prices of its products when they face such competition, at the same time reducing the base over which general expenses can be recovered. That tends to increase the price of the remaining products and therefore to invite the development of new compatible pieces of hardware.

IBM is thus faced with a fundamental strategic alternative. One possibility is to compete at the level of unit prices, which would force IBM to cut down on market development expenses and more generally on its lifestyle, maybe to the point of renouncing the age-old "full employment" policy. The alternate possibility is to exploit its systems skills and market leadership to maintain a competitive advantage at the total system level, offsetting higher prices for each unit. This dilemma is a variation of the "box strategy" versus "systems strategy" issue[14].

A task force convened in Armonk in the second quarter of 1971 to hammer out a proposed action plan to implement that second strategy. Its key assigned objectives were:
- to propose a system architecture and a product plan creating a significant competitive advantage through a major technological breakthrough,
- to make existing computers obsolete,
- to restore a technologically justified basis for re-bundling and a return to functional pricing.

---

14   see previous chapter

One of the major constraints of the project was that any change in the structure of the offerings, whether concerning equipment, software or services, would have to be justified by unquestionable technological arguments and not only by marketing or financial motives. At that time, IBM was the target of several lawsuits, including one by the Government of the United States, and was more cautious than ever not to engage into any action that might be interpreted, even remotely, as an abuse of a dominant position.

The task force soon assigned itself a second major objective, that of facilitating application development. To that effect, the new system had to include all features which could possibly contribute to reducing application costs in proportion with the expected reduction of hardware costs. Otherwise, manufacturers could capture only a decreasing share of the computer expenses of enterprises. On the contrary, a system with decisive advantages in application development efficiency would enjoy a compelling competitive advantage and hopefully justify higher prices as long as its technological leadership would allow a functional pricing approach.

The result was a revolutionary architectural proposal combining a large number of highly innovative ideas. IBM believed that it had a significant advantage in the mass production of very large capacity storage (semiconductors and disks), in software management of memory hierarchies and in microcode technologies. The entire system was therefore designed around a memory of apparently infinite capacity, implemented in a hierarchy of physical devices totally managed by the machine. That physical hierarchy appeared to the user as a "one-level store" where each chunk of data was addressed through a unique identifier assigned at the time of its creation. The system was able to move data within the storage hierarchy in a transparent way and to make it available on call irrespective of its current location.

That apparently unlimited storage capacity, combined with the low costs projected for memories, made it possible to use a single operating system for the whole range. That system would provide all the necessary technical devices in support of easy application development and computer center operations, in all operational modes and at all levels of system price and performance.

In order to support the current and future evolution towards data base and real-time operations, the task force further recommended a drastic redistribution of the traditional functions of hardware and system software. Successive layers of programming were defined between circuitry and application programs, with the ones closest to hardware (called microcode) implemented in very fast read-only memory. Most functions so far implemented in the operating system and its extensions would be microcoded, using several levels of microcode, and certain complex software functions would end up etched in silicium at the very heart of the system.

In the end, the proposed "machine" included everything which constituted base software for previous systems including System/360, including communications management and database management. Similarly, the "central processing unit" now incorporated a high amount of both semiconductor and disk memory, as well as the equivalent of a significant part of the transmission and input-output control units. Apart from application programs, where IBM had no ambition, only input-output devices such as terminals and very high capacity storage devices remained physically separate and therefore vulnerable to competition. That very integrated structure, based on highly specific component units, should preserve the integrity of the sector, in the face of narrowly focused attacks from compatible machines.

That project, which by the end of 1974 kept virtually all IBM development resources busy on a full-time basis, was discontinued in the beginning of 1975, and replaced by a strategy of compatible evolution preserving the 360/370 base. The reasons for canceling the project have obviously not been stated publicly, even inside IBM. They can be roughly summarized as follows.

In their search for maximum exploitation of all current or foreseeable developments, the designers of the system had accumulated technological bets, a large number of which were individually critical for the entire project. Even assuming that each of those bets seemed a reasonable one when viewed separately, a straightforward probability analysis showed that the odds in favor of success of the total project were indeed rather weak. It was therefore highly probable that the project would come across formidable difficulties resulting in delays. In fact, while the 1971 task force had proposed an announcement date of mid-75 (four years later), the announcement date expected in 1974 was early 78, still four years away after three years of hard development work.

Furthermore, in spite of planned tools to facilitate the migration of the old applications, conversion to Future Systems raised serious issues of costs, logistics and customer workload. On the contrary, avoiding those problems by continuing to use Future Systems in 370 compatibility mode deprived users of most advantages of the new system. One could therefore fear that, when FS arrived on the market, its advantage over 370-compatible machines developed in the meantime would not be perceived as compelling by prospective customers. Now the sheer magnitude of the work required for the Future Systems project had dried up all other developments inside IBM, leaving the field open to announcements from the other manufacturers. Finally, the range of alternate possibilities open to customers was far larger than at the time of System/360, now including inexpensive used IBM equipment in addition to compatible or non-compatible competitive hardware.

Whatever reasons motivated IBM executive management of that time to accept "the most expensive failure of its history", that decision has a profound significance: by forgoing Future Systems, IBM was renouncing its explicit project to return to the industry structure which existed in the beginning of the sixties, when its technological leadership gave it a quasi-monopoly on all sectors of industry. The announcement of the 3033 in 1977 meant that data-processing would no longer know revolutions but only a gradual evolution. Moreover, by dropping Future Systems, IBM was accepting to no longer be the master of the game but simply one player among others, taking part in a competitive game of which it would no longer set the rules.

Towards maturity

During the seventies, the IBM world evolves towards a more complex structure. The market breaks down into segments where secondary suppliers compete with the leader in the niche that they have chosen (for example compatible or used equipment), or offer additional elements that the leader has chosen not to provide (for example in software or services). In that world of multiple suppliers, IBM is no longer fighting only the Univac and Control Data, but the likes of Amdahl, Hitachi, Memorex and Storage Technology as well.

That move towards fragmentation of the sector is essentially confined to the IBM products: System/360 and its successors the 370, 4300, 30xx. In the competition between the various "worlds", that situation tends to make the "IBM world" more attractive, both because it benefits from the contributions of other suppliers, and because competition from compatibles and used equipment results in improved product quality and diversity, together with a decline of prices. From the viewpoint of Honeywell or Remington Rand, companies like Amdahl, Hitachi, Memorex or Computer Associates are objectively the allies of IBM.

Simultaneously, the leader sees an increase of the share of the market covered by its architecture and corresponding products, while its own share of that market decreases at well as its profit margins and the influence that it can exert. That direct competitive pressure forces IBM to reduce prices, erodes its market share and its margins, and has indirect repercussions on the other manufacturers (the other "worlds") through the competition between them and IBM.

In summary, the structure of the computer industry changes significantly in the period 1968 to 1980. The spectacular attempts to dismantle the existing structure through legal action do not produce any real results in the end. All the accusations of unfair or illegal practices do not stand the test of legal examination, which amounts to saying that the industry structure prevailing in the seventies is the result of normal competitive market behavior and economic forces. But at the same time, the dominant position of IBM begins to be challenged and gradually eroded through the action of a growing number of smaller enterprises, which exploit the weak spots of the leader by focusing on selected market niches. The profound implication is that IBM, and later the other traditional vendors, will gradually be forced to compete on a box-by-box and niche-by-niche basis, a situation which IBM will painfully recognize by canceling the Future Systems project.

The stage is now set for a gradual dis-integration of the large computing vendors and fragmentation of the industry into separate segments. At the end of the seventies, a sensible prediction could be that the IBM architecture would be increasingly dominant and eventually overtake most of the industry, the IBM company becoming one of many competitors within that "world" and holding a declining market share. But that foreseeable process is going to be disrupted, and in the end accelerated, by the sudden appearance of the brand-new world of microcomputers, with a completely new structure.

Chapter 3 - Another industry emerges (1975-1993)

The micro-computing revolution. IBM creates a competitive world. Specialization and creativity. The illusion of the general public. Two separate worlds. UNIX, a standard or a laboratory? Whither the information industry?

The beginnings of micro-computing (1975-1981)

The first personal computers appear on the market in 1975, as a result of converging developments in three main areas:

- integrated circuits, introduced in the mid-sixties, which have steadily improved with arrival of monolithic memories and microprocessors in the early seventies,
- input-output displays, which existed from the beginning of the sixties, but whose cost has considerably declined while their capabilities increased,
- removable disks, first introduced in 1962, which have been revolutionized with the arrival of the "floppy disk" used from 1971 in certain large computers.

Although those technological foundations are due to large computer and component manufacturers, the birth of micro-computing results from a blossoming of individual initiatives, attempting to build a low-cost personal system by assembling a microprocessor, a screen, a keyboard and a floppy disk.

While previous attempts made by traditional manufacturers in personal computing were targeting professional users, the new suppliers address the hobbyist market. The first microcomputers are indeed sold as kits through magazines for electronics hobbyists. For that reason, the newly-born sector of micro-computing immediately takes a structure similar to that of high fidelity equipment: small independent specialized manufacturers assemble equipment using off-the-shelf components, and distribute their products through mass distribution channels, without any other service than that of the distributor. Specialized distribution chains are created, such as Computerland in 1976. New enterprises enter the competitive arena, such as Texas Instruments, Osborne or Sinclair, each one offering its particular system. Software companies also appear, such as Microsoft, Digital Research, Software Arts or Micropro, and offer the first ready-to-use word processors and spreadsheets in 1979.

As early as in that 1976-1981 period, Apple establishes itself as the leader in micro-computing by offering an original integrated system aimed at the general public. Around this system, an array of software of a new type develops, typical application examples being word processing (with Wordstar in 1979) and spread-sheets (with Visicalc in 1979). Moreover, instead of just selling equipment at the best cost through distributors, that company, under the impetus of its founders, becomes the prophet and the church of a new culture. Thus emerges around Apple a mysticism of user-friendly micro-computing opposed to rigid conventional large data-processing, which takes on the accents of one more crusade against large wicked IBM. This attitude will gradually spread to the world of business, even though the microcomputer itself actually penetrates it only in homeopathic quantities.

The IBM Personal Computer, an open system at last

IBM always sought to be present in personal computing. It introduced the 610 and later the 1620 in the fifties, then the 1130 (the first individual computer using a disk operating system) in 1965, and even the first portable machine in 1975 with the 5100. Nevertheless, it remained uninvolved in the new micro phenomenon until 1981, although the new religion had attracted within the company a growing number of followers whose voice was increasingly strong. It is likely that the prevailing association of micro-computing with the general public market has diverted the attention of IBM leaders from that sector during several years, despite the visible rise of Apple.

IBM finally reacted, but in a completely unusual manner. The Personal Computer launched by IBM in 1981 used an Intel processor, disks purchased from Tandon and an operating system subcontracted to Microsoft. Like the micro-computing pioneers of 1975, IBM only carried out the assembly and wholesale marketing, retail sales being implemented by independent distributors. Better still, the system included a "bus" device allowing the addition of extension cards provided by other manufacturers. Similarly, the selected operating system (MS-DOS) facilitated the development and the incorporation of software by third parties. In a word, the IBM Personal Computer, unlike all the other IBM machines, was a system deliberately open to software and extensions from other suppliers. The commonly accepted explanation for that unusual decision is urgency, but here again the belief that the market involved had little if any relationship with the traditional markets of the company was probably at least an implicit consideration in those decisions.

In a way, IBM elected to follow the Tandy approach rather than the Apple approach, which happened to be the traditional IBM approach. In order to be the number one supplier for micro-computing, just as IBM is the reference supplier for enterprise data-processing, Apple followed the IBM model, as Digital Equipment did a few years earlier on the occasion of the mini phenomenon. On the contrary, to oppose Apple, IBM took on the role of a catalyst of a galaxy of independent enterprises, counting on their creativity and dynamism to make its equipment the *de facto* standard.

Was that maneuver only a temporary expedient to get a foothold in the market while getting ready to regain control with genuine household products? The announcement of the PS/2 and OS/2 in 1988 would tend to support that view, but in the meantime too many systems and compatible extensions for the original PC have been sold, too much software has been written for the backwards journey to be possible. Even assuming that IBM's intention was to take the market back to proprietary systems, that move clearly did not happen and most probably never will[15].

An exploded world

In 1977, when Apple displayed an ambition to take the leadership of the emerging field of micro-computing, it conformed to the typical integrated structure of traditional data-processing. Still today, the Apple company provides, directly or through its affiliate Claris, the quasi-totality of elements installed by users of the Apple architecture, and remains in complete control of the evolution of hardware and base software, even though it subcontracts part of their implementation. This has changed only very recently starting in 1994, with the use of the PowerPC chip and the move towards separate licensing of the MacOS operating system.

In contrast to the unifying action of Apple, the approach selected by IBM to enter this market encourages an exploded structure, where many equipment suppliers coexist and no one of them exerts overall leadership of the sector any longer. The different units of the computer are produced by different manufacturers. Producers of equipment and producers of software form two distinct sectors, and the only mandatory contact with the customer is the distributor.

Suppliers selected by IBM for components and for the operating system soon acquire a durable monopoly position. Intel provides three quarters of the microprocessors used in PC's, the remainder being provided by suppliers of "clones", including IBM itself. Symmetrically, the MS-DOS operating system from Microsoft is installed on practically every PC, after having virtually eliminated all its predecessors and competitors. In contrast, many companies jump into the systems market by assembling a processor, a screen and disks acquired from specialist firms, and complementing them with the MS-DOS system from Microsoft. As early as 1982, the number of brands of IBM-compatible PC's based on Intel processors is estimated at 60, and the total volume of their sales already exceeds that of Apple. Apart from IBM in the early years and more recently Compaq, none of these firms will ever reach a market share higher than 15% and most will satisfy themselves with less than 3%.

That new market of micro-computing attracts traditional manufacturers as well as office equipment companies, and also innumerable newcomers. It quickly becomes the place of a fierce competition, resulting in a dramatic and continuing decline of prices and profits. Similarly, the high production volumes of Intel and Microsoft (several tens of millions of chips or copies of MS-DOS per year) allow a constant decrease of the prices of those basic components. At the same time, the technological progress of components, including microprocessors, memories, disks and displays, entails a continuous and no less dramatic increase of performance.

Those different effects of the competitive dynamics finally add up to an extraordinary variety of the offerings and to prices bearing no relationship to those

---

15   see part 4 (chapters 14 to 16)

of traditional data-processing. The following table, based on studies by the Meta Group, gives a comparison of costs per Mips[16] and costs per Megabyte[17] of central memory, for the PC and for the large computers.

Evolution of costs-logic

$/Mips	micros	mainframes	ratio
1990	700	100000	>140
1995	60	55000	>900

Evolution of costs-memory

$/MByte	micros	mainframes	ratio
1990	90	6000	>65
1995	6	1500	250

Such considerable gaps, which moreover widen with time, could give an impression of different universes based on radically different technologies, but that is not the case. Those dramatic gaps are simply a consequence of high production volumes for monopolistic sectors like components or software packages on one hand, of the intensity of competition for fragmented sectors like equipment on the other hand. Of course, for players of the latter sectors, where no monopoly effect comes into play to keep the profit levels high, the low level of prices comes with lower margins and a more modest lifestyle.

Through its wide availability and moderate prices, the microcomputer opens the gates to individual creativity in the areas of software and all forms of exten-sions (cards, attachable units, etc.). While large data-processing was by necessity reserved to large organizations, the development of a micro software package or even of an extension card only requires, in addition to a good idea, moderate and controllable investments which an individual or a small team can easily afford. Countless small enterprises with very specialized products emerge, many of which survive only for a short time or remain modest players, while others prosper or become dominant players in their niche.

One sees therefore a blossoming of extensions and software of all sorts, implementing especially many new ideas in user-friendliness which had been neglected in the traditional data-processing environment, but which the structure of microcomputers enables. In that area, thanks to often innovative and attractive technical solutions, microcomputers take a serious advantage over conventional sys-tems. The Apple world remains on the leading edge, largely due to its somewhat elitist choice of a powerful processor and a large memory. Apple is also the first to implement with its equipment (Lisa in 1983 and especially the Macintosh in 1984) the revolutionary concepts invented and developed in the sixties at the Palo Alto Research Center of Rank Xerox, such as the mouse, windows and icons. PC users will have to wait until 1984 for a graphic interface remotely comparable to that

---

16 Million of instructions per second: a unit of processing speed.

17 Million of bytes: a unit of memory capacity.

available since a long time with Apple, and until 1990 for a competitive graphic system to be available on the PC, with Windows 3.

All those smaller dedicated enterprises seek to reach the largest possible market, but most are not capable of putting in place their own sales and distribution
network. On the other hand, the sales network of the large traditional manufacturers, is adapted neither to the PC customer population nor to the logistics required
for large quantities at a low unit cost. For that reason, distribution organizations are
created, ranging from local shops to departments of large general department
stores, and including chains specialized in micro-computing. The modes of distribution soon become as important a sales consideration as the features of the equipment.

On the other hand, the rise of micro-computing has no great impact on computer services. Existent service companies satisfy themselves with acquiring the
skills required to incorporate microcomputers, as needed, in the systems that they
develop for their customers. The specific service requirements of microcomputer
users are mainly addressed by the dedicated distributors, some of which happen to
be subsidiaries of service companies.

The micro-computing industry thus appears as made up of complementary
and specialized sectors:
- components,
- equipment,
- operating systems,
- application software packages,
- distribution.

In contrast with the structure of conventional data-processing, each player
specializes in a single one of those activities, and very few firms operate in several
sectors. The most striking exceptions are Microsoft which is present in both types
of software packages, a few equipment manufacturers like Dell that choose to be
their own distributors, and IBM which is present in all sectors including components, and still attempts to return to a traditional structure with the PS/2 and OS/2
complex,.

The PC world also distinguishes itself from the traditional world by the
nature of leadership. In the conventional world, the undisputed leader is a supplier
of equipment, generally IBM. In the PC world, while hundreds of firms share the
equipment market, none of them exceeding a 15% market share, both Intel and
Microsoft are virtually in a monopoly position in their respective sectors. Those two
firms dominate the PC world insofar as their products are the ones which unify the
sector, and their decisions determine its overall evolution.

In summary, the rise of micro-computing translates into a radically different
industry structure from that prevailing for conventional data-processing. The separation between manufacturing and distribution is the rule, with most manufacturers
moving their products through several channels and most distributors marketing
products from several different manufacturers. Enterprises producing only software
are many. Among manufacturers of equipment, most produce only a specific type
of unit such as disks, printers, central units, and even extension cards or particular

units like scanners or modems. Contemporary computing can be characterized as "exploded computing " (the title of a book of J.M. Desaintquentin and B Sauteur[18]); this qualifier applies as well to the structure of that industry.

As was partly the case for System/360, IBM has created with the PC an industry that it does not control and where it occupies a minority place. Indeed, in 1992, all the PC compatibles and the PS/2 add up to close to 90% of the market, versus 10% for Apple and 2% for the other architectures (Commodore, Atari). But in those 90%, IBM is a minority contributor, although still number one, with approximately 15% of total sales, when it represented some 32% in 1986. In the meantime, suppliers of compatibles have exploited technological progress to cut market prices in a continuous and dramatic fashion, some at the price of their survival.

Disconnected markets

At the beginning of the eighties, micro-computing is still essentially a matter for individuals in the general public. Apple and its cohort of followers of the true faith are alone in prophesying that micro-computing will someday overturn large data-processing in enterprises. In practice, the two sectors and the two markets do not communicate: suppliers of micros and suppliers of large data-processing equipment are generally distinct enterprises belonging to two different worlds, while micro customers are individuals and customers of large data-processing are enterprises. That idea that micro-computing addresses a separate market has survived for a long time. Even IBM has deemed necessary to introduce a specific machine called the "PC Junior" in 1983, before pulling it back for lack of sales in 1985.

One may think that this mirage of the general public, although costing a lot of money to many an ephemeral enterprise, has nevertheless played a positive role. What would have happened if the pioneers of micro-computing (the Steve Jobs, the Bill Gates) had foreseen at that time that they would someday be competing directly with big businesses like IBM, who dominated the data-processing market? Believing that they were operating in a new market, disconnected from the market of large data-processing, probably gave them the necessary boldness. Similarly, the same belief that micro-computing addresses the general public and not enterprises kept out the traditional manufacturers, which nevertheless possessed all the necessary technologies and had already introduced personal computers for professional usage. The successful start of micro-computing results partly from the same misunderstanding of its true potential by pioneers who have promoted it and by the large manufacturers who have neglected it.

IBM's entry into the personal computer market radically changes the image of the microcomputer by somehow bestowing on it a guarantee of seriousness, and considerably widens its market by opening up the enterprises. But microcomputers spread there mainly for forms of usage and populations of users thus far unconcerned by conventional data-processing, such as word processing in business offices or decision-making assistance for individual managers.

---

18   "L'Informatique éclatée" Masson - 1991

In large enterprises as for the general public, micro-computing has until now essentially allowed the satisfaction of personal computing requirements that were not satisfied by central systems. When micro-computing arrives, the central needs of enterprises are largely satisfied by conventional data-processing, which is also getting ready to address individual needs with "timesharing" technologies. Micro-computing conquers that latter area before the large computers succeed in establishing themselves there. The spreading of word processing and spreadsheet computing did not take away existing workload from central systems, but it enabled the satisfaction of a latent still unsatisfied need. In so doing, it has made obsolete the concept of "computing utility" and has given the death-blow to that market where many services companies were still operating.

Even now, the replacement of large systems by microcomputers has remained marginal as compared the total number of large systems installed. Migrating existing applications to microcomputers assumes that those can somehow be assembled into complexes equaling the large systems in functions and in power. It also demands a heavy investment in the redesign and redevelopment of applications, which has seldom been justified by a potential gain of operating costs in the eyes of large systems users. Moreover, such an operation carries a risk that few DP executives have deemed reasonable to incur.

But the advantage of micros continues to grow with time and increases the competitive pressure to make the whole of data-processing benefit from the lower costs resulting from very large scale distribution. To achieve that requires the development of simple and efficient means to distribute applications between interconnected systems, or to build large systems from the same cheap components as PC's. Those are the real stakes attached to the ongoing developments in the areas of client-server architecture, distributed systems and multiprocessors.

The innovative dynamics of the micro sector result in increasingly satisfactory solutions to those technical problems, which have so far constrained the upward expansion of micro-computing technologies. In particular, a third "world" which we have not mentioned yet, namely the Unix movement, plays a key role in this process of innovation, despite its relatively small importance in term of volumes.

The Unix world

In the beginning of the eighties, when the PC tidal wave begins to surge, a few companies, including most prominently Sun Microsystems, seek to penetrate the market without having to support the heavy investment required for developing and maintaining an operating system. It turns out that a system called Unix is highly popular in the academic circles that those new suppliers are precisely targeting.

The Unix operating system is an adaptation for small computers of the General Electric Multics system[19], developed around 1969 on the initiative of the Bell

---

19   Multics, developed around 1960, was a "time-sharing" system enabling many independent users to simultaneously exploit a large computer in an interactive manner, through a

Laboratories. For a long time, its utilization has been confined to a few American universities (most notably Berkeley) where it formed a basis for studies and experimental work in computer research and education, resulting in many extensions and competing versions. Facilitating the exchange of those developments has always been a very important objective in this academic environment, leading in particular to a major rewrite of the system in a high level language (language C) in 1973.

In the beginning of the eighties, Unix appears as an available system, not protected by a manufacturer, designed for easy evolution, and benefiting from the innovative dynamics of the most active research centers. Adopting it enables manufacturers to rely on an independent source of base software and to concentrate their efforts and their investments on hardware. It also provides a significant competitive advantage in the scientific market. Thereafter, almost all manufacturers will include Unix systems in their catalog alongside their proprietary systems, supporting them with highly variable promotional and marketing efforts depending on how strongly Unix competes with their traditional offerings.

Contrary to the launching of the PC, the industrial beginning of Unix does not bring a major change in the structure of the industry. In particular, no autonomous component industry appears. Newcomers such as Sun develop new proprietary microprocessors, while traditional manufacturers (Hewlett-Packard, IBM, Digital Equipment) use their existing microprocessors in their Unix systems, before developing specific microprocessors for their Unix machines.

Rather quickly, the development of processors supporting Unix turns to the utilization of the Risc concept (Reduced Instruction Set Computer[20]). Initially though, each Unix hardware manufacturer considers the possession of an original processor as part of its competitive advantages and restricts its utilization by other vendors. Only recently did the monopolistic logic of the component industry begin to cause the creation of associations where the main Risc component manufacturers attempt to enroll other equipment manufacturers in order to increase their production scale[21]. Nevertheless, in 1993, the distribution of each of these microprocessors does not exceed a few hundred thousand copies (500000 for Sun's Sparc, 200000 for Mips from Silicon Graphics or the Hewlett-Packard Precision Architecture), which is tiny when compared to the Intel processors and way below the optimal production scale.

Concerning the operating system, the hope of some manufacturers to do without investing in its development will soon be disappointed. In 1983, ATT, the legal owner of Unix, who until then had allowed its liberal distribution, reacts to the sudden commercial success of the system by charging high royalties. That weakens considerably the very reason for hardware manufacturers to select Unix, its inex-

---

reasonably user-friendly interface for the time.

20   A microprocessor architecture favoring simplicity and therefore execution speed, based on a limited and homogeneous instruction set, complex operations being implemented by combining those simple instructions at the software level.

21   see chapter 7

pensive availability in source form. Moreover, the uneven industrial quality of implementations by academic laboratories forces manufacturers to undertake rewrites or additional developments, which result in more competing versions and adds still more fuel to the usual disputes between supporters of the various versions of Unix.

Each manufacturer therefore turns to the development of its own specific system, built of an assemblage of standard elements and proprietary elements, while still remaining true to the dream of a universal operating system and participating in permanent standards efforts through neutral organizations such as XOpen, or alliances like OSF[22] and more recently COSE[23]. The intensity of the standards effort in the Unix world is the direct counterpart (or the reverse side) of the proliferation of alternate solutions and of the resulting controversies. If no such phenomenon occurs in the PC world, the reason is simply that the whole industry rallied very early, rightly or wrongly, behind MS-DOS and later Windows.

In summary, the current structure of the Unix (and Risc) world is closer to the traditional structure than the PC world. As in the traditional world, competition takes place essentially between complete computer solutions made up of a vendor-specific combination of hardware (using a proprietary processor) with a proprietary derivative of the Unix operating system. The structure of the Unix world differs from the classical structure only by the multiplication of alliances purporting to share those elements which require heavy investments, such as components or operating system modules, and by the related intensive standards activity. The phenomenon of alliances and the system standardization movement, often presented as concerning the totality of data-processing, are in fact largely confined to the Unix world and indeed only concern one tenth of the market, strictly speaking[24].

The use of Unix is growing faster than data-processing as a whole, but remains at a modest level both in absolute numbers relative to micros and in value when compared to the total software revenue. The number of Unix systems installed in 1992, all versions together, was estimated at approximately 2.5 million, versus more than 130 million MS-DOS and Apple microcomputers. At the same time, the market share of Unix systems in the total market was approximately 13%. But the potential strategic importance of Unix is much greater than its quantitative place. The Unix world is the laboratory from which will emerge the practical elements for resolution of problems related to the replacement of large systems by networks of systems or processors coming from the micro world, with similar levels of price/performance.

Contrary to a widespread opinion, the Unix world is quite the opposite of a standardized world. On the contrary, the Unix world is the place where the specific competition between operating systems is the most intense. In the traditional world, it is partially eclipsed by the hardware-related competition, and it no longer exists in

---

22   Open Systems Foundation

23   Common Operating Systems Environment

24   see Chapter 12

the PC world because of the general adoption of MS-DOS and now of Windows. The Unix world must devote so much effort to standard definition precisely because it has a glaring need for standards and there is no dominant supplier to impose them.

Conversely, thanks to these efforts, the Unix world is producing standards for the whole industry. Innovation being the other face of competition, the Unix world is the privileged center of innovation for all areas related to operating systems, including systems architecture and structure, multiprocessing, distributed systems, availability, security, etc. Moreover, the performance level of most Unix systems is similar to that of traditional minis. Unix suppliers have therefore an immediate competitive motivation to endow Unix with all the functions of minicomputers, which are themselves derivatives of large systems, as well as to attack the large systems head-on through the development of multiprocessors. The very dynamics of the Unix world and its position at the junction of traditional data-processing and micro-computing make it the birthplace of upheavals yet to come.

An overview in 1993

The history of the computer industry, as well as the combined action of competitive dynamics and technological progress, has resulted in a relatively complex industry structure, where three industrial worlds coexist, each with its own logic:

- a traditional world inherited from the sixties, still highly concentrated in spite of gradual fragmentation of the IBM world,
- the world born from the PC in 1981, where a highly fragmented structure has led to new standards of price and affordability for computers,
- the Unix world, which went from academic stage to commercial stage in 1983, and is the laboratory where the data-processing techniques of tomorrow are being elaborated.

According to their membership in those three worlds, industrial players are more or less specialized and form more or less identifiable sectors. Players in the traditional world and in the Unix world generally offer a complete range of products and services, including hardware, base software and services, while specialization by nature of product is the rule in the PC world. In the traditional world and the Unix world, competition between players is based on the totality of this basket of products and services, including components. Consequently, each player develops and produces its own processors and its own operating systems, even though in this last area the Unix world pretends to implement one standard system. The PC world has adopted a single processor architecture and a single operating system, and the competition between players of each sector concentrates on the specific products of that sector. Finally, each player in those three worlds can aim at markets of various sizes: the entire computer market for most traditional manufacturers, where IBM is the example, more narrow niches for the more recent suppliers.

These three worlds are still evolving side by side more than competing head to head, no matter what some "small is beautiful" enthusiasts have pretended, and even if some players are simultaneously present in two or three of those worlds. In

1992, traditional data-processing was estimated as still representing 45% of sales, micro-computing 41% and the Unix world 13%. Neither the PC world nor the Unix world offers yet a technically viable and sufficiently believable alternative to large systems, which could overcome the inertia of user organizations, justified by risks and costs of conversion. The client-server concept is not yet considered as mature by the majority of users. In the Unix world, the abundance of alternate solutions and the resulting incompatibilities (in spite of standardization efforts) add up to a complexity of choice that still turns away the bulk of the market, except for a few niches like graphic workstations where those difficulties have been locally solved. The industry has not evolved to a new structure as a whole, but three worlds with different structures are living side by side with relatively minor overlap.

Nevertheless, these three worlds have a mutual influence. Plummeting micro prices and constant progress of their performance pull the prices of Unix worksta-tions downwards, which by continuity also pulls downward the prices of traditional midrange systems. The rise of micros and workstations has strongly slowed down the progress of large systems and caused a regression of the minicomputer market, which were the stars of the seventies and eighties.

But while the decline of prices continues in micros and still widens the price differential with traditional data-processing, the performances and functional rich-ness of small systems are approaching those of traditional systems, especially thanks to Unix-based developments. Competitive tensions exasperate, and those worlds with the most dynamic internal competition are acquiring more and more competitive advantages relative to the other worlds, precisely in areas where compe-tition is most active: prices for micros, operating systems for the Unix world.

The current situation is unstable. It seems likely that, by the end of the cen-tury, the three worlds will merge into a single industry structure where the competi-tive and sectoral logic of the PC world will prevail, and which will offer technical solutions combining the best of Unix, of the PC world and of the traditional world. What will the structure of this new world be? What forms of integration or specialization will be dominant among the four possible dimensions of specializa-tion: by type of equipment, by market, by nature of offering or by stage of produc-tion?

In parallel, at the same time as that evolution occurs, data-processing is invad-ing all sectors of activity. Widespread products like cars, domestic appliances, audio-visual equipment or games contain an increasing amount of "intelligence". Is the future of data-processing to become invisible by being completely integrated into products specialized by function? In the same movement, will the computer indus-try merge into the other industries and disappear as a separate industry? Those questions will be looked at again in part four, after conducting a sector by sector analysis of the underlying mechanisms which govern the structuring of industry,

Chapter 4 - The structure of the industry

In search of a structure. Generalists and specialists. Main products and secondary products. Do sectors match markets? Expense structures and models of enterprises.

The subject of the present chapter is to analyze a few figures concerning firms that constitute the computer industry, in order to establish an applicable classification and to attempt to find indications of a structure and of typical behaviors.

On the whole, statistics that are regularly published concerning the computer industry do not care to define a typology of firms in a precise way. Most postulate a traditional breakdown of the market into broad segments such as large systems, midrange systems, personal computers, workstations, peripherals, software and services. But that segmentation of the market does not necessarily match the specialization of firms. In reality, many firms operate in several of those segments. For example, almost all firms included under large systems or midrange systems also provide software and services. Conversely, many commentators lump together packaged software and services into one sector, which would only make sense if the majority of firms present in one activity was also present in the other.

Many analysts follow the official industry statistics by placing each firm in the sector defined by its main product or service. The industry sectors thus defined parallel exactly the market segments, but that simplifying approach eliminates the problems of firms with multiple products, by ignoring the actual content of the offer of the different companies and the relative frequency of the various combinations. To obtain a more accurate picture of the computer industry, we must analyze the content of the offer of each enterprise, and identify representative combinations and groups of firms offering similar baskets of services or products. If, in addition, it turns out that the firms which belong to each of those groups have other features in common and distinct from the other groups, that will tend to indicate that the structure thus defined is indeed relevant.

Few sources provide a reasonably reliable analysis of the revenue breakdown for a sufficient number of enterprises. We will use a listing published each year by the Datamation magazine, where the worldwide revenue of the top 100 American data-processing companies (and occasionally a few non-American ones) is broken down into ten areas by nature of product or service, and therefore by market segment. The ten segments are: large systems (large), midrange systems (mid), PC, workstations, communication hardware (com), other peripherals (peri), software (soft), maintenance, other services (serv) and miscellaneous (other). The following discussion exploits the statistics for years 1992 to 1994.

For 1992, our sample of 100 large US companies totals a computer revenue close to $211 billion, or 63% of a worldwide market which other statistics, such as those from McKinsey that we will use later, evaluate at $338 billion for the same year. It leaves out mainly large European firms like Siemens, Olivetti, Bull and ICL, or Japanese firms like NEC, Fujitsu, Hitachi, Toshiba, Matsushita or Mitsubishi, as well as many services companies very active in Europe. In addition to being limited to US vendors, that sample of the top 100 companies is obviously biased in favor of the larger ones. We will discuss later to what extent those limitations of the sample could cause a distortion in our findings, and how they should be modified to give a more accurate representation of the structure of the worldwide computing industry.

Let us keep in mind that the figures provided are certainly inaccurate. Some are clearly "guesstimates" produced either by the firms or the authors of the survey, and not derived from any sort of accounting system. When they rely on the statements of enterprises and their internal accounting reports, they refer to implicit product definitions which may differ from one firm to another. For example, some equipment manufacturers report zero maintenance income, which can mean charging maintenance as part of hardware, rather than providing no maintenance. Therefore, we will refrain from interpreting those figures as more than estimates. Considering the general character of our conclusions, we will nevertheless consider that the image of the industry which they present is probably a reasonably accurate representation of the worldwide situation.

Secondly, those statistics do not include the activities of component manufacturing on one hand, of distribution on the other hand, as part of the computer industry. Firms specialized in those areas do not appear in the classification. Intel and Motorola are mentioned, but only for their secondary activities in large systems and extension boards for the Intel, for midrange systems and communication devices for Motorola.

Notice incidentally that it is inaccurate to consider the total revenue of the computer industry as being equal to the sum of revenues of the firms mentioned. For instance, suppliers of peripherals and software packages sell a significant share of their production to equipment manufacturers, which in turn charge those products back to their customers as part of their packaged offerings. That revenue is therefore counted twice.

A classification of actors

Firms by number of sectors

nb segments	10	9	8	7	6	5	4	3	2	1
nb firms	2	1	1	4	4	1	6	12	32	37
market share %	37	7	5	5	3	0	4	9	12	18

Let us use the 1992 figures to sketch a classification of the firms in our sample. Of the 100 firms present, 69 are present in only one or two segments. Together, those 69 specialists add up to 30% of total industry revenue. At the opposite, eight firms are present in seven or more segments and occupy 54% of the

total market. Between those two classes, 23 firms are present in three to six segments, for a total market share of 16%. Therefore, although specialized firms are a
large majority in terms of numbers, more than half of the industry revenue comes
from a small handful of generalists.

The generalists

The eight main generalists are the historic equipment manufacturers and suppliers: IBM, Digital Equipment, Hewlett-Packard, NCR/ATT, Unisys, Wang, Data
General and Texas Instruments.

The share of equipment in their revenue ranges from 39% for Unisys to 70%
for ATT/NCR, Hewlett-Packard and Texas Instruments. However, the history of
these firms allows to consider the sum of equipment and maintenance as more significant than hardware alone, since all those firms only maintain their own equipment, and none offers third-party maintenance services. The share of maintenance
for those generalists varies considerably: from 0% for Texas Instruments to 31%
for Digital Equipment and Data General, and 42% for Wang. One can propose two
possible explanations for those variations: on one hand, the maintenance techniques
and billing policies used by each firm can end up in different proportions between
maintenance revenue and the corresponding hardware revenue; on the other hand,
some firms have seen their equipment sales decline, but still derive from their
installed inventory a revenue stream out of proportion with their current sales of
equipment; it is probably the case of Data General and Wang. By adding maintenance to the hardware activity, one obtains a total ranging from 60% for Unisys and
64% for IBM to 89% for Data General.

Those eight generalists are therefore still dominated by their original activity
of equipment manufacturers. Among the other firms, which are present on less
than seven segments, two exhibit that same feature without being clearly specialized
in a specific hardware segment: Control Data and Wyse, which we classify as generalists.

Generalists

Name	Lg	Mi	PC	Sta	Sof	Per	Co	Ma	Ser	Oth
IBM	13	9	12	3	18	12	3	12	10	9
Digital Equipment	0	18	3	8	6	21	2	31	11	0
Hewlett-Packard	1	10	6	12	3	36	5	2	5	20
AT&T/NCR	1	5	10	0	3	22	32	16	11	0
Unisys	25	0	6	8	9	0	0	22	17	13
Wang	0	16	15	0	4	13	3	42	7	0
Data General	0	30	6	7	2	15	0	31	9	0
Texas	20	10	20	0	4	20	0	0	20	6
Control Data	21	0	0	25	19	0	0	26	13	0
Wyse	0	0	19	19	0	63	0	0	0	0

In summary, the ten firms in the above table can be considered as generalists.
Those firms account for 54% of the total revenue for the 100 firm sample. At the
worldwide level, we would have to add Fujitsu, NEC, Hitachi, Siemens-Nixdorf,
Toshiba, Olivetti, Bull, ICL and Mitsubishi, respectively ranking second, third, sixth,

eighth, tenth, twelfth, thirteenth, seventeenth and twenty-sixth in order of decreasing total DP revenue, which would again increase the share of generalists in the
global market.

For most of those generalists, software packages and services activities are
ancillary services that are provided only in relation to their main activity of equipment sales, and do not account for more than 20% of their revenue. Appreciating
the "ancillary" nature of a service involves a dose of subjectivity. For example,
firms considered as specialized in hardware, like NCR, Unisys or Control Data
make between 11% and 17% of their revenue in services other than maintenance.
The case of Control Data is particularly interesting, since that company has moved
part of its services activity into a subsidiary called Ceridian, but still retains a share
higher than 12 % of its own revenue.

One can therefore think that a services share of 12 to 15% represents a normal level of ancillary assistance in support of equipment, and does not justify considering a firm as genuinely mixed. Now, for IBM, services other than maintenance
account for only 10% of revenue, which is less than for the five firms mentioned
earlier. Although this figure is characteristic of a purely ancillary service activity, and
is also rather lower in relation to hardware than for other manufacturers, the size of
IBM makes it number one in the services market, and often leads to consider it as a
services company in the same way as specialized firms.

The specialized companies

Although partly subjective, this distinction between main services and ancillary services[25] is valid for all enterprises. The mere presence of an actor in a segment does not necessarily mean that it plays an important role in the segment, nor
that the corresponding production is an important part of its activity. For example,
the revenue of Microsoft, which everyone agrees to regard as specialized in software, includes 8% in services and 1% in equipment alongside with 91% in software
packages. Similarly, Lexmark is indisputably specialized in peripherals (precisely
printers) which account for 98% of its revenue, the 2% that it makes in PC's being
incidental.

Since counting Microsoft, Lexmark and many other similar companies among
the generalists would be a severe distortion of reality, we must consider as specialized all firms that offer one main service plus ancillary services in support of the
main service. For firms offering mainly products (equipment or software packages),
ancillary services may include maintenance or assistance in the utilization of those
products, or even software packages or peripherals related to those products,
acquired from third parties and resold as part of a complete system. In a symmetric

----

25   In this book, the terms "products" and "services" are often used to mean both products
     and services, for the sake of brevity. The cases when they should be understood in the
     restrictive sense should be apparent from the context. In fact, as will be discussed in chapter
     10, making a sharp distinction between products and services is not essential for the
     purpose of this book.

fashion, services companies can integrate into their offer equipment that they buy and resell, which is a frequent situation in systems integration.

With those remarks in mind, we can consider as specialists not only the 37 firms that are present in only one segment, but also 41 of those that are present in 2, 3 or 4 segments. We thus end up with a total of 78 specialized firms distributed as shown in the following table. The detailed list for each area of specialization, with the percentage of their revenue realized in each segments, is given in the appendix (tables A-II to A-XII):

Number of specialists by segment

	lge	mid	PC	stat	soft	peri	com	main	serv	other
1 segment	0	1	4	0	8	7	3	0	13	1
>1 segment	3	2	5	3	7	6	2	1	11	1
total	3	3	9	3	15	13	5	1	24	2

Most of these allocations are obvious, but a few cases require some additional explanation. In the categories of central systems specialists, two types of firms coexist: those which market only processing units, requiring their customers to turn to other suppliers for peripherals and services (like Convex, Stratus and most PC manufacturers), and those which offer more complete systems entailing significant revenues in the ancillary segments. That second category includes Amdahl for large systems, Tandem for the midrange, Apple or CompuAdd for micros. We have also considered that significant revenue in maintenance or services is not necessarily the indicator of a genuine mixed activity, where services would be marketed independently of equipment.

Note finally that Motorola and Intel only appear in the Datamation statistics as suppliers of midrange systems and communication peripherals for Motorola, of large systems and extension boards for Intel. Although essential to the whole data-processing industry, their main role of component manufacturers is not taken into account in this classification. In our classification, those two firms are assigned to a different category, that of components, and are not counted among the communications and peripherals specialists.

Mixed firms

The above classification into ten "generalists" and 80 "specialists" (including Intel and Motorola) leaves out ten firms which can be considered genuinely "mixed" in various ways. Those firms are distributed as follows (see table A-XII in the appendix):
  - one (Prime Computervision) is an equipment company offering maintenance, software and related services, and could have been included in workstation specialists, except that its important maintenance activity concerns in a large part different equipment inherited from the acquisition of Prime;
  - one (Ask) offers mainly software, complemented by equipment and services;
  - three (Dun and Bradstreet, Reynolds & Reynolds, National Computing Systems) supplement with equipment and software an offer focused on service and maintenance;

- two (Lockheed, Datapoint) offer equipment and services in almost equal proportions;
- two (Sterling Software, Nynex) offer almost equal proportions of software and services;
- one (MAI), offers services and maintenance in an almost balanced manner.

Apart from Prime/Computervision, whose history is that of an equipment manufacturer, the share of services in the mixed firms offer is high. Indeed, almost all started as services companies and have added to that activity the sale of equipment or software packages.

1992-1994 trends

Differences between years 1992 and 1994, as reported in the Datamation figures, may involve either a real evolution of the composition of the offer of firms or the reclassification of the same activities in different categories. Typical examples of the latter are the merging of peripheral revenue into the related central systems, different breakdowns between maintenance and other services, and even merging maintenance with the equipment or software maintained. In addition, maintenance and other services have been combined into a single category in the 1994 statistics. This is most unfortunate since it precludes any serious analysis of trends involving the services area, which is actually extremely heterogeneous and would warrant being split into its various constituents rather than treated in bulk.

Movements by category

	1992	out	in	1994
generalists	10	3	0	7
mixed	9	5	2	6
large	3	1	0	2
midrange	3	0	0	3
PC	9	3	1	7
stations	3	0	0	3
software	15	1	7	21
peripherals	14	1	7	20
comm	6	3	11	14
maintenance	1	0	0	1
services	25	13	4	16
other	2	2	0	0

Seventy-one firms are present in both the 1992 top 100 and the 1994 top 100. Of those 71, only three change category:
- Texas Instruments from generalist to mixed (28% PC, 20% software and 52% peripherals), after getting out of large, midrange and services,
- Wang from generalist to mixed (60% services, including maintenance which was 42% in 1992, 28% PC, 10% midrange and 2% software), after getting out of peripherals and communications,

– Wyse from generalist to peripherals(80% peripherals and 20% services), after dropping PC's and workstations.

Twenty-nine firms disappear from the 1992 top 100, either by leaving the business, being absorbed or dropping below the 100th rank. The twenty-nine new firms entering the 1994 top 100 can be either startups, new names resulting from mergers or fast-growing existing firms. The detailed changes are given in the following table.

Revenue by category (M$)

	1992 M$	92 share	1994 M$	94 share	CGR%
generalists	114039	53.5	116093	46.4	0.9
mixed	4510	2.1	4778	1.9	2.9
large	3554	1.7	2561	1.0	-15.1
midrange	2860	1.3	3136	1.2	4.7
PC	18486	8.7	31792	12.6	31.1
stations	5932	2.8	8020	3.2	16.3
software	12015	5.6	19066	7.6	26.0
peripherals	18260	8.6	27201	10.8	22.0
comm	4749	2.2	10010	4.0	45.2
maintenance	800	0.4	828	0.3	1.7
services	24764	11.6	26839	10.6	4.1
other	1225	0.6	0	0.0	

The growth rates for each category shown in the preceding tables should be compared to an overall growth rate of 8.9% for the total revenue of the top 100. Large systems specialists show an absolute decrease in both revenue and numbers. Generalists and mixed firms, as well as specialists in midrange systems, maintenance and services grow more slowly than the market, so that their share of the overall market erodes. In particular, the generalists fall below 50% of the market. Of the ten generalists in 1992, three restrict their range to the point of becoming mixed or specialists. In the mixed firms, five out of nine disappear from the 1992 top 100, and the two new entrants into the category are generalists cutting down on their range. Conversely, many software and peripherals firms, including communications, make it to the top 100 and capture a growing share of the total revenue.

PC specialists capture an increasing share of the total market, but fewer firms show up in the top 100. In services, the number of specialists in the top 100 decreases together with their market share. This can mean either that the share of non-specialists increases, or that large specialized firms grow more slowly than the overall industry, resulting in increased fragmentation of the sector.

The overall trend is towards increased specialization of firms and increased fragmentation of the industry.

Correspondence between sector and market

Let us now examine how the different markets are served. For each of the ten main segments retained by Datamation, let us consider all firms that realize a non-zero revenue in that segment. Those firms may belong to any of the categories defined above, but they will most often be either generalists or specialists of the segment concerned. The following figure shows, for each segment, the respective market share of generalists, specialists of that segment and other firms (specialists of other segments or mixed firms). The detailed figures are given in the appendix (table A-XIII).

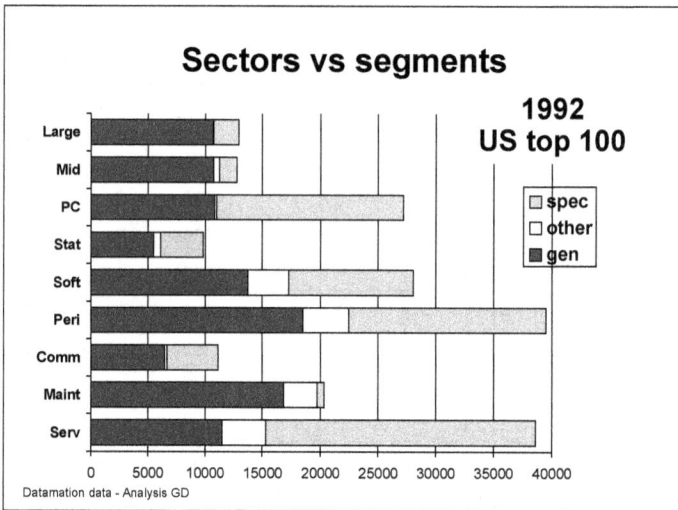

The ten generalists largely dominate the large and midrange systems segments, as well as the maintenance segment. They are a clear minority only in the segment of services other than maintenance. For PC, workstations and communications peripherals, specialists of the segment account for virtually all the remainder of the market, leaving only a marginal place to specialists of the other segments and to mixed firms. That split is less clear for software, other peripherals, maintenance and services. In the maintenance segment, the specialized firm even occupies only a marginal market share, leaving the second place to specialists of the other segments and to mixed firms.

A more detailed segment by segment analysis is given in the appendix. Tables A-XIV to A-XXII contain, for each segment, the list of those firms in the sample of 100 that are present, ranked in decreasing order of their share of that market (shown in column 4). Only firms with a market share of 1% and higher are listed. In addition, those tables show for each firm its category of specialization (column 2) and the percentage of its total computer revenue realized in that segment, which measures its degree of specialization in that segment (column 3).

Because it only includes the US top 100 firms, the sample is biased in favor of large companies. In particular, all firms which are among the top 100 appear in all segments where they are active, even with segment revenues which might be lower than those of specialized firms not present in the top 100. The tables in the appendix show in boldface characters the companies which would certainly remain in the same relative position even if the sample was extended to smaller companies. The other firms might be displaced by smaller ones, but more specialized in that segment.

Large systems (table A-XIV)

Eleven firms are present, of which seven of the ten generalists, which realize together more than 80% of the revenue, with specialization not exceeding 25%. Three real specialists occupy together less than 20% of this market, and only one other firm (Intel) is marginally present.

The companies with the two highest market shares are generalists, in decreasing order IBM and Unisys, which together realize nearly 80% of revenue. The large systems market is therefore dominated by those two suppliers. Specialists appear only at the third place, with shares not exceeding 12%.

The situation is similar in 1994. IBM and Unisys still account together for 80% of the market. With the disappearance of Convex and the decline of Amdahl, the two remaining specialists now represent only 15% of the market. Texas Instruments and Hewlett-Packard, two generalists, have left that market, and Silicon Graphics starts reporting some of its revenue as large systems. In general, the order of the major firms and their market shares remain similar, although there is a slight trend towards increased concentration.

Expanding the sample to the entire worldwide industry would result in adding a handful of Japanese and European generalists (NEC, Fujitsu, Hitachi, Siemens, Bull, ICL), but very few other companies. This would increase the share and the domination of specialists in the large systems market.

In summary, firms specialized in large systems are too few and occupy too small a share of that market to be considered as forming an autonomous sector. One can expect the competitive behavior of large systems suppliers to be governed not by factors specific of that segment, but by generalist strategies that also address the other markets in which the dominant suppliers operate.

Midrange systems (table A-XV)

In 1992, the situation is very similar to that of large systems, with only a few different names. Fourteen players operate in that segment, among which seven of the ten generalists, which account for 84% of revenue. The total market share of the three specialists is 12%. Four other firms are present (Reynolds and Reynolds, Ask, Motorola and Sun), with market shares ranging from 0.3% to 1.6%.

Here again, the three highest market shares are those of generalists, which are in decreasing order IBM, Digital Equipment and Hewlett-Packard, and together realize 75% of the revenue. Specialists appear only in the fourth, sixth and ninth place, with shares lower than 7%.

In 1994, the generalists still dominate the segment, now occupying the first four places and a total of 80% of the market. The new entrants are either generalists (Unisys, Control Data) or PC specialists (Apple, Dell) who start reporting part of their revenue as midrange systems. It is likely that part of the growth in this segment is simply due to a reclassification of existing revenue based on fuzzy definitions, rather than genuine intrinsic growth. Compared to the large systems segment, there are more changes in order and market shares of the firms, and a visible trend towards less concentration.

In the same way as for large systems, taking in consideration the entire worldwide industry would add the same Japanese and European vendors and thus strengthen the dominance of generalists. This would however be mitigated by the addition of a few specialists both from the US and the rest of the world. But in the end, as for the large systems, one can not speak of an autonomous sector for midrange systems.

PC (table A-XVI)

The situation is clearly different for the microcomputer segment. In 1992, nine of the ten generalists appear among the 21 firms present, but their revenue only adds up to 40% of this market. On the other hand, nine specialized firms occupy close to 60% and appear as high as the second to sixth places. Mixed firms other that generalists play a very minor role. The segment is therefore satisfied by two types of firms: specialists on one hand, for which micro-computing represents more than 65% of their activity, and on the other hand firms for which this segment represents a minor part (less of 20%) of their activity.

In 1994, the share of specialists increases to almost 66%, even with the disappearance of Commodore, Tandy and CompuAdd from the top 100. The same nine generalists are still present although two have moved to the mixed category, but their combined market share drops below 33%. There does not seem to be a significant change in segment concentration.

If we took into account the entire worldwide computer industry, we would see appearing on this segment a few other non-American generalists, but also a large number of enterprises too small to show up in the sample retained by Datamation. In number of players, this would give a very clear majority to specialized firms.

One can therefore consider that there is indeed an autonomous sector of suppliers specialized in microcomputers, which includes a large number of small firms. That sector is competing on the market with the large generalists, and gradually taking over the larger part of the market.

Workstations (table A-XVII)

The case of workstations is somehow intermediate between that of midrange or large systems and that of PCs. In 1992, sixteen firms are present here, including seven of the ten generalists, which still represent 56% the market. On the other hand, although there are only three real specialists (Sun, Silicon Graphics and Intergraph), they account together for 38% the market and occupy respectively the first, fifth and seventh places.

That division of the market does not change much in 1994, although six of the 16 firms present in 1992 do not appear any longer, all the leavers being neither generalists nor specialists. The combined share of "other" firms drops from over 6% to around 4%. The lower number of actors, together with the increased combined share of the top ones, indicate a trend towards more concentration.

Here again, we can consider that there is an autonomous sector of suppliers specialized in workstations, competing on the market with the large generalists. But contrary to the case of PCs, this specialized sector is formed by a small number of firms. Taking into consideration the entire worldwide industry would probably not modify this conclusion.

Software (table A-XVIII)

A striking difference with the preceding segments is the number of players present, which is as high as 52 in 1992 and 53 in 1994, more than half of the sample population. Moreover, many small or non-American firms are active in this area, so that taking into consideration the whole industry would reinforce that characteristic. One can say that the majority of firms that make up the computer industry are present in the software segment.

It is especially the case for generalists, which together represent 49% the software revenue of our sample for nine active firms in 1992, while 15 specialists represent some 38%, and 32 other firms, specialized in others areas or really mixed, add up to 13%. A generalist, IBM, is in the top position with 40%, but specialists appear rapidly: Microsoft is second with 10%, Computer Associates third with 6%, Novell fourth and Lotus fifth around 3% .

In 1994, although the total number of firms is only one higher, there is considerable turnover relative to 1992. Nineteen of the 52 firms disappear, including most notably six of the nine services firms present and five of the sixteen mixed and generalists. Only one services firm and one mixed enter in 1994, against seven software specialists and 19 other specialists. In net, the number of firms active in software goes from 16 to 9 for generalists and mixed firms, from 15 to 21 for specialists, from 9 to 4 for service firms, and from 12 to 19 for other specialists. The combined market share of generalists decrease from 49% to 40% and that of software specialists increases from 38% to 47%, other specialists and mixed firms going from 12% to 13%.

Although many companies including most generalists report a secondary activity in software, the specialized software companies represent a large and fast-growing share of the market. An autonomous sector does exist for software, again in competition with generalists.

Peripherals and communications (tables A-XIX and A-XX)

The situation in peripherals, where 37 firms are present in 1992, is intermediate between that of PCs and that of software. Here again, eight of the ten generalists occupy in total a little less than half of the market, IBM being in the lead with 20%. But 13 specialists represent some 40%, the market share of the largest being close to 8%, while 16 other firms, mixed or specialists of other areas, add up to 13%. In 1994, the number of generalists and of "others" decreases and the number of specialists increases. The corresponding market shares go from 47% to 38% for generalists and from 40% to 49% for specialists.

For communication peripherals, the number of players (13) is lower than for the other peripherals, in total and for each category. Only 5 of 10 generalists are present, with 58% of the market, along with five specialists for 33% of the market, and three other firms for the remaining 9%. In 1994, the number of firms in the top 100 increases to 21, mainly with the arrival of 10 new specialists. The market share decreases to 46% for generalists and increases to 42 % for specialists.

To really understand that segment, it would be necessary not only to consider communication peripherals separately, but also to distinguish the various functional families such as printers, disks, extension cards, terminals, etc. Those families define separate markets, which are more different from each other than for instance large systems, midrange systems and stations. In each of those segments, along with gen-eralists always present to some extent, one finds a large number of specialists play-ing an important role despite their often modest size.

Maintenance (table A-XXI)

Twenty-six firms, including eight of the ten generalists, report maintenance revenue. The 8 generalists account for 83% of the total revenue and in particular occupy the first five places. A single firm, Bell Atlantic, can be considered as spe-cialized in maintenance with 77% of its revenue, 20% being software and 3% ser-vices; it appears in the eighth place with a market share of 3%. Seventeen other firms, generally specialized in hardware or services, share 14% the market. No sepa-rate figures are available for 1994.

There are probably other firms specialized in maintenance out of the sample, especially out of the USA, but their share of the total market is certainly modest. One cannot therefore consider the maintenance as an autonomous sector, but as an ancillary service attached to products, although a few exceptional firms have spe-cialized in that area.

Services (table A-XXII)

This is the area where the number of players is highest, with 57 of the 100 firms of our sample appearing. It is also in services that the number (25) and the share (60%) of specialists are the highest. This particularity is probably still more striking at the level of the entire worldwide industry, because there exists, in Europe as in the USA and elsewhere, a multitude of service enterprises too small to appear in the US top 100, but which account in total for a non-trivial share of revenue. Nine of the ten generalists are present and occupy together 30% of this market, especially IBM which occupies the first place with 17%. But 22 other firms of our sample, for which service is also a secondary activity, nevertheless account for 10% of revenue. No separate figures are available for 1994.

Services clearly attract many firms of highly variable size, and represent an autonomous sector although in competition with generalists.

Segment concentration

A concentration index for each segment can be computed from the market shares. The most commonly used by industrial economists is the "Herfindahl index", which is equal to the sum of the squares of the market shares. It is easy to see that the Herfindahl index is equal to 1 in a monopoly situation and close to zero if the segment is served by a very large number of very small firms[26].

Value of the Herfindahl concentration index

	1992	1994
large	0.437	0.446
midrange	0.260	0.175
PC	0.155	0.145
stations	0.148	0.179
software	0.187	0.125
peripherals	0.085	0.086
comm	0.183	0.111
maintenance	0.206	na
services	0.062	na

The large systems segment stands out as more concentrated. Peripherals and services are highly fragmented, and communications is moving towards the same high level of fragmentation. There is a general trend towards more fragmentation except in large systems and workstations, but more visibly in midrange systems and software. That confirms the above observations for some of the individual segments.

Conclusions

As a rule, one cannot associate with each market segment a group of firms that would at the same time implement virtually all the revenue of the segment and be only marginally present in others. It is therefore important to clearly distinguish between the concepts of "market segment" (the potential or current buyers of a product) and that of "industry sector" (the firms that offer products which are close substitutes of each other). Industry sectors cannot be correctly defined by a simple match with market segments.

The major split of the industry is between generalists and specialists. After separating the generalists, the remaining firms fit rather nicely into sectors aligned with the market segments, with the exception of a few mixed firms which play a marginal and diminishing role.

---

26   More specifically, it is easy to see that for N firms of equal size, $H=1/N$. H is therefore equal to 1 in the monopoly case and decreases towards zero when N increases to infinity.
   Moreover, for any given number of firms, H is minimal when all firms are of equal size and increases with inequality of market shares. Industry concentration as measured by the Herfindahl index is a function both of the number of firms and of the distribution of market shares. We will see in chapter 7 that this is indeed a valid view of concentration.

To obtain a complete summary, it would be necessary to add two other specialized sectors: components and distribution. Intel and Motorola would then leave the peripherals sector where the Datamation classification artificially places them. Furthermore, the peripherals sector (and segment) should be divided into different sectors according to the nature of the products, as the Datamation classification does for communication peripherals. A storage sector would include firms like Seagate, Conner, Quantum, Maxtor, Storage Technology, Western Digital, Micropolis and EMC, while a "paper output" sector could include Canon, Xerox, Lexmark and Kodak in competition with Hewlett-Packard. In the same manner, the services sector should be broken down into specialized sectors, considering the wide variety of forms of services.

The generalists are the traditional large vendors which were already active in computing in the seventies, like IBM, Digital Equipment, Hewlett-Packard, NCR, Unisys, Data General, Texas Instruments, Control Data and a few smaller ones, plus at worldwide level firms like Fujitsu, NEC, Hitachi, Siemens, Bull or ICL. Their basic strategy is to attempt to meet all the requirements of their customers, by offering the full range of hardware units needed to build a system, plus software and services. Some focus on specific market segments, but the larger ones aim at the entire market and try to be all things to all people. In contrast, the specialists try to do one thing well. Most of them entered the industry more recently, generally after the introduction of the PC in 1981.

The competitive coexistence of generalists and specialists in every market segment is a key feature of the computing industry. The generalists are always present, with a place ranging from significant to dominant (30% to 84%). They dominate the large and midrange systems and the maintenance segments, and are dominated by the specialists in the PC and services segments. In the workstations, software and peripherals segments, generalists and specialists play more balanced roles. However, the overall trend is towards more specialization in each segment. The number of generalists and their combined market share decrease in all segments except possibly maintenance. The mixed firms are already marginal in numbers and in market share, and gradually vanishing. In particular, software and services are already and increasingly separate sectors.

The behavior of suppliers on most segments is not entirely determined by considerations specific to that market, but also by the more general strategy of a few generalists. In the confrontation between generalist strategies and specialist strategies, specialist strategies relate only to that segment and may be closely tailored to the specific conditions. Generalist strategies in each segment are the local by-product of more general strategies and may not match as closely the requirements of the segment, but that disadvantage may be compensated by the breadth and consistency of the product line. However, the trends indicate that specialist strategies are gradually taking over.

Expense structures and models of enterprises

Another way to classify enterprises is to analyze the breakdown of their expenses. Statistics provided by McKinsey[27] indicate for a certain number of firms, in addition to their DP revenue and profit, the percentage of their revenue that they spend on Research and Development on one hand, on sales, administrative and general expenses on the other hand. It is easy to derive from that data the allocation of their total expenses (income less profit) between Research and Development (R&D), commercial and administrative expense (SG&A), and finally cost of production. Relating those expense categories to total expenses, rather than to income, eliminates the differences in profitability that would increase the dispersion of percentages. It also allows to focus on the way companies operate internally, irrespective of whether they are successful or not on the market.

Those ratios are given in the appendix in table A-XXIII for the year 1993 taken as an example. Firms are ranked in decreasing order of the ratio of costs of production to total expenses.

Those ratios vary within very wide ranges: from less than 20% to nearly 90% for costs of production, from 0% to nearly 30% for R&D, from 6% to over 70% for SG&A. It seems obvious that firms spending 85% of their revenue for cost of production versus 4% for R&D and for marketing and general expenses are probably very different from firms where production costs are only 25% of revenue versus 15% for R&D and 45% for marketing and administration. Such differences certainly reveal radically different forms of enterprises obeying different behavior dynamics, which should lead to consider them as belonging to distinct categories.

It turns out that a close look at those figures clearly shows a distribution of firms into relatively homogeneous groups.

Manufacturers of PC's and of PC peripherals (Western Digital, Quantum, Conner, Seagate, Maxtor, Micropolis) have the highest costs of production, with ratios between 65% and 90% of total expenses. For most of those firms, R&D varies between 2 and 4% for PC manufacturers, which merely assemble standardized products, between 4 and 8% for peripheral manufacturers which develop more original products. Sales and administration costs vary between 6% and 10% for firms that rely on indirect marketing through retailers, while firms like Dell or Compaq show higher ratios. In total, such ratios are characteristic of an enterprise strategy based on a small number of standard products and of a price-based rather than product-based competition. The only microcomputer specialist to deviate from that pattern is Apple, with ratios similar to those of traditional manufacturers.

At the other extreme, software packages have the lowest relative costs of production, always below 50% of revenue and most of the time under 35%. Conversely, sales and administrative expenses are the highest, being always more than 30% except for SAP, and often exceeding 50%. R&D expenses typically represent

---

27   McKinsey & Company, Inc : Report on the Computer Industry (1991, 1992, 1993 and 1994)

between 8% and 20% of revenue, the case of Ultimate being probably a mistake in the figures.

The differences between those types of enterprise appear more clearly on the following diagrams, where each firm is represented by a point having its R&D percentage on the horizontal axis and its SG&A percentage on the vertical axis. Year 1993 is used as a reference. The three gray areas show where most microcomputer firms (lower left), software package firms (upper right), and generalists (intermediate area) concentrate.

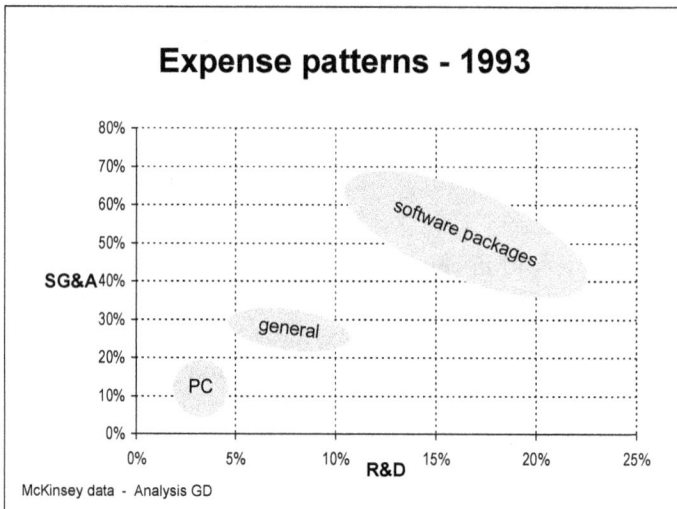

Expense patterns - 1993

McKinsey data - Analysis GD

Leaving aside for the moment a few odd cases such as Apple, which as we have already seen belongs in fact to the generalist category, or also Ultimate and Novell, we see that those ranges are sufficiently narrow and disjoint to represent different types of enterprises. Moreover, one observes that those ranges are very stable in time over the recent years, the only visible move being a drift of the PC area downward and to the left, showing most probably an increasing management pressure on "indirect" expenses.

The case of software packages calls for some comments. Its very low reproduction costs automatically entail high values for the other two categories of expenses, R&D and general expenses, placing therefore the area of software packages at the upper right of the diagram. But the points representing the different enterprises are relatively dispersed. It is likely that the size of the area observed for software packages can be explained essentially by the fact that in this sector, the distinction between development, production and marketing has different interpretations depending on the enterprise. For example, the borderline between R&D and production may have been located in different places by different firms, or documentation expenses may have been considered as development costs by some, as commercial expenses by others. For that reason, one should not attach too much importance to the abnormal points mentioned earlier.

Setting aside those possible inaccuracies, the position of firms on the diagram, and their possible movements in time, give a good indication of their mode of operation and of their strategic choices. The percentage of R&D will tend to increase when the firm seeks to offer original products, as opposed to merely assembling standard products. The share of marketing and administrative expenses also reflects in part the originality of products, which tends to demand specific marketing efforts, but is mostly dependent on indirect or direct marketing, the weight of advertising and more generally the lifestyle of the enterprise.

Those explanations help in interpreting the place of the other firms. Specialized system manufacturers have SG&A rates similar to those of generalists, except Amdahl and Cray that have lower rates, while their R&D rates are usually higher than those of generalists. This is in particular the case for workstation suppliers. Peripheral manufacturers have more modest sale and administration expenses, probably because an important share of their production is marketed indirectly through systems vendors, while their R&D rate makes them similar to either generalists or PC vendors depending on the purpose of their products.

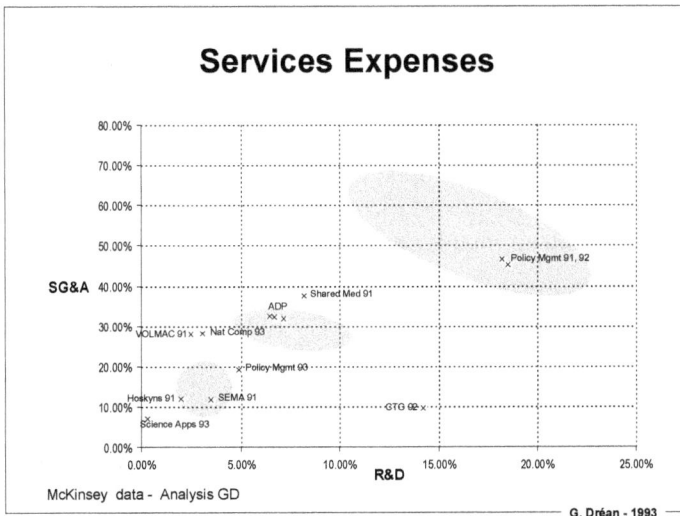

Services are scattered all over the diagram, confirming that it is a very heterogeneous set of activities. In that category the proportion of firms that publish such information is also the lowest, which may cast some doubts on the reliability of the few published figures, for the same reasons as for software packages. Nevertheless, one can observe that companies as Hoskyns or Sema, which offer integration or development services, are located close to the PC area, while the expense structure of processing firms like Policy Management, ADP or Shared Medical Systems places them close to generalists and even software package vendors.

Summary

By combining this classification approach with the analysis of products and service combinations, we reach the following conclusions:

There is a unique model for firms specialized in software packages, which are generally totally absent from the equipment market and offer only a minimum of ancillary services such as maintenance or services. Those firms have a strong R&D activity and an overdeveloped commercial activity, but a low production cost in relative value. We will call that model "development-oriented".

Firms where the equipment dominates belong to two distinct types:
- a "production-oriented" type associated with the PC-compatible microcomputers, where R&D, sales and administration activities are reduced to the lowest possible level, and which are therefore totally dominated by production.
- a "classical" type with enough R&D activity to develop their own products and a strong marketing activity. This type includes the traditional generalists and their more specialized competitors offering selected types of equipment including peripherals associated with traditional systems. It also includes the workstations specialists, as well as Apple in the micro sector.

The generalist manufacturers belong to the classical type and seek to offer a wide range of equipment including peripherals, as well as the maintenance, software and services related to that equipment. This model is that of the first times of data-processing. Firms following that model always try to provide their customers with complete systems, even if the different products and services have become independent from each other from a marketing and charging viewpoint, and also in the internal organization of enterprises. Firms like Prime/Computervision, workstation vendors, as well as Apple in microcomputers, also follow the "classical" model.

Specialized equipment manufacturers have elected to limit themselves to a specific niche, whether it is central units or peripherals. As a rule, those manufacturers try to provide only a minimum of ancillary software or services. The oldest ones, like Tandem, Stratus, Evans & Sutherland or Memorex remain close to the classical type, while manufacturers of IBM compatibles and associated peripherals conform to the "production-oriented" model which has become the rule in micro-computing since 1981. This separation is consistent with the historic separation between the traditional world and the PC world. The functioning of the Unix world and of the Apple world looks more like the traditional world than PC-compatible micro-computing.

In the area of services, two extremes types appear. In "professional" assistance and development services, the cost structure is similar to that of micro-computing equipment, with high production costs and low R&D and marketing costs, places these firms in the "production-oriented" category. At the opposite, the cost structure of processing services companies resembles that of software packages, with high R&D and marketing costs and puts those firms in the "development-oriented" category. Not only does the overall sector of services group together two diametrically opposed forms of enterprises, but the similarities of cost structures with other sectors seem paradoxical. Software development services behave like micro hardware firms and not like software packages, while processing services behave more like software package companies than like equipment firms.

The expense structure of mixed firms makes some of them look close to one of the above dominant models. For example, MAI normally adheres to the production-oriented model, Datapoint to the classical model and Ask Computers to the development-oriented model.

Conclusions

The examination of figures, despite some reservations on their reliability and the limited coverage of the sample, allows us to allocate most firms in the computer industry to specific industry sectors. Those sectors can in turn be related to a broader perspective and to a small number of enterprise models.

The main distinction is between generalists and specialists, the latter forming in turn different sectors according to their activity. In addition to specialists and generalists, there are relatively few firms whose main activity is split in comparable shares between two or three segments. In most cases such firms are in a transient situation, for example enterprises offering "turnkey" systems that are in the process of restricting their offer to software (like Computervision or Ask), or on the contrary service companies trying to complement their offer with specific equipment. In any case, those mixed enterprises occupy only a marginal place in those market segments where they are present.

By analyzing the expense structure of each enterprise, we have identified among those specialists two contrasting personalities: development-oriented at one extreme and production-oriented at the other extreme. Development-oriented companies have high R&D expenses and overdeveloped marketing and general expenses, as exemplified by the producers of software packages. Production-oriented companies have minimal commercial and R&D expenses, and are exemplified by the assemblers of PC's and associated peripherals. The development-oriented model also applies to processing services and most probably to components manufacturing, and the production-oriented model also applies to development, assistance and consulting services.

The breakdown of the industry into specialized sectors generally conforming to either of those two models is characteristic of the "new world" which appeared in the late seventies with the microcomputer. Older firms such as the generalists and specialists of traditional systems are in an intermediate situation between the two extreme models. However, the more recent sector of workstations, as well as the Apple company, also fit that intermediate "classical" model. The entire services sector has been placed in the "old world" column, since most services firms existed well before 1980 and the emergence of the "new world" caused little if any change in that sector.

Classification of sectors		
	old world	**new world**
development-oriented	(processing services)	components software packages
	generalists large/midrange peripherals	workstations Apple
production-oriented	development services	PC peripherals PC's

Those conclusions would be globally unchanged if we considered the totality of the worldwide industry instead of a sample of the largest north-American firms. The biggest difference would be the appearance among the large players of firms not specialized in computers, like Fujitsu, NEC, Hitachi, Siemens, Canon, etc. This phenomenon is typically Japanese and somewhat European. In the USA, non specialized industrial groups are no longer playing a major role in computers since their failed attempts of the sixties. Furthermore, taking small players into account would result in an even more pronounced contrast between concentrated sectors like conventional equipment, which includes few players outside the big ones, and fragmented sectors like microcomputer hardware, software packages or services, where small firms are present in high numbers.

The view that the computer industry is moving from a state dominated by generalists to a new order dominated by specialized companies has been already expressed. The preceding analysis provides a more accurate and more complex picture. Generalists still coexist with specialists in all market segments, and the transition towards the dominance of specialists is at different stages and proceeds at different paces depending on the segment. The transition is well under way and going fast for PC's, software packages and peripherals, but very slow for large systems, midrange systems and workstations. We have found companies like Apple and the workstation specialists, which both belong to the "new world" and follow the same model as the old world generalists. Finally, we have identified profound differences between specialized companies.

That picture raises a few questions. Assuming as we do that the rise of specialists is unavoidable, how far will it go? Will all the remaining generalists be eventually eliminated or somehow forced to specialize, including IBM, Digital Equipment, Hewlett-Packard, Fujitsu and NEC? What will happen to the younger firms which still live by the same business model, like Apple, Sun or Silicon Graphics? We will return to those issues in chapter 14 after taking a closer look at the structure and dynamics of each sector.

Chapter 5 - Structure and performance

Growth by sector. Considerations on compared profit levels. Production cycles and the dispersion of profits. There are no good and bad sectors. Profitability and services. Profitability versus growth.

Observers are often puzzled by the diversity of firm performances in the computer sector. Until the end of the eighties, data-processing was considered as a prosperous industry, but in the last years a succession of disasters has occurred. Some of the formerly most successful firms are going through successive years of declining business volumes and financial losses, which calls for painful restructuring. At the same time, other firms, generally younger, smaller and more narrowly specialized, are posting year after year growth rates of 30% and more, and net margins higher than 20%.

Starting with that observation, as expressed in the published results of enterprises, the subject of the present chapter is to discover possible correlations between performances and the types of enterprise which we have identified in the previous chapter. We will measure performance by two indicators: revenue growth rate and net profit ratio, obtained from available industry statistics including various trade journals and the annual McKinsey reports on the computer industry, more specifically the recent issues covering years 1985 to 1993[28]. We have eliminated a few firms for which the computer activity represents too small a part of the total for the figures to be representative of that activity, and those for which the category was unknown. The sample of firms includes firms other than those in the US top 100 used in the preceding chapter, and may change from year to year depending on the availability of figures, but for the purpose of this chapter, the size of the sample is more important than its consistency.

In the analyses that follow, we use the classification of enterprises according to the nature of their production that we have presented in the preceding chapter. This analysis differs from those regularly published in the press, which look at market segments defined by the different products and services that make up the computer offer, independently of their source. For enterprises that are specialized in each of those segments, their growth rate reflects essentially how market demand for the products of the segment evolves, and how well the products of each enterprise meet that demand. Revenue growth is therefore more dependent on the market than typical of each enterprise, except when it is possible to single out cases where an enterprise evolves differently from other enterprises in the same sector, and when this difference of behavior corresponds to a difference of personality.

---

28   McKinsey & Company, Inc : Report on the Computer Industry (1991, 1992, 1993 and 1994)

We have seen in the preceding chapter that each segment is served by enterprises of different natures, and that conversely some enterprises are present in several segments. It is therefore interesting to compare in each market segment the behavior of specialists to that of generalists and mixed firms. Profit ratios, by integrating costs of production and therefore the economic characteristics of each enterprise, can provide indications of how competition operates in each of the different sectors, as we will see in the following chapter.

Growth rates

The rate of revenue growth is the most easily available indicator of firm performance and the most commonly used as a measure of success. It is generally accepted that rapid growth of an enterprise is an indication that it does satisfy market demand in a better way than its slower competitors, and that growth is therefore the just reward of know-how and efficiency. Moreover, the most rapidly growing firms increase their market shares at the expense of the others and thus acquire new competitive advantages which will fuel their success even further.

The growth rates for the firms of our sample, for years 1986 to 1993, are shown in the appendix in table A-XXIV.

From a bird's eye view, revenue growth at the enterprise level is generally strong for communication peripherals, services and software packages, low or even negative for generalists and mixed firms, highly irregular for PC's, other peripherals and workstations. Ranges of variation are very large in each category, with often both high upper bounds and strongly negative lower bounds. One does not perceive any simple relationship between sector and enterprise growth. It is not sufficient to select a high-growth segment such as PC's, peripherals, services or software packages to automatically benefit from the growth of demand; and conversely, operating in a globally regressing sector like generalists or conventional systems does not inevitably condemn individual enterprises to recession.

The most obvious observation is that generalists and most mixed firms are undergoing a recession since 1990, and in all cases grow less rapidly than specialized firms offering the same products separately. The figures seem to indicate that simply offering an extended but closely coordinated range of diversified products and services has become a handicap as compared to a strategy of specialization on just one product or service from the same set. The exception represented by Hewlett-Packard can be taken as an *a contrario* confirmation of that thesis: this company has always behaved differently from most other large traditional generalists by operating as a conglomerate of independent specialized divisions rather than striving to offer a fully integrated range. At any rate, the place of generalists within the computer industry is regressing, and also that the other mixed firms. The data-processing industry is gradually becoming dominated by specialized firms.

Nevertheless, revenue growth is far from being a perfect indicator. On one hand, it integrates the effect of mergers and acquisitions, of breaking down enterprises into separate units, and more generally all the other possible variations in enterprise perimeter. Furthermore, growth rate is not necessarily a good indicator of firm health. An enterprise can both grow rapidly and lose money, therefore con-demning itself to regression and even disappearance in the long run; on the con-trary, a drastic reduction of the activity perimeter, and therefore of revenue, can be an effective way to restore profitability. Finally, as we will see thereafter, there are sectors where a high market share is not an advantage *per se*, and where growth is therefore not necessarily the overriding objective. For all these reasons, we will con-centrate on profitability rather than growth in most of the following discussion.

Profits compared

The following analysis focuses on the net after tax profit of enterprises, which is readily available for most enterprises. However, it is a meaningless figure for our study when the computer activity is only one of a range of productions of the enterprise and is not individualized as such. This is the case for example of many large Japanese groups or service companies. We have therefore eliminated firms not specialized in computers and those whose profitability is not published.

The net after tax profit rate is only one of the possible profitability indicators. Most financial analysts prefer using the rate of profitability of the invested capital (*return on invested capital* or *ROIC*) or the profitability of assets (*return on assets*), which have a more direct economic meaning[29]. Unfortunately, those indicators are not eas-ily available for a sufficient number of enterprises. Moreover, most commentators who are not professional economists concern themselves more with profit on sales as a measure of profitability.

Let us however keep in mind the economic meaning of this ratio, which is fundamentally an accounting and more specifically a fiscal concept. The net profit after taxes is what is left of the income of the enterprise after paying its employees, its suppliers and creditors, depreciating its assets according to accounting rules and paying taxes. This net profit can be used on one hand to pay the shareholders for the capital they have invested, and on the other hand to increase the investments of the enterprise above the level that can be financed by the depreciation of past investments. The "normal " profit level of an enterprise is therefore dependent upon its investment requirements and its growth rate. An activity requiring high and increasing investments, such as components, demands high rates of profit, while a moderately capital-intensive activity, like most services, can live with more modest profitability, even in periods of growth.

Finally, profit itself is not a complete and totally reliable indicator of com-pany performance. Because reported accounting profits are the base for taxation in most countries, many firms would rather spend more of the money they earn than declare higher profits and pay more taxes. Profits must therefore be viewed together

---

29   see chapter 6. Basic economic theory shows that, under certain general conditions known as "perfect competition", the economy evolves towards a state of equilibrium where the return on invested capital is equal to the market interest rate <u>for all firms</u>. In that state of equilibrium, net profit on sales for each firm is equal to that market interest rate multiplied by the capital intensity ratio (invested capital divided by sales), which is a characteristic of the firm.

with the general standard of living of the firm. A very prosperous firm may be both profitable and lavish, to the extent that it will have no motivation to squeeze expenses if profits are already sufficiently high. A firm encountering difficulties can still arbitrate between reducing its expenses and standard of living or accepting a degradation of its profitability.

Analysis by category

For each category, the following diagrams show the lowest and highest profit rates reported each year from 1985 to 1994 by firms in the sample, together with the average of the category (total net profit divided by total revenue) and the median of the category (the level such that the number of firms with a higher profit is equal to the number of firms with lower profit). The detailed figures are given in the appendix (tables A-XXV to A-XXXIV).

These graphs and these figures must be interpreted with caution. Certain categories such as large and midrange systems, stations or communication peripherals are represented by only very few firms. Minimal and maximal values can be out of line in relation with the other values, and thus give a false picture of the distribution of profit levels around the median. An important gap between the average and the median can indicate a potential size advantage or disadvantage, but can also be the result of abnormal figures for a large firm. For those reasons, the following comments must refer to the detailed data tables in the appendix.

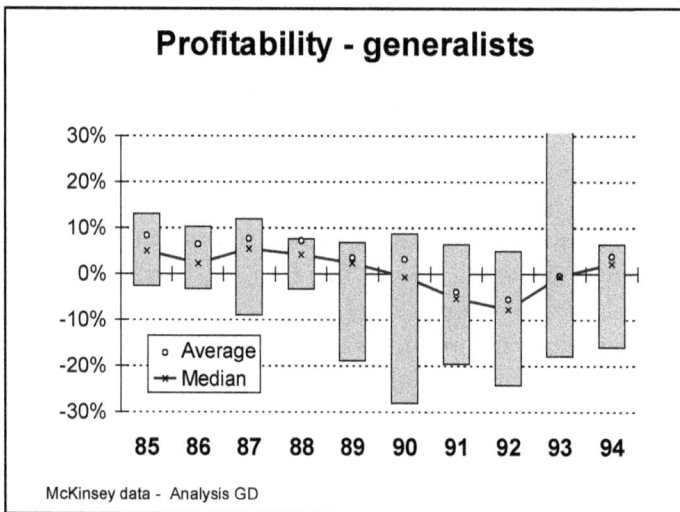

Profitability - generalists

McKinsey data - Analysis GD

Generalists (table A-XXV) are in good shape until 1987/1988, except Wang and Data General, while Bull is barely positive. Since 1989, one sees a general declining trend: Digital Equipment and Bull are in the red since 1990, IBM since 1991, and Unisys from 1989 to 1991. The only enterprise that obtains an almost stable result is Hewlett-Packard, which nevertheless drops from 7% in 1985 (third rank) to 5% in 1992 and 6 % in 1993 and 1994, which are among the best performances of the category for those three years.

Wang is unexplainably out of line in 1993 with a reported profit of 38%. Not counting Wang, the best performance for 1993 is Unisys with 7.3%, making the 1993 range totally consistent with 1992 and 1994. The generalist sector seems to be in a phase of recovery from its five-year decline from 1988 to 1992.

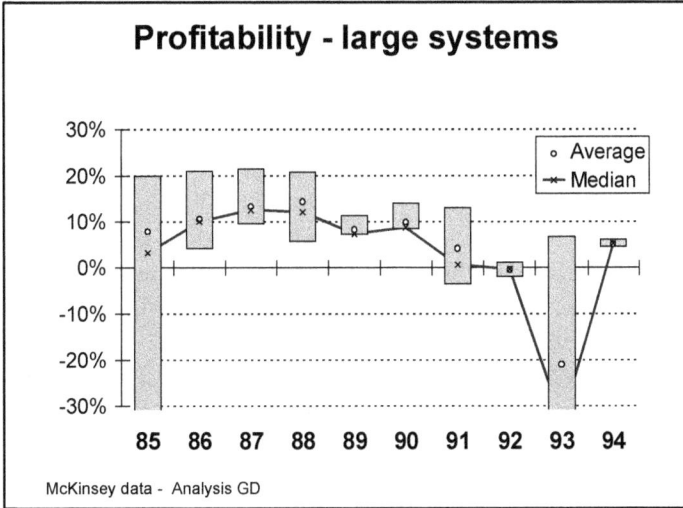

Profitability - large systems

McKinsey data - Analysis GD

Large systems specialists (table A-XXVI) are too few (3) to be described otherwise that in terms of their individual history. In the years of their splendor (1985 to 1988), their results are among the best of the entire computer industry. They then begin to fall dramatically starting in 1991. At a closer look, one sees that Convex and Amdahl fall together from more than 8% to zero or less in 1991, while Cray that in 1989 had already fallen from over 20% to around 13%, joins them around zero in 1992. In 1993, Amdahl continues to fall together with Convex, while Cray improves to almost 7%. No data is available for Convex in 1994, but the other two specialists are now back to a normal profit level.

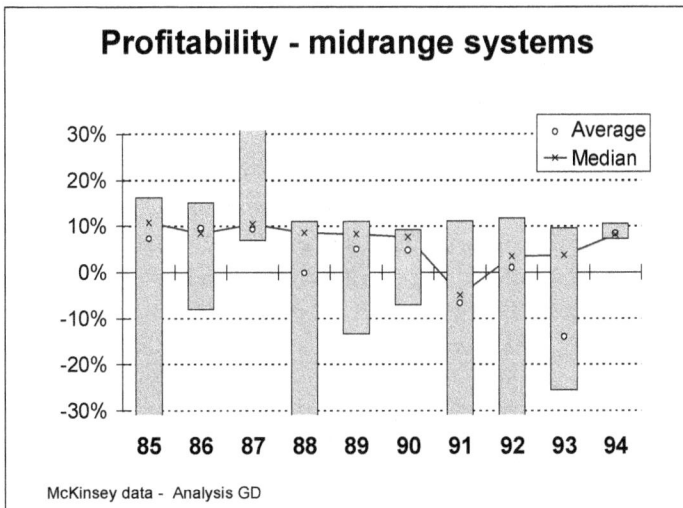

Profitability - midrange systems

McKinsey data - Analysis GD

The midrange systems category (table A-XXVII) is also the place of bumpy individual histories. Stratus is alone in achieving satisfactory and stable results. Tandem plunges in 1993 after vacillating in 1991 and 1992, Sequent and Pyramid oscillate between the best and the bad, while Norsk Data reaches the bottom since 1989, and returns to profitability in 1993 by losing close to 40% of its revenue. Here again, firms are too few (5) to support any statistical conclusion. The overall aspect of the ranges is similar to that of generalists, the dispersions being still higher in 1991 and 1992. In 1994, profit data is available for only three firms, which happen to be extremely close together, as in the large systems case.

For hardware specialists of the traditional type, year 1991 is a discontinuity. In years 1985 to 1990, the median profit for all those categories is close to 10%. One observes very good successes in particular niches (Cray, Pyramid), and except for Norsk Data, only firms in their starting phase are in the red. Beginning in 1991, profits start to decline, maximums become modest except for Stratus, and many firms show a deficit. However, for both large and midrange systems, 1993 and 1994 seem to be years of elimination of the weaker firms and return of the few survivors to normal profit levels. That might indicate that a major shakedown is now over, with the surviving firms now well-positioned.

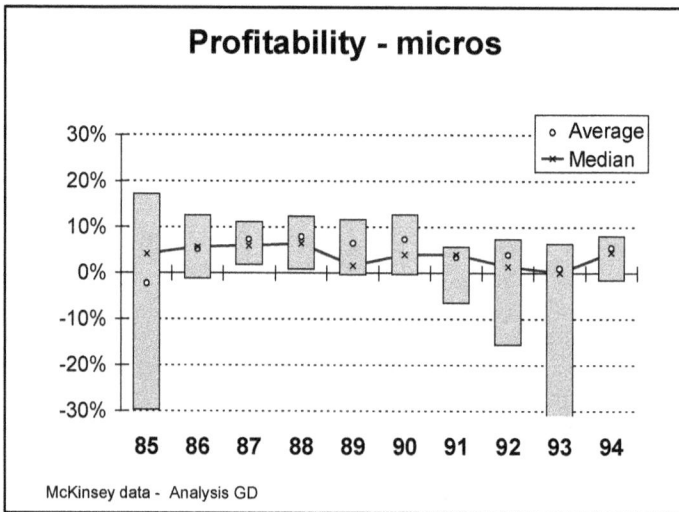

The category of PC specialists (table A-XXVIII) contains 8 to 10 firms depending on years (only 6 in 1994). It shows a more stable evolution, although one can observe a similar downward trend since 1991. Dispersions are relatively low except in 1985 and 1993, and widen slightly in 1992 because of important losses by Everex and Commodore. In 1993, apart from the Commodore disaster, no other firm goes below -1.4%, which corresponds to a range similar to that of 1991. From 1986 to 1992, the average profit varies in a narrow band between 3% and 6 %, but tends to decline since 1991. The maximum, close to 13% in 1990 (Compaq), is steadily declining (8.5% for AST in 1991, 7.3% for Apple in 1992, 6.4% for Compaq in 1993). 1994 shows a more encouraging trend with a maximum of 8% for Compaq, and higher average and median.

Profitability - workstations

McKinsey data - Analysis GD

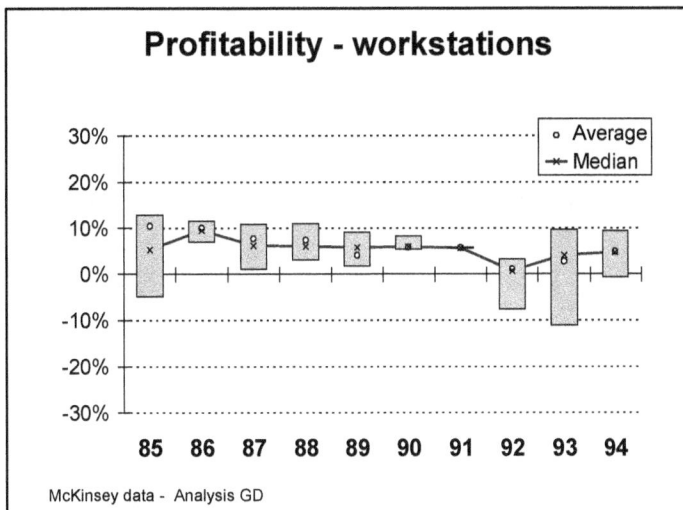

Workstation specialists (table A-XXIX) are also few (3) and always located within narrow ranges, with a general declining trend and average levels similar to those of PC. Considering the size of the sample, this category of specialists does not seem to behave differently from the PC's.

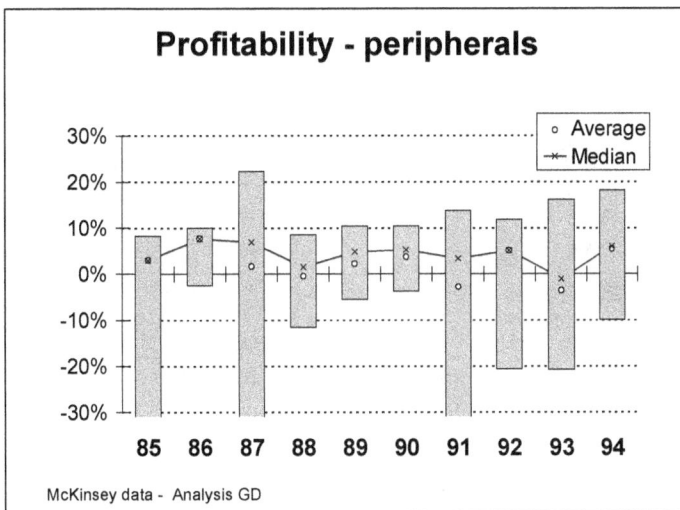

Profitability - peripherals

McKinsey data - Analysis GD

The category of peripherals (table A-XXX) includes 9 to 17 firms according to years. Rather bumpy individual histories also appear (Memorex Telex, Maxtor, Storage Technology, Tandon). Each year, at least one firm approaches or exceeds 10%, while several are in the red, but the positions of individual firms vary considerably from year to year. One does not perceive a clearly unfavorable trend until 1993, when the majority of firms is losing money, and almost all post declining profits, except EMC which happily exceeds 16%, the number two reaching only 8%. Again, 1994 is a year of recovery, with only one of 12 firms in the red, and improving maximum, minimum and averages.

Profitability - communications

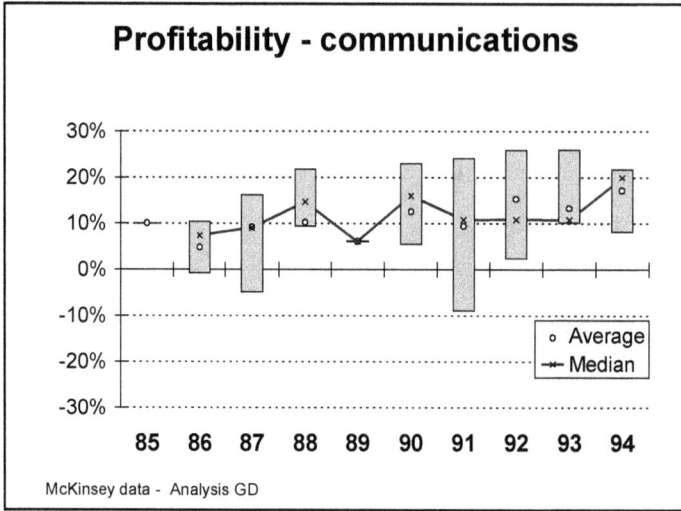

McKinsey data - Analysis GD

Three communications specialists (table A-XXXI) stand out with excellent performance since 1990, even if one firm has known losses in 1990.

Profitability - software packages

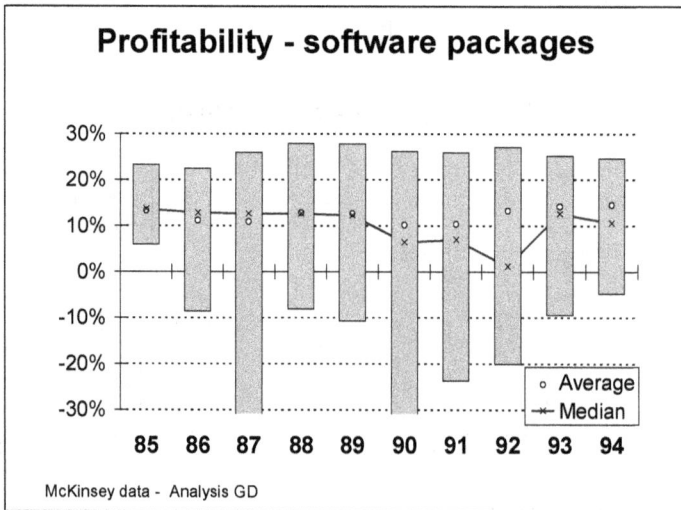

McKinsey data - Analysis GD

The category of software packages (table A-XXXII), which includes 13 to 16 firms according to years, presents a rather different aspect from the preceding categories. In particular, one does not observe any clear discontinuity in 1991. The median profit goes through a relative low point from 1990 to 1992, but returns to its previous level in 1993, while the average always remains above 10%. The dispersion is constantly high, with maximums always above 20% and even exceeding 25% since 1989. But one also observes negative results each year since 1986 (even ignoring startups), some of which are spectacular like Mentor Graphics and Ultimate since 1991, Informix in 1990, or Borland in 1989, 1991 and 1992. Even Novell who was in the lead ahead of Microsoft in 1991 and 1992 with more than 25%, falls into the red in 1993. Note nevertheless that although the minimums are strongly negative, the number of deficient firms is small for any given year: one out of 13 in 89, three in 1990, 1991, 1992, five in 1993, two in 1994. Averages are always above 10% except in 1991.

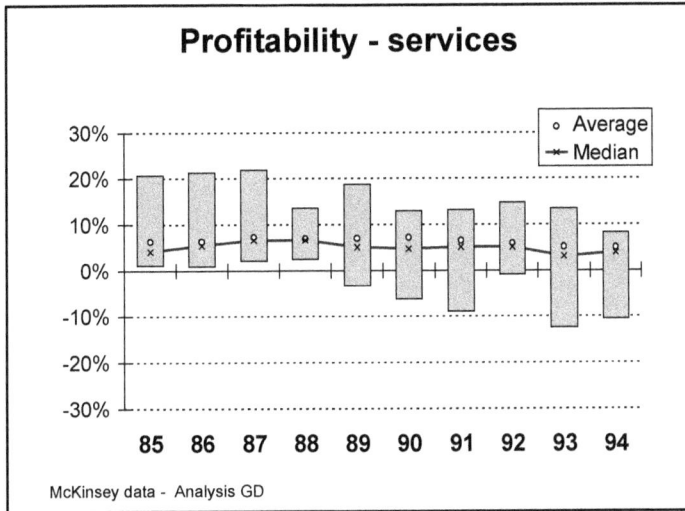

Profitability - services

McKinsey data - Analysis GD

The services sector (table A-XXXIII) is represented by 14 to 21 enterprises according to years, but only 7 in 1994. Its aspect is different both from the categories of equipment (large and midrange systems, PC, workstations and peripherals) and from that of software packages.

As for PC's, the average profit for the totality of services remains remarkably stable between 4% and 6%, with a very slight declining trend since 1992. The dispersion is always relatively low despite the large number of firms and the heterogeneity of the sector. In 1990 and 1992, a single firm was in the red, and all others achieved more than 2%. In 1991, the last three firms fell to -9%, -3% and 0%, and the other 18 remained above 2%. Only in 1993 did the situation begin to degrade a bit more., Despite the lower number of firms, the 1994 figures seem to be consistent with the previous years.

If one distinguishes between sub-sectors, the average profits are just as stable: between 9% and 11% for processing services, between 4% and 5% for assistance and development from 1985 to 1991, with a decline in 1992.

The recent maximums are steadily between 13% and 15%. For the previous years Volmac appears as an exceptional phenomenon by reaching 21% before 1988 and 19% in 1989, while its immediate follower is always in the range of 13% to 15%. Such high performances are always from north-American application processing companies such as Shared Medical Systems, First Data, ADP, Policy Management, all of which (strangely enough) are absent from the 1994 sample. The suppliers of more conventional services show profits usually under 8%. Each year since 1989, one or two companies of the sector are in the red (among those of the sample).

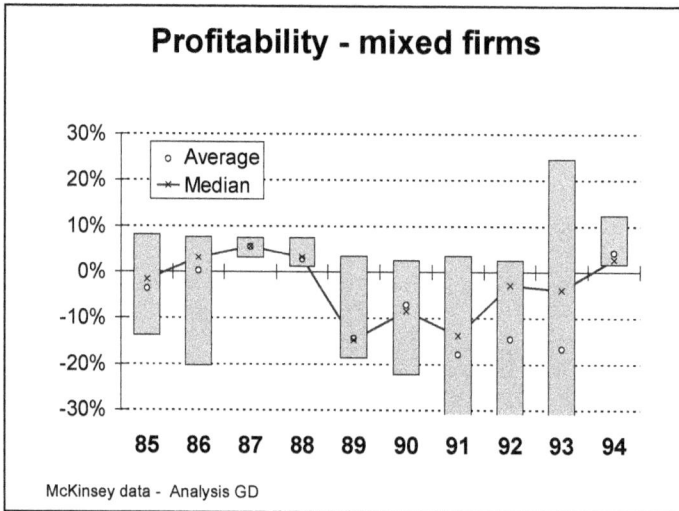

Profitability - mixed firms

○ Average
✳ Median

McKinsey data - Analysis GD

Since 1989, the average profitability of mixed firms (table A-XXVI) is almost always negative, and the maximums are lower than 9%, going down to 4.3% in 92. The year 1993 seems abnormal because of MAI, which after considerable losses from 1989 to 1992, goes up suddenly to the exceptionally high figure of 24% (but having lost in 93 almost 60% of its 1992 revenue). Setting aside this abnormal case, the majority of firms is in the red in 1991 and 1992, often very significantly. The general trend is unfavorable, and it seems clear that the results of mixed firms are always worse than those of the firms specialized in the individual services that make up their offering. In 1994, the sample is reduced to four firms, which show globally better results than in the previous years. That may be a result of a shake-down of the sector, similar to large and midrange systems, leaving only the few firms fit for survival.

A first general conclusion is that for almost all combinations of category and year, net profit varies within large and even very large ranges. Moreover, it is neces-sary to take into account the number of firms represented, which is sometimes too low to support any significant conclusion. Average values are therefore of little sig-nificance, and the individual features of each firm count at least as much as the sec-tor or the category to which it belongs. Anyway, the low range of all categories is often negative, meaning that all categories occasionally include firms losing money. This is the most common situation for midrange, peripherals, software, generalists and mixed firms, and less frequently but more so in the recent years for large sys-tems, micros, workstations and services.

Over the period, all categories contain firms with positive profits and firms with negative profits. In other words, there are neither accursed categories nor blessed categories; some firms manage to make money in traditional large systems, and others manage to lose money in software packages. But to quote McKinsey: "companies with viable strategies and good execution can be successful in any segment[30]". It is not entirely trivial to add that conversely, a non-viable or poorly exe-cuted strategy will lead to failure in all segments.

The dispersion of profits

One can wonder why the performances of firms of the same specialization vary in such wide ranges. A first case is that of startups, where the initial years are years of investments often matched by heavy operational losses, as is the case for Convex, Sequent or Teradata in 1985, Exabyte and Sybase in 1987. A large disper-sion of results can also reveal the heterogeneity of a sector which groups activities presenting different features. In the area of peripherals, communication devices exhibit a different behavior, but the distinction between micro peripherals and oth-ers does not show striking differences. For services on the other hand, although sub-sectors evolve in parallel, development services clearly always occupy the lower part of the services profit range, and processing services the upper part.

In homogeneous segments and after eliminating startups, the dispersion of results can be related to the different ways in which firms can respond to market conditions. The management of enterprises constantly devotes considerable effort to try to reach a satisfactory result. One must admit that, with few exceptions, nega-tive results are not the sign of an incompetent or sloppy management, but of a deeply rooted impossibility to do better within the limits of the accounting period, after exploiting all the opportunities for improvement that are really available.

In subsequent chapters, we will examine the time relationship between expense buildup and revenue buildup in the enterprise, which we will identify as a major determinant of firm structure and culture[31]. At this point, let us just remind that in industrial reality, the enterprise makes the decisions concerning expenses, but the market has the final saying concerning revenues. More precisely, the enter-prise first commits expenses in the hope of future revenue, and only at a later time can it observe the corresponding results. Revenues from each accounting period serve in part to pay for the production of the products sold, but also to invest in preparation for the next periods. If the revenue of a period happens to be lower than expected, it is generally impossible to reduce expenses in the same proportions without reducing investments in the period and thus jeopardizing the future of the enterprise.

That logic leads to the assumption that a large dispersion of profits in a homogeneous sector is related to situations where commitments of expenses have become irreversible when the corresponding revenues materialize. This is especially true when investments are high and only produce their results after a long period. In such cases, the enterprise has a long "base cycle". On the contrary, if invest-ments are low or produce revenue quickly, the "base cycle" of the enterprise is short and it is possible to adjust expenses to income without really jeopardizing the

---

30   McKinsey & Company, Inc : 1992 Report on the Computer Industry

31   see chapter 9

future. In such sectors, enterprises will be generally able to avoid excessive losses even faced with significant downturns of revenue.

Conversely, when by chance income happens to exceed estimates, this will only entail relatively few additional expenses for firms with long cycles, which will thus post high profits. Short-cycle enterprises will only be able to realize that extra income by accepting additional expenses which will bring profit back towards the anticipated level.

In summary, a large dispersion of profits for a given period would be characteristic of sectors where the expense-revenue cycle is long and where variable costs are a small part of average costs.

Applied to the evolution of the profitability ranges, this assumption would allow to formulate the following predictions:
- in an emerging sector, average profits are low and dispersion is high. As players progress on the learning curve, the average increases while the limits of the range narrow.
- a slowdown of activity translates into a decline of revenues relative to estimates, and a general profit decline, therefore a declining average profit. In sectors with long cycles, enterprises will only be able to adjust expenses in a very limited way; the average profit will therefore decline significantly and some enterprises will post important losses that will translate into a collapse of the minimum. In sectors with short cycles, enterprises will be better able to adjust their expenses; thereby, the decline of the average profit and especially of the minimum will be less pronounced.
- a firm can be durably in the red only in a sector with a long cycle, where the hopes that its investments represent can justify its survival. In a sector with short cycles, a deficient firm must recover quickly, and can do that more easily than an enterprise with a long cycle, or must disappear. At the overall level, a sector with short cycles will not see the minimum point remain far below zero, while in a sector with long cycles the minimum point may stagnate at strongly negative values.

Profitability factors

To complete this exploitation of industry statistics, let us examine two questions related to the profitability of firms.

Profitability versus share of services

According to a preconceived idea, many equipment firms seek to develop their services activity in order to improve their profitability. Let us therefore look for a possible correlation between net profit and the share of services in the revenue. Notice first that services other that application processing do not exhibit appreciably better profitability than PC's, workstations or some peripherals, and are notably worse than packaged software.

The following diagram shows the 1992 profit figures of the firms that offer equipment, services or both, plotted against the share of services in their revenue.

We have eliminated extreme cases corresponding to abnormal situations, for example startups.

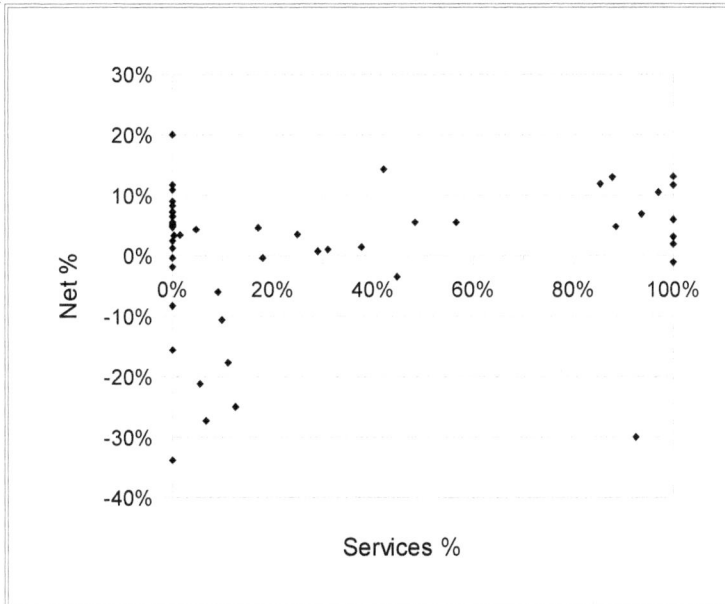

For specialized services enterprises, which appear at the right end with a service share equal or close to 100%, profits concentrate between -1% and 13% (except Ceridian and Grumman which are still lower). At the other extreme, for firms whose share of services is less than 20%, profits are widely dispersed between -30 and 25%, but the large majority of firms is located between -2 and 12%, in practically the same range as services firms. Intermediate cases remain in the same range as the pure services enterprises, with only a very slight upwards trend.

The correlation coefficient between the rate of profit and the share of services is equal to 0.16, which indicates a very weak correlation between those two factors. Contrarily to a well-anchored idea, there is therefore no statistical reason (and we will see later than there is no logical reason) to believe that developing services enables manufacturers to improve their results. The analysis of the actual figures can at the very most lead to believe that aiming at a share of services higher than 20% may be a way to limit the risk of losses, but at the same time putting an upper limit on the possible gains.

Relationship between profit and growth

The last question that we will explore with the help of industry statistics is the relationship between profitability and the growth rate of firms. In their analysis, the McKinsey researchers have concluded that the financial results are not directly correlated with revenue growth. Indeed the correlation coefficient between those two figures is low when computed for the complete set of firms in the sample.

Does this conclusion hold true for each category of enterprises considered separately, since we have reasons to believe that their dynamics are different? The following table shows the same correlation coefficients, now computed category by category, and separating the periods 1986 to 1988 on the one hand, 1989 to 1993 on the other hand. We have introduced that separation because we have seen earlier that 1988-1989 seem to mark an abrupt change in the behavior of several sectors. When the number of observations for a category and a period is lower than fifteen, the value of the correlation coefficient has been considered as not significant (ns). We have used the decomposition into subcategories according to the weight of production costs, as discussed in the preceding chapter.

Correlation between growth and profit

	86-88	89-93	86-93
general	0.57	0.26	0.41
large	ns	ns	0.54
midrange	0.43	0.72	0.66
PC	0.08	0.61	0.40
stations	ns	ns	-0.10
periph micros	0.09	0.51	0.43
comm	ns	ns	0.61
periph other	0.19	0.41	0.33
services devpt	0.56	0.04	0.19
services fm	ns	ns	0.40
services processing	-0.72	0.43	0.08
mixed	0.62	0.56	0.57
software	0.50	0.56	0.52

It appears that the conclusion of the McKinsey report that profitability is not correlated with growth rate is validated for development and processing services as well as workstations. But there is, over the entire period, a positive although modest correlation between growth and profit for all the other sectors. A comparison of periods 1986 to 1988 on the one hand, 1989 to 1993 on the other hand is surprising. PC's and peripherals change from a zero correlation to a relatively strong correlation, while generalists and development services follow the reverse evolution, and processing services change from a strongly negative correlation to a positive correlation.

One can think that the explanation of this observation relates to the sketch of firm operations that we have used earlier to explain the variations of profitability. Most enterprises manage their actions, and especially their expense commitments, on the basis of an annual budget where the revenue side represents the hopes or ambitions of the firm for the subject period, and where the expense side is prepared is such a way as to yield an acceptable result by difference. The budget for each period takes into account the results of the preceding period: if those are satisfactory, the budget will generally tend to extrapolate them by reproducing the current ratios. Otherwise, the budget will seek an improvement either by assuming an acceleration of the growth of income, or by cutting down authorized expenses. At this stage, firms set profit objectives which depend on their situation and can vary from one firm to another, the growth rate of each firm being only one parameter of this situation. Should each firm implement exactly its plans, there would thus not necessarily be any close correlation between profit and growth.

In reality, because of the time lag between expenses and the corresponding revenues, expenses really committed are most often very close to the planned budget, while revenues can deviate much more significantly. The improvement in profitability resulting from revenue growth higher than assumed in the budget will therefore tend to be large if the base cycle of the enterprise is long, and small if the cycle is short. The same will be true for the profit erosion resulting from a lower revenue growth.

According to this model, sectors where profits are dispersed should also present the largest correlation between profit and growth, although this correlation should not reach very high values. This assumption verifies well for generalists and midrange systems for high correlations, for workstations and services except facilities management for zero correlations, for large systems in the intermediate case. Results are less clear for PC's where correlation is medium and dispersion is small, and for software packages where correlation is also medium, but the dispersion is large.

One can also think that a weak correlation, and even a paradoxically negative correlation, can be related to services going through difficult periods or in recession. Some firms can then implement a strategy of withdrawal which preserves their margins by accepting a reduction of their revenue, while other firms that continue with growth objectives achieve negative results.

Conclusions

The analysis of the performance of enterprises in our sample is far from validating the conventional views concerning profitability. It does show the difficulties and the recession of generalists and of most traditional manufacturers, especially since 1988, and the consequent rise of the specialized firms. Data-processing is gradually changing, from an industry dominated by a handful of generalists, into the business of a large number of specialists, each offering one element of the system. This transition is currently close to its turning point, since generalists still account for approximately half the total industry revenue.

It does not seem that this evolution leaves much room for mixed firms, that would base their strategy on the association of selected products or services, too limited to turn them into generalists. Many enterprises offer services or software as ancillary support of their main products, but the performance of the few firms offering in similar shares hardware and services, or software packages and services, are not likely to attract many followers. In particular, contrary to a widespread idea, we have not observed any relationship between profitability and a high proportion of services, beyond the usual 10% to 15% which commonly supports products.

Beyond obvious differences in activities, we have been able to identify different behaviors according to sectors, which the expense structure partly explains. In particular, we have seen that the characteristics of the time relationship between the expenses required to introduce a product on the market and the revenues generated by the sales of that product have a profound influence on the way the firm oper-ates. That relationship is linked to the production cycle, and therefore to the nature of each product as well as to the strategy implemented by each firm. The differ-ences between short-cycle productions and long-cycle productions seem to account reasonably well for the dispersion of profits and the correlation (or the absence of correlation) between profit and growth rate.

But, whatever global features one may attach to each sector in particular, this analysis brings to light the high dispersion of results within each category, and therefore the importance of individual strategies appropriate to the sector and of the quality of their execution. The following chapters will look at each sector in turn, in order to identify its economic characteristics and structure, the strategies available to the players and the appropriate success factors, in particular as they relate to company organization and culture.

Part two - Hardware and the basic mechanisms

A... E... I... That is true... Three cheers for science!
Molière

In the following chapters of this book, we are going to search for rational explanations to the phenomena that we observe in the computer industry. Let us first summarize the main structural findings that become apparent after the preceding historical and statistical survey.

Data-processing in its beginnings is a single product, inasmuch as all firms offer complete and equivalent ranges of products and services. Moreover, rather rapidly, all firms active in data-processing happen to be specialized in that product. Data-processing thus structures itself as a well-delimited sector, since it is formed by specialized firms, and a homogeneous sector since all firms conform to the integrated model. After the main firms have absorbed the component manufacturing activity in the sixties, the sector acquires its total autonomy from the electronic and electrical industries, while remaining homogeneous.

The number of firms active in the computer industry grows as compared to unit-record from which it was born, thanks to the entry of many competitors, of which only the most specialized survive. This does not erode the growing supremacy of a dominant player, IBM, which occupies constantly 60% to 70% of the market. Until the end of the sixties, the industry essentially retains its concentrated and homogeneous structure, with a relatively small number of players dominated by one firm with a clear majority position.

From the beginning of the seventies, one sees a progressive disintegration of the industry along several dimensions: by nature of services following the separate billing of services, by market niche with the minis and the compatibles, and later a vertical disintegration of part of the sector with the appearance of suppliers specialized in components or subassemblies. This disintegration increases again in the eighties with the rise of a new part of the industry, whose structure is exploded from the outset, and which gradually conquers an important share of the territory of traditional data-processing. Simultaneously, computer technologies spread to all sectors of activity and modify dramatically some industries, to the point of blurring the borderlines of those sectors.

This evolution has structured players of the computer industry into relatively well defined classes of enterprises, but which correspond only imperfectly to the structuring of the market according to products and services provided. Specialized firms are the most numerous, but most market segments are dominated by a handful of firms which offer virtually all forms of products and services. Apart from those generalists, few firms offer a specific combination of different services, and the existing combinations themselves are in small number. Those classes of enterprises, defined by their services, seem to relate in turn to a few main models, which differ by the structure of their accounts and their behavior in reaction to market risks.

The forces driving that evolution have been in all cases the decisions of firms. Those of the dominant player, IBM, have been particularly influential. The objective of those decisions has always been to exploit the technological progress potential in the best interest of the firm. Initiatives from organizations external to the industry, especially of public authorities, have had in the end only little effect. On the other hand, market reactions have acted in favor of the offerings most in tune with demand, and have sanctioned and even eliminated enterprises whose behavior was too far from the expectations of customers.

Such are, briefly summarized, the facts of which we intend to seek the causes. How to explain that trend towards disintegration? Why does only a limited set of services combinations seem viable? Can one justify in each sector the relative sizes and market shares of the players present? How to explain the fall of the supremacy of IBM and the current problems of generalists? What logical relationship links types of enterprise to the selection of products and services, and performance to types of enterprise? How to describe interactions between data-processing and other industries?

Those questions are fundamentally questions of economics. Economic theory is therefore the first place where we wish to turn in our search for the more basic explanations. But we will find out that there is no chapter of economic theory that is capable of explaining completely the structuring of a productive sector and the evolution of that structure. Even more seriously, the central paradigms on which most of the economic science relies ignore by construction concepts that intuition and experience designate as fundamental for the structuring of industry, including product differentiation, specific firm behavior, competition between producers or technological evolution. This will force us to develop part of our own analysis tools.

Concerning questions linked to the coexistence of services of a different nature within a same enterprise, which contribute to explaining the specialization of firms, our belief is that they cannot be answered by economic calculation alone, but relate to more basic qualitative incompatibilities. For that reason, we will try to show the relationships that exist between the nature of productions on the one hand, the organization and the culture of the enterprise on the other hand.

Chapter 6 - The economic mechanisms

An evolutionary view of the industry. Gaps in the economic theory. Production equilibrium, scale of production and industry structure. Oligopolies, monopolies and imperfect competition. Competitive forces and profitability. Industry, sectors and trades. Concentration, fragmentation and profitability. The borders of the information industry. Sector evolution and life cycles.

The economic study of industry structures and of the behavior of productive firms is the subject of a discipline called "industrial economics"[32], which purports to analyze and to explain, among other things:
- the number and the size of enterprises present in each industrial sector, which determine in particular the degree of concentration,
- the horizontal diversification of enterprises, that is to say their propensity to offer a diversified product line and to operate on several markets,
- the vertical integration of enterprises, that is to say their propensity to carry out all successive operations required for the production of their products.

This discipline only exists as such since the seventies, although its subject has been approached earlier, for example by Marshall or Chamberlin. We will retain in particular one of its basic propositions, which is consistent with one empirical postulate of the present book: industry structures result from the action of competition and economic forces.

We will therefore lay down as a principle that the different features related to the structure of industry are neither the fruit of chance, nor of phenomena external to the framework of the economy, but that they can be explained by the action of economic forces which should be identified. The present chapter contains a summary of the main results of economic theory applicable to our purpose, as well as a more precise analysis of competitive phenomena, derived from the works of Michael Porter.

Concepts of industrial economics

The evolution of industry structure

Enterprises derive their subsistence from the sale of products and services[33], which they produce using certain resources. The markets where the enterprise obtains those resources and sells its products, as well as the technological, legal,

---

32 For the reader who would wish a more complete view of industrial economics, the book by Rainelli "Economie Industrielle" (Dalloz, 1993) presents a good recent summary and contains many references.

institutional and economic surroundings, form the environment in which the enterprise lives.

Since markets are limited by assumption, productive firms are competing
against each other. Although competition on the markets for factors of production
is sometimes important, the most deciding competition takes place on the market
where the enterprise offers its products. This market enables demand to sanction
the behavior of suppliers by acting directly on the economic performance and the
financial health of enterprises, who try to anticipate that sanction by organizing to
offer products capable of satisfying the market. Through the immediate selection
of products, the market indirectly selects those organizations and forms of enterprise which are best adapted to the permanent satisfaction of demand. That indirect selection of firms determines the structure of the industry.

To reach their objectives, firms must make a multitude of decisions of variable importance, which relate to different time scales. In particular, the nature and
the price of products made available on the market at any given time result largely
from decisions taken a long time earlier. Such decisions are based on a subjective
projection of demand, internal to each firm and strongly influenced by its features,
and which can turn out to be quite different from the real demand. When supply
and demand meet on the market, the product offering has been determined by productive firms on the basis of internal estimates, and the demand which is actually
expressed at that time can differ considerably from the assumptions that have
presided over the determination of the offer.

For example, when a firm introduces in 1994 a product whose design and
development have lasted a year, with the hope that sales of that product will be significant after two years, one can at best hope that the definition of the product integrates the idea that the firm had in 1992 of the demand at that time and in 1996. In
any case, the real demand in 1994 did not contribute in any way to the definition of
the product. If Sperry Rand and IBM created computers in 1951 and Apple created
the micro in 1977, it is obviously not because the market of that time was asking
for it.

The offer of products and services results from decisions taken by industrial
players according to their possibilities, their objectives, the image that they have of
their competitive environment and the idea that they form of the market. In particular, the determination of prices, which plays a key role in the competition between
firms and rival technologies, is part of the competitive strategy of each firm. For
that reason, contrary to the usual view, we believe more realistic to consider that,
when transactions do happen on the market, there is no direct causal relationship
going from demand to supply. In other words, in the short term of market
exchanges, supply precedes demand.

On the other hand, through the market, demand exerts feedback on the offer
and on the evolution of the firm and of the sector.

---

33 In this book, we will frequently use the term "product" to designate services as well as
    products. The distinction between these two concepts will be examined in following
    chapters, mainly chapter 10 "Disentangling software and services".

At the most immediate level, the market sanctions the behavior of entrepreneurs by buying from those who have made the best choices and implemented them in the most efficient manner, as perceived by potential customers. From its commercial results and those of its competitors, as well as from the other reactions of customers, the firm derives indications about the real demand of the market. If results are not satisfactory, it can immediately adjust its prices and commercial conditions, but changing the quantities produced or features of the product demands a certain time, during which the relative position of the firm is likely to decline.

If serious gaps persist between supply and demand, and if they have an important negative effect, the management of the firm is going to seek out the causes and try to correct them. The firm will attempt to reduce its operating costs with all the more energy that it feels in trouble. It will react to the failure of a product not only by designing different products, but also by modifying its product design process, if only by replacing the people responsible for the failure. It can thus reconsider its production processes and facilities, its methods, management systems, structures, conduct and people. It can also discover that the actions of the enterprise are not consistent with the intentions of its leaders, and re-examine its information, authority and control mechanisms.

For each supplier, the demand that has really developed for its products, in volume and in price, determines its revenue, its financial balance and therefore its viability and its survival. Suppliers whose products durably meet a strong demand will prosper and grow, while those who make too many mistakes will have to throw in the sponge and disappear.

The financial performance, which determines the survival of the firm, is therefore a measurement both of the match of the offer with the market and of the firm with its environment. Natural selection thus operates at three levels: the selection of products by the market, the selection of organizations and behavior inside each firm, and finally the selection of firms and enterprise models. The industry is thus evolving according to a Darwinian process where the market plays the role of the environment and the deep personality of firms that of the genetic material, each firm determining its supplier behavior according to its personality.

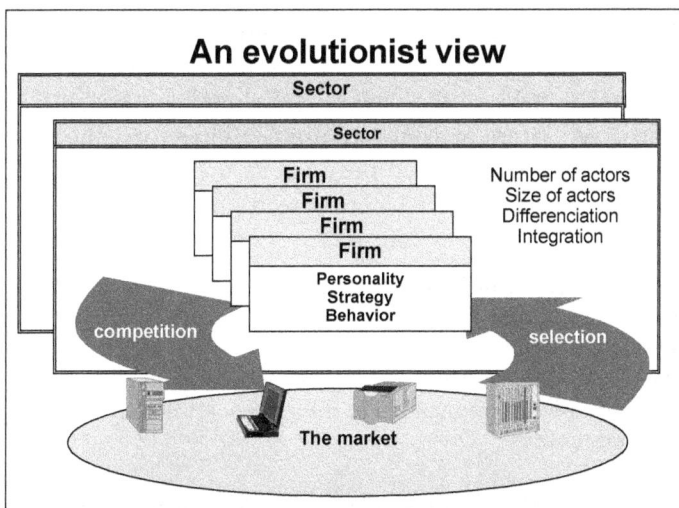

An evolutionist view

=This model is analogous to natural selection in biology. Each enterprise is similar to a living organism whose behavior results from an active search for the best possible adaptation to its environment, but is constrained and partially determined by its internal features: skills, resources, organization, management systems, value system, patterns of behavior…, that we will generally designate as its "personality". By determining the evolution of each supplier according to the success of its products, the market also makes a selection between the different enterprise personalities, in the same way as the environment indirectly selects the genetic material through the behavior of individuals. Thus "species" of enterprises can appear and evolve.

Classical production theory

Contemporary economic theory[34], which results from developments started by Adam Smith in the XVIIth century, revolves around the reference model of neo-classical economics. This model assumes a very large number of agents, each one very small relative to the market, and all conforming to the same model called "*Homo economicus*", which itself is a simplified model of individual human behavior.

Classical and neoclassical economic theory studies transactions between those economic agents by assuming that the size of each one is negligible as compared to the size of the market. That implies the existence of a very large number of suppliers and buyers for each good, each of which is too small to have an influence on market prices. The price of the good is determined by the confrontation of total demand and total supply, and becomes a given for each supplier.

Reciprocally, at the prevailing market price, each supplier can sell any quantity of the good that he can produce, provided that this quantity remains a very small part of total supply and demand. If he tries to sell above the market price, he will not sell anything at all. If he tries to sell below the market price, he will not sell a higher quantity and will therefore lose money. Except for the initial groping required to discover the market price at the beginning of each session, price is not a competitive parameter and the only adjustment variable available to each supplier is the quantity that it produces.

Each supplier uses certain means of production which, for economic purposes, can be summarized by a "production function" relating production cost to the quantity produced. The total production cost for a certain quantity is generally formed of a fixed part, independent of the volume of production, and of variable costs which vary with volume. In most real cases, the variable cost initially decreases when volume increases, then starts to increase when volume passes a certain threshold (the so-called "law of diminishing returns"). Therefore, the average cost per unit produced initially decreases when the quantity increases, then starts to increase above a certain "optimal quantity". In other words, for a given production facility,

---

34   Readers wishing to refresh their knowledge in economics are invited to refer to a classical textbook, for example the excellent "Economics" by Samuelson (McGraw Hill), which has known many successive editions.

Most such books describe the status of the major schools of thought around the fifties and contain a comprehensive bibliography. The present book will only give references to more recent or less known works.

there is an optimal production volume that minimizes the average cost and therefore maximizes supplier profit, since the selling price is determined independently of costs and volumes.

The optimal production quantity and the corresponding average cost can be different for each supplier according to its production facility, which be more or less efficient in exploiting available technologies. In the same way as there is an optimal production quantity for a given production facility, there is an optimal production scale for a product and a given state of technology. That scale is such that it provides the lowest possible unit production cost by making optimal usage of the available technologies, and thus provides maximum profitability for suppliers who operate at that scale.

The increase of productive capacities and the exploitation of new technology requires investments. An industry will attract new suppliers and new investments as long as the return on capital invested in that industry is higher than the market interest rate. These new suppliers and the additional quantities offered will cause a decline of prices and profits. In the opposite case, suppliers and capital will tend to desert that sector as long as the equality of those two rates is not re-established.

In summary, the sector will evolve towards a state of "long-term" equilibrium where:
- the prices and quantities exchanged correspond to the point of equilibrium between the interests of suppliers and those of buyers,
- each supplier operates on a scale at least equal to the optimal production scale,
- the return on invested capital is equal to the market interest rate.

It must be noted that the existence of a state of equilibrium does not imply that the real economy is in that state. In reality, the balance can be displaced by the evolution of technologies even before being reached. In fact, it is extremely rare to observe a stable equilibrium, especially in an area which evolves as quickly as data-processing. In general, even if economic theory tends to favor the study of states of equilibrium, which can more easily be handled by the tools of mathematics, we will rather retain its conclusions relative to the mechanisms and trends of evolution.

Oligopolies, monopolies and imperfect competition

The reasoning of classical economics assumes that in all states of the economy, including short-term equilibrium and long-term equilibrium, the quantity produced by each supplier is insignificant compared to the total quantity exchanged, which amounts to saying that the optimal production scale is extremely low compared to the size of the market. That reasoning no longer holds when the optimal production scale becomes equal to a significant share of the market, and it collapses when the average cost is indefinitely decreasing, which defines an effectively infinite optimal production scale.

Those last cases are less rare than classical economists want to admit. For example, if the variable cost is the same for each unit produced, the average cost of each unit is equal to the sum of that variable cost and the quotient of fixed cost by the quantity produced, and therefore decreases endlessly when that quantity increases. In industrial production activities, that assumption generally holds true over a very large range of volumes, and is even accepted as always valid, whatever the volume, in management decision-making. In that case, the same reasoning as above shows that the first supplier to obtain an advantage over its competitors will eventually eliminate all of them. Moreover, as soon as one supplier reaches a sufficient market share, its actions can have an influence on the market price, and it can manipulate prices as part of its competitive strategy.

In first approximation, one can nevertheless say that the relationship between the optimal production scale and the global size of the market determines the final structure of the sector. If the optimal production scale is very low compared to the size of the market, many suppliers can operate profitably, and the competitive situation approaches the so-called state of "pure" competition so dear to classical economists. If on the contrary the optimal production scale is equal to or higher than the size of the market, one finds a monopoly situation where only one supplier can survive. In intermediate cases where the size of the market is a small multiple of the optimal production scale, one finds a situation called oligopoly, where a small number of firms are competing for the market.

The monopoly case, where the good is offered by a single supplier, has been formalized and treated very early. Contrary to suppliers on competitive markets, the monopolist has the power to set the price of the good unilaterally. One shows that it can maximize its profit by limiting the quantity offered and selling at a higher price than that which would prevail in a competitive situation. The monopolist is protected from the entry of competitors by the level of investments that they would have to support to implement a competitive production facility. That situation enables him most often to earn durably higher profits than those corresponding to the interest rate of invested capital (economists call that difference "excess profit").

By so doing, the monopoly satisfies demand only partially, and introduces a form of rationing and abnormally high prices compared to what "pure" competition would allow. For that reason, classical economists consider that monopolies entail a degradation in the overall efficiency of the economy, and recommend that public authorities should either prevent their development or break them up when they exist, or submit them to regulations that will re-establish consistency with the general interest.

The concept of economical production scale is basic for the comprehension of a sector of activity, because it determines at the same time the number of firms that will be able to operate in a viable manner, the form of the competition that will prevail and the level of profitability that those firms will be able to hope for. It will be the first criterion for distinguishing between firms and between sectors in our model. It will also appear among the main considerations in our analysis of competitive dynamics.

Industry structure in classical economics

Classical theory describes productive agents as competing against each other for the supply of goods on certain markets. The market paradigm allows all agents to intervene at any given time on all markets as buyers as well as suppliers. However, for most goods, some players are always suppliers and others are always buyers. With each good (or market) is therefore associated a relatively stable group of agents producing that good, which form the "industry" associated with the market. Inasmuch as the set of buyers of the good is itself only a part of the totality of agents, one uses also the term of "market" to designate "the set of potential or actual buyers of the product[35]". A market[36] and an industry are thus associated with each product.

The theory also assumes that each sale or purchase decision is independent of other decisions of the same agent on that market and on the other markets. Markets are viewed as being totally independent from one another. Economic phenomena can then be studied separately for each good or market. The economy is seen as a juxtaposition of separate markets, each associated with an isolated good. Interactions between those markets are limited to tradeoffs made by consumers in allocating their resources to the acquisition of different goods, and by suppliers in allocating production factors.

In that vision, two distinct suppliers produce either identical goods, which are complete substitutes of each other, or totally different and independent goods. Moreover, one supplier is implicitly associated with one and only one product. If it offers several products, classical economic theory treats them independently by assuming implicitly that the supplier behaves on each market in the same way as if it operated exclusively on that market. Classical economic theory thus postulates an industry structure built by juxtaposing groups of firms such that all firms of a group offer the same good, and that all groups, therefore all products, are independent of each other.

That hypothetical structure obviously does not correspond to reality. It is extremely rare for two different firms to offer the exact same good. Each supplier strives to make its offer different from that of its competitors. Except in a few markets for food or raw materials, which are not in the scope of the present book, there are no rigorously identical products. All products are different to some degree and can be more or less substituted to other products, so that grouping real products into homogeneous families comparable to the abstract products of economic theory is a largely arbitrary exercise.

The concept of product or good itself is less obvious than it seems: for example, a transportation service between Paris and Lyon cannot be substituted to a transportation service between New York and Chicago. It is therefore not the same product although it is the same sector of industry. Two products, even very similar, are never identical, and conversely two very different products can have a mutual influence, for example software packages and disk drives[37]. Moreover, different products are often related at the stage of their utilization or at the stage of their

---

35   Kotler, Principles of Marketing (Prentice Hall, 1980).

36   This meaning of the word "market" is different from the usual economic vocabulary, where it usually stands for the institutional or physical device which allows transactions between suppliers and buyers.

production. For example, market demand for software packages depends on the number of computers in use, and demand for electronic components depends upon demand for computers. Those interdependencies are all the more significant that one tries to study an industry like data-processing, where a large number of product types coexist and are linked by complex relationships.

Until the thirties, economic theory represented the world as a juxtaposition of markets belonging to one of two types: those whose functioning is correctly approached by the model of pure competition, and those whose functioning obeys the model of monopoly.

The most ambitious attempt to formalize a general model is due to Chamberlin[38]. In this model, one considers that each supplier is a monopoly for the good it offers, and that two goods offered by two different suppliers are neither totally identical nor totally different, but exhibit a certain degree of substitutability characteristic of that couple of goods. The cases of pure competition and of monopoly become particular limiting cases, the first one corresponding to a situation where the offers of many suppliers are totally substitutable, the second to the situation where the product of a certain supplier has no substitute. In the general case, the behavior of each supplier resembles more that of a monopolist than that of the infinitely small supplier of the classical theory, whence the name of "monopolistic competition" given to that model.

Unfortunately, neither Chamberlin nor his followers have been able to derive from those ideas a sufficiently operational analytic system to serve as the basis of a new theory. The difficulty is in the definition of demand for each product: since all products can be substituted to each other in varying degrees, and are therefore more or less competitive, the demand curve for each good is dependent on all the other markets, products, and suppliers. Until now, no way has been found to describe the interrelations between products in a manner both sufficiently rigorous and sufficiently simple to serve as the basis for redefining the concepts of competition, market and industry. In other words, Chamberlin's approach, however appealing, is only of little use in resolving the problems addressed in the present book.

Existing economic theory is thus incapable of setting rigorous criteria which would allow to isolate any part of the economic system in order to study it independently of the rest. As Chamberlin himself wrote: "A market or a sector cannot be defined in an objective manner. The economic world can be considered as a network of interdependent markets and sectors, whose borderlines are chosen in a way to obtain a convenient representation, but which are essentially arbitrary".

------

37 That influence can take many forms: generally, the use of software packages creates a demand for disk storage capacity, but some data compression software packages reduce that demand.

38 E H Chamberlin, The Theory of Monopolistic Competition (Harvard University Press, 1933)

Competition and industry structure

To analyze more finely the competitive processes which preside over the structuring of the industry, we must turn to sources which describe competition in a more exhaustive and detailed manner than does economic theory. We will use for that purpose the works of Michael Porter, which have become classics in that area[39]. While building upon the relevant economic concepts, such as barriers to entry or optimal production scale, Porter's analysis complements them with many other considerations derived from the experience of enterprises, and represents a comprehensive study of the behavior of firms in competitive situations.

Porter's five forces

According to Porter, competition in a given industry is governed by the action of five basic forces:
- the threat of new entrants,
- the rivalry between existing competitors,
- the pressure exerted by replacement products,
- the bargaining power of customers,
- the bargaining power of suppliers.

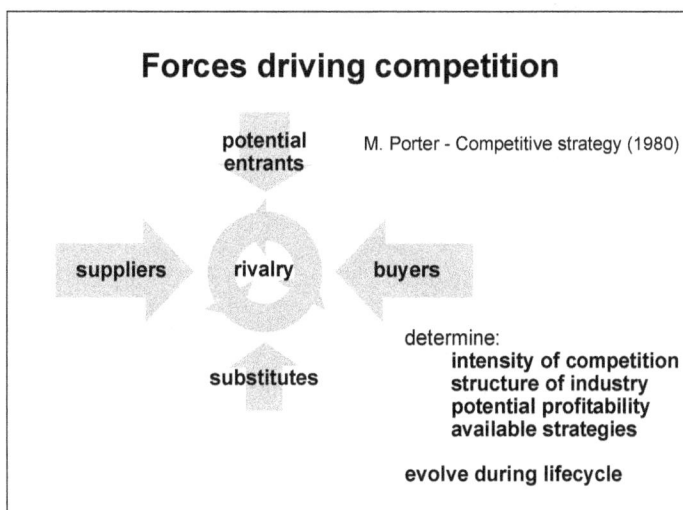

Forces driving competition

potential entrants

M. Porter - Competitive strategy (1980)

suppliers   rivalry   buyers

substitutes

determine:
**intensity of competition
structure of industry
potential profitability
available strategies**

evolve during lifecycle

Each of those forces summarizes many factors related to the product or service concerned, to the system of production, to the firm or to the sector of industry. The interaction of those five forces determines in particular the intensity of competition and the potential profitability level of the sector, the number of competitors present and the distribution of market shares, the rules of the competitive game and the available strategic choices.

---

39 The two reference books by Porter are "Competitive Strategy" (1980) and "The Competitive Advantage" (1985), both published by The Free Press, New York.

The sector concept

Relying on the study of competition to understand the structure of industry demands a sector by sector analysis. Customer choices, and therefore competition, take place only between firms offering products than can be substitutes of each other in the sense that they can satisfy the same customer need. Products that are not substitutes define therefore as many separate sectors which structure themselves independently, at least in the first analysis. For example, the printer sector or that of data-processing software packages are as distinct from computers as the compact disks sector is from that of electronic components.

Porter uses the term "*industry*" to designate "the group of firms producing products that are close substitutes for each other". It includes in effect all the players that are competing for a given market and that are structured by the action of competitive forces. That term has been replaced rather happily by that of "*secteur*" (sector) in the French translation, because what it designates is far more narrow that what is usually meant by the word "industry". In this meaning, the present book will use the term "sector" and retain the word "industry" in its wider and fuzzier sense. This concept of sector is different from the concept of market or market segment, which is defined as "the set of actual and potential buyers of a product"[40].

According to that definition, data-processing does not constitute a single industry or sector, but is composed of a large number of sectors corresponding to as many substitutable products. The products of Intel cannot be substitutes for those of Lotus, nor can those of EDS for those of Compaq. Within equipment, printers and disk drives form two distinct sectors, in the same way as spreadsheets and word processing in software. In the sense of Porter, not only do components, equipment, software and services constitute distinct sectors, but those sectors themselves must in turn be broken down into sub-sectors, that can obey different production logic and competitive dynamics, and thereby adopt different structures.

Like the classical economists, Porter recognizes that it is difficult to set exact borderlines for a sector, in the same way as to separate candidates to entry from existing competitors or to distinguish replacement products from current products. But the very nature of its purpose allows him to explicitly avoid the issue. The businessman whom he addresses knows what are his products and relevant competitors, and basically there is no need for the borderline of the sector to be drawn in a rigorous fashion provided that all competitors are somehow taken into account according to the importance of the threat that they represent.

We will need to adapt some concepts and tools to the purpose of the present book. Porter's books are targeted at business executives to help them formulate efficient strategies considering their particular activities and their particular environment. In this spirit, they seek to draw an exhaustive inventory of all factors which might be taken into account, even if their individual analysis must remain incomplete or vague. Conversely, Porter implicitly assumes that his readers are located inside a particular firm belonging to a given industry structure, and that each of

---

40   Kotler, Principles of Marketing

them knows pragmatically which firms he must take into account when defining his competitive strategy.

We will therefore have to adapt that model in order to identify general and objective criteria for structuring the industry, and to take into account relationships of covariance or antagonism between products and therefore the corresponding sectors, as well as the fact that most firms offer several products and thereby oper-ate in several sectors.

For example, most software package firms are present in several application areas, and almost all equipment firms also offer services. When many firms are present in a same configuration of elementary sectors, one can consider that this situation defines a composite sector. But it is often useful to consider those sectors as the juxtaposition of elementary sectors which can obey different logic or be in different phases of sector evolution.

On the other hand, we will be able to simplify the model proposed by Porter by retaining only those elements that are in direct relationship with the industry structure. Some factors can appear as important for determining the strategy of a particular firm, but can be considered as minor for the study of the global struc-ture; we will therefore be able to leave them out of our model. Similarly, we will be able to ignore those factors that do not concern the computer industry, or that act on all firms in the same manner.

The correct method is to concentrate first on sectors as "elementary" as pos-sible, corresponding to indisputably substitutable products. Only in a second step, after having studied "pure" sectors, in the sense of pure substances in chemistry, will we be able to take account similarities and interrelations between sectors.

In a first approach, we will restrict our discussion to the four main traditional categories of components, equipment, software and services, at the same time seek-ing to identify potential differences in the action of competitive forces inside each of those categories.

Competitive forces and profitability

The classical model of economic equilibrium indicates that each industry sec-tor tends towards a situation where the profitability of invested capital is equal to the market interest rate, which is the same for all firms and all sectors. The profit rate of the firm, expressed in percentage of revenue, is equal to the product of the capital profitability rate by the ratio of capital to revenue. It follows that, under the assumption of "pure and perfect" competition, the average profitability of a sector depends only on the capital intensity of that sector. It will be high for strongly capi-tal-intensive activities like electronic components, and low for activities like advice and assistance services, but in all cases it will be just high enough to pay interest on invested capital at the market rate.

That assumes, among other assumptions, that suppliers can freely enter and leave the market without incurring particular expenses, and vary their production by infinitely small quantities.

The presence of barriers to entry or to exit, or of fixed stages in production variation, changes the above conclusions. New suppliers will appear only if the profitability of the sector is high enough to justify their initial investment and the associated risk. At the opposite, with obstacles to exit, unlucky suppliers will not leave the sector as long as their profitability will remain sufficient to avoid having to pay the price of exit. In summary, the presence of barriers to entry tends to main-tain the profitability of the sector above industry average and that of barriers to exit below industry average. In both cases, the convergence process is stopped and firms present in the sector can durably obtain different profit levels.

The same considerations also govern the number of active firms and the intensity of competition in each sector. The presence of obstacles to entry tends to reduce the number of competitors and constitutes a concentration factor for the sector, while obstacles to exit tend to maintain the number of competitors at an artificially high level, and constitutes a dispersion factor for the sector. Further-more, the intensity of competition tends to increase with the number of competi-tors. If it is possible to leave the sector easily, ailing firms will be able to quit rather than continue the struggle. If on the other hand, for some reason or another, firms engaged in a sector encounter difficulties to leave, some will choose to fight with their back to the wall and thus exasperate competition.

The threat of new entrants and the competition between existing suppliers contribute therefore to determining the profitability of a sector. In the same way, the threat of replacement products places an upper limit on the price of the prod-uct and therefore on the possible profitability, while the bargaining power of cus-tomers and suppliers determines the extent to which firms of the sector can impose their conditions and thus retain the value that they create. In summary, a sector is all the more favorable for incumbent firms that obstacles to entry are high, obstacles to exit low, threat of replacement products remote, and the relative power of customers and suppliers limited.

The most important barrier to entry is a high economical production scale. Such a situation imposes important investments and capital requirements on the candidate to entry, as well as a minimal production volume and ceiling prices that are those of firms already in place, thus increasing its risk. This is consistent with economic theory, which shows that the optimal production scale increases with the ratio between fixed costs and variable costs of production.

Sectors of the computer industry

The borderlines of data-processing

Although economic theory comes to the conclusion that it is impossible to isolate any part of the economic system to study it independently of the rest, real-ism forces us to limit the scope of the present study in a more precise manner than we have done until now.

We can define the computer industry as "the set of organizations that pro-duce goods or services which enter into the composition of computing systems or are used in their implementation". This definition assumes in turn that we can define precisely what a computer system is, which is less obvious than it seems.

Data-processing and computers have long been synonymous, but the constant decline of the cost of components has allowed to integrate elements of computers into all kinds of objects, most of which existed before data-processing, and some of which belong to everyday life. Airplanes, cars, cameras, musical instruments, telephones, machine tools contain microprocessors of varying power and in varying numbers. Should we therefore consider those objects as computer systems, and the airspace, automobile, photographic, musical and telephone industries, as branches of the computer industry? In the same spirit, where should we put calculators, electronic games or flight simulators?

For the moment, we will decide arbitrarily to focus our study on so-called "general purpose" computers, keeping in mind that the technologies and components of data-processing are also used in other machines, but for particular purposes corresponding to the specific functions of those machines. Only after having examined the computer industry in that narrow sense will we return to the question of computerized objects and try to understand the industrial phenomena that manifest themselves at the borderlines of data-processing *stricto sensu*.

The definition of the computer industry that we have retained invites us to establish an inventory of products and services that "enter the composition of computing systems or are used in their implementation".

As seen by their users, computing systems (which we assimilate to computers) are always built from interconnected equipment, and execute software which defines their application functions. The hardware part can be as simple as the combination of a central unit, a screen, a keyboard and a printer, or include a complete network of processing centers, each comprising many computing and storage units, accessible from thousands of terminals. There exists a large variety of hardware devices distinguished by their primary function (computing, storage, presentation and production of information in different physical forms, communication between computer systems ...), as well as by the modes of execution and performances of those functions. Those various pieces of equipment can be acquired separately from competitive suppliers.

Software defines specifically services that the computer system can provide to its users. All computer systems contain therefore an important amount of software, which is usually divided into several categories: system software directly related to hardware, utility programs implementing service functions, general applications common to many users, applications specific to a particular group. All those programs can be obtained in different manners: some general programs are developed by entrepreneurs and can be acquired on the market like any other product; one will then speak of "software packages". At the opposite, they can be developed specifically for a particular user, who can assign that work to his own personnel or to a services company. Let us note right now that, in contrast with hardware, which always implies a simple classical relationship between supplier and customer, software can be acquired in three different modes of economic relationship: industrial production for software packages, service or "self-service" for specific develop-ments.

In addition to software development, other services may be used in the com-position or the implementation of computer systems: communications, integration, training, management, maintenance, etc. Moreover, to the horizontal breakdown as perceived by users can be superimposed a vertical decomposition corresponding to a specialization of production stages, where production of the final good is per-formed by a complex of different firms.

At this point, our attempt to find clear borderlines for the computer industry meets a second difficulty: among all goods and services used by computer systems, and among sectors who produce them, which ones must be retained as belonging to the computer industry? It is clear for example that even if computers are enclosed in metallic cases, this does not suffice to make metallurgy a branch of the data-processing industry. But conversely, many commentators quite happily merge the telecommunications industry with data-processing. Inasmuch as a very large number of computer systems do incorporate telecommunications services provided by specialized operators, we must ask ourselves whether telecommunications ser-vices satisfy our definition.

Here again, our position will be utilitarian and not dogmatic. In case of doubt, it seems better a analytic discipline to start by considering two sectors as dis-tinct and to study explicitly their relationships, even if we eventually conclude to their sameness, rather than to postulate *a priori* that they form only one sector. In that precise case, telecommunications services provide the function of transporting information, which is not specific to computer systems. Even in the framework of computer systems, that transportation function can be implemented by other means such as mail or road transportation, which can thus be substitutes to telecommuni-cations and could therefore also be candidates to enter the scope of our study.

In general, we will adopt the following empirical rules:
- leave out those industries for which data-processing is a minority customer and not the dominant customer,
- leave out those industries that existed before data-processing, that is to say before 1950.

We will thus retain a narrow definition of the computer industry, which in particular does not contain telecommunications, considered as a distinct industry. At a later point in our study[41], we will examine firms that play an important role in computing without it being their dominant activity, as well as firms whose activity is strongly influenced by computing, two criteria that apply to telecommunications. Understanding the implications of that proximity will enable us to return later to the question of their possible merger.

---

41   see chapter 16.

The structuring factors

Economical production scale

A high optimal production scale, for example due to a very high ratio of fixed costs to variable costs, constitutes the most important obstacle to entry. One extreme case of this situation is electronic components, where investments are counted in billion dollars while marginal costs are very low. It is also the case for software packages, whose cost of reproduction per copy is very small while the fixed development cost can be high.

For hardware, the situation depends on the strategy adopted by the supplier. A manufacturer can limit himself to assembling component and units acquired on the market, in which case his variable expense will be predominant and its economic production scale will be low. Economies of scale appear when moving to a more industrial type of production demanding investments, or when the manufacturer produces himself, in total or in part, the components that he uses.

Services cannot be characterized in a simple way. Some, like advice and assistance services, have a very low production scale and therefore are virtually exempt from obstacles to entry. Others, like telecommunications, demand considerable hardware investments entailing high fixed expenses and therefore a production scale forming an almost insurmountable obstacle to entry. Already, we see that the sector of services is very heterogeneous and will have to be subdivided into sub-sectors.

Another barrier to the entry of a new competitor is formed by those costs that customers must support when changing to a different product, and the other disadvantages related to that change. Those obstacles depend upon the differentiation of the product, the loyalty of the existent customer base, and the switching costs for the customer. A candidate to entry can reduce those costs by choosing to copy existing products, especially when they are subject to a standard or a norm. That barrier to entry will therefore be important for original products not subject to standardization, low for services and standardized equipment and very low for ordinary services such as technical assistance or the program development.

Other obstacles

The need for capital is directly related to the cost structure for the activity under consideration and therefore to the scale of production, although it involves the absolute magnitude of the need while the production scale only involves the ratio of capital to variable cost. For example, components and software packages both have a high production scale, but the capital requirements for the software package activity are much lower in absolute value, and so are the barriers to entry.

Capital requirements form a particularly severe barrier to entry when capital is used to finance sunk costs, which cannot be recovered even in the event of a total stop of production. It is the case for example for research and development and marketing expenses, or for the costs of construction of production facilities when those facilities cannot be used for any other purpose and therefore have no usage value if production is stopped. This last situation can result from a rapid evolution of production technologies, for example in the case of electronic components.

A firm possessing original technologies can make the entry of competitors difficult by forbidding them access to those technologies through patents or any other protective arrangement. Even in the absence of such industrial property provisions, the investment and the time necessary to acquire a competitive skills level can represent a significant obstacle to entry.

This type of barrier to entry forms a major obstacle in the components sector, and is also present for so-called "professional" services where skills are essential. The situation is more confused for software packages, for which legal protection is not fully efficient and constitutes a major current problem.

In the case of data-processing, the main source of obstacles to exit is the use of specialized assets which lose all their value if production stops. Other potential sources are real or assumed strategic relationships with other activities of the firm, as well as government restrictions. Concerning this last point, governments which support a national industry want to ensure the existence of a national generalist manufacturer. By continuing to support it at the time when all generalists are in trouble, they contribute to maintaining a number of generalists higher that simple competitive logic would warrant.

The power of customers

The motivation of customers to engage into strong bargaining with suppliers, and their relative power in those negotiations, are all the more high that:
 - customers purchase high volumes relative to the size of suppliers,
 - the cost of purchases is an important part of customers' expense,
 - products are little differentiated and switching costs are low,
 - customers are financially fragile,
 - customers have the capability to produce themselves the goods that they purchase (threat of backward integration),
 - the product is not critical for the activity of customers,
 - customers have a good information on the products, the market and the suppliers.

In their great majority, computer suppliers address a diversified customer set which covers all branches of activity and does not form a group exhibiting particular features. The importance of purchases for the customer is very variable according to applications and market segment, but is in most cases medium. Switching costs are high for non-standard equipment, low for standard equipment and most services, but high for some services of a monopolistic type like telecommunications. The threat of backward integration exists only for the majority of services, where it is significant.

Within the computer industry, we can apply the above analysis to cases where products of one sector are used by another sector. By eliminating the trivial case, not specific to data-processing, of using computers for administration purposes of to support internal activities of the firm, the two cases to be looked at are that the supply of components to manufacturers and the supply of hardware and software packages to the suppliers of certain services.

We have seen that the sector of components is highly concentrated while that of equipment is fragmented. Moreover, components represent a critical part of equipment, and the component suppliers can exercise a credible threat of entry into the hardware sector. On the other hand, hardware manufacturers form a critical outlet only for those component suppliers that are highly specialized in computers. The component sector therefore enjoys a high bargaining power over its customers the equipment manufacturers and can in a large measure impose its conditions and pocket the largest share of their combined added value.

In the case of service suppliers that incorporate equipment or software packages into their services, as is the case for processing services, systems integration or facilities management, both sectors are fragmented. On the one hand, those purchases are more critical for service companies than for manufacturers, and on the other hand manufacturers can exercise a constant threat of forward integration into services, while the opposite is hardly credible. The power of equipment and software packages suppliers is therefore relatively higher than that of their customers the services providers. This conclusion must however be mitigated by the role of prescriptor and distributor that those latter firms can play.

Concentrated sectors and fragmented sectors[42]

We can now complement the distinction between sectors that we have outlined based on the optimal production scale.

A high optimal scale of production due to a high ratio of fixed costs to variable costs, and/or a strong product differentiation entailing high switching costs for the customer in the event of a change of supplier, constitute strong barriers to entry and make the sector a **concentrated sector** where competition involves a small number of large firms. A typical example is microprocessors.

A high production scale implies high fixed costs and capital requirements, which we will not consider therefore as independent structuring factors. Other factors favorable to the concentration of a sector are mainly the use of protected or rare technologies and the absence of obstacles to exit.

---

42 In the original French text, we have preferred translating the word "fragmented" used by Porter by "*dispersé* " (dispersed) rather than the more direct equivalent "*fragmenté*". On one hand "dispersed" is a better antonym of "concentrated", and on the other hand this choice allows us to reserve the word "*fragmenté* " to designate an industry where the different goods are produced by distinct specialized firms, as opposed to an "integrated" industry (see chapters 14 and 15). In the English version, we return to the terms used by Porter, although this creates an ambiguity in the use of "fragmented".

Types of sectors

Entry barriers		
concentration profitability	**concentrated** strong competition medium risky profits moderately attractive	**highly concentrated** moderate competition high stable profits very attractive
	highly fragmented intense competition low risky profits unattractive	**fragmented** high competition low stable profits moderately attractive

ease of exit

security

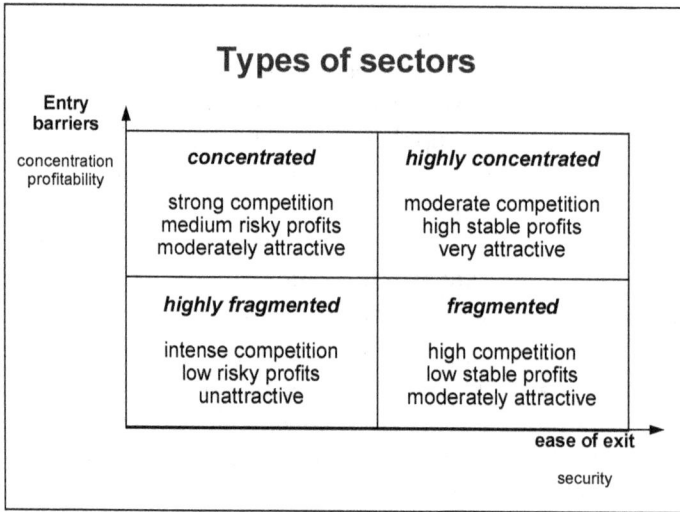

In concentrated sectors, firms can hope to reach a high profitability, but market share plays a deciding role. Several studies have tried to understand whether there exists a stable configuration of market shares, based on the fact that competition is most intense between firms of similar size and should become more moderate between firms of very different sizes. Empirically, one often observes a trend towards a configuration where a leader occupies 55% to 65 % of the market, a challenger approximately 30%, with some secondary firms sharing some 10 to 15%[43]. It was for example the case of data-processing until the eighties, with IBM in the role of the leader, and it is now the case of microprocessors with Intel, of system software packages and each of the main utility programs with Microsoft, or networking software with Novell. We will try to explain that phenomenon in the next chapter, using components as an example.

Conversely, low barriers to entry entail a ***fragmented structure*** where a large number of firms are competing. In such sectors, market shares are lower, the largest firm having seldom more than 15% of the market and the top ten accounting most often for less than 50%. The potential profitability is also low, even for the most efficient firms. This situation can result from a small optimal production scale due to moderate fixed costs, as well as to commoditization or standardization of products, which facilitates changes of supplier. It is aggravated by the utilization of commonplace technologies or the presence of obstacles to exit.

Several sectors, as defined by Porter (the group of firms producing products that are close substitutes for each other) can use similar production facilities and therefore share all structuring factors related to the production system, even if their products are not substitutes. We will use the term "trade" to designate such a group of sectors. It is for example the case for the assembly of hardware devices, which

---

43   This observation has been proposed as a rule by Henderson, the founder of the Boston Consulting Group. His "rule of 3 and 4" states that "in a stable industry, there are only three significant competitors and their revenues are in the ratios 4-2-1".

can produce printers as well as computing units; it is also the case of software packages, since a spreadsheet and a communications management system, although they are not substitutes, rely nevertheless on the same production process.

The action of the forces of competition at the level of a trade works somewhere between a sector in the strict sense and an industry in a broader sense. The similarity of the production facility will lead some players of the same trade to be present in several sectors, possibly to derive a competitive advantage from that presence and to protect that advantage by establishing connections between products belonging *a priori* to distinct sectors. This phenomenon has dominated the sector of equipment before standardization started to isolate the different types of units from each other and to allow partitioning between sub-sectors. It is now playing an increasingly visible role in software packages, where leaders like Microsoft or IBM, and their immediate challengers such as Lotus or Novell, seek to cover as extensive an area of applications as possible. We will return to this discussion in chapter 11, devoted to software packages. On the other hand, the functioning of the market, and in particular the substitution effects between competitive products and the distribution of market shares, must be analyzed separately for each elementary sector.

Data processing products and sectors

At this stage of our study, we can therefore predict that the components sector will be characterized by a low number of players and a high profitability, the equipment sector by a relatively large number of players and medium profitability, that of services by a large number of players and a low profitability. For the sectors of hardware and software packages, we have not been able to characterize in a simple manner such factors as product differentiation and cost of changing supplier. The structuring of those sectors has therefore to take into account the standardization phenomenon: a high degree of product standardization lowers the barriers to entry, and therefore increases the number of competitors and decreases the potential profitability as compared to a sector where competitors offer more differentiated products.

The packaged software sector presents paradoxical features to the superficial observer. At the same time, obstacles to both entry and exit seem low, and economies of scale are very high, the largest share of costs being supported in the development phase. Also, one observes in that sector the coexistence of a large number of firms with very high profit levels. The key consideration is that packaged software firms do not constitute a single sector, but as many sectors as there are areas of application (operating systems, network management, word processing, spreadsheets, utilities, ...). The dispersion here is only apparent and applies to the global level. Each elementary sector conforms to a logic of concentration, which explains the strong profit levels observed.

The services sector is still more heterogeneous, since it contains various types of services based on production facilities which are very different in terms of their economic features, especially their scale of production. Even in a first approximation, services cannot be analyzed as a homogeneous sector, or even as a trade viewed as a set of firms with production facilities having similar economic characteristics. This explains the diversity of situations in an area where different trades and sectors coexist, as we will see in chapter 13.

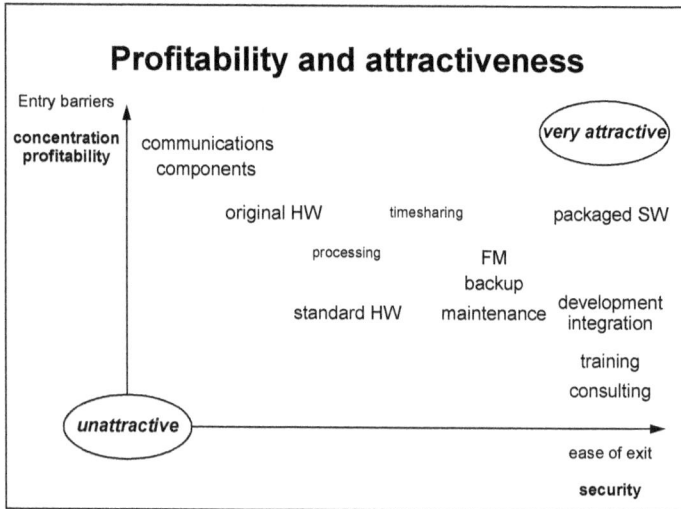

Life cycle

The five forces of competition evolve in time, and with them the structure and the features of sectors, which generally go through a life cycle including succes- sive phases of emergence, growth, maturity and decline. As a rule, as the sector evolves towards maturity and decline, the power of customers increases, the prod- ucts become standardized, competition tends to intensify and profitability tends to decrease. But occasionally some newly created sub-sectors resume the cycle from its beginning, and may exhibit a very different structure from that of the sector from which they originate.

To illustrate that analysis, let us apply it the to the entire macro-sector of data-processing, delaying the study of each component sector to the related chap- ter.

The first group of evolution factors relates to the market. The customer set served by data-processing is constantly expanding, but at different paces depending on sub-markets: large organizations, small enterprises, independent workers and individuals. Those different populations have different requirements and purchasing behaviors, which contribute to a growing market segmentation and constantly open new opportunities of specialization to suppliers. Similarly, the needs evolve towards increased diversification of applications, as well as a diversification of user attitudes regarding customization and integration of their systems. Most large enterprises wish to have customized systems, smaller ones and individual users want ready-to- run standard system. Such differences create different requirements concerning software packages and services, therefore again more opportunities for supplier specialization.

Rapid growth enables competition to concentrate on the acquisition of new customers, while a slowdown forces each player to seek its growth at the detriment of others, thus stirring up competition. Data-processing has globally moved from a regime of rapid growth to a regime of slower growth, but pockets of decline and pockets of rapid growth coexist with zones of moderate growth.

Market penetration is variable according to segments. High for the large organizations and the very technical small enterprises, it is moderate for other small enterprises, and relatively low for individual workers and home use. Depending on the product and the market, the rate of penetration can correspond to the emerging phase, the growth phase, the maturity or the declining phase. The same applies to the learning curve of buyers, whose skill levels are extremely diverse.

A second group of evolution factors relates to the technological evolution, which can bring innovations to the product or to the production process, changes in the production scale or innovations in the commercial area. For data-processing, the most significant phenomena take place in the area of components, where the continuous miniaturization constantly increases the ratio of fixed expenses to variable expenses, which raises for each successive generation the optimal production scale, the capital requirements and the obstacles to entry. On the commercial side, the growing importance of direct marketing to individuals or groups, rather than to specialized purchasing units of large enterprises, gives a growing weight to the distribution activity in the totality of the sector.

In summary, that quick survey of the main structuring factors confirms the heterogeneity of the macro-sector of data-processing and points to segmentation approaches. As long as the market remains globally in expansion, maturation of the sector is compensated by the explosion of the market into distinct segments which offer opportunity for specialization to productive firms, thus giving birth to new sectors that can take on different features from those of the sector from which they originate. A sector in maturity phase can thus give birth to a new sector where the dynamics will be those of an emerging sector. The life cycle concept does not have much significance for the totality of data-processing: multimedia software packages are in the introduction phase, while large and midrange systems are entering the decline phase and processing services have passed the decline phase. The position in the life cycle constitutes a new differentiating factor within data-processing, which contributes to destroying the relevance of any global analysis.

Chapter 7 - Components, a concentrated sector

An overview of the semiconductor industry. Production technologies and cost formation. Technical and economic tradeoffs. Memories and processors. Fixed costs, variable costs and production scale. Competition and sector structure. Stable configurations and the allocation of market shares. Risc versus Cisc. Towards the end of progress?

The driving force behind the entire evolution of data-processing is the progress of electronic technologies, which is essentially realized in components. In the same way as their performances govern the totality of computer system performances, we must expect that the economics of their production exert a dominant influence on the structure of the entire industry.

In this chapter, we will apply to the production of electronic components the conceptual elements that we have summarized in the preceding chapter. To that effect, we will begin by reviewing the history and the current structure of this sector of activity, then the technological considerations which govern the production of components and the economics of the sector.

We will limit our discussion to integrated circuits (memories and microprocessors), which constitute the most "noble" part of computers and which have the most profound and the most original influence on the evolution of the industrial sector. Among other components, the two most critical areas are displays, where the technology of flat screens is analogous to that of memories and benefits from developments in micro-electronics, and the various input-output and information storage units, where micro-electronics combines with high precision mechanics.

History

Initially, computers used the same electronic components as other equipment and manufacturers obtained them from suppliers like General Electric, RCA, Sylvania or Raytheon, for which data-processing was only a very marginal customer. The emerging computer industry was thus distinct from that of components, which existed before computers. Many component suppliers will then attempt to enter data-processing, and all will quit sooner or later.

Around 1960, computer equipment manufacturers gradually begin to produce themselves, totally or partly, the components of their machines. This move happens with the appearance of specific components such as memories and later integrated circuits, the design of which can no longer be separated from that of the machines where they are used. Starting in 1964, following IBM, each computer manufacturer designs and produces the major part of the components that it uses. At the same time as the computer industry thus separates from the industry of general purpose electronics, the production of components becomes integrated in the activity of each supplier. Until today, that integration remains a feature of the traditional data-processing industry.

Conversely, microprocessors developed by computer manufacturers find applications in other industries. In response to those new requirements, new specialized enterprises are created, such as Intel in 1968. Those two movements combine when IBM decides to use Intel components in its microcomputers launched in 1981, returning the PC world to the initial situation where hardware manufacturers obtained their components from outside suppliers. Such specialization between the component industry and the hardware industry in the PC world has been confirmed by the blossoming of manufacturers using Intel components, as well as by the appearance of Intel-compatible component suppliers like AMD or Cyrix. The most remarkable point is without doubt that, despite IBM's efforts to get back into the PC component market, Intel's dominance has become stronger with time.

Not only the world of the PC, but also its alternative Apple conforms to the same model by using processors built by Motorola. The whole world of microcomputers relies on the utilization of microprocessors supplied by specialized firms, separate from the equipment manufacturers. The exception — a most notable one — is IBM, which produces most of the components that it uses, some on the basis of licence agreements with Intel.

On the other hand, the Unix world has preserved the structure of the traditional world, each of the main manufacturers (Sun, Hewlett-Packard, IBM, Digital Equipment, Silicon Graphics) using its own processor. It turns out that a majority of those manufacturers have chosen to use in their Unix machines processors based on the Risc concept (*Reduced Instruction Set Computer*). In each case, design and manufacturing of the processor are the subject of a partnership between the equipment manufacturer and one or several firms specialized in micro-electronics. Thus Motorola is associated with IBM, Hitachi with Hewlett-Packard, Texas Instruments and Fujitsu with Sun and Mitsubishi with Digital Equipment. Furthermore, around each processor, consortia have been formed which group equipment manufacturers that use this processor in their machines. In that sense, the industry structure associated with Risc components, which was initially similar to that the traditional world, begins to present some features of the PC world. But each major manufacturer of Unix hardware continues nevertheless to consider the possession of an original processor as a key competitive advantage.

In the last years, a growing number of equipment manufacturers, generalists or specialized, offer systems built from off-the-shelf components, and some traditional manufacturers like NCR or Unisys have even abandoned the manufacturing of components to use those of Intel. This move seems to represent a basic trend that we will seek to explain in the rest of this chapter.

The segment and the sector

The next table gives the list of the top 10 suppliers of electronic components for computers in 1992. The column "components" gives their revenue in that area in million dollars, and the column "semi-conductors" shows their total revenue in electronic components, all applications included.

Components revenue - 1992

	components	semiconductors
Intel	4690	5064
Motorola	1464	4635
NEC	1158	4976
AMD	637	637
Hitachi	616	3902
Texas Instruments	530	3052
Mitsubishi	487	2 307
Toshiba	457	4765
National Semiconductors	395	
Philips	287	2108

Notice that, except for Intel and AMD, computer components are only a minor share of the total production of semiconductors. A 1992 estimate places the total revenue of the semiconductor industry at 59 billion dollars (130 billion for electronic components), of which 27 billion (45 %) was used in computers. Those 27 billion break down into approximately 25% for microprocessors, 30% for memories and the rest for other components (special chips, cards, …).

Some component suppliers are at the same time data-processing generalists, like Texas Instruments or the Japanese NEC, Hitachi and Toshiba. But for all those firms, the activities of component production and of computer manufacturing are managed in a totally independent manner, according to the conglomerate model and not the model of integrated generalist manufacturers.

Several computer manufacturers produce their own components, but do not appear in this table since their production is reserved for their own needs and is not available on the market. The most important is of course IBM, whose component production is similar in value to that of Intel (even if its breakdown is somewhat different), and which therefore takes place among the top producers. It is also the case of Digital Equipment, Hewlett-Packard, Sun and Silicon Graphics. But it is necessary to note that all these firms have made alliances with more specialized or more important component suppliers: IBM with Motorola for its PowerPC program, Digital Equipment with Mitsubishi, Hewlett-Packard with Hitachi, Sun with Fujitsu and Texas Instruments, Silicon Graphics with NEC. Moreover, all these firms are moving to offer their components on the market.

Technical issues

Technology summary

Microchips used in computers are small rectangles of silicon carrying engraved circuits. The sides of those rectangles are around one to three centimeters in length. Electronic circuits etched on the chip can perform information storage and processing functions. Some chips contain only memory, while microprocessors contain mainly processing circuits as well as the memory directly necessary to the operation of those circuits. We will return later to the difference between memory chips and microprocessors, which plays an important role in the dynamics of the industry.

The width of the lines etched on the silicon, to constitute for example a conducting wire, is characteristic of a technology level. For microprocessors recently put on the market, the line width is less than 1 micron (μ), which is one thousandth of a millimeter. For the most recent chips, line width is around 0.5μ. It is difficult to visualize what those dimensions mean. Let us imagine that a chip such as the PowerPC is enlarged in such a way to allow the movement of human beings instead of electronic pulses. That would require replacing the 0.5μ lines by paths 1 meter wide. The chip would then be the size of a square with sides over 20 kilometers long, and the average distance between two adjacent paths (the width of flower-beds or the thickness of hedges) would be 6 meters. The complexity of such circuits is therefore equivalent to that of a labyrinth of 1 meter wide paths which would totally cover the Paris region according to a 6 by 6 meter mesh. Such complexity contributes to explaining the importance of research and development expenses required for the design of microprocessors.

The width of the lines and the space between two neighboring lines determine the density of circuits. It is limited mainly by three factors:
- the laws of electron propagation in solids, which for very low distances involve still poorly known quantum phenomena,
- radiation effects and electromagnetic interference between neighboring circuits,
- the precision of photo-lithography techniques used in manufacturing.

With current technologies, a typical chip contains 4 million bits of memory, or approximately 3 million transistors for microprocessors. With a line width of 0.35μ, memory chips of the next generation will contain 64 million bits, and microprocessors over ten million transistors.

The theoretical limits are still far away. At the research stage, it is now possible to implement elements measuring a few nanometers (one millionth of a millimeter), which is hundred times more narrow than current commercially available circuits, and therefore potentially ten thousand times more dense. At the manufacturing stage, one begins to master, in the laboratory environment, the techniques which will allow etching 0.1μ wide circuits on an industrial scale, which is the current horizon for manufacturing techniques, and promises chips with 256 million bits of memory or over 100 million transistors.

The overall performance of the chip is determined on the one hand by its architecture, on the other hand by the clock speed, which determines the number of state changes of the active components per unit of time. The architecture of a chip, which defines in particular the repertory of instructions which it is able to rec-ognize and execute, also affects its performances through the following factors:
- the quantity of information which flows in parallel between the different functional blocks of the chip (32 bits for most current chips, 64 bits for the latest ones),
- the quantity of information which flows in parallel between the chip itself and the rest of the computer, and which can be different from the flow inside the chip,
- the possibility of executing several operations simultaneously inside the chip. A chip is called "superscalar" if it contains several processing units capable of executing different instructions in parallel. It is called "pipeline" if succes-sive stages of a same instruction are executed by different units, allowing the execution of several successive instructions to be simultaneously under way. Those two approaches can be combined in the same chip.

A chip, as defined by its architecture and its technology, can operate at differ-ent clock speeds. The maximal speed is limited by the possibilities of removing the heat produced by the circulation of electricity in the chip, as in all electrical conduc-tors. The higher the density of circuits and the clock speed, the higher the heat dis-sipation per unit of area (some current circuits radiate as much as a material heated to 1200 °C, 6 times hotter than a cooking plate). It is possible to decrease heat dissi-pation and power consumption by reducing the operating voltage, but this also decreases the intensity of signals, which must be distinguished from the electronic noise present in circuits. Most recent chips operate under a tension of 3.3 volts, ver-sus 5 volts for the previous generation. The constant reduction of operating voltage is a key feature of technological evolution.

A given chip can operate in a relatively large range of speeds. More than of the chip itself, the maximum clock speed is directly dependent on the heat removal capacity, which itself depends on the environment where the chip is supposed to function. A portable computer cannot include any specific device for heat removal, so that chips used in them will not be able to exceed a certain density and a certain frequency. On the contrary, a large computer can contain very powerful cooling devices which enable maximum densities and clock frequencies for the applicable electronic technology.

Chip manufacturing

To operate correctly, a chip must be free from any defect that could disturb the movement of electrical impulses. At the human scale which we have used above, the occupants of our labyrinth would move at a speed of 600 meters per second and should meet no significant obstacle in their 1 meter wide paths. In other words, the quality of current microchip manufacturing must be the same as that of a 20 kilometers by 20 kilometers square where no irregularity larger than a few tens of centimeters would remain. This demands that the production of components takes place in an extremely purified atmosphere.

The production cycle begins with manufacturing a cylindrical crystal of pure silicon from smelted silicon. Current techniques allow to obtain cylinders 20 cm in diameter and 1,5 meter long. This cylinder is then sliced into wafers approximately half a millimeter thick, and many identical chips will be manufactured simultaneously on each wafer.

On the silicon wafer, circuits are formed of a certain number of layers, (typically between 5 and 15), each supporting a particular drawing implemented with a particular chemical substance (a doping agent or a metallic conductor). Each of these layers is created in a cycle of four main operations: deposit of a photosensitive resin, photo-lithography, etching and doping. Wafers are thus submitted to a series of successive thermal and chemical processes in order to etch the patterns corresponding to the different levels and to the different active substances used in the process, and finally to deposit the substances which constitute the circuits. That process uses a sequence of masks, which must be positioned with an accuracy consistent with the dimension of the circuits themselves. That manufacturing process demands equipment allowing stable positioning to precision lower than the micron, able to withstand cycles of extreme heating and cooling, enclosed in anti-vibration rooms built in turn within antiseismic constructions. The substances used, generally in the gaseous form, are numerous, often toxic, and must also be exempt of any impurity larger than 0.2μ, so that their circulation demands very particular and expensive systems.

At the end of the process, each chip is tested individually in order to mark for later elimination those which include defects due to imperfections of the silicon or of the manufacturing process. The wafer is then cut into chips, defective chips are eliminated, satisfactory chips are equipped with their connectors and coated with a protective resin. The percentage of satisfactory chips, or yield, is the main measure of the quality of the process. It is usually low at the beginning of production, and cannot be expected to stabilize at an acceptable level until after many months.

Economics of production

The determinants of performance and costs

When they design a new chip, manufacturers obviously seek to obtain the best performance at the lowest possible cost. The manufacturing cost of a chip is roughly proportional to its area and inversely proportional to the yield of the manufacturing process. On the other hand, cost is almost independent of the functional content of the chip: ignoring development costs, the cost of a 16 Megabit chip is almost the same as that of a 4 Megabit chip, and the cost of a processor is the same for 3 million transistors as for 1 million, assuming of course the same area and the same yield. The cost per function (bit of memory or logical function) is therefore all the more low that the density is high. This mechanism explains the unceasing search for higher densities and consequently the constant cost decrease of information processing, at the rate of about 20 % per year.

The dimensions of chips result primarily from a tradeoff between yield on one hand, functional content and practical packaging considerations on the other hand. Large chips can be rich in functions and their cost per function can be low. At the opposite, the yield of the process is roughly inversely proportional to the probability of finding a defect on a chip, which given the origin of defects is proportional to the size of the chip. Assume for example that each silicon wafer contains on average, after processing, 5 small defects placed at random. If one hundred identical chips one centimeter square have been manufactured on that wafer, at most five contain a defect and will have to be eliminated. The yield will therefore be 95%. If one had manufactured on the same wafer only 10 chips four centimeters square, it is still probable that five would contain a defect, and the yield would now only be 50%. Incidentally, if one wanted to use the entire wafer for a single giant chip, that would only succeed from time to time in an unpredictable manner. This phenomenon leads to favor small chips.

Whatever is the density of circuits, it is impractical to reduce the dimensions of chips below certain limits. They are connected to the outside world, specifically to the rest of the computer, through hundreds of pins (typically between 200 and 500). Placing those connectors on the chip impose a minimal size which varies depending on the number of pins and the connection technology used. Moreover, the number of pins increases with the number of bits processed in parallel, and more generally with the functional content of the chip. For those reasons, the size of chips varies between slightly less than a centimeter and approximately 2.5 cm per side, and those dimensions are not very likely to change significantly.

Thus, the progress of electronic technologies translates first into increased content, storage capacity and number of logical functions on each chip, and secondly by faster switching speeds and the capability to operate at low voltages. The functional enrichment of logical chips can translate into improved performance if used to implement an appropriate architecture. For each level of electronic technology, the possible clock speeds and therefore the real performance of the chip in a given environment, are actually determined by the "ancillary" cooling and packaging technologies.

Memory and logic

The differences between memory chips and logical chips or microprocessors have important industrial implications. While many circuits are simultaneously active on a logical chip, only a small part of a memory chip is active at any given time. In a processor, the risk of interference between neighboring circuits and the heat production is therefore higher than for a memory chip of equivalent technology and speed. For a same line width, circuit density and switching speed can be higher for a memory chip than for a logical chip. For example, the same 0.5 micron technology is used for processors such as the 2.8 million transistors PowerPC and for 16 Megabits memory chips. Counting only one transistor per bit, the density of the memory chip (1 cm by 2 cm) is 80000 transistors per square millimeter while the density of the processor is approximately 20000 transistors per square millimeter.

A memory chip implements the relatively simple function of storing information represented by binary elements and retrieving it upon request. At the functional level, two memory chips of different generations or technologies differ only by their capacity and speed. The structure of a memory chip is therefore highly repetitive and relatively stable from one generation to the next, which limits design efforts and costs. Moreover, testing a memory chip is a relatively simple operation, almost identical from one generation to the next.

On the contrary, logical chips implement complex functions which vary from one chip to another. Each new technology eventually demands the development of a new chip, because it is of limited interest to produce the same chip in smaller dimensions. Each technological jump enables placing roughly two to three times more transistors on the chip. However, a logical chip containing three times more transistors cannot be derived from its predecessor in a simple manner, but implies a new architecture. Also, the very nature of logical chips requires very complex test programs, which must be redeveloped practically from scratch for each generation.

For all those reasons, memory chips are simpler to design and easier to manufacture than logical chips. As soon as technological R&D enables the manufacturing of higher density chips of a new generation, that technology can be used in memory chips which will appear first on the market. Using that same technology for logical chips requires additional investments and delays to design the microprocessors and to build the development support system and the test procedures. That period is also used to complete the qualification of the new technology and to solve manufacturing and yield problems. Memories can thus always remain one technological generation ahead of processors, so that the short-term evolution of microprocessors can easily be predicted from current developments in the area of memories, the time difference being approximately two years.

For example, pilot lines are beginning to produce 64 Megabits memory chips, with a line width of 0.35 microns and density higher than 300000 transistors per square millimeter. Considering the lower density of processors, this technology will allow to produce, in 1996/1997, logical chips with more than 8 million transistors in the size of the PowerPC, and 25 million for the size of the original Pentium.

This situation also allows memory chip manufacturers to offer the utilization of their production lines to firms specialized in microprocessors, but that only design them and subcontract manufacturing to third parties. Those "fabless" firms (without manufacturing) can thus limit their investments to the R&D necessary for design of the processor, and to turn the totality of manufacturing costs into variable costs.

The formation of costs

A basic feature of the component industry is the enormity of production investments. Production lines require a complex of very high precision equipment based on leading edge technologies and operating in extreme environmental conditions concerning purity of the atmosphere, physical stability, circulation of fluids or temperature control. A chip manufacturing line using current commercially available technologies costs between 600 and 800 million dollars for the smallest industrial production unit. A less expensive production line is not conceivable, or would entail prohibitive costs of production per chip. The capacity of such a unit line is approximately a million chips per month.

A new generation of components appears every two years or so. Since the middle of the eighties, the cost of a production line has increased by more than 50% for each technological generation. That trend is expected to continue, barring a revolution in processes which is not currently foreseen. Production lines for 64 Megabit memory chips, which will be on the market to 1996, or for microprocessors of the same technology which will appear in 1997/98, will cost significantly more than a billion dollars. For example, Toshiba estimates that the optimal size of a component factory represents an investment of roughly 3 billion dollars (300 billion yen) for an annual production of similar value.

On the other hand, the raw materials used are either cheap, like silicon which costs approximately 70 dollars a kilogram in purified form, or consumed in very small quantities in each chip. One estimates that the total cost of raw materials, reactive agents and fluids used in the production of semiconductors, including masks, is around 13% of the value of the production. Production uses little personnel, so that manpower costs, inasmuch as it is legitimate to consider them variable expenses, are relatively low[44]. The marginal production cost of each chip (the additional cost incurred to produce one additional chip) is probably less than 50 dollars on average for all types of chips.

We have seen that tens or hundreds of identical chips are manufactured simultaneously on each silicon wafer, defective chips being eliminated at the end of the process. The marginal cost per wafer is roughly proportional to the area of the wafer, whatever its content. The cost per chip is therefore inversely proportional to the number of chips per wafer on the one hand, to the yield on the other hand. Assuming that yield problems have been solved, the marginal cost of a chip depends therefore only on its surface and not on its content. Increased circuit density allows therefore to reduce cost per function, and for the same content a smaller chip is less expensive than a larger one. For example, the marginal cost of the PowerPC (approximately 100 mm²) is three times lower than that of the Pentium (approximately 300 mm²). But let us keep in mind that this difference is of limited significance, the variable cost of production representing only a small part of the average cost and of the selling price.

Research and development costs cover not only the design of the chip, but also the R&D on technologies, the development of manufacturing processes, and the cost of the pilot lines. Those costs have been estimated by Intel at 500 million dollars for the 486 processor and 750 millions for the Pentium. For memories, the following table gives estimates by Siemens for R&D (column 2) and production

---

44   It would be more logical to treat personnel costs are fixed recoverable costs, since staff is hardly sensitive to volumes produced, but corresponding expenses can be suppressed if production stops.

(column 3) in million dollars. These figures are consistent with the previous ones, considering that the planned production investments by that manufacturer cover several unit lines.

Fixed Costs for memories

	R&D	production	introduction
64Kb	120	190	
256Kb	400	180	1985
1Mb	350	1300	1988
4Mb	380	1600	1990
16Mb	510	3700	1993
64Mb	1000	6000	1996

Note finally that all those investments are "sunk costs" by definition, since they lose their whole value when production stops or when changing to a new technology.

Competition, prices and market shares

Let us translate into economic terms the characteristics of the production of highly integrated micro-electronics components, which we have just described.

General configuration of the sector

As we have seen in Chapter 6, the sector of components is a concentrated sector characterized by very high obstacles to entry. One can expect that few enterprises can afford the above levels of investments, and that therefore only a very small number of firms will be present.

The economical production scale is at least equal to the annual production of one line, which is around 1 million chips per month or 12 millions per year, about one quarter of the worldwide market. The above estimation by Toshiba, which applies to more recent production technologies, would even increase that scale to a magnitude of 30 million chips per year. Moreover, R&D investments themselves are also important, and additional economies of scale can therefore be obtained by multiple production lines in the same firm. Throughout the range of reasonable volumes of total production, average unit costs are indefinitely decreasing. In such cases, economic theory concludes that all competitors will be eliminated and a monopoly will be formed.

It seems that ratios of this magnitude are exceptional in other industries, especially concerning the relationship between the economical production scale and the total size of the market. For comparison purposes, a study of efficient plant sizes conducted in 1975[45] evaluates that size below 3% of the USA market for almost all industries, the maximum being less than 15% of that market. Apart from the pure monopoly, the economic literature has paid little attention to such extreme

---

45   Scherer et al : The Economics of Multi-Plant Operation, an international comparison study
      (Harvard University Press, 1975)

cases of oligopolistic concentration, which leads us to admit in advance that our conclusions are not necessarily applicable to other situations.

The actual structure of the microprocessor sector is that of an asymmetrical oligopoly formed by a half-a-dozen firms of very unequal sizes. Taking all architectures as a base, the market shares of the top three are respectively 81%, 10% and 5%. Restricted to Intel compatibles, the top three occupy 93%, 6% and 1% of the market. At the same time, this sector is the place of a severe price competition and of continued investments resulting in the renewal of products according to a 2 year cycle, each time with dramatic improvements of the price/performance ratio. Therefore, although this sector is close to a monopoly by the distribution of market shares, it is very far from the classical monopoly by the vitality of competition.

Note also that this kind of sector structure, featuring very unequal market shares, with a dominant supplier exceeding 60%, is widespread in the real economy. Until in the eighties, it applied to the totality of the data-processing industry, which then formed a single sector,. It appears again today in the case of system software packages and large utility programs. Several authors had already observed that, in many sectors, stable configurations were characterized by very different market shares, and sought an economic explanation to this phenomenon, without nevertheless looking at such extreme cases.

Note in passing that the theory of "contestable markets" does not explain this situation. Baumol and other authors have shown that if barriers to exit are low, for example if investments required for entry can be recovered upon exit, the simple threat of entry by new competitors suffices for prices to evolve towards those that would result from pure competition. In our case, permanent costs are not only very high, but also unrecoverable ("sunk") since they are incurred even if the firm decides to cease production[46]. Assets that constitute the essential part of fixed costs have no market value outside of their utilization for the production of components, and it is unlikely that a competitor would want to buy them in the event of production stop. Those sunk costs constitute real and severe barriers to entry and prevent components from being a contestable market. According to classical economics, it should appear as a natural monopoly, or at least evolve rapidly to a monopoly situation.

It is difficult to believe that such a frequent phenomenon does not have a solid economic explanation, more convincing anyway than the classical thesis of Gibrat according to which the inequality of market shares is simply a result of chance[47]. Indeed, simulations of the so-called "Gibrat effect" lead to maximum market shares of around 40% after more than 100 years, while in our case the share of the leader is much higher, and the asymmetric distribution is established in just a few years.

---

46   An example of the contrary would be an airline service between two cities, where fixed assets such as airplanes can be reassigned to other relations if that line is closed.

47   It can be shown that if a population of identical firms evolves each year according to growth rates which are randomly distributed around an average value, their sizes tend towards an unbalanced distribution.

It looks as if the process of evolution towards monopoly stops underway to let several secondary firms subsist durably alongside the dominant supplier, thus maintaining enough competition to translate into both low prices and high investments. Let us try to show that this type of configuration is related to specific features of the sector, namely the ratio of fixed costs to variable cost and the duration of the product cycle, and is characteristic of strongly concentrated sectors.

Production scale and bounded rationality

For constantly decreasing costs, is the optimal production scale truly infinite, or rather equal by definition to the size of the market?

In classical theory, the definition of the optimal production scale rests on the assumption that firms will exhaust all opportunities of reducing the average cost of production. In particular, they will continue to decrease prices in attempting to increase the quantities produced and sold, as long as the reduction of selling price remains less than the expected cost reduction, however small that reduction may be.

It is not at all obvious that, in the real world, manufacturers reason in that manner. The behavior postulated by economists would assume that on the one hand the relationship between cost and quantity is known with certainty, and on the other hand that producers decide to simultaneously decrease their selling prices and increase their production capacity at the expense of heavy investments. In reality, the relationship between production volumes and cost is uncertain, and so is the relationship between prices and quantities really sold, especially in a competitive situation. It is therefore more likely that suppliers act more prudently and only commit to a price decrease if the benefit that they can expect seems sufficiently certain.

Viewed from the demand side, it is clear that when the price gap between two substitutable products is low, the other choice factors become relatively more important. For example, a price difference lower than 15% is not necessarily conclusive if other factors of differentiation between products exist. At that level, suppliers will seek to differentiate by other features or to push up volumes by actions such as advertisement rather than by cutting prices.

The equivalent behavior on the cost side is to only seek a reduction of costs by increasing quantities produced if this reduction is of sufficient magnitude. For the sake of simplicity, we can consider that the average cost is equal to the sum of the variable cost, assumed to be constant, and of the quotient of fixed costs by quantity produced. As soon as this second term is under a certain threshold, say 10% of variable cost, the remaining cost reduction potential is at most equal to those 10%. In an uncertain future, it is unlikely that suppliers will engage into action programs (and therefore expenses) aiming to reduce the average cost further by increasing volumes.

The above view of enterprise decision-making is consistent with practical business experience. It has been introduced into economic analysis by Herbert Simon[48] under the term "bounded rationality". Simon's view is that firms do not

---

48   Simon H A, March J G Organizations John Wiley, New York, 1964
     Simon H A Models of bounded rationality, The MIT press, Cambridge Mass 1982

attempt to maximize any single variable such as profit, but seek many objectives and try to satisfy a large number of constraints, many of which are of a qualitative rather than quantitative nature and cannot easily be expressed in mathematical form. The above discussion can be summarized by saying that when conventional models show only minor variations between alternative courses of action, decisions are made on the basis of other, non quantified considerations which nevertheless become the most important in the situation.

Let R be the ratio of fixed costs to variable unit cost. If the number of units produced is equal to R, the contribution of fixed costs to the average cost is exactly equal to the variable unit cost, and the potential for reducing the average cost through increased volumes is 50%. If on the other hand the number of units produced is for instance equal to ten times R, the share of fixed costs in the average cost is equal to one tenth of the variable unit cost, or one eleventh of the average cost, and the cost reduction potential through increased volume is not higher than 9%. At that level of production, it is likely that suppliers will no longer consider price and quantities as the major competitive parameters. For all practical purposes, that production volume will play the same role as the optimal production scale in classical theory.

In the case of constant variable cost, we can therefore replace the concept of optimal production scale by that of economical production scale, which is measured by a small multiple (between three and five) of the ratio of fixed costs to variable unit cost. In the case of components whose commercial lifetime is a few years, the annual economical scale of production is thus of the same order of magnitude as the ratio of fixed costs to variable unit cost.

We have seen that for the manufacturing of components, even without taking R&D expense into account, fixed costs amount to 600 to 800 million dollars for one production line, and that variable cost is approximately 50 dollars per chip. The ratio of fixer costs to variable unit cost, and therefore the annual economical scale of production is therefore between 10 and 20 millions. That figure can be considered as the order of magnitude of the annual production required for average cost to become practically insensitive to volume.

Chronology of costs and prices

For a generation of microprocessors, the sequence of decisions is as follows. The producing firm first engages into a development effort which determines the physical and functional features of the product as well as its performance, and then builds the required production facilities. Those preliminary phases last two to four years, during which the firm accumulates expenses which constitute fixed sunk costs. When the production facility is operational, the product is launched on the market and the supplier chooses a selling price. From that point on, the competitive market determines the quantities sold, and therefore the average cost and the general economic balance of the program. In response to the market, the supplier can act on the selling price, and in a limited measure on the variable part of production costs. But the product itself, as well as the fixed costs, the production capacity and the level of variable unit costs have become intangibles.

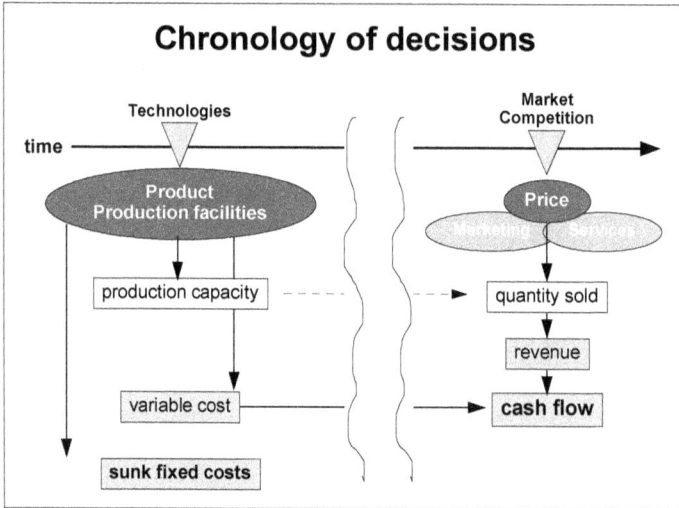

Chronology of decisions

time

Technologies

Market Competition

Product Production facilities

Price

Marketing   Services

production capacity - - - - - - - → quantity sold

revenue

variable cost - - - - - → cash flow

sunk fixed costs

In other words, as soon as a microprocessor has been introduced on the market, the only variable that the supplier can control in the short run in his struggle against competition is price. Modifying product features, or significantly changing its costs, demands new development efforts which will bear their possible fruit after several years and at the expense of additional sunk costs.

Economic analysis shows that, contrary to a common idea, the selling prices of goods are not directly determined by their cost, but by the market. Indeed, the market mechanisms themselves tend to bring that price close to marginal cost, but from the viewpoint of each supplier, the market price is determined by the action of competition. It is up to the supplier to adjust costs in order to keep them lower than selling prices and thus return a profit.

In a sector such as components, where costs are essentially formed by fixed sunk costs, prices are even more independent from costs than in any other sector. Assume that competitors engage in a price war, resulting in continuous price decrease. The best interest of each supplier is to continue production as long as the selling price remains higher than the marginal cost of production[49], which thus forms the lower limit below which prices cannot decrease. Such conduct seems suicidal, because suppliers could no longer finance the necessary investments for the next generation. It could nevertheless appear if some players estimated that their accumulated profits are sufficient to finance their new developments and wanted to increase their market share, or if some players decided to stop investing and attempted to maximize their residual revenue by increasing their market share. In any case, the value of this pricing floor is very low: some tens of dollars for microchips.

---

49   more precisely, as long as his revenue, which is the product of unit price by quantity sold, is at least equal to the sum of variable costs and fixed recoverable costs.

Although the fact is familiar to economists and a large number of business people (but not all...), it is useful to insist that fixed costs play no part in the above rationale, inasmuch as they are sunk costs. At the time when the enterprise must make its product pricing decisions, nothing can prevent those costs from being incurred or change their level. Firms wish eagerly that all costs be covered by revenue, but if competition establishes the market price at an insufficient level, they will nevertheless prefer selling at those prices as long as they remain higher than the marginal cost of production. In other words, fixed sunk costs do not appear in the determination of prices except as the expression of a wish, and can therefore be left out of the operational reasoning.

Market share distribution and survival price

A particularity of the microprocessor market is that its total size, in other words the number of units sold, is hardly sensitive to selling prices. The microprocessor represents only approximately 10% of the selling price of a microcomputer, and memory chips are a similar percentage. Even if the price of microprocessors was zero, that would only allow a reduction of 10% in the price of the complete system, and the total number of units sold would not change much. Conversely, the price of processors could double or even triple without reducing in the same proportions computer sales, and therefore the number of processors sold.

It follows that despite the highly concentrated character of the sector and the existence of a dominant supplier, the formation of microprocessor prices does not obey, even remotely, the classical logic of monopoly. The theory stipulates that monopoly suppliers set prices at the level which maximizes their total revenue, that is to say the product of unit price by volume. If they could agree on a such a strategy, component suppliers would benefit by setting prices at a level at least five or six times higher that current levels, because their total sales volume would certainly not be reduced in the same proportions, and therefore their revenue would be higher.

The formation of prices in this sector results therefore entirely from the action of suppliers competing for shares of a market whose total size is practically independent of their actions. In such a struggle, every bit gained by one is inevitably lost by another, which increases the probability of retaliation by the dominant supplier if attacked by a challenger. On the whole, it is in nobody's interest to start or to extend a price war which would probably end in declining profits for all players, and even to the disappearance of some of them. One can assume that all players are aware of that situation, and that they will avoid engaging into this suicidal path, without any need for explicit collusion or illegal agreements.

A configuration where a few firms would share the market in equivalent proportions cannot be stable. In a such case, each supplier would operate on too low a scale to benefit from all possible economies of scale. At least one of them would certainly attempt to increase his volumes by acting on the price, which would start a sharp round of competition. In a sector where variable costs are by assumption low relative to selling prices, a small volume advantage translates into significant additional financial resources. Their beneficiary can either forgo part of those resources to reduce prices and increase again his volume advantage, or use them to obtain other advantages through marketing actions or improvements in the product or associated services. Any size advantage is thus a competitive advantage which can be exploited to increase size further. An even distribution of market shares is therefore unstable in a concentrated sector.

On the contrary, if market shares are very different, those who enjoy very large shares will be less prone to increase them further by reducing prices. Incidentally, most authors agree that it is generally not in the best interest of the leader of a sector to hold 100% of the market by eliminating competition. As for those competitors with low market shares, which are thereby just viable, it is likely that they will hesitate to take the risk of reducing their prices further. Competition will therefore tend to become more moderate, prices will stabilize, and the configuration will become stable.

Classical oligopoly theory shows that, to preserve their market share and their profit, dominant suppliers should set their prices at the level of the production cost of secondary suppliers (the "limit price"), which discourages secondary suppliers from seeking to increase their share. That assumes that the production cost of dominant suppliers is lower than for secondary suppliers, and that consequently the dominant suppliers make a profit by selling at the limit price.

That reasoning does not explicitly mention fixed costs, which are integrated in the production cost of secondary suppliers and therefore in the limit price. For a sector where new products are introduced every two years at the price of heavy investments, one understands the mechanics better by saying that in order for a firm to survive, the revenue that it obtains from the sale of current products must cover variable costs, administrative and commercial expenses, plus the research, development and production investments required for the next generation. Using its current sales volumes and its estimates for the next generation, each firm determines more or less consciously the "survival price" which enables it to remain in the race.

Research expenses required to develop a new chip, as well as the cost of a line of production, are roughly the same for all firms, and their contribution to the survival price is therefore inversely proportional to the market share of each firm. The survival price of the leader is thus much lower than for marginal firms. In the event of a price war, the leaders will therefore be able to resist much longer. If necessary, they will be able to reduce their prices to a level where they will still survive while marginal firmsl have disappeared.

When the distribution of market shares corresponds to a situation acceptable by all players, although not necessarily optimal for any one, the behavior just described tends to perpetuate that structure at least for the duration of one technology generation.

Who can then reasonably challenge that equilibrium and stand a reasonable chance of succeeding, and how can he attempt to reach that goal?

A possible candidate to entry finds by definition an already occupied market and prices already established for existing products. To have some chance of succeeding, he must either offer a clearly better product for a similar price, or a similar product for a clearly lower price, and even if possible combine a price advantage with a better product. At the same time, he must facilitate the migration of current users to his product.

Products in place are the result of investments amounting to hundreds of millions of dollars. Whatever is the genius of the new candidate, it is highly unrealistic to expect that he will be able to offer a superior product for a much lower investment. As for market prices, they are established around a few hundred dollars per unit, which is close to the average production cost of the less well placed of existing suppliers. The candidate to entry would therefore have to sell approximately one million copies of his new chip to simply cover his development costs. To conquer a place on the market, he will be have to either spend more or sell at a lower price, and in any event to support variable costs, marketing and management expenses, … so that the minimum sales volume required to reach profitability quickly exceeds a million copies.

Faced with that equation, is it reasonable to invest over a billion dollars to be capable of producing, two or three years later if everything goes well, a product which will hopefully be competitive with the chips that Intel, IBM/Motorola, Sun, Digital Equipment and Silicon Graphics will have put on the market in the meantime? The wise businessman will answer no and will invest his available funds in other ventures. That situation, which Porter calls a case of "entry deterring price" justifies the prediction that there will be probably be no more new entrants into the microprocessor sector.

Among incumbent suppliers, the leader has no interest in starting a price war which would bring him even closer to a monopoly situation and could expose him to the attacks of public authorities and of courts. On the other hand, we have seen that marginal firms can only survive by taking advantage of sufficiently high prices. Being reasonably able to attempt to destabilize the leader demands both volumes high enough to support a decrease of price and the availability of sufficient financial and professional resources to develop a superior product. In addition, the challenger must enjoy technological advantages in production, so that his survival price is similar or lower than that of the leader for the market shares that he can reasonably hope to reach. That combination of conditions can only be satisfied by the number two of the sector, provided that he has the firm ambition to become number one. One can think that such is the case for the PowerOpen consortium formed between IBM and Motorola.

Component pricing

The formation of component prices reflects competition for market shares by a small number of players, and cannot be separated from the strategy and tactics of those players. Moreover, each player reacts to the actions of others, and one can therefore expect prices to evolve over time.

Pricing decisions will aim therefore to optimize the economics of the production program not necessarily over its entire duration, but perhaps rather within a horizon limited by uncertainty concerning the reactions of competitors and of the market, as well as by the possibility for the firm to act again on its prices. Finally, if

the economist can afford to be concerned only by the global balance of multian-
nual programs, the business manager must worry about the accounts of each
reporting period and therefore consider accounting effects even if their economic
meaning is debatable.

Investment costs incurred before the launching of the product appear in the
firm's profit and loss statement through annual depreciation provisions that are
constant or decreasing. However, in the early commercial life of a component, production capacities and demand are generally limited and the yield of manufacturing
lines is also low, therefore quantities produced are low. Those two combined effects
result in an apparent average cost which starts from a high level and decreases with
time. But that is only due to an accounting effect resulting from the depreciation
conventions selected, and is deprived of any economic significance.

Nevertheless, the selling price will have to be high in order for the enterprise
to present balanced accounts in the early periods. Fortunately, the performances of
the new component can probably justify a higher price than its existing competitors, especially when switching costs (costs of replacing the old component by the
new one) are low.

The highest conceivable price would maximize total revenue, and be such
that an increase of that price would entail a decrease of quantity sold by a percentage higher than the percentage of price increase. We have seen that the lack of
demand elasticity places this maximal price at a level clearly higher than commonly
practiced prices. In total, unit prices of components can *a priori* be set in a very
wide interval, going from a few tens of dollars (the marginal cost) to a few thousands of dollars (the revenue-maximizing price). In reality, observed prices are
spread between 100 and 3000 dollars, the majority of microprocessors being sold
between 200 and 500 dollars.

A more efficient but totally compatible component can be introduced at a
high price, while the price of a component with a new architecture will need to be
sufficiently low to compensate for switching costs. In any case, the supplier will
tend to set the introduction price at the highest level which will enable him to sell
all the current production, and to decrease price only to the extent necessary to sell
a supposedly growing production. The market leader will naturally adopt a prudent
compatibility strategy and high prices, while the challenger (or challengers) will
probably attempt to conquer market share through more aggressive prices, while
still retaining an important potential price reduction margin.

A typical example is Intel's Pentium, which was introduced on the market at
almost 1500 dollars while its closest predecessor, with which it is totally compatible
but two times faster, sold for less than 500 dollars. One year later, the price of the
Pentium had decreased to around 800 dollars. Its real strategic challenger the PowerPC by IBM/Motorola, was introduced under 500 dollars for a similar computing
power, but it has to conquer a market and cannot directly replace existing processors. No matter what some manufacturers are saying, those prices and their evolution have only little to do with the evolution of costs, but result from a progressive
adaptation of prices to market demand and competitive actions.

As we have seen, it is precisely that process which leads to a stable configuration of the sector, at a price higher than the marginal production cost. Moreover, the only firms that can survive in the long run are those which derive from their current products enough marginal profit to cover the investments required for the next generation. Marginal profit is defined here as the difference between revenue and total variable production cost. In practice, the firms will consider that their minimum prices are significantly higher than marginal production cost, parting thus from economic theory. Anyway, each generation will become obsolete and will cease to be marketed before the price reaches that lower limit, whether theoretical or practical.

Thus, competition drives prices along a path that would make them always tend towards the same value of about 100 dollars, whatever are the functional content, performances and technology of the chip. But before prices reach that limit price, technological progress enables the introduction of a new generation which restarts the cycle from a higher level. In reality, the prices of the latest generation chips are presently spread between 1500 and 400 dollars, a range which will probably be restricted to an interval of 600 to 300 dollars as a result of the action of the PowerOpen consortium. Previous generation chips, which remain usable in low-end systems or particular applications, cost between 100 and 300 dollars.

Chip designers and silicon foundries

In the preceding discussion, we have assumed implicitly that all suppliers perform all stages of production from R&D to manufacturing. In reality, some vendors only design and market microprocessors, and subcontract manufacturing to third parties, usually producers of memory chips. Those producers support the investments required for technology research and production, and their economical production scale is in the several tens of millions of chips, all types and models included. Non-manufacturing vendors restrict their investments to the design of the processor, and report the totality of manufacturing costs as variable cost. Some of those vendors reduce their research and development effort even further by offering more or less exact copies ("clones") of existing chips.

Assume that the investment required for the design of a microprocessor, in addition to the development of the basic technology, is 200 million dollars and that the variable unit cost, which is the selling price of the foundry, is around 200 dollars. The ratio of the two is then equal to 1 million and the economical production scale is of that same order of magnitude. Even relative to the microprocessor market alone, rather than to the totality of components, this figure is sufficiently lower than for the foundry to make room for more processor vendors than founders. Nevertheless, it must be noticed that no supplier other than Intel and Power Open has yet reached that threshold of 1 million processors sold.

The cost of designing a chip can remain relatively small in a certain number of specific cases. The most obvious one is when an existing chip is merely implemented in a new technology. We have seen that the interest of a such operation remains limited, since other constraints such as minimum size will prevent the new chip to take full advantage of the new technology, which only chips of a new design can exploit. Nevertheless, that approach enables extending the commercial life of existing architectures and to compete with the newer architectures by using cheap and efficient clones of older architectures.

That approach can also be used for ancillary chips whose functional content is frozen and which would have nothing to gain from a new design. Finally, a particularly interesting case is that of processors specialized in computations which are parallel by nature, for example image processing. Such chips are formed of identical cells operating in parallel, and therefore are in many ways similar to memory chips. Each technological leap forward does not demand a redesign of the basic processing cell, but enables putting more of them on the chip and thus easily translates technological progress into cost and performance improvements.

For a vendor offering real clones and subcontracting their production, the survival price is relatively high even if development costs are limited, because variable costs are high, due to subcontracting, and volumes are normally low. Since the chip being copied can be only that of the leader or possibly of the challenger, the survival price of the clone vendor may be higher than that of the original, or similar at best.

Even if survival prices are similar, the useful market life of the clone is necessarily shorter since its introduction on the market can only be later than that of the original, with a possible time lag of about one year. When the leader has introduced the successor of the cloned processor, it can cut the prices of the old chip down to marginal cost if necessary, and anyway down to the survival price of the clone vendor. In summary, neither the separation of designer and foundry roles, nor the clone phenomenon can modify in depth the dynamics described above. The existence of those phenomena is significant because it contributes to preserving in the sector some "contestability" in the sense of Baumol, but their importance in terms of volumes can only be marginal.

Conclusions

In a concentrated sector such as electronic components, stable configurations are strongly unequal. Any advantage in market share tends to amplify, so that a slight advantage in know-how, a little bit of luck or simply being first on the market, may end in a dominant situation, except if the leader commits big mistakes or if one of its challengers goes through the efforts necessary to dethrone him. In any case, balanced configurations are unstable by nature.

The challenger holds the key to stability. He may decide to implement an aggressive strategy if he has reasons to believe that his survival price is particularly low. If he starts a price war, the first effect will be to accelerate the elimination of marginal suppliers before hopefully taking market share away from the leader.

Concerning profitability, we have seen that the largest suppliers are also the most profitable. Since market shares are very unequal, that makes the average profitability of the sector very high, which does not imply that all firms operate at that level of profit. Quite on the contrary, the smallest firms only survive at the mercy of leaders, and are condemned to disappear in the long run if the leader and top challenger decide to engage into a price competition.

Let us repeat here that this inequality is neither fortuitous, nor the result of disloyal or illegal dominance maneuvers, but constitutes an intrinsic feature of concentrated structures. Competition in the component sector, as in all highly concentrated sectors, is similar to a contest where prizes are known in advance: the first prize is a market share above 70%, the second price is 10 to 15%, and the third prize is 5%. The only uncertainty is the order of arrival, which results from the action of competition between firms. The fact that one firm occupies 80% to the component market is an inescapable consequence of competitive dynamics. It turns out that Intel has won the first prize. History could have awarded that prize to IBM or Motorola or another vendor; but it could not have allowed five, ten or fifty suppliers to share the market equally.

The technological progress potential offers to each competitor, and even to new entrants, a permanent opportunity to take the advantage with a new generation of more powerful and less expensive chips. In other words, even if the action of competitive forces results in designating a winner who will hold 70% of the market, the title is put at stake again every two or three years. The stakes are indeed high (and we will see that they do not cease to increase at each round), and the leader in place is more likely to be able to collect or to borrow them. But as long as some technological potential remains unexploited and a credible challenger exists, the leader is compelled to be moderate in his prices and can retain his position only by constantly investing in the exploitation of new technologies. In a concentrated sector where a technological progress potential exists, the realization of this potential is guaranteed by the importance of risks for the leader and his challengers. Competition takes the form of successive bets where the challengers stake billions to dethrone the leader, and where the leader does the same to remain in place.

One should therefore not be surprised by the quasi-monopoly situation nor by the high profitability which Intel enjoys, which are perfectly consistent with economic theory. One must not believe either that such market shares, whether they are today Intel's or yesterday IBM's, are indications of megalomaniac maneuvers. Outside of industry-fiction, no firm is going after dominating the world. But competition being what it is, one of them will necessarily win the top prize and then do everything possible to keep it.

Perspectives

Technology perspectives

Technological progress translates mainly into an increase of circuit density, the dimension of chips remaining almost constant because it is determined by the constraints of the manufacturing process on one hand, of connection to the external world on the other hand. By the end of the century, memory chips with 256 million bits and microprocessors with 30 to 50 million transistors are expected. The beginning of the XXIst century will probably see memory chips with 1 billion bits and processors with more than 100 million transistors.

In order for that progress to be effective, that transistor potential must be used in an economically efficient manner, either to increase the processing speed through increased parallelism, or to place new functions on the chip.

In the case of memories, the progress translates simply into increasing chip capacities at each generation, resulting in decreasing cost of storage per unit of information. For processors, exploiting the technological progress demands a new chip design for each generation.

A single computing unit can comfortably be implemented with a few hundred thousand transistors. Supercomputers of the sixties contained a total of around 150000 transistors, distributed between many cabinets, and the Intel 386SX processor, which is still very widespread, contains some 275000 transistors. Until now, technical evolution has consisted in integrating on a single chip functions which were previously located on separate chips or even separate cards or cabinets. As a result, a 1990 chip contained within a 2 by 2 centimeters square all the functions which required a large hall in the sixties.

In the most recent microprocessors, the transistor potential is used in several manners. First of all, parallelism and therefore performance are increased by processing 64 bits in parallel instead of 32, or by simultaneously executing several instructions in different stages (the so-called "pipeline" architecture). Those two approaches increase the number of transistors per computing unit to the neighborhood of 1 million. Beyond that point, one can locate on the same chip two or three computing units and the logic required to manage them, like in the Pentium or the PowerPC (the so-called "superscalar" architecture), and thus make use of 3 million transistors. Finally, one can integrate into the chip functions thus far implemented by separate components, such as floating-point computation, or entirely new functions such as energy management.

It is clear that this movement can only continue, and that functions currently implemented on separate components are going to find their place inside the microprocessor, at the same time as new functions will be added into it. But while a simple increase in parallelism does not necessarily imply modifications in the communication conventions between the chip and the outside world (its instruction set), functional enrichment demands a parallel enrichment of the instruction repertory.

This inescapable evolution brings back to its correct proportions the current debate between the advocates of architectures called Risc ("reduced instruction set computing") and Cisc ("complex instruction set computing"). In the middle of the seventies, a school of research proposed a new concept in computer design where the repertory of instructions executable by the hardware would be reduced to its simplest expression, around a dozen instructions, all more complex operations being implemented by programming. The idea was to simplify the hardware in order to make it as fast and cheap as possible, and to compensate in that way the slowdown that would result from the execution of an additional layer of software.

In the eighties, those ideas have been incorporated in the design of micropro-cessors used to support the Unix operating system[50]. Since then, the debate between Unix and the other systems has been paralleled by a debate between the advocates of Risc machines and the manufacturers of other machines, nicknamed Cisc for the occasion. In the beginning of the nineties, Risc microprocessors have effectively been one generation ahead in the exploitation of technologies, which has been commonly interpreted as reflecting an intrinsic superiority of the Risc approach.

It is now becoming apparent that this advance was only a matter of circum-stances. The absence of constraints related to compatibility with existing processors or to the requirement to anticipate high-volume production have allowed to take full advantage of the architectural simplicity inherent in the Risc concept to design new chips and to bring them to market on a very short cycle. The submicron tech-nologies have therefore been implemented first in new processors of the Risc vari-ety, but it could be expected that those same technologies would quickly spread to the entire range.

The Pentium processor from Intel, introduced on the market in 1993, fills this gap by being situated at the same technological level and at the same power level, and by using the Risc design philosophy in the implementation of a processor with a rich instruction set compatible with its existing processors. On their part, IBM, Apple and Bull, associated with Motorola in the Power Open association, have decided to use the same PowerPC components in PC hardware and in Unix hardware. The sector of PC processors and the sector of Unix processors are now in the process of merging.

Until now, the sector of Risc components could be considered as a particular competitive sector from which processors of the Intel 80X86 type were absent, and where the dynamics of concentration operated only inside a relatively small market. Now the competitive concentration dynamics, characteristic of highly monopolistic sectors are at work in a single market segment going from PC's to Unix systems, before eventually spreading to large systems. The following round of competition will no longer be decided on the artificial opposition between Risc and Cisc, but on the ability of the promoters of the current Pentium, Power, Alpha, Sparc, PA-RISC and Mips processors to continue investing the billions of dollars required for devel-oping and producing their successors. Some will succeed, and will offer the proces-sors of the future at price levels which will remain those of micro components, say 200 to 400 dollars independently of their functional content and of their perfor-mance. The only suppliers that will survive are the very few who will be able to reach a market share consistent with an optimal production scale measured in tens of millions of units.

The Risc versus Cisc debate is therefore in the process of being quickly over-taken by events. Besides, it is difficult to visualize how a chip incorporating several tens of millions of transistors, richer in functions that an entire supercomputer of the eighties, could satisfy itself with a "reduced" instruction set. From the two ini-tial efforts, reducing the number of different instructions and simplifying the struc-

---

50   see chapter 12

ture of each instruction, only the second one will remain visible at the chip level. On the other hand, it is probable that each of the functional blocks which compose the processor will be designed according to the Risc philosophy, with a local reduced instruction set. In other words, the Risc concept will remain as a set of architectural principles concerning the internal structure of processors in general, and not as a distinctive feature of some. The few microprocessors that will survive will somehow be Risc on the inside and Cisc on the outside.

Industrial perspectives

Competitive dynamics guarantee that exploitation of the technological progress potential, which is still considerable, is going to continue for at least the next ten years, at a pace where circuit density will double every two or three years. That evolution comes with a growing complexity of microprocessors and increasingly drastic production constraints, entailing an escalation of R&D expenses and production investments, which roughly double for each new generation. On the other hand, the marginal production cost of each chip remains almost the same from generation to generation, and can even tend to decline if the improvement of density is partly used to reduce chip dimension and to improve the yield of the manufacturing process. The discrepancy between fixed cost and marginal cost of production aggravates with time, increasing the economical production scale and making the sector increasingly monopolistic.

Note in passing that the possible emergence of other technologies than those of silicon, such as gallium arsenide, supraconduction or optical technologies, would not substantially change those conclusions. The fundamental cause of fixed costs is the width of the line and the number of layers, which in all likelihood will remain the same whatever the technologies. Alternative technologies can eliminate or alleviate the heat dissipation problems or enable higher switching speeds, but they have only a minor chance of reducing manufacturing costs, and would probably demand higher development costs.

Faced with the inexorably increasing fixed cost of production lines, which is already close to a billion dollars and will certainly exceed 2 billions in 1998, several players are exploring the potential of new production technologies which would reduce the unit cost of production lines to less than 500 million dollars, with a capacity reduced in similar proportions. Such "minifabs" would have the additional advantage of allowing significantly shorter production cycles, and therefore both increased flexibility and lower production scale. Assuming that those new technologies are viable, one can nevertheless expect that their advantages will apply mostly to relatively short series, and that traditional plants will preserve their economic advantage for microprocessors produced in very large series. In any case, the appearance of "minifabs" would probably do little more than introducing a plateau of a few years in the process, and their cost would then resume a growth parallel to that of current integrated factories.

Let us return to the question of sector configuration. As we have seen, the configuration becomes stable when the market shares of players are in a constant ratio and when the market share of the smallest is close enough to the optimal production scale. This combination of conditions determines the number of firms in the sector. Assume for example that the ratio of market shares between two successive competitors is equal to 2 as proposed by Henderson. Market shares are then in the ratios 1, 2, 4, 8, 16, etc. Since the market share of the smallest firm is consistent with the economical production scale (EPS), one concludes that two firms will entirely cover the market if the market size is equal to 3 times the EPS, three firms will cover a market equal to 7 times the EPS, four firms for 15 times the EPS, etc.

However approximate this reasoning can be, the conclusions to which it leads are not so far from reality. A Dataquest study estimated the number of manufacturing lines required in 1991 at 48, which according to the preceding reasoning places the efficient number of firms between 5 and 6, a number close to the actual number of suppliers. The same study estimated at 18 the number of lines in 2001, which corresponds to 4 or 5 firms, and by extrapolating that trend one finds 7 lines and therefore 3 firms in 2011. One is tempted to predict that the years to come will see the number of "foundries" decrease by one for each cycle of a few years. We should then refine our model of price evolution by suggesting that the final prices for each generation will be established at a level allowing the survival of all players except the weakest.

Already, Hewlett-Packard has thrown in the sponge in 1994 by creating an alliance with Intel. That it is the first to quit, although it may not have been the less well placed in the race, can be explained by two reasons. Among all secondary players, Hewlett-Packard is probably the one whose culture is most remote from the demands of the component production activity. On the other hand it is also the one for whom this withdrawal creates the fewer strategic problems, contrary to other firms which are basing their hardware strategy on the use of proprietary components.

This trend to a reduction of the number of players can be countered only by an expansion of the market, which explains the efforts of component manufacturers to find new applications, whether in the automotive industry, in home electronics or in multimedia.

In addition to traditional suppliers in the USA and Japan, countries like Korea or Taiwan are investing massively in the construction of semiconductor plants, the economic reasoning of manufacturers being distorted by important public subsidies. The plants under construction in Taiwan alone in 1994 will almost have enough capacity to satisfy the current worldwide demand for memory chips. One can therefore expect that the industry will go through an excess capacity situation in the years 1996-1997, entailing on the one hand a price war and on the other hand an accelerated search for volume sales, including new applications. This situation will be favorable to "fabless" vendors and to the diffusion of components, memory and processors, into a growing number of applications other than data-processing in the usual sense.

At the opposite, the resulting sharp competition between manufacturers will accelerate the disappearance of the less effective, that is to say the smallest. Some of those that both design and manufacture microprocessors will cease to manufacture and subcontract that activity, as Hewlett-Packard has already done. Others will consolidate their manufacturing capacity through the formation of alliances or joint ventures. As long as an excess capacity situation will last, it will be favorable to the existence of a relatively large number of microprocessors suppliers, most of them "fabless". But the next generation (1997?) will undoubtedly see by reaction a severe selection among manufacturers and consequently a high mortality rate among the smaller processor vendors, which might even to lead to a situation of under-capacity in 1999/2001.

What will happen when the number of microprocessor suppliers is reduced to three or even two, and when microprocessors will include one or two hundred million transistors, which will probably happen around 2010? Will there remain any competitive motivation to invest the billions of dollars required for doubling density again? Will there remain candidate functions for using an additional hundred million transistors on the chip? At the time these lines are written, one is tempted to reply by the negative and to admit that the progress of components will stop in the first twenty years of the XXIst century. But nothing is less sure. Perhaps the incorporation of electronic components in a growing number of objects will expand the market to the point of more than compensating the increase in economical production scale. That is obviously what the players of this industry are hoping for, and one of the fundamental stakes in their current efforts in the multimedia area.

Chapter 8 - Hardware, a fragmented sector

Emergence of an autonomous sector. Components, boards and boxes. The limits of auto-
mation. A fragmented sector. Market fragmentation, niches and profitability. Available strategies.
The PC model spreads. Innovation and proliferation of hardware. A healthy sector.

Hardware, of all sizes and all functions, accounts for approximately 60% in the total revenue of the computer industry. All users of data-processing are necessarily customers of one or several hardware suppliers, while they could to a large extent do without software vendors and especially services companies. Moreover, through the phenomena of compatibility and standards, the other offerings arrange themselves around hardware, which somehow appears as the central sector that governs all the rest of the industry.

At the same time, the hardware sector is often considered as a sector in difficulty, or at least the most affected by the crisis that is shaking the computer industry. Some commentators have even written that hardware manufacturers are condemned to zero margins, and therefore to disappearance in the long run. However hasty and absurd that forecast may be (can we imagine data-processing without hardware to support program execution?), it is symptomatic of the questions raised by the evolution of the hardware sector, which we are going to try to answer in the present chapter.

History

Hardware has long been the center of the whole computer offering. The first actors were all hardware manufacturers, and until 1970 hardware has been the only billable offering. All the rest, software, maintenance services, training, support services,... was provided free of charge in support of hardware, and their cost was covered by the billing of that last item. Moreover, each manufacturer offered the complete array of hardware and performed its integration at the customer site. The whole computer industry therefore summed up to one sector producing integrated systems. Revenue was based exclusively on hardware, even though suppliers performed many complementary activities necessary for the production of such systems, including services and software development.

That integrated offer started to crack towards the end of the sixties with the appearance of the IBM compatibles. Some firms then undertook to offer separately units meant to replace the equivalent IBM units. The offer of those firms could be strictly limited to hardware, inasmuch as they could rely on IBM to provide the other elements, for instance software and services, without which their offering would not have been viable. Incidentally, it is often IBM's refusal (real or alleged) to provide services in support of competitive hardware that started the first lawsuits brought against IBM.

During the same period, in relation with the rise of compatibles, IBM decided to charge separately for software packages and the various services, and was imitated more or less rapidly by the other system suppliers. The revenue of manufacturers thus split between the categories of hardware, software and services, albeit without implying a real change in their activities nor an internal reorganization which would have rendered those activities more autonomous. The only firms truly specialized in hardware remained the manufacturers of compatibles, a sector which remained relatively marginal because it was limited to the IBM sphere and subject to vigorous competition from the dominant manufacturer.

The arrival of the PC in 1981 comes with a real revolution in the distribution of industrial roles. In the universe of PC compatible micro-computing, the adoption of operating systems developed by Microsoft (and a few others) entails the separation between the sector of software packages and the hardware sector. Similarly, the generalized utilization of Intel processors reduces the activity of PC manufacturers to assembly operations. On the other hand, the simplicity and the destination of products exempt manufacturers from providing services, while the nature of the target market invites them to leave the marketing of their products to specialized distribution firms. Those distributors can play the role of service providers and in particular of systems assemblers, which enables some manufacturers to specialize even more by type of unit.

Therefore, a new activity of hardware assembler appears with the PC. We have seen in Chapter 4 that this activity possesses a characteristic expense structure: the cost of products sold typically exceeds 75% of revenue, of which 65 to 70% is represented by purchase of components and sub-assemblies from other suppliers. Research and development expenses represent only 2 to 4% of revenue, while general expenses, including marketing expenses, revolve around 15%. For those enterprises, the net result after taxes only very rarely exceeds 5% of revenue. Those ratios are very different from those of traditional manufacturers, where R&D represents 10 to 20% of revenue and general expenses can be as high as 40 % to cover in particular a very strong marketing activity. Those figures do represent two different trades: on one hand the production of standard hardware from off the shelf components, on the other hand the design of original hardware calling for more integrated production and significant marketing efforts.

We have also seen in Chapter 4 that the hardware assembler model is largely represented in the area of PC and peripherals, by many firms of highly different sizes which together provide close to half of hardware revenue. On the other hand, this model has remained very marginal in the other areas, where the assembly activity remains linked to the other activities within each firm. It is therefore important to first examine that assembly activity in isolation, as it exists in those specialized firms. We will indeed find in that analysis reasons to believe that the pure assembler model is going to generalize gradually to all segments. The industry structure prevailing in microcomputers of the PC type thus foreshadows the entire hardware industry of tomorrow.

Technology and economics

Let us quickly examine the physical structure of a microcomputer to identify the main assembly steps that lead from electronic components to a complete system. Incidentally, the techniques used are the same as for the professional electronics or the general electronics such as high-fidelity equipment or television sets.

At the lowest level, components are placed on cards around 10 by 30 centimeters, which receive chips of different kinds and also support conductors connecting chips to each other and connectors connecting the card to the rest of the computer. Those components are most often somehow fastened to the card, which constitutes a well-defined functional unit. All microcomputers contain a "motherboard" supporting the basic functions: processor, main memory, intermediate memory (or cache), adapters for pluggable units, local bus to manage the exchange of information between components, possibly specialized processors. It can be complemented by specialized cards implementing functions such as communications, graphic input and output, sound input/output, etc.

The motherboard is installed in a box which also contains internal units such as disks, power supply and cooling device, as well as empty slots for extension cards and additional units. Finally, the complete system is generally built by interconnecting, through external cables, separate boxes such as a central processing unit, a keyboard, a screen, a printer, etc.

The manufacturing of cards resembles that of components, albeit on a totally different scale: conductors deposited or engraved on the card are about half a millimeter wide and the dimensions of components that are inserted there are measured in centimeters. That manufacturing operation is largely automated, but uses assembly techniques which are commonplace in the general electronics industry and not specific to the computer sector. The corresponding investments remain reasonable, leading to an economical production scale measured in tens of thousands.

On the other hand, the final assembly of cards into units is essentially a manual operation, that can be performed by installation or maintenance personnel, and even by the user himself, except for some particular miniaturized systems such as portable computers.

In 1974/1975, the very first microcomputers were sold as kits by amateur electronics magazines. Still today, one can find in specialized shops all the elements required for assembling one's own microcomputer: processor, memory chips, motherboard, disks, keyboard, screen, … sold separately or in kits. Even in computers that come completely assembled, users can easily add or replace a large number of elements such as memory, extension cards, disk drives and even the microprocessor, without any special training or special tools. The complete assembly of a microcomputer is within the capability of a reasonably skillful amateur, and requires only a few hours.

Depending on the cost of manpower, the cost of manual assembly of a microcomputer is typically between 20 and 40 dollars, while the cost of purchased elements is between one and four thousand dollars depending on the configuration. There are few ways and little motivation to reduce the assembly cost through automation techniques, which would not bring a very substantial competitive advantage. In any case, by selecting production modes demanding only modest investments and where virtually all costs are variable, a very small production scale becomes economically viable.

In summary, the assembly of hardware involves two successive operations obeying different economic logics. While component manufacturing is similar to a heavy industry, card manufacturing follows the logic of a small industry and final hardware assembly is a craft industry. It is natural enough for the structuring of the hardware sector to reflect those differences of scale. A few large enterprises cover the totality of the path, becoming fewer and fewer as the upstream component industry concentrates and becomes more autonomous. A second category is formed by large and medium enterprises, which cover all stages of assembly and thus preserve their ability to offer original products, either by incorporating special units or by the assembly techniques themselves. Finally, many small firms are specialized in card assembly or in final assembly. For this last type of manufacturers, variable costs are far higher than fixed costs, and the production scale can be minimal.

Hardware assembly is therefore characterized by a small economical production scale, associated with low barriers to entry and a standardization of products that facilitates the change of supplier by eliminating switching costs. Those features define a fragmented sector, where a large number of competing firms coexist, reaching only low market shares. In that sector like in other fragmented industries, the largest firm obtains rarely more than 15% of the market and the first ten most often total less than 50%. Moreover, the potential profitability and the average profitability are also low in such a sector, even for most efficient firms which hardly reach or exceed 5%.

In reality, while microprocessor manufacturers are fewer than a dozen (and we have seen that their number can only decrease), there are thousands of suppliers of microcomputers in the world. Some operate on a worldwide scale, others operate only in a single city. Some have put in place their own distribution network, others rely completely on specialized distributors. The existence of a specialized component industry and of independent software package vendors has enabled the existence of a large number of assemblers implementing highly diversified strategies.

It is also important to note that the weakness of obstacles to entry in hardware assembly makes all threats of integration believable. Upstream, component manufacturers may wish to offer complete systems, as Intel is doing in a limited manner for highly parallel systems and Motorola for communication systems. Service or software package companies may want to exploit in the form of hardware the skills acquired in their basic activities, by offering for example application-oriented terminals. Large industrial customers may also wish to assemble the systems that they are using, and even possibly put those products on the market. All those threats also contribute to limiting the profitability of the sector.

Segmentation and strategic options

Competitive strategies

Let us return on the analysis of competitive behavior presented by Porter, which we have introduced in Chapter 6.

Whatever is the sector where it operates, the firm must seek a distinctive advantage over its competitors, and to that effect endow its products with specific features that provide potential customers with reasons for choosing them rather than those of the other firms.

As a rule, the price of a product compared to competitive products is the most important competitive factor, and it always intervenes in the choice of customers whatever strategies are implemented by the suppliers. The enterprise can therefore choose price as its major competitive advantage. On the contrary, it can forgo offering the lowest prices, but endow its products with exceptional features that justify their purchase by at least part of the customer population. One then speaks of a differentiation strategy.

Secondly, the enterprise can seek a competitive advantage that is applicable to the whole market, or on the contrary that is specific to a limited segment. In the first case, it implements what Porter calls a leadership strategy, in the second case a concentration strategy.

In combination, those two independent choices define four generic strategies: global cost-based leadership, global product-based leadership, concentration on the basis of costs, concentration on the basis of products. Porter calls those strategies "overall cost leadership", "differentiation" and "focus", grouping under that last item the two strategies addressing a particular segment. In its implementation, each strategy requires particular resources, skills, organization and management systems. Each firm must therefore opt for one of the four generic strategies. Any attempt to pursue a mixed strategy, deliberately or because of failing to decide, necessarily puts the firm in a weak situation. In chapters 9 and 14, we will expand upon those issues of compatibility of different strategies and different products within a same firm.

Generic strategies

Nature of the advantage

Scope of advantage	product uniqueness	low cost
whole sector (industrywide)	differentiation	overall cost leadership
particular segment	product-based concentration (focus)	cost-based concentration (focus)

In fragmented sectors, where by definition a large number of firms operate, most will adopt a concentration strategy aimed at a particular market segment. If some choose a global leadership strategy, they will have difficulties in succeeding, because they will compete in each segment with specialized firms better adapted to particular needs. Global leadership by products is doomed to failure in a varied and vast market, while attempts at global leadership by costs will succeed at best in segments particularly sensitive to costs. The fragmented character of a sector can nevertheless be purely circumstantial and not caused by a deep structural feature, in which case a strategy of leadership can succeed. But in all cases where the sector is fragmented for structural reasons, such as a low economical production scale or a very diversified demand, one can consider that leadership strategies are not viable. All players will adopt concentration strategies (focus strategies in Porter's terms), which differ only by the choice of segmentation criteria and may thereby be aimed at market segments of very different sizes.

Available strategies

The market can be broken down into segments along several dimensions. A first set of criteria relates to the product itself: functional nature of the product (complete systems versus isolated units such as extension cards, printers or screens), standards used, catalog of functions, level of performance, price range, modularity or integration, portability, dimensions, aspect, etc. A second type of criteria relates to the target customer: individual or enterprise, activity sector, type of usage, purchasing habits, etc. Finally, the segmentation can integrate other considerations such as distribution channel or geographical location of customers.

In the selected segments, the supplier will be able to opt between the two basic competition strategies: based on prices or based on qualities of the product. The essentially manual character of assembly operations leaves few opportunities to reduce costs by investing in sophisticated production facilities. Firms opting for price-based competition will therefore most often decide to restrict themselves to the assembly of relatively standard products using components commonly available on the market, to avoid research and development expenses. On the other hand, firms that choose product-based competition will have to support higher research and development expenses to define specific differentiated products, and even to design and produce themselves certain partly original components or sub-assemblies.

For those reasons, obstacles to entry as well as economical production scale are as a rule higher for specialization strategies than for price-based competition. This raises in an acute fashion the problem of distribution channels: while firms offering inexpensive standard products can rely on generalist channels, specialized manufacturers must be sure that the channels that they use are indeed capable of reaching and convincing the particular market segment that they are aiming at.

Before the arrival of microcomputers, specialized computer distribution was only represented by some forerunners such as leasing companies or used equipment dealers. On the other hand, electronic hardware distributors like Tandy have been at the origin of the microcomputer wave at the end of the seventies.

Today, distribution channels used by micro-computing have considerably diversified. Some manufacturers practice direct sales by mail or in their own retail outlets. According to their market targets and their strategy, the other vendors use either distributors specialized in computer hardware, large generalist distribution channels such as chain stores, or computer services companies that integrate their products into complete systems. The diversity of the modes of distribution naturally complements the diversity of vendor strategies and the diversity of the market.

For suppliers that have chosen a specialization strategy, the potential sources of competitive advantage can be very different and vary from one firm to another: functions, performance, quality, delivery time, but also appearance, esthetics or dimensions. The objective of each supplier is to sufficiently isolate those market segments where he operates and to protect them by high enough obstacles to entry. Those segments can then become pseudo-sectors where concentration dynamics will operate internally, and where it will be possible to find better levels of profitability. The joint action of specialist players thus tends to fragment the market into segments of a size equal to a small multiple of the economical production scale, and to turn the fragmented sector into the juxtaposition of a large number of concentrated sub-sectors.

But obstacles to mobility between segments, which in that case play the role of obstacles to entry, are most often relatively low and not strongly defensible. Moreover, the large number of possible segmentation dimensions makes every prospective customer the target of several strategies, and forces him to choose between offers ranging from inexpensive standard systems to more costly tailored systems. In particular, competitive strategies based on general criteria, including price, are present and often effective in virtually all segments. The pressure on prices is present everywhere, and profits cannot be much higher than the sector average, even for firms that succeed the best in a specialization strategy. It follows also that a well-executed low price strategy will lead to high volumes even though volume does not constitute a compelling advantage *per se*.

The key of the success is not necessarily market share. The rule of the competitive game is no longer to offer the best of all possible solutions in order to conquer the whole computer market, but to define for an identified market segment an offer such that the firm can derive from one or several of its own features a competitive advantage valid for that segment. The only condition related to the market share is that the size of the target segment must be consistent with the investment required to realize the competitive advantage.

For a given supplier, the choice of one or several segments and of a strategy must rely on the specific advantages of the firm. Low manpower costs will naturally orient the firm towards a strategy of price-based competition. Similarly, command of a technology will orient towards concentration on products and segments where that technology can be exploited to create an advantage. Exceptional familiarity with a class of users will push the firm towards specializing in satisfying the needs of that market segment. Even so, the distinctive features on which the competitive advantage relies must not be exposed to straightforward imitation by competitors, and must therefore embody a particular know-how of the firm.

The range of viable strategies depends on the segment and on the supplier. There are no good and bad segments irrespective of the supplier, and there is no strategy which is good or bad independently of the segment and the supplier. In other words, the question "what is the correct strategy for hardware vendors? ", like the question "what is the right distribution channel? " cannot receive a general answer. Diversified and conflicting strategies coexist and will continue to coexist.

Sector characteristics

In total, the rules of the game that govern the activity of hardware assemblers are characteristic of a fragmented sector.

The production of hardware includes several different sectors depending on the nature of the hardware. We have focused the preceding discussion on the assembly of central processing units, which often include disk storage units. Similar considerations would apply to the different peripherals, which are themselves produced by assembling components of various natures, some of which belong to the electronics industry while others relate to precision machinery or micromechanics.

Some sectors such as PC's imply a pure assembly activity and therefore a low production scale. Those sectors are populated by many firms, the most important of which occupy less than 15% of the market. The profitability of those firms is in a narrow range, the average level being consistent with that of other assembly industries, typically between 4% and 6% for the most successful firms. Competition is lively and translates both into the frequent appearance of new products according to a cycle of about a year, and by a continuous price war. That form of competition constantly challenges the acquired positions, and market share never gives a definitive competitive advantage. The relative positions of firms change from year to year, their mortality rate is high as well as their birth rate. This sectoral dynamics thus exhibits features exactly opposite to those of the component sector.

Some suppliers implement a more important development activity, either because the sector where they operate demands it, as for electronic cards or certain types of peripherals, or because they choose a product-based differentiation strategy in fragmented sectors. In the first case, a more concentrated sector structure and more dispersed profitability appear. Extreme cases of high technology, like laser print heads or flat screens, may even create a situation of asymmetrical oligopoly similar to that of microprocessors. The second case can bring to the enterprise higher margins than the average of the sector, inasmuch as its differentiation investments provide a deciding advantage on a healthy isolated market, like for instance high-performance microcomputers.

In a general manner, the progress of standardization lowers the obstacles to entry and favors the multiplication of pure assemblers, at the same time reducing the number of sectors where research and development efforts are necessary. One can therefore expect the hardware industry to become increasingly fragmented, which implies in particular that positions are constantly unstable, and that profit levels higher than the normal 4 to 6 % are increasingly rare.

Miniaturization and its limits

We have seen that, at the most basic level, technological progress translates into an increase of the capacity of each chip, whether memory or processing functions. It follows that the implementation of a given level of function and performance requires fewer and fewer components. In the most recent computers, the microprocessor incorporates functions so far implemented by separate specialized chips located on the motherboard, for instance floating point computation, power management or cache memory. Similarly, at the same time as functions migrate from the card to the microprocessor, other functions such as sound and image processing migrate from extension cards to the motherboard, pending their eventual incorporation into the forthcoming 100-million transistor microprocessor. In summary, for a given level of function and power, the number of separate pieces decreases and assembly becomes increasingly simple.

That continuous integration movement is not new. Not so long ago, the full functional content and performance that fit today in a box 40 by 40 centimeters required several large cabinets installed in a large air conditioned room.

That overall evolution can be exploited in two ways: either to reduce the number of assembly levels or to reduce the complexity and the size of each level. By following the first path, the central unit of future microcomputers equivalent to current machines may soon be reduced to two chips on one card, plus a couple of disk drives and a few external connectors, at the expense of system modularity and extendability. Choosing the second path allows preserving modularity and ease of adding extensions and replacement functions. To that end, manufacturers can deliberately choose to locate optional functions on separate cards or removable components on the motherboard.

Although circuit miniaturization is the very essence of progress in components, it encounters external limitations at the other levels. We have seen that it is hardly useful or practical to manufacture chips smaller than 1 cm. By the same token, a removable card must be large enough to be easily manipulated. At system level, miniaturization is also limited by the constraints of man-machine communication, which require the size of keyboards to be compatible with human fingers, the dimensions of displays to be consistent with the constraints of human vision, and the size of printers to be that of the printed page. The physical dimensions of machines cannot therefore decrease below certain limits defined by considerations totally foreign to data-processing, and therefore unaffected by technological developments in that area. On the contrary, the dimensional standards of computing equipment generally conform to standards already recognized in other neighboring areas: the credit card format for removable cards (the PCMCIA format), and the A4 format for portable computers.

Furthermore, reducing dimensions does not always constitute a concrete advantage. An office computer must be equipped with a comfortable screen and keyboard, and the other units can be installed in a place where they are not obtrusive. For a same set of functions, different forms of implementation are possible, and therefore several different systems meeting the same functional need can be proposed. In a fragmented sector with a low economical production scale, one can anticipate that all such possible alternative offerings will coexist and that the customer will have a wide choice.

The evolution of industry structure

Since the sixties, the traditional computer industry combined in the same actors all the roles going from component manufacturer to systems assembler. In contrast, the PC world has been built from the very start on a clear separation of those roles, which are now played by separate sectors.

That distribution of roles allows each player to follow its own economic logic to its conclusion. It is the single common explanation for the vitality of the hardware sector, the number and diversity of vendors, the raging price war and the continuous improvement of the price/performance ratio, the variety of offers, the price/performance discrepancy between microcomputers and conventional systems, but also the modest profitability and the high mortality rate of enterprises in that sector.

Let us remind once more that differences between the world of micro-computing and traditional data-processing cannot be explained by technical reasons. In reality, the same technologies are exploited in both cases, and the causes of the differences must be sought in the respective industry structures.

Can we then predict that the world of midrange and large systems, which has so far essentially preserved its integrated structure, and that of workstations which has been built on the same model, are going to convert to that separation of roles which accounts for the dynamism of the micro-computing world?

At the same time as the assembly of microcomputers simplifies, current assembly techniques will allow assembling high-end systems at the same cost as the small systems of today. In particular, it is possible to place several microprocessors on the same card and several of those cards in the same box. Such multiprocessor systems offer a computing power which is a multiple of the power of elementary processors and will exceed the power of the largest current computers for the current price of a PC. For example, without modifying the box or the assembly techniques, it is possible to place two processors on each of the four cards that often compose a PC, and thus go from one 20 Mips[51] processor to 8 processors of 200 or 300 Mips each, for a relatively low increase in total cost.

The physical parameters which determine assembly costs, namely the dimensions of cards, chips and wires, remain stable in time, since the consequences of technological progress are essentially internal to the chip. Contrary to the case of components, the same assembly techniques can be used for different generations, and the economical production scale of cards or complete systems remains virtually constant. In an expanding market, there is room for a growing number of competitors, and therefore the fragmentation and the variety of the sector will tend to increase.

---

51   million instructions per second

Hardware equipment produced according to the PC model, and indeed the existing PC manufacturers, will therefore increasingly be in direct competition with traditional computers. In that confrontation, they benefit from considerable advantages in price and variety of the offer. Such competition takes place today in the area of low-end minicomputers, where high-end micros are constantly gaining ground. In the area of graphic workstations, the specificity of Risc processors still maintains a dividing line with microcomputers, but the imminent merger of microprocessors into a single sector is going to enable PC's to become directly competitive. By structuring itself in the same way as the PC world, that new segment combining microcomputers and workstations will gain even more strength to compete with traditional hardware, using in particular multiprocessors based on inexpensive off-the-shelf processors. There are already, at the high end, isolated segments such as massively parallel processors or large file servers built from standard chips, that constitute as many starting points from which the PC model will propagate to the whole range of functions and power levels.

In the long term no market segment will escape those dynamics. The extreme fragmentation of the PC sector will thus spread to the totality of data-processing. Simultaneously, the very lively competition will cause a decline of prices and margins which will extend the features of the PC world to all data-processing, in particular its characteristic price/performance ratio. Anticipating that foreseeable evolution, IBM has already announced that its entire range will eventually rely on the PowerPC chip.

In summary, vendors who elect to use components available on the market and limit themselves to the assembly of hardware can concentrate their efforts on reducing prices on the one hand, satisfying particular segment needs on the other hand. By doing that, they constantly increase the competitive advantage of products designed according to that model and spread their success to the entire market, thus obsoleting the suppliers who conform to the traditional model.

The concentration of the upstream sector of components and the standardization of microprocessors thus entails extreme fragmentation and diversity of the downstream sector of hardware. In this latter sector, each attribute of the product or of the distribution system becomes a possible differentiating and competitive factor, and thereby a potential area of innovation. Players are pushed to innovate constantly, by identifying market segments that present specific needs and by developing diversified products closely matching those needs. The whole sector of hardware becomes a competitive machine for identifying and satisfying specific needs at the lowest possible cost, leading to continual decrease of prices, improvement in functions and performance, and diversification of the offerings.

This dynamics extends beyond the data-processing sector in the usual sense. The continuous decline of component costs leads to the incorporation of data-processing functions into a growing number of industrial products. It has been the case since a long time for expensive objects like airplanes, military vehicles or machine tools, more recently for more common equipment like cameras, audio, telephones or automobiles. Following calculators or electronic games, one sees now appearing new objects of a computing nature, such as electronic diaries or pocket repertories.

This phenomenon will spread gradually to all sectors, and will tend to blur the borderlines between data-processing and other industries.

A sector in full health

That vision of an extremely lively and creative hardware sector is at the opposite of currently fashionable ideas that view the current industry crisis as the beginning of a gradual vanishing of hardware manufacturers behind software and service providers, and even of their eventual disappearance.

That gloomy forecast is twice superficial. In 1992, the hardware sector represented over 200 billions dollars, or 64% of the total industry revenue, and was growing at a rate of 5.7% compared to 91. Even if the software package sector (12% of the total with 37 billion dollars) and the services sector (close to 50 billions) are growing more rapidly, hardware remains by far the single most important sector. In any case, it is difficult to imagine data-processing without hardware to execute programs, and hardware without manufacturers to produce it. The sector of hardware is in no way threatened by disappearance.

The source of that misconception resides in a superficial analysis of the phenomenon of transition from the old industry structure to the new structure, which we will cover in detail in Chapter 15. Three aspects inherent to a fragmented sector structure are involved. First, market shares and profits are normally lower in such sectors than in the concentrated sector which traditional data-processing used to be, resulting in the appearance of a recession. Second, positions are more volatile by nature and the mortality rate of enterprises is high, but is compensated by a similarly high birthrate. Finally, the media offer extensive coverage of the difficulties of large traditional suppliers, who must at the same time adapt to declining market shares and profitability, and often abandon some of their activities where they have ceased to be competitive. But that does not prevent the prosperity of firms that are capable of behaving in accordance with the rules of the new sector structures, although they may not reach the high market shares that would render them visible.

In any case, the health of an industry or of an industrial sector must not be judged solely on the affluence of the players which constitute it, but mainly according to their collective capacity to satisfy the demand of the market. In addition, financial difficulties and even the disappearance of such or such an enterprise are not necessarily symptoms of bad health for the totality of that industry. Just as in the study of living organisms, the health of the species called "computer hardware manufacturers" must not be confused with that of each separate individual. Measured as it should be, by the rate of new product introduction and the evolution of prices and performance, the computer hardware industry is in full vivid health, even if its new logic no longer allows the comfortable margins which some generalists used to enjoy.

Chapter 9 - The differentiation of enterprises

The process of dis-integration. Different characteristics according to activity. The "Seven S" model of McKinsey. The contingency approach of Lawrence and Lorsch. Segmentation, differentiation and integration. Uncertainty and the limits of rationality. Cycles, horizon and culture. Segmentation options and overall company structure. Segmentation and personality. Personalities by sector. The consequences of inadequacy.

In the two preceding chapters, we have seen that productions with different cost structures give birth to different sector structures: concentrated sectors when the ratio of fixed costs to variable unit cost is high, fragmented sectors in the opposite case. The hardware sector appears as a heterogeneous sector, where the manufacturing of components on one hand, the assembly of hardware on the other hand, obey radically different production logics and competitive dynamics. The structure of production costs, and in particular the ratio of fixed costs to variable unit cost, plays a fundamental role by determining the degree of concentration, the potential profitability and the diversity of the sector, as well as the viability of the strategic options available to each player. We will see later how those same considerations apply to software and services activities taken separately.

First, we will complement the distinction between concentrated sectors and fragmented sectors, by inquiring to what extent differences between forms of production can entail differences in the internal features of enterprises. For example, the management methods and cultural attitudes required to succeed in a concentrated sector are probably different from those that allow to succeed in a fragmented sector. If such is the case, a single firm will meet with considerable difficulty in trying to operate successfully in both environments, and therefore incompatibilities will exist between activities of a different nature.

The survey of the whole computer industry, that we have undertaken in the first five chapters, leads us to assume that the combinations of products and services offered by the different firms do not arrange themselves at random. Some combinations are very frequent, others are very rare, and the industry in its totality is organized around a small number of enterprise models. Traditional generalist suppliers, diversified and integrated, coexist today with the new world of the PC, essentially formed of specialized firms. The generalist model is the oldest, but also the less numerous and that which includes the largest proportion of firms in trouble. One also observes that the few really mixed firms, which supply services of different natures in similar proportions, are always less efficient than firms specialized in each individual component of their mixed offer. In a general manner, the entire computer industry is evolving towards a more elaborate specialization of enterprises, not towards increased diversification of their offer and vertical integration of production stages, contrary to the traditional views of economists.

Those issues of diversification and integration are generally approached in a purely quantitative manner, based on a comparison of respective advantages and costs. Moreover, most studies implicitly assume that no *ex ante* considerations prevent varied productions from coexisting efficiently within the same organization. We believe on the contrary that to succeed in productions of different nature, enterprises must possess qualities different enough to render certain types of production incompatible within the same organization. Enterprises that nevertheless attempt those product combinations will necessarily fail to be competitive in either one, and even in all related markets.

For each elementary type of production, we will try to identify what enterprise features are associated with competitive success in the corresponding sectors. That will enable us to approach the issues related to the coexistence of different productions in one single enterprise. We will thus clarify those aspects of industry structure that concern the diversification or the specialization of enterprises, and the integration or "dis-integration" of production. Are traditional integrated suppliers going to continue their movement of dis-integration? Will the computer industry preserve the current specializations? Will it evolve towards new combinations featuring for instance a strong services component, as commentators often predict, or on the contrary will it specialize even further?

The personality of enterprises

Porter already noted that different strategies require different and incompatible qualities. A strategy based on the control of costs demands a constant supervision at very detailed levels, strict quantitative objectives and a culture that encourages thriftiness. On the contrary, a strategy based on the qualities of the product demands encouraging creativity and individual autonomy through a rather qualitative motivation system, and by a general lifestyle attractive for high-level professionals. Those strategies are associated with incompatible enterprise personalities, to such an extent that a firm which would neglect to opt clearly between the two would be doomed to failure, a situation which Porter calls "being stuck in the middle".

If such differences exist within one sector of activity between firms that choose different strategies, one can *a fortiori* expect the qualities that make enterprises successful to be radically different depending on whether they operate in a concentrated sector or in a fragmented sector.

For example, in the production of components, a long time span separates the design decisions and the investments in new production lines for a new chip on one hand, market introduction and production of revenue from sales of that chip on the other hand. Current decisions commit heavy investments in the short run, and entail long-term consequences that will have become irreversible when it becomes possible to observe them. It is therefore vital to uncover all potential issues as early as possible and to find solutions in advance. To that effect, it is mandatory to develop explicit long term plans, to submit them to criticism, to encourage dissent as long as irreversible decisions are not taken yet, and to implement an issue management system efficient enough to produce positive results.

Strategic Factors		
	product based	**cost based**
Investments	research	production
Key skills	research marketing	production distribution
Culture	creativity risk taking vision	thriftiness discipline attention to details
Organization	flexible	hierarchical
Management	delegation	centralized
Motivations	long term	short term
Objectives	qualitative	quantitative

Such a management system is necessarily resource expensive, because the enterprise spends significant time addressing in advance problems that may never occur in reality. Those reflections require delays that can only be afforded in long cycle activities where time is available, but can also introduce delays in the outcome of projects. That mode of operation implies a company culture where the voicing of disagreements is encouraged as long as the debate remains open, but where everyone must rally behind the decisions of the firm when they are taken. A typical example is the traditional management system of IBM until in the eighties.

On the contrary, in the activity of hardware assembly, the cycle of development and production is short, and any decision that does not pass the test of the market can be corrected rapidly. Current decisions therefore do not commit the firm for a long period in the future. Moreover, being the first on a new market, offering a new product earlier than competitors and operating at a lower cost are as many potentially deciding competitive advantages. A possible strategy is therefore to spend as little time and efforts on preliminary studies as possible, and to leave it to the market to place a judgment on products. Inasmuch as specific investments have been low and a replacement product can be introduced quickly on the market in case of failure of the previous one, that strategy can be a winning one on a very volatile market.

The corresponding management system must give a free hand to innovation, while severely limiting preliminary investments, but also measure the reaction of the market and the profitability of each product in real time. The company culture must value short term profit, boldness in innovation but also complete submission to the whims of the market and the ability to react immediately to external signals, including dropping without any hesitation products that do not find the hoped-for success. It seems obvious that an organization well adapted to such activities will automatically be poorly adapted to the long-cycle activities described earlier, and vice versa.

The Seven S's of McKinsey

To analyze the internal features of enterprises, which govern their behavior and somehow constitute their personality, we will use the "Seven S's" model proposed by McKinsey[52]. In this representation, the elements of enterprise personality are:

- its **Strategy,** the set of plans and rules of action prepared in order to reach the objectives of the firm,
- its **Structure,** which defines the assignment of responsibilities within the firm,
- its management systems and procedures (**Systems**), meaning the formal information and decision-making mechanisms,
- its **Style,** the habits and modes of behavior that prevail inside and outside of the enterprise,
- its personnel (**Staff**),
- its **Skills** and know-how,
- its **Shared Values,** common models of behavior and references.

A central theme of Peters and Waterman's book is that the least formal and the least directly controllable variables (the "*soft*" variables: shared values, style and skills), are also those that have the biggest influence on people behavior and therefore on the success of the firm. An essential role of management consists therefore in modeling indirectly the company culture and management style through its own behavior and through actions of a symbolic nature, more than participating directly in decisions. This view is opposite to the rational school represented by Taylor.

Our purpose is not to summarize that book, which attracted significant readership and elicited many comments. For some executives, it only describes their daily experience. For others, on the contrary, its theses belong to daydreaming and are harmful for the enterprise. We believe that the diversity of reactions can be partly explained by the fact that the relative weight of each of the Seven S's in the success of the enterprise varies depending on the type of activity. That is precisely what we are attempting to prove, and a subject that Peters and Waterman have not addressed in their book. In other words, certain forms of activity call for a strong implication of each employee and can largely do without formalized systems, while others demand very strict control systems that relegate individual motivations to a secondary position. We will return to this idea later.

Organization, culture and personality

The "Staff" and "Skills" variables describe the inventory of people and of their capabilities, in other words the raw materials of which the firm is made. The other variables describe the cement which unites people around common objectives, enables them to work together towards common objectives and makes them an enterprise rather than an amorphous crowd. Clearly, the activity of the enter-

---

52 Peters TJ, Waterman RH : In Search of Excellence (Harper & Row, 1982)

prise defines the nature of skills that must be present, and thus skills characterize an activity in a certain way. But our purpose is to see how different organizations or cultures can be associated with different forms of production, and if possible to understand why two firms with identical skills bases can nevertheless be two enterprises with different personalities. For example, a software package company and a programming assistance company are both formed by programmers, but differ by their organization and their culture. In that sense, the skills of the enterprise are distinct from the skills of individuals that compose it.

Furthermore, all enterprises incorporate people with different skills, such as engineers, salespeople and accountants. One could therefore believe that it should always be possible for the people and skills required for any combination of activities to coexist efficiently. If there are incompatibilities or conflicts, their origin must be sought in the specific style and values of each population concerned.

Like structure and systems, strategy is typically the domain of executive management. Nevertheless, we will not consider it an intrinsic feature of the enterprise, but rather as a management tool allowing to assemble a large set of decisions into a consistent whole underpinned by a long term perspective. To play a useful role, the strategy must necessarily be translated into operational decisions or actions pertaining to the other variables, for example a recruitment policy that will concern the "Staff" and "Skills" factors. It can also materialize as a choice of structure and management system.

In most enterprises, structure and systems are subject to formal descriptions developed under control of executive management and published in the form of organization charts and procedure manuals. Adherence to those descriptions is verified permanently, sometimes by specialized audit departments, and all changes are subjected to thorough studies and specific implementation programs. Structure and systems therefore constitute highly formal components of the personality of the firm, placed under the direct explicit control of management.

We will call "organization" of an enterprise the combination of its structure and its information and management systems, which determine how decisions are made and executed. Systems and structure are strongly interdependent. The structure is the anatomy of the enterprise: it tells how the enterprise is built and how tasks and responsibilities are allocated. Systems are the physiology: they tell how the enterprise works and what are its decision and information processes. By itself, the structure defines by default a hierarchical decision system that can be sufficient in a small simple enterprise. In a more complex organization, systems are needed to define in addition the horizontal relationships between peers, the transverse relationships between distant units and the global business processes.

Unlike organization, shared values and behavior styles are essentially the unconscious and involuntary results of the history of the firm. At no time can the culture be subject to a global decision. At the very most the selection of people recruited can favor certain attitudes and behavior, and the rewards and punishment system can play a conditioning role within the enterprise. But it is the accumulated history of the firm that creates the legends, the heroes and the villains, in other words the mythology which expresses the value system and on which individuals model their behavior.

We will call "culture" of the enterprise the combination of its style and value system, consisting of the set of references, shared values and standards of behavior that consciously or unconsciously govern the actions of each individual. Executive management has only an indirect and limited influence on company culture, and is indeed also motivated by cultural factors which are part of its culture. Organization and culture together constitute the "personality" of the firm.

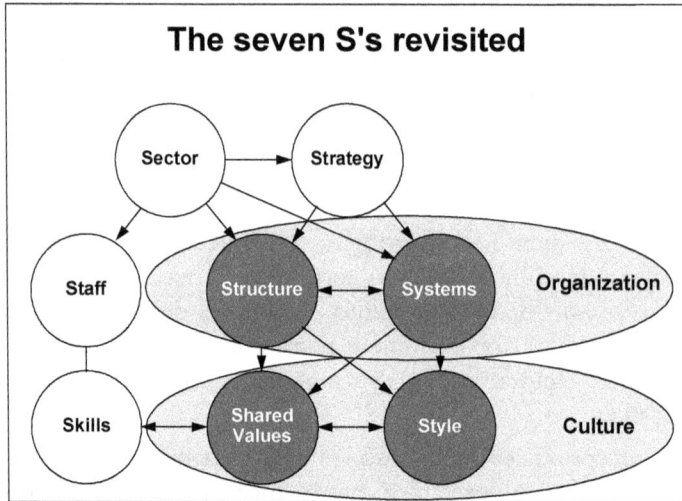

The "contingency" approach to organization

Let us first consider the organization, that has been the subject of numerous works and of multiple often contradictory theories. In their vast majority, those works attempt to define general laws or empirical rules applicable to all enterprises in all situations, whatever in particular the nature of their production. That approach is equivalent to postulating that organization rules are independent of the nature of the activity of the firm.

Beginning in the sixties, several authors have challenged that postulate, but it has been necessary to wait until 1967 for finding the seminal concept of the "contingency" school expressed and developed in the now classical book by Lawrence and Lorsch[53]. For those authors, no organization or management system is best under all circumstances. On the contrary, the required type of organization varies depending on the nature of goods or services provided, the resources used and the economic environment at a given time. The question which their works attempt to answer is "what kind of organization does it take to deal with different environmental conditions? ".

In the rest of this book, we will rely on those works for two basic reasons. First, in any event, the contingency theory appears as the only approach consistent with the actual experience of business leaders who had the opportunity to know

---

53 Lawrence PR, Lorsch JW : Organization and environment (Richard Irwin, 1967)

sufficiently different environments. Second, the discussion and the elements of explanation proposed by Lawrence and Lorsch form a good base for our attempt to characterize those organizational forms that are best adapted to the different sectors of activity.

Segmentation and differentiation

The objective of organization is to distribute the tasks of the enterprise efficiently between employees and units. In the first analysis, one can represent the activity of organization as the distribution of activities, resources and responsibilities of each unit to subunits at the next lower level. That division expands in a recursive manner from the total enterprise level downwards, until the elementary units become indivisible, being reduced to a single individual or an indivisible piece of equipment.

That division, which most authors call segmentation, leads to the creation of a hierarchy of units, each one with assigned resources and responsibilities, and where the responsibilities of each unit are the union of the responsibilities of its subunits.

By introducing differences between units in their activities, responsibilities and objectives, segmentation also introduces differences in attitudes and behavior. Apart from objectives (which determine "goal orientation"), those differences concern mainly:

- the "time orientation", or how people project their actions in time, in particular the relative weight of the short term and the long term,
- the "interpersonal orientation", or the relative importance given to the execution of tasks on one hand, relationships with colleagues on the other hand.

Those differences induce in turn differences in the internal organization of each unit, as resulting from the next lower level of segmentation.

From their experimental studies, Lawrence and Lorsch conclude that differences of objectives, time orientation and people orientation, as well as differences of internal organization observed between units (including "formality of structure"), can be explained by three criteria: the clarity of information available for decisions, the probability of causal relationships linking decisions to their consequences, and the reaction time of the environment to actions of the unit. Those three factors characterize the degree of uncertainty of the environment in which the unit operates. In a relatively certain environment, short term objectives dominate, employees are more motivated by the correct execution of their tasks than by personal relationships, and the organization tends to be very formal ("mechanistic"). On the contrary, in an uncertain environment, objectives are in the long term, the quality of personal relationships becomes an important motivation, and the organization is more informal ("organic").

Differentiation and uncertainty		
	low uncertainty	high uncertainty
Power	centralized	distributed
Structure	formal	flexible
Number of levels	high	low
Procédures	formal	indicative
Objectives	short term	long term
Relations	task- centered	people-centered
Organization	mechanistic	organic

Integration

In order for the organization to function correctly, the activities of its different units must be integrated through coordination devices. Generally, the need for integration increases with the level of differentiation of the units involved. Integration devices are not necessarily formal. They can use exclusively the hierarchical channel or rely on direct contacts between units. Their implementation can involve only representatives of the units involved, or it can be assigned to specialized integration units. Methods of conflict resolution can be diverse: confrontation, avoidance, tradeoffs, decisions imposed by the hierarchy, etc. For example, units that share a culture valuing dialogue and dedication to the general objectives of the enterprise probably have a natural tendency to solve their conflicts by direct contact without a need for formal procedures, even if their objectives and local personalities are highly differentiated,.

Integration mechanisms are most efficient when each conflict resolution decision is made at the point of the organization where the three ingredients of an effective decision meet: the power to implement the decision, the required information and the skills necessary for decision-making. The optimal decision level varies therefore depending on the situations, on the origin and volatility of the information, on the complexity and degree of specialization of the activities involved, etc. For Lawrence and Lorsch, "in more certain environments, conflicts might be resolved and integration achieved at the upper levels through the management hierarchy; in less certain environments, conflict resolution and the achievement of integration might have to take place at the lower levels of the hierarchy". That difference explains the differences between the organizations and cultures best adapted to each environment.

In summary, an organization is well adapted to its mission and to its environment if on the one hand its level of differentiation is sufficient to enable it to execute its strategy efficiently considering the uncertainties of the environment, and if on the other hand its level of integration is consistent with its level of differentiation. The enterprise will then be able not only to operate efficiently in its environment, but also to find the correct solutions when the environment changes and adaptation is required.

Lawrence and Lorsch's conclusions reconcile the traditional Taylorian theses and those of the "human relations" school by observing that the autocratic hierarchical organization recommended by the classical school is well adapted to stable and certain environments, while the flexible and participative organization advocated by the human relations school is well adapted to changing and uncertain environments.

Uncertainty, organization and culture

Let us now bring together the concepts of segmentation, differentiation and integration with the model of the Seven S's that we have presented earlier.

The steps leading to the organization of an enterprise can be summarized as follows. At each successive level, moving down from the top of the enterprise, management takes segmentation decisions which create units of the next lower level, each assigned specific tasks and objectives, and inheriting a local environment. The specificity of objectives and local environment entails a cultural differentiation between units, which management must take into account in the implementation of formal integration devices that constitute the management system. Inasmuch as the units thus constituted must segment in their turn, their own culture and local environment will intervene in their organization decisions, possibly conflicting with the culture of higher levels.

Segmentation results from conscious and controlled management decisions. It defines the structure in the sense of the seven S's. On the other hand, differentiation happens spontaneously in each unit as a result of its formal definition through segmentation on one hand, of its environment on the other hand. Differentiation is therefore of a cultural nature.

The segmentation mechanism, by allocating missions to each specific unit, assigns it to care for a specific part of the external environment. In addition, for each unit, the other units form an environment internal to the enterprise. The local environment characteristic of a unit is thus composed of three generic pieces: all or part of the external environment of the enterprise, the other units and the organization levels above. The internal environment generally includes a conventional more or less formalized part made of standards, procedures, etc., defined by the higher level or other units. For example, the product catalog is a subject for decision at the enterprise level, while it is part of the environment for its sales department.

Coordination mechanisms can be more or less formal. Their formalized part constitutes the systems in the sense of the seven S's, while their informal part belongs to the culture. In other words, management systems can be defined as the formal part of coordination mechanisms, while culture includes in particular the informal part of the coordination mechanisms, together with the people orientation and the time orientation, which depends in particular on the cycle of the activity.

Although they did note that the required organization type varies depending on the nature of goods or services provided, Lawrence and Lorsch have especially

taken into account the influence of the external environment and of the function within the enterprise (research, sales, production...). They have spent little effort on relating the features of the organization to the goods and services produced. We now intend to show that the organization and the culture of an enterprise are influenced by the features of its production activity, in particular:
 - the time relationship between expenses and revenues, or the duration of the basic cycles of production,
 - the production scale, which as we have seen depends on the ratio of fixed costs to variable costs.

Differentiation factors relate as much to the nature of the activity of the unit or of the firm than to the environment. Two firms operating in the same environment, but with different cycles of production can have different time orientations. Indeed, "the primary time orientation ... is related to the time span of definitive feedback[54]", that is the time required before being able to know the real result of decisions made earlier. As we will see later, that period, which constitutes somehow the time range of decisions or the horizon of the organization, is a good expression of uncertainty, and strongly contributes to modeling the organization and culture of enterprises.

The limits of the rational model

Most theories, whether concerning organization, management or economics, rely explicitly or implicitly on an image of "Rational Man". When making a decision, Rational Man is supposed to be aware of the complete set of possible actions among which he will choose. Secondly, he knows with certainty, at the time of decision, the consequences of every possible action, or at least he can allocate probability values. When he must take uncertainty into account, Rational Man does it by adjusting future values in such a way as to make them equivalent to certain present values. Third, Rational Man is able to rank all possible sets of foreseeable consequences from most desirable to least desirable. Rational Man is then supposed to make every decision by comparing the consequences of every possible action. Given those assumptions, decision theories can concentrate on the best techniques to be used for comparing alternate decisions, ranging from mathematical programming to elaborate game theory.

Experience of real life in enterprises does not fit that rational model. On the one hand, a very large number of decisions are made without detailed analysis, in a reflex manner. In each organization, preset action schemas are associated with classes of recurring or expected situations and problems, and those schemas are executed when perceived symptoms seem sufficiently similar to the memorized symptoms. When those schemas are explicit, they are most often part of the management system of the firm. They can also be implicit and even unconscious and then be part of the culture.

On the other hand, in real life, neither the costs nor the benefits of a decision can be known with certainty at the time when the decision must be made. Their values, and the probabilities attached to the consequences of possible actions only

---

54 Lawrence et Lorsch, op cit

represent highly subjective estimates. Finally, it is generally accepted that "most human decision-making is related to the discovery and to the selection of satisfactory choices and not of optimal choices[55]". Those views are the basis for the so-called "bounded rationality" model of management decisions introduced by March and Simon.

Those facts explain the relatively modest place of pure economic rationality in the reality of industrial life, and considerably limit the practical interest of elaborate mathematical models, as well as their relevance in the explanation of micro-economic phenomena. They give on the other hand an essential place to cultural factors that form the personality of the enterprise in its day-to-day operations. Indeed, reflex decisions are determined by empirical rules, instructions and value scales that belong essentially to the culture of the decision maker. When they result from conscious management action, those rules and values can express a rationality consistent with the interest of the enterprise. But they can as well be independent from such interests, and in any event they remain of a general and essentially qualitative nature.

For the most important decisions, which are subject to specific study and analysis, cultural factors again come into play to eliminate at the outset those lines of action that would not be consistent with the personality of the enterprise as perceived by the decision maker. Finally, even for actions whose consequences can be expressed in the form of financial streams, the decision cannot rely on the exact knowledge of certain figures, but only on expenses and revenue estimates, both subject to uncertainty. All decisions involve some risk that can only be appreciated subjectively.

Indeed, the prudent decision maker will ask experts to prepare as elaborate and well-supported estimates as possible. Those experts can even be wise enough to present their estimates as ranges of variation or alternate scenarios, assigned suitable probability coefficients (which anyway are largely dictated by their own subjectivity). It nevertheless remains that, at the moment of decision, the decision-maker relies on his own feeling of what is in his view the most likely. His decision owes at least as much to his prejudice, his experience, his wishes or his affectivity that to economic reasoning. Confronted with identical choices, managers will not take the same decisions in an organization where culture values risk taking and in an organization that leads to prudence, or in an organization that glorifies individual responsibility and another one which advocates shared responsibility.

If the consequences of a decision could be known with certainty, the decision would become automatic as soon as the relevant information is available. Provided that the objectives of the enterprise are clear for everybody, the decision would be the same whatever is the point where it is made. In addition to its hierarchical aspect, the organization would be reduced to a matter of information flow, and possible cultural differences would be of no importance.

In reality, on the contrary, the organization must both specify who should be involved in every decision and therefore use his personal culture, and ensure that

---

55 March JG, Simon HA : Organizations (John Wiley and Sons, 1958)

everybody's culture is consistent with the rationality of the firm in the area where he is involved. The quality of the organization and the validity of the culture there-fore precondition the pertinence and the efficiency of decisions and actions of the enterprise. In particular, in case of changes in strategy or environment, the person-ality acquired by an enterprise continues to dictate an important part of its conduct, even if a rational analysis would lead to a significantly different behavior.

Revenues, expenses and uncertainty

Since we must admit that virtually all decisions of the enterprise rely on uncertain information and imply a real risk of error, we must regard as essential the possibilities of correcting a decision when it appears that its actual consequences are not in line with the estimates or expectations that motivated it. That raises two questions: first, how is the information enabling to measure the real consequences of a decision made available? And secondly, when a decision turns out to be incor-rect, what can be done at that time to correct it? Those two questions go back to the time relationship between the formation of expenses and the formation of rev-enues, which we have mentioned in Chapter 5 when looking at how enterprises react to business conditions.

Apart from the fact that, for any decision or product, the real costs (the expense stream) and benefits (the revenue stream), are both unknown at the time of decision, it so happens that for most decisions, a major part of the expenses must be committed before the corresponding revenues are acquired. In other words, expenses chronologically precede revenues. In that sense, virtually all impor-tant decisions of the enterprise imply investments, even if the accounting vocabu-lary restricts the word "investment" to expenses for which the benefits are expected in subsequent accounting periods.

Concerning a product, and relative to the usual production cycle going from research and development to production and marketing, expense streams occur in all stages, revenue streams occur only during the marketing phase. Moreover, expenses result from a unilateral decision of the enterprise, even if their exact amount can depend on external factors. Revenues, on the other hand, depend not only on factors which the firm can the control, such as quality and price of the product , but also on external factors such as the general business conditions, the actions of competitors, the decisions of customers, etc. Costs are immediate and virtually certain while benefits are at least partly future and uncertain. In other words, decisions generally have an immediate direct effect on expenses, while their effect on revenues is indirect, risky and deferred. Management can control expenses, it can only hope for revenues.

In short cycles, the consequences of decisions appear rapidly, and there are ways to act quickly on expenses if necessary without producing consequences in the long term. For long cycles in the contrary, consequences appear long after the decision, when significant expenses have already been incurred, on which it is too late to act. Whatever new decisions are made to correct the effect of previous deci-sions, they will never be able to cancel those past expenses. On the contrary, they will most often initially entail new additional expenses, the potential justification of which will in turn not be known before the end of a period that can last months or years.

The horizon of a decision can be defined as the time required to observe its consequences, or more precisely to be able to compare its actual consequences to the estimates that have motivated it. A decision can indeed rely on estimates covering many years in the future, and although some of its consequences may appear rapidly, it will only be possible to judge whether the estimates that motivated it are valid after some years.

Cycles, organization and culture

A type of production or an activity can be characterized by the duration of the longest of the cycles that govern it. For example, of all functional activities, selling is a short cycle activity and R&D a long cycle activity. The cycle of the production activity is very variable according to types of production. It can be as short as the sales cycle for advice or assistance services or for the assembly of hardware. It can be very long for component manufacturing, software development, or telecommunications services.

The longer the cycle of an activity, or the more remote its horizon, and the more unstable its environment, the more uncertain are the related decisions. In real life, every decision relies largely on the observed consequences of similar past decisions. If the cycle is short and the environment is stable, the consequences of recent decisions are well-known and constitute a good basis for estimating the effect of new decisions. On the contrary, if the cycle is long or if the environment is changing, the consequences of past decisions are either unknown yet, or too old to serve as a reference in the new environment. Current decisions must therefore be taken in a situation of high uncertainty. The duration of the cycle of an activity is therefore a factor determining uncertainty in the sense of Lawrence and Lorsch, and therefore a key differentiation factor between units.

In a unit with short cycles, results are close to decisions, and therefore responsibilities are clear. Possible errors can be corrected without delay. Inasmuch as managers are attentive to the reactions of the market and act rapidly in case of problems, the market itself can serve as an operational control device. In such units, the key to good management is to constantly adjust expenses to actual revenues.

On the contrary, in a unit with long cycles, results are remote from the corresponding decisions and responsibilities are diffuse. Errors can be corrected only with great difficulty, and in any event slowly. It is therefore vital to make as few mistakes as possible, and to that effect to conduct internal studies elaborate enough to correctly analyze the needs, opportunities, risks and the different foreseeable lines of conduct. The sanction of the market comes too late in the cycle for the market to serve as a base for operational control. The key to success is to make fewer strategic mistakes than competitors. This concern may translate into expensive controls, checks and various assurances, and also entail slower reactions to the hazards of the environment.

Horizon and culture	
short cycles	**long cycles**
results close to decisions clear responsibilities	results remote from decisions diffuse responsibilities
realism reactivity control ajustment	vision planning confidence perseverance
mechanistic organization	organic organization
sales	R&D
equipment assembly consulting, assistance	components, packages telecommunications services

Personalities and structure

Let us now examine the influence of the enterprise activity on segmentation decisions that define its overall structure by distributing the activities, resources and responsibilities of each unit to subunits of the next lower level.

The overall organization of the enterprise results from applying the segmentation process in a recursive fashion, starting from the top level down to the individuals. At each level, segmentation can be "homogeneous" if the activities assigned to each subunit are virtually the same as those of the enclosing unit, but are limited in their scope or area of application (a generalization of spatial segmentation or divisional organization). Segmentation will be "heterogeneous" if the objectives and tasks of each subunit are only a part of those of the global unit, but cover the same area of action (a generalization of functional segmentation). In the global structure, segmentation of the homogeneous type and segmentation of the heterogeneous type can alternate at the different levels of the hierarchy. For example, a sales organization, which results from a heterogeneous functional segmentation, can be organized by regions, which follows the homogeneous geographical segmentation mode. Each region can in turn be organized on the functional mode into units for sales, promotion, administration, logistics, customer support, etc. Those successive segmentations should however be consistent with the economical scale of the different activities.

At each level of the structure, the nature of segmentation, functional or spatial, induces significant differences in the relation between successive hierarchical levels and between units of a similar level, and therefore in the subsequent segmentation context. For the totality of the enterprise, the predominance of one or the other form of segmentation, especially at the highest levels, induces differences in management systems and in the culture of the firm.

Segmentation is necessary for distributing the work efficiently, but it can also have the objective of breaking down a unit with long cycles in such a way that some or all of its subunits will operate according to shorter cycles. Indeed, the manager of an organization generally wishes to structure it so that the responsibilities of his subordinates are clear, and to make controls and adjustment mechanisms easy and effective. One way to achieve that is to isolate the long cycle activities in the staff of the global unit, or in one or more specialized units if required, so that all other units operate according to shorter cycles. Segmentation options thus depend on the activity through its economical scale, which determines the economic viability of possible fragmentations, and also through its base cycle, that can orient the definition of subunits.

The homogeneous organization

In a "homogeneous" segmentation, the activities, objectives and environments of the different units are of a similar nature, and their cycles are similar in length. That will very probably result in closely related cultures, similar in turn to the culture of the top level of the enterprise. Homogeneous segmentation thus favors spreading throughout the enterprise the values and behavior models of its leaders, without requiring any particular additional action. Conversely, the homogeneous culture thus created has a high probability of being moderately tolerant towards the other cultures, which could nevertheless be favorable to some activities.

Operating in different fields of action, units have only few opportunities and motivations to cooperate. They are juxtaposed rather than interdependent. On the contrary, since the results of each unit are expressed in the same manner and can be easily compared, while being independent of each other, relations of competition and rivalry can easily develop. The common management of all such units may elect to favor such competition and to exploit it to increase overall performance.

The results of a unit are simply the sum of the results of its subunits, and its success depends only upon the success of the subunits. No specific activities must take place at the enclosing level, and therefore there is no need for a sizable staff. The only coordination requirements consist in avoiding that actions of subunits might be detrimental to the whole, for instance in the form of competing products, competing proposals or disparagement. The enclosing unit is also likely to impose minimum cooperation between the subunits when needed.

Since the differentiation between subunits is low, the need for integration is limited. On the other hand, since the culture does not naturally call for dialog between units, coordination mechanisms will need to be formal. In summary, the management system of a homogeneous organization will be a simple but relatively formal system. For those reasons, management of a unit organized in the homogeneous mode can oversee a large number of subunits, which works in favor of "flat" structures.

The heterogeneous organization

By definition, units resulting from a heterogeneous segmentation have different activities and objectives, which add up to the global objectives of the next higher unit enclosing them. The subunits are only involved with a limited part of the environment of the enterprise, and they operate in their own local environment, where a significant number of elements are determined by the other units of the enterprise. They can function according to very different cycles, some according to cycles notably shorter than the rest of the enterprise. Those units will therefore probably develop very different local cultures, where the values and behavior models may be significantly different from those of executive management of the enterprise. Maintaining a single cultural identity for the firm and a level of shared motivations sufficient to resolve conflicts will demand specific actions on the part of leaders, without which the enterprise may not function correctly. On the other hand, if that global culture is sufficiently healthy, the organization will be tolerant towards local cultural differences between subunits. A unit resulting from heterogeneous segmentation can more easily segment itself in a homogeneous manner than the opposite.

Units execute different pieces of one activity. They are therefore interdependent and must develop mutual cooperation relationships and be able to resolve occasional conflicts between units. Depending on whether management has succeeded or not to develop in the enterprise a cooperative dialog culture and a clear conscience of the general interest —which again does not happen by itself without specific actions— conflict resolution will be achieved rather spontaneously through confrontation and direct contact, or on the contrary will demand formal procedures and a constant involvement of management.

The success of the global unit depends not only on the success of its subunits, but also of the quality of integration and therefore on specific actions at the global level. Integration can require substantial staff teams and even special integration departments. Each level of the structure can efficiently control only a limited number of subunits, which tends to favor a pyramidal structure. The number of subunits per level must remain low if management of the global unit is frequently involved in integration actions and conflict resolution, which will result in more levels of management. A high number of hierarchical levels being a factor of inefficiency, a culture enabling conflict resolution to take place at the lower levels clearly works in favor of firm efficiency.

The global structure of the enterprise

At the global level of the enterprise, one can imagine distributing activities and responsibilities to major units using three dimensions of segmentation:
- products if the range of productions of the enterprise is wide and diversified,
- functions (Research, Development, Production, Sales, Personnel, Finance, Administration,...)
- market or geographical activity zone.

Since our purpose is to relate enterprise personalities to forms of production, we will only look for the moment at enterprises offering a single type of product or at least a sufficiently homogeneous range, leaving aside the case of diversified enterprises. Having thus discussed the organizational implications of different forms of production, we will then be able to evaluate to what extent they can coexist within a unified organization. If on the contrary there are sufficiently severe organizational or cultural incompatibilities between different productions, that leaves no other choice than segmentation by products, which is in fact equivalent to creating a conglomerate of operationally independent enterprises.

With that in mind, the major choice for a single-product company is between a functional segmentation and a segmentation by market, or spatial. In the functional segmentation, each subunit is assigned a part of the activities of the enterprise and implements that part for the entire field of action (markets and locations) where the enterprise is present. The cycles of the subunits can be different from the global cycle, and can also vary from one subunit to another. In the spatial segmentation, each subunit exercises the totality of the main functions of the enterprise, within a limited part of the field of action of the firm, for example in defined geographical limits. All subunits have the same cycle, which is also that of the whole enterprise.

The activity of the enterprise, through its economical production scale, is a key factor in this choice. If indeed, as a result of segmentation, one of the subunits would be forced to operate on a scale lower than its economical production scale, that unit and therefore the enterprise would lose a competitive advantage. If therefore the field of action of a unit is just large enough to enable it to reach the economical production scale, further segmentation of that unit must preserve the integrity of the production facility, and can therefore only be functional. That remains true when considering functions other than production, as soon as the field of action of a unit is just sufficient for any one of its major functions to reach its economical scale of operations.

For that reason, the most natural segmentation for an enterprise with a homogeneous production is functional. At least product definition can only be done at the level of the complete enterprise. Spatial segmentation is a viable alternative at the highest level only if two conditions are satisfied: first the definition of productions requires only very limited resources that can be managed as a staff activity, and secondly production can be economically performed on a scale lower than that of the entire enterprise. That last condition is equivalent to saying that the enterprise operates in a fragmented sector where it occupies a significant market share. Such a combination of conditions rarely occurs in industrial production activities, but is frequent in many service activities.

Similarly, an enterprise with a long production cycle will be more prone to adopt a functional segmentation which will shorten the cycle of some of its constitutive units, while an enterprise with short cycles will be more inclined towards a spatial segmentation.

Divisions and subsidiaries

Having examined the personality of enterprises offering homogeneous products, we can now return to diversified firms and to their organization in product divisions. This type of organization relies on homogeneous segmentation, since each division is responsible for the whole range of activities concerning its products. The differentiation between divisions relies mainly on the scale and cycles of production associated with their respective products, and possibly on their markets inasmuch as the products of different divisions may address different markets.

From the above considerations, it follows that in order not to be penalized relative to its more specialized competitors, all the products of a division must imply cycles of similar duration. Otherwise, the organization and culture of the division will necessarily be poorly adapted to a part of its activities, where it will not be competitive. By exception, a division mainly responsible for long cycle products can also offer short cycle products. Its reduced competitiveness for those products will need to be compensated by significant integration advantages or by internal subsidies which may deteriorate the competitiveness of the major product. For those reasons, the short cycle products can only be ancillary to the main, long cycle products.

To what extent should that specialization of divisions materialize by a separation into separate legal entities? In other words, can divisions with different personalities coexist within one enterprise in the legal sense of the word? The answer is theoretically yes, provided that the executives of the enterprise are aware of the cultural differences, and are able not only to tolerate differences in organization and management systems, but also to adjust their own behavior to those differences. The personal qualities demanded to satisfy those conditions are truly exceptional. An executive raised in an environment of long cycles will loath appearing as finicky and petty as required for efficiently managing a short cycle activity. Conversely, an executive accustomed to short cycles will want to intervene more than advisable in long cycle activities, and will thus mess up operations and rapidly alienate the key persons.

Most executives want their companies to adapt to them, not the reverse. It is even more unrealistic to expect the same person, supposed to carry ultimate responsibility, to adapt his behavior to such different activities and cultures. A "democratic" leader adapted to long cycles can at best force himself to control the detail of an activity if required, but refraining from intervening would genuinely be superhuman behavior for an autocratic leader. Although it is not an absolute guarantee, introducing the protection of a separate legal personality, and especially the distance of a board of directors between mutually incompatible executives and activities seems anyway a wise precaution.

Personalities by sector

We can now summarize the choices of organization and personality features that characterize the main types of services and activities, as identified in Chapter 6, and relate them to the associated type of sector. For components and hardware, which we have already analyzed, we will thus be able to describe enterprise models that exist in the sector of hardware and to evaluate their past and future viability. We will see in passing to what extent an inadequate personality may translate into a competitive disadvantage, depending on the situation of the environment.

For the other activities, especially software and services, we will return to the issue of enterprise personalities in the chapters that cover them specifically[56].

Note first that there is a close correspondence between the production scale and the duration of the cycle. A long cycle generally implies that an important part of the expenses resulting from a decision, for example installing a production facility, is committed in an irreversible manner long before the corresponding revenues materialize, and in particular before production volumes are defined. Long cycle activities also tend to require high investments and fixed costs, and therefore a relatively high production scale. Besides, it is difficult to identify in the real world, or even to imagine, activities that would present both a long production cycle and a low economical scale, while the opposite case of short cycle combined with high scale seems possible. In any case, neither one nor the other appears in the computer industry.

Concentrated sectors

Concentrated sectors, of which the component industry is an extreme example, are made of a small number of relatively large enterprises of very different sizes. Production cycles are long and the economical scale is high, leading to dominance of the heterogeneous functional segmentation. The enterprise is a complex assembly of differentiated units, linked by an elaborate management system, and controlled by reference to an overall plan developed with a long range planning system consistent with the duration of the basic cycles. Objectives, culture and motivations are different in different functions, and coherence of the enterprise must be ensured by a strong company culture transcending functional cultures.

The culture of a long cycle enterprise must promote planning, long term vision, confidence and perseverance. The typical hero is the infallible visionary or guru. When the company executives themselves do not belong to that category, which is the case in many large enterprises, there can be a gap and even a conflict between their own culture and the dominant culture in the enterprise. More generally, in order to function efficiently, a long cycle organization must be capable of integrating units with different cultures, and will generally be reasonably tolerant of subunits adapted to short cycles.

The qualities of an enterprise well adapted to long cycles are consistent with those that Porter deems necessary for succeeding with a strategy based on the qualities of the product: encouragement to creativity and individual autonomy, flexible organization, delegation, long term motivation, rather qualitative measurement system. If competition becomes tougher, such an enterprise will therefore spontaneously react by seeking to improve the qualities of its products. On the other hand, implementing a cost-based competition strategy encounters deep cultural obstacles. If the enterprise decides to engage into such a strategy, for instance to fight the dominant form of competition, that will demand vigorous management action to change organization and culture. To succeed within acceptable delays, such action will benefit from being isolated in a specialized part of the organization.

---

56 see chapters 11 and 13

That enterprise personality is typical of large scale industrial production activities. We will find that it also matches the development of software packages, and even some services activities like telecommunications or application processing, which obey the logic of concentrated sectors.

Fragmented sectors

In fragmented sectors, like the assembly of hardware from standard components, a large number of enterprises occupy relatively small market shares, but nevertheless sufficiently different for enterprises to be of different sizes.

Among those enterprises, the size of the smaller ones is close to the economical production scale, however low that may be. Their segmentation is therefore of the heterogeneous functional type, but their small size limits the effects of differentiation and its consequences for management system. The chief executive or a small group of leaders can make all important decisions and thus handle most long cycles, and create the company culture through their personal example and direct action.

The size of large enterprises in such a fragmented sector is by definition higher than the economical production scale. The most natural trend will be to favor a homogeneous segmentation by markets, into units which include both marketing and production, and small enough to allow coordinating the functions and controlling the operations as close to the market as possible. The formal management system will use unit accounting statements similar to those of the firm itself. If management nevertheless seeks economies of scale, production and sales may be kept separate, but an adequate management system will have to enable quick mutual adjustments.

In order for the enterprise to function correctly, its culture must emphasize strict controls and the capability of quickly adjusting to reality. The behavior model, or the hero in this culture, is the pragmatic hard-nosed business manager. Long term vision and perseverance in following through an idea are rather poorly appreciated because they are useless and may even delay adjustments to the real situation. That culture is pervasive throughout the organization and greatly facilitates the relationships between managers at all hierarchical levels. Conversely, that culture is all the more intolerant towards different cultures that it is homogeneous throughout the enterprise. An organization adapted to short cycles will therefore very be unlikely to tolerate in itself a suborganization adapted to activities with long cycles.

The qualities of the enterprise adapted to short cycles are consistent with those that Porter considers as adapted to a cost-based strategy: a psychology emphasizing discipline and thriftiness, constant supervision at very detailed levels, centralization of authority, quantitative short term objectives. If faced with an escalation of competition, such an enterprise will naturally tend to react by a cost-based competition strategy, whatever is the nature of the competitive attack. If the enterprise decides to engage into a competition based on product qualities, it must not only modify in depth its organization and culture, but its existing personality can discourage the high level professionals that would then be needed.

That enterprise personality is found in many professional services activities such as consulting, assistance and development. The homogeneous and constraining character of the company culture, especially in small firms, makes it difficult to tolerate units obeying a different logic, for instance adapted to the development of products on a longer cycle. That is one of the reasons why, while product firms are often successful in offering services, it is extremely rare for services firms to succeed in industrial production activities, including software packages.

Adaptation issues

The nature of the activity and the strategy defined for the enterprise lead executive management to select an organization (structure and systems) that forms the controllable part of the firm's personality, and contributes to mold its culture. One enterprise can clearly have only one organization, or else it is actually separated in two or more different organizations forming a conglomerate rather than an enterprise. A first way to look at the issue of compatibility between productions is therefore the following: inasmuch as the optimal organizational choices are different for different activities or different strategies, to what extent can the enterprise live with a hybrid organization, or is it compelled to opt between two incompatible solutions? In other words, to what extent are activities or strategies mutually exclusive because they require different organizations?

A similar issue appears if the enterprise wants to change activity or undertake a new activity. The organization that exists at this moment is assumed to be suitable for current productions, but may be inadequate for the new productions contemplated. If a change of organization (structure or management systems) is required for the new productions, the organization can in theory be adjusted almost immediately, but the new organization will only function if it is compatible with the existing culture.

Now culture is the most stable element of enterprise personality, because it is diffuse and implicit and cannot be decreed. The culture of an enterprise exists by definition only in the mind of each employee, and can be extremely different from one group to another. Acting on the company culture involves acting on representations and value systems implicitly present in the mentality of each employee. Management has only few means to act directly on it, and must content itself with influencing culture through the example of its own behavior and through the selection of behaviors that it wishes to encourage. In any case, culture is a given for most decisions.

Whatever actions management undertakes, the culture of the enterprise changes only very slowly. If a change of activity or strategy encounters cultural incompatibilities, either directly or through the organizational changes that it implies, those incompatibilities will subsist for a long time. Meanwhile, it is likely that the enterprise will not be competitive in its new activities, and even run the risk of seeing its competitiveness decline in its existing activities. The adaptation time will be all the more long that the enterprise is large and that its previous personality has made it more successful. If competition is fierce enough to eliminate poorly adapted enterprises, strategies or orientations inconsistent with the existing culture are thus doomed to failure, and cultural incompatibilities must in practice to be considered as deterring.

However, one has to accept that in practice, many executives are not sensitive to those issues. Most believe that organizational forms, management methods and styles which lead to success are the same in all activities, or rather that the behavior and recipes that have enabled them to succeed so far will continue to work no matter what they undertake. One can therefore expect that all combinations of products and services will be attempted, including the most illogical and unviable. There again, competition on each relevant market, especially with specialized enterprises, will determine success or failure of mixed enterprises. Those that offer incompatible combinations, whatever are the reasons for this incompatibility, will be eliminated and the market will thus select the viable combinations.

What happens when an organization adapted to a certain type of cycle undertakes activities involving a very different cycle?

An organization adapted to long cycles necessarily has higher operating costs and higher inertia. If applied to short cycle activities, it will tend to bring out products later than firms adapted to short cycles, with products less well adapted to current demand. At the same time, it will have to cover higher operating expenses. Such an organization will therefore be penalized to the point of being condemned to failure if short cycle products constitute the largest share of its revenues and if the situation is strongly competitive. If on the other hand short cycle productions are both secondary and strongly related to the main long cycle productions, it can nevertheless operate in relatively satisfactory fashion, possibly by subsidizing the ancillary productions. Moreover, it is always possible to implement within the "long cycle" organization a "short cycle" organization for those secondary services.

At the opposite, an organization adapted to short cycles will be impatient to put products on the market without necessarily taking all the time necessary for preliminary studies, while limiting the corresponding investments to a minimum. Anyway, it will probably include few employees capable of long term analysis and planning. That situation may result in poorly designed products and insufficient quality, and a production facility more suitable for short series and therefore more expensive for large scale production. If products do require long cycles, the enterprise will not be able to correct those competitive disadvantages when it notices them, and will attempt all kinds of short term fixes which are likely to do more harm than good.. In summary, undertaking long cycle activities in an organization adapted to short cycles is almost certainly doomed to failure, all the more so that such an organization could not tolerate long enough the existence of subunits having the organization and culture required by long cycles.

In summary, the working of competition and the resulting phenomenon of natural selection have the effect of closely associating certain forms of production with certain enterprise personalities. An enterprise adapted to long cycles will only be able to succeed in new productions if their cycle is of similar duration, or for secondary productions from which it does not expect high profits. An enterprise adapted to short cycles has practically no chance of succeeding in long cycle activities. We will see that it is probably the reason why no services company has ever succeeded in software packages.

The consequences of inadequacy

In our attempt to analyze the structuring of industry, we have sought to uncover the relationship between forms of production and enterprise personalities. But in the development of that personality, the nature of production is not the only factor. In order to be efficient, the organization and culture must also be adapted to the environment of the firm, in particular to the market situation and to local conditions, as well as to the position of the firm in its cycle of evolution (emergence, growth, maturity, decline), and to the intensity and form of competition.

In a mildly competitive situation, the degree of firm adaptation may be of little significance. If competition is not intense enough to eliminate less well adapted firms or force them to change, firms with radically different personalities may be able to continue to coexist in the same sector. In a situation of very low competition, a sector can even be dominated by poorly adapted organizations, if all competing firms are built on that same model. This is for instance the case for ancillary services, as long as all competing firms treat them as ancillary and no specialized enterprise approaches this market with an adapted personality.

Inadequacies between production and personality can thus be without immediate effects, and only manifest themselves at the detriment of the enterprise upon the occurrence of external events such as an escalation of competition or the appearance of better adapted specialized competitors. On the contrary, the revealing event can be internal, like the launching of a new production or the desire to make an existing activity more profitable, or the implementation of new production techniques which modify the scale or the horizon. Finally, an inadequate personality can be imposed in an untimely manner by a new executive coming from another type of sector, or by the controlling company following an acquisition, or simply for lack of sufficiently taking cultural factors into account on the occasion of structural changes.

The traditional generalists

Those considerations help us in interpreting the past evolution of the computer industry. Until the end of the sixties, the industry was entirely dominated by generalists, each offering a diversified range of services dominated by hardware. Software, maintenance and other services were considered as ancillary services, mandatory for the sales of hardware and strongly linked to it.

Competition concerned a virtually identical offering for all suppliers, which constituted in fact a single integrated product. Data-processing was therefore a single sector, which took on the features of its dominant production, hardware: high investments, high production scale and long cycles made it a concentrated sector. Relatively few competitors could coexist and market shares were very unequal, in accordance with the dynamics of that type of sector (see chapter 7). The personalities of all competing enterprises were adapted to the long cycle of their main production, which besides was their only revenue base until the end of the sixties.

The introduction of separate billing in 1969 did not radically modify that situation. Independent competition on ancillary services appeared only very slowly, and those services remained largely subsidized by hardware revenue. The poor adaptation of traditional generalists to short cycles did not translate into a real disadvantage, for lack of competitors specialized in the services activity.

On the contrary, when firms specialized in compatible hardware emerged around 1970, those firms did represent a significant threat, all the more so that they selected different modes of production corresponding to radically different personalities, adapted to short cycles and/or low economic scale. A winning strategy for those new entrants was to specialize in the pure assembly of a single type of equipment and to refrain from undertaking long cycle productions such as components or the development of original hardware or software. By adapting their resources, but also their organization and their culture to that type of activity, they were able to derive a substantial advantage from their lower costs, their quick reactions and capacity of adjustment.

When generalists wanted to respond, their personality turned out to be a serious handicap which largely explains their difficulties and their more modest place in micro-computing. They first had to accept the idea that the organization principles and management techniques that had made their fortune in the past were leading them to failure in the new environment. Then they had to sort their activities according to economic scale and respective cycles, and to bring about mutations in their organization and corresponding culture. To that effect, they had to segment their organization according to those scales and cycles, and accept that the so far integrated management system and homogeneous company culture break down into differentiated subsystems and subcultures. During that process, some of the units thus constituted might appear uncompetitive on their markets, which forced firms to drop the corresponding activities, beginning with the most concentrated, for instance electronic components.

In summary, the appearance of specialists compelled the generalists to a genuine cultural and organizational revolution that came on top of a reduction of their market shares and margins, due to the rise of specialists. That revolution demands a significant amount of time, which increases with the size of the enterprise and the strength, homogeneity and pervasiveness of the traditional company culture. That tends to explain why IBM and Digital Equipment have remained in difficulty longer that Unisys or ICL. Finally, that challenge to the large generalists leads them to discontinue some of their activities, thus adding to the specialization phenomenon which is at the root of their difficulties.

The case of Hewlett-Packard reinforces that thesis *a contrario*: that firm actually operates according to a model where divisions specialized by product are individually vying for the achievement of their individual objectives rather than for coherence of the total product range offered by the enterprise. The firm thus functions as the juxtaposition of specialized enterprises and its personality is therefore closer to that which suits short cycles and small to moderate production scales. Once a relative disadvantage, that personality feature has become an advantage which partly explains why Hewlett-Packard has known neither the performance downfalls nor the agonizing redirections of other large vendors.

Part Three - Software and services

The time has come, the Walrus said, to speak of many things:
of shoes and ships and sealing wax,... of cabbages and kings.
Lewis Carroll

Many commentators like to group into the same category all productive activities that do not end in a tangible material good, and to attribute to those activities properties that would both be common to all its constituents and separate them radically from hardware products. Thus is born the concept of a "software and services" sector.

Our approach will be more cautious. Believing, like Descartes, that one needs to "divide each difficulty... into as many fragments... as would be required to better resolve them", we tend to think that all-encompassing statements are a variety of obscurantism. The preceding chapters have shown that the activities of computer hardware production break down into sectors with contrasting characteristics: a concentrated components sector and a fragmented hardware assembly sector. Those sectors are differentiated by the number and the size of firms present, by the range of viable strategies and corresponding models of competitive behavior, as well as by the mechanisms of price and market share formation. We have also seen that different sectors and different strategies are associated with different types of enterprise, of organizational forms and of cultures.

One often speaks of a "software and services" sector. Is that group of activities sufficiently homogeneous to constitute a sector in the sense of Porter, defined as a set of firms offering closely substitutable products, or even a "trade" as we have defined in chapter 6, that is to say a set of sectors obeying the same production logic? If not, is it possible to easily divide it into homogeneous sectors or trades? In other words, since the structure of production costs appears as a powerful explanatory factor for our study, are there elements of that structure which are characteristic of software and services as opposed to hardware, or of services as opposed to products?

To answer those questions, we will apply to software and services the tools of industrial structure analysis that we have introduced in the second part, that is to say the concepts of competitive sector and the concepts of concentration and fragmentation, as well as of differentiation of enterprises. We will thus find, within the so-called "immaterial" pseudo-sector, internal differences much stronger than similarities between the various activities that compose it. We will therefore conclude that the opposition with hardware is more artificial than real.

To develop a clear understanding, it will first be necessary to examine critically the traditional distinctions between "products" (or "goods") and "services". That analysis will lead us to the conclusion that this distinction has little to do with the economic features of the production process that govern the structuring of industry and its competitive dynamics. Software, which is ubiquitous in all data-processing, includes a range of extremely diverse activities ranging from packaged software products to custom development services. In particular, for economic purposes, the production of software packages can in every respect be assimilated to that of industrial products.

We will therefore treat separately the software package industry (Chapter 11), which itself is formed of a complex of more or less strongly concentrated sub-sectors, individually subject to their own competitive dynamics, and in strong interaction with each other. Among those sub-sectors, that of operating systems (Chapter 12) is particularly critical, and can be compared to electronic components both because of its central place in the totality of data-processing and by its strongly monopolistic dynamics.

Finally, the genuine services, far from being a homogeneous sector, even after separating out software packages, constitute in reality a complex of sectors where diverse economic logics operate. We will discuss the different types of services in Chapter 13, with special emphasis on the issues of coexistence of different services within one firm.

Chapter 10 - Disentangling software and services

In search of a definition of services. Immateriality, inseparability, intangibility, variability, perishability, etc... A typology of products and services. A largely irrelevant differentiation. What is software? Programming and writing. How much does a program cost? Varieties of software and the diversity of actors. Software packages are products.

In the previous chapters, we have used the case of hardware to verify that the analysis of competitive dynamics correctly accounts for phenomena of industry structuring, provided that it is conducted sector by sector, a sector being defined as the set of firms offering substitutable products. We have also acknowledged (see chapter 6) that this concept of "substitutability" is essentially relative, and therefore that the definition of sectors cannot be rigorous. Nevertheless, it is clear that taking sector structure into account has a strong explaining power. In reality, the specialization of enterprises according to their production logic plays a key role in the general operations of the industry and in the evolution of products.

We have also seen that the behavior of enterprises, and in particular the actions that translate into the introduction of products on the market, are determined by a set of internal factors which belong to the "personality" of each enterprise. The market, by selecting products best adapted to demand, also selects enterprise personalities best capable of satisfying that demand. In situations of strong competition, the sanction of the market closely associates enterprise personalities with each sector and strategy, forcing mixed firms to either specialize or explode, as can be observed in the history of data-processing in the last ten years. We will now apply the same tools to an examination of the other sectors of the computer industry.

The analysis of industry statistics, which we have started in chapter 4, can provide us some leads. A majority of players, all specialties together, report software activities, most frequently as a secondary activity representing less than 30% of revenue. But there are also many firms specialized in software, for which that activity represents more than 70% of their revenue. The picture is the same for services, with only slightly different figures. Software and service activities are therefore exercised both as secondary activities by many non specialized suppliers and as the main activity of suppliers specialized in one or in the other.

Some firms specialized in software also offer services in an ancillary fashion and *vice versa*, but service specialists and packaged software specialists are two practically disjoint populations. In the sample of 100 enterprises that we have analyzed in chapters 4 and 5, only four offer software and services in an almost balanced manner (Nynex, Dun & Bradstreet, Ask, Sterling Software), and none of those five enterprises is really a major player in either sector. Moreover, no one of the leading software package vendors (Microsoft, Computer Associates, Novell, Lotus, Oracle, …) has ever been a services company.

We have also observed (see Chapter 4) that firms specialized in software packages exhibit a characteristic expense structure, with very low production costs, high R&D costs and oversized marketing and general expenses. On the other hand, firms specialized in service conform to different types regarding the structure of expenses. Most are exactly at the opposite of software specialists, with a very high share of production costs and very low R&D and marketing costs, while those with a cost structure closer to software packages typically perform application processing activities. All those facts tend to indicate that many different forms of services exist, and therefore that services are neither a single sector nor even a homogeneous trade. In addition, industrial software development, usually designated by the term "software packages", seems radically different from a services activity.

Services and products

A critical review of usual definitions

First of all, let us try to specify what distinguishes a service from a product. Neither the dictionary, nor the economic literature proposes a fully satisfactory definition of services. Indeed, for each proposed definition, it is easy to find examples of activities which official statistics as well as commonsense classify among services, and that nevertheless do not satisfy the definition being considered.

Most dictionaries define services as "activities intended to satisfy a need, but that do not result in material goods". That definition parallels that proposed by Kotler in his reference book on marketing[57]: "any activity or benefit that one party can offer to another that is essentially intangible and does not result in the ownership of anything". Kotler expands upon that definition by suggesting that services can be distinguished from products by four characteristics:
  – intangibility: services cannot be seen before they are bought;
  – inseparability: a service cannot be separated from its source, it does not exist when its source is not present;
  – variability: a service is not the same depending on who provides it and when and where it is provided;
  – perishability: services cannot be stored.

It is obviously very easy to illustrate each of the above criteria by appropriate examples, and even to present cases which satisfy all four criteria. But it is just as easy to find, for each criterion, examples of services that do not satisfy it, and indeed services that fully meet all four criteria seem to be rare. It looks as if the wide variety of offerings actually form a continuum with "pure products" at one extreme and "pure services" at the other, with no clear dividing line anywhere in between. We will now review the proposed criteria and verify that no single one allows to establish a dichotomy which would be consistent with both usual language

---

57   Kotler P : Principles of Marketing [Prentice Hall, 1980]

and the official nomenclature. That review will also help us to identify the relevant dimensions of the product-services continuum.

Note in passing that, like the definitions found in dictionaries, Kotler's definition is essentially negative, in that it defines services by the absence of some features of products. Attempts to provide a positive definition are hardly more successful at justifying a clear distinction between services and products. Let us mention for example a definition proposed by Peter Hill in 1977: a service is "the transformation of the condition of an individual, or of a good belonging to some economic agent, resulting from the activity of another economic agent, upon requirement or with the approval of the first agent". Such a definition cannot apply to hotels, to the telephone service, to any form of rental, to interim services, except by considering that a hotel service consists in "transforming a person in the street into a person lodged in a hotel". Even if one would accept to take such verbal acrobatics seriously, they would then work just as well for the most indisputable products ("transform somebody without a car into somebody possessing a car"). In short, although that definition has some virtue by specifying the agents and the type of relationships that unite them in a transaction, it does not allow to clearly tell a service from a product.

Materiality and separability

If the fundamental characteristic of services is that they "do not result in material goods", how should we call the activities of a tailor, a construction company or a publisher, which the official nomenclature includes among services although their production is visibly material? Those examples also violate the other supposed "inseparability" feature. In the above examples, the result of the service activity not only continues to exist when the production activity has ceased, but can even be the subject of new transactions independently of the initial producer: the suit, the house or the book can be resold by their buyer to a third party.

A simple solution would be to consider that such activities should in reality be included in products, and that the official nomenclature is erroneous. This approach would have the disadvantage of concealing important differences with usual industrial products. For instance, such goods are designated as being the property of the buyer even before they exist, their definition is negotiated between the producer and the buyer, and the act of production most often does not begin before a contract is established between supplier and buyer. But those features also apply to certain forms of products where the buyer can choose among a large number of options, for example automobiles or computers.

Transfer of property

Traditionally, computer manufacturers have offered to their customers, for the same equipment, a choice between rental, leasing and purchase. Do they operate in different sectors for that reason? Can one really say that they offer a product in the case of sale and a service in the case of rental, and then what about leasing? In reality, their core activities are identical whatever is the financing formula used. Concerning the customer, his choice applies first to the equipment, and the financing mode is a secondary decision. In that case, the transaction concerns a product beyond any doubt, and the possible rental service is a modality of the transaction rather than a distinct service.

Neither the materiality of the object of the transaction, nor the possibility of dissociating it from its source, nor the modalities of transfer from supplier to buyer constitute criteria allowing to distinguish definitely services from products. On the other hand, those considerations can be summarized into a criterion that we will call "transfer mode" which constitutes one of the relevant dimensions of classification.

At one end of the continuum is the case of "pure" products that are the subject of a real transfer of property from supplier to buyer. Note that, by definition, such a transfer is possible only for material goods separable from their source. At the other extremity are "pure" services that have no material existence and cannot therefore be subject to appropriation in the first place, and *a fortiori* not to a transfer of property either.

Between those two extremes, we find very frequent cases where the transaction consists in granting the customer a right of usage on a good belonging to the supplier. That good can be perfectly material and more or less separable from its source. The usage rights can be more or less limited, either in time or in the extent of actual rights granted to the customer. For example, a tool or car rental service involves a temporary transfer of usage rights on a separable material good; hotel services include a temporary transfer of usage right on an inseparable material good (the bedroom); an interim personnel service can be assimilated to a temporary transfer of usage right on persons. A case specific to data-processing is that of software packages, where the license contract grants to the user a definitive usage right, without any transfer of property, since the licensee may not sell the package to a third party. In reality, setting aside that prohibition, which is not a severe constraint anyhow, customers ignore such contractual subtleties and everything happens as if there was a transfer of property.

Intangibility and variability

Some services have a tangible aspect. For example, it is possible to visit a hotel bedroom before renting it. Some hotel chains even make it a rule to offer identical accommodations in all their establishments worldwide, thus giving to their services a character of invariance in time and in space that is usually considered as characteristic of products. In other words, certain services share with products the features of being defined *a priori* by the supplier and listed in a catalog, and to be offered only in that standard form. For example, bus lines are catalog services, while taxis offer a custom service.

A commonly used way of improving productivity in services is to standardize or to systematize all or part of the service, which can also address a consumer desire to have a reliable description of the service that he contemplates acquiring. Whatever are the motivations, such a step tends to give services some of the invariability features of products. Incidentally, the term "product" is frequently used to designate a service defined *ex ante* by its supplier and which can be provided in an identical manner to all buyers.

It is possible to object that, even if it is formally defined by its provider, the service actually rendered can deviate from that description and vary depending on customer and circumstances. In particular, the contract can contain the description of the target result, but guarantee only that the service provider will do his best to achieve that result, not that the final product will conform to its contractual description. However, the existence of such uncertainty does not allow differentiating clearly services from products either, since even the most carefully defined products can also fail to meet their specifications.

Here again, there is a possibility of a continuous variation from tangible goods precisely defined and whose conformity to their specification is considered as certain, to intangible services whose definition is purely indicative. This definition itself can exist *a priori* in the catalog of the supplier without any room for variation, or it can be obtained by choosing between predetermined options or by combination of predetermined elements and specific elements, or it can result entirely from a specific negotiation between customer and supplier. In the same way as for the materiality and separability criteria, there is no dichotomy between products, assumed to described in an inflexible catalog, and services that would always be intangible and uncertain. Reality is a continuous range of definition forms, where it is impossible to draw anywhere a borderline that would unambiguously separate services from products.

That criterion concerning the definition mode is largely independent of the preceding criterion which concerns the transfer mode. It is of course unlikely that a good defined only in an indicative manner may be the object of a definitive transfer of property or even of usage, but a good defined by negotiation or on a catalog can involve the different modes of transfer.

Customer - supplier relationship

Each one of the two criteria related to the transaction that we have retained above has an impact on the duration and on the nature of the relationship between customer and supplier, and can thereby exert an influence on the organization and the culture of the producing enterprise. For a good defined by a catalog, as for a service defined in a purely indicative manner, no durable relationship is required for specifying the object of the transaction, while such a relationship is mandatory if the definition is negotiated.

A definitive transfer of property or usage requires only a one-off relationship at the moment of transfer, and can easily be handled indirectly through an intermediary. On the contrary, a temporary transfer implies a permanent and generally frequent direct relationship between supplier and customer during the duration of the transfer. Exchanges that do not involve any transfer correspond to Hill's definition and imply some form of cooperation between supplier and customer during the entire time when the service is rendered.

In the restrictive definition implicitly accepted by most authors and commentators, a good defined by catalog and subject to a definitive transfer of property can unambiguously be called a product. The only distinctive feature of services would then be the duration of the relationship between the producer and the consumer, plus the fact that such relationship involves the production system of the supplier. That feature can indeed have a profound influence on the organization and culture of the enterprise. It can for example forbid separating the sales function from the production function, or demand that production units possess a capacity of negotiation and adaptation far exceeding that of the usual factories in conventional industries.

Perishability

Services are often characterized by the fact that they must be produced every time they are consumed and at the very moment of their consumption. This criterion can be interpreted in two ways: it is trivial for services that cannot be dissociated from their source, and in that case it is equivalent to the inseparability criterion that we have examined earlier. When on the contrary a service gives birth to a transferable material good, that good has all the features of a product and can in the same way be perishable or not. A non-transferable service, for example an education course or a show, will on the other hand be perishable in the above sense.

That criterion of perishability also has an economic translation: production costs for a perishable good are incurred by the supplier even if the service is not consumed, and the value of production not sold is zero. From that viewpoint, the perishability criterion concerns the economics of production, and can therefore be related to considerations of production scale and sector structure.

Once again, although that criterion applies to the majority of service activities, it can as well be satisfied by many products and therefore cannot be used to discriminate between products and services. First of all, perishable products do exist, whose value decreases rapidly with time. More generally, for products as for services, the share of total costs formed by fixed production costs is incurred whatever volume is produced and sold. For products with permanent costs much higher than variable costs, the quasi-totality of costs are incurred even if the production is not sold, in just the same way as for services and perishable products.

Conversely, as for products, the cost of services can be split in different proportions into fixed costs and variable costs, or into sunk costs and recoverable costs. Investments in production equipment can range from almost zero for consulting services to enormous volumes for telecommunications or air transportation. Many services include a share of genuinely variable costs such as supplies. Finally, although the share of personnel in the cost of services is often important, some services like telecommunications are essentially provided by automated equipment.

Summary

In short, wherever one places the borderline between products and services, one will always find offers that are located right across that borderline. One is therefore tempted to think that reality cannot be described as the juxtaposition of two separate worlds of services and of products, but as a multidimensional continuum where the different types of offers can fall somewhere between "pure" products and "pure" services. Incidentally, certain administrative regulations introduce a distinction between "supplies", "works" and "services", supplies corresponding to standard products while works can imply the creation and transfer to the customer of a material good defined by him.

It is of course always possible to agree upon more or less arbitrary border-lines that would allow to assign each activity, enterprise or trade into one or the other of the two categories. But apart from the fact that the resulting classification would not always satisfy common sense, the real question is whether such a dichotomy would help to understand the economic mechanisms. To that end, it would be necessary that each one of the "services" and "products" groups thus defined possess characteristics common to all their elements and distinct from those of the other group. In other words, each "product" should be closer to all the other products than to any "service". We have seen that this is not the case. Let us conclude therefore that introducing a basic distinction between products and ser-vices does not contribute in any way to the study of industry structures.

In any case, those criteria related to the form of the exchange bear no rela-tion with the structuring factors of sectors. Classifying a production among services or among products according to those criteria does not say anything concerning the structure of production costs nor the production scale, not more than concerning obstacles to entry and to exit, all considerations that govern sector dynamics. Porter's analysis based on competitive forces applies to services as well as products, and will result in identifying concentrated sectors and fragmented sectors in ser-vices as well as in products.

A typology of services and products

If we accept that the distinction between a product and a service concerns the transaction between the producer and the consumer, distinguishing a service from a product requires answering the following questions:
- what is the object of the transaction (a material good, a change of condition of the buyer, of a good belonging to him)?
- how is the object of the transaction defined? (unilaterally by the supplier, by more or less open negotiation)?
- what guarantees does the producer offer (none, of means, of result)?
- what is the nature of the transaction (transfer of property, definitive transfer of usage, temporary transfer of usage, no transfer)?

Those four criteria are largely independent from each other, and each one may accept more than two answers. Possible combinations of answers are therefore numerous, even if some appear unlikely. Some unambiguously match the intuitive concept of product (a material good defined unilaterally by the producer, whose conformity is guaranteed and the property of which is transferred). Others define forms of offerings that common sense includes among services, for example access to a skill defined unilaterally without guarantee (consulting) or a change of condi-tion without transfer of property or usage, where the definition can be unilateral (public transportation), negotiated (taxis, maintenance) or practically non-existent (medical care). But other combinations, although commonplace, are more ambigu-ous, for example cases of temporary transfer of usage of a material good defined unilaterally with guaranteed conformity (rentals, hotel services) or transfer of property of a material good defined through negotiation (construction enterprises).

The following diagram represents that continuum in a simplified manner by restricting it to two dimensions. One dimension combines the mode of definition (indicative, negotiated or by catalog) and the related question of guarantees of conformity. The other one is the mode of transfer (of property, definitive usage, temporary usage or no transfer), which depends itself on the object of the transaction. On the resulting map, the pure products are located at the upper right (definition by catalog, transfer of property), pure services at the lower left (indicative definition, no transfer), but there exists a large variety of combinations, illustrated here by the most common computer services.

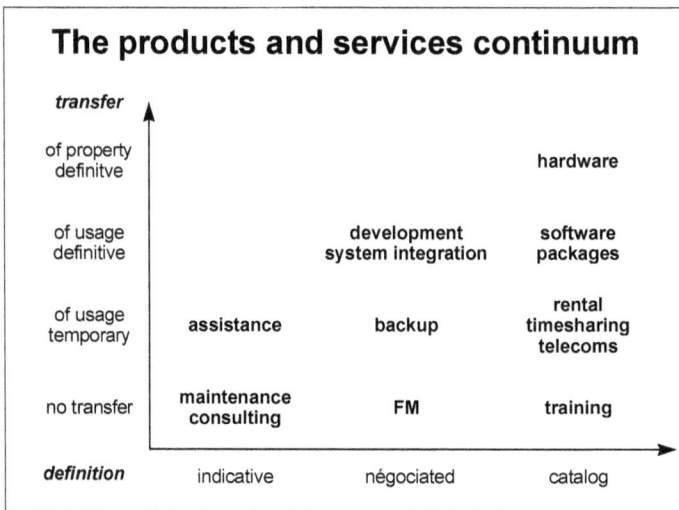

The products and services continuum

transfer			
of property definitve			hardware
of usage definitive		development system integration	software packages
of usage temporary	assistance	backup	rental timesharing telecoms
no transfer	maintenance consulting	FM	training
definition	indicative	négociated	catalog

One will note in particular that software packages are extremely close to a pure product, from which it is only distinguished by the contractual transfer mode, and on the other hand as remote as possible from services such as assistance or consulting. We will see later that, from this viewpoint as well as that of economic logic and associated industry structure, software packages must definitely be classified among products and not among services.

Conclusions

In summary, the alleged dichotomy between products and services is a much too simplistic view of reality.

Concerning modes of transaction, there are intermediate forms of exchange between pure products and pure services, that can be analyzed along several independent dimensions and represent a large variety of offerings. Concerning economic logic, there is no industrial dynamics specific to services and that would be different from that (or those) which apply to products. In reality, one can observe in services a variety of dynamics and structures similar to that which prevails for products, and the same types of structure will concern services as well as products.

Services do not form one sector in the sense of Porter ("a group of firms producing products that are close substitutes for each other"), because even when reduced to computer services, services are too diverse to be substituted to each other. There are many sectors in services. Similarly, services do not constitute a trade in the sense that we have introduced in chapter 6, namely a group of sectors that would have enough common features to be governed by the same dynamics. Concerning productive firms themselves, some forms of service call for structures and company cultures close to those that characterize industrial products, while others call for radically different structures and cultures. Some forms of service are less compatible between themselves than they are with certain forms of products.

The only real difference that we have been able to recognize is that in the so-called services, the act of production always involves the customer more or less directly. Thereby, the production facilities of the services firm are directly exposed to the view and to the judgment of the market. In a product activity, the attributes of products put on the market are isolated from those of the organization that has served to produce them, for example by the contractual or commercial description that comes with them. Also, it is easy enough to avoid that possible malfunctions in production might show on the market as defective products. For services, on the contrary, the very quality of the production facilities is visible, every possible failure is perceived by the customer, and therefore poorly adapted structures or culture are a formidable handicap in competitive situations. In other words, in the area of services, the degree to which the personality of the enterprise is well adapted to the nature of its production and to the expectations of the market takes on a much more decisive importance than for products. We will see in chapter 13 how much those problems contribute to structuring the services sector and to explaining its difficulties in adjusting to the evolution of market requirements.

Towards a service economy?

Despite the absence of a satisfactory definition of services activities and their fundamentally heterogeneous character, several authors have proposed ambitious theses concerning the place of services in the economy, that various commentators of computer evolution sometimes rediscover. A frequent opinion is that services are intrinsically more profitable than products, develop more rapidly and will end up replacing them.

That thesis relates to the "postindustrial" school illustrated mainly by Daniel Bell[58]. It holds that the share of services in the economy increases inescapably, so that the development of services can be considered as an indicator of economic progress. That thesis is often disguised under the form: "a sector is mature when services overtake hardware", and is used by some computer commentators to forecast the definitive supremacy of services and the regression or even the disappearance of equipment manufacturers.

At the other extreme is the so-called "neo-industrial" thesis, whose inspiration goes back to the classical concept of value and whose main present advocates

---

58   Bell D : The Coming of Post-Industrial Society [Basic Books, 1973]

are related to the Marxist current. That thesis postulates with Adam Smith that only the production of material goods is a genuinely productive activity, and therefore that services activities are unproductive by definition. Services are therefore para-sitizing the economy, their growth is in no way a sign of progress and must be con-trolled if not prevented.

Apart from the fact that the "neo-industrial" thesis relies on an erroneous and arbitrary conception of the formation of value, how can one put forward this sort of conclusions in the absence of an *a priori* definition of services? In practice, the authors in question avoid the issue by only retaining as examples of services those activities whose features do support the theses that they wish to prove, thus underlining involuntarily the wide diversity of services and of the dynamics that govern them.

Moreover, those theories address mostly the concerns of sociologists, who are seeking to characterize the activities of individuals, rather than the concerns of economists who are interested in enterprises and in their productions. A large part and even the majority of workers of the "tertiary sector" exert their activity in industrial enterprises. The multiplication of "knowledge workers" does not allow in any way to conclude that services enterprises are expanding to the detriment of industrial enterprises. Finally, even if it appears that services offerings take a grow-ing place in the economy as a whole, that does not imply that services are replacing products within each individual sector. There are on the contrary many examples of the reverse movement, for example the replacement of household employees by electrical appliances. In the particular case of data-processing, we will return in chapters 13 and 15 to the competition between products and services and to the potential validity of the "postindustrial" thesis, often presented as obvious.

The diverse forms of software

A possible reason for the widespread assimilation of software and services is the choice of the word "software" itself, in contrast with "hardware". Hardware being a product, then software must be a service. Let us therefore look at software from the perspective of its production dynamics and the ensuing industrial struc-tures.

Software is the very essence of data-processing. It is ubiquitous at all levels: processor chips contain microprograms, as do most functional units like printers or extension cards. At a more global level, the functions of a computer system are defined by programs, which implement the general functions provided by operating systems and utility programs, or specific functions that constitute applications and endow the system with usable capabilities. The development of programs forms the heart of the activity of computing professionals, and many services consist largely in developing software. Software is, properly speaking, the soul of hardware, that is to say what animates it[59]. A computer can be defined as "a machine for exe-

---

[59]   The French word for "soul" is "*âme*", which comes from the same latin root (*anima*) as the word "*animer*" (to animate).

cuting programs", and hardware is only an empty inert body capable of receiving a large variety of souls in the form of programs.

In what follows, we are going to attempt to analyze the technical and economic features of software-related activities, in order to identify the types of players, their place in the industry and the economic dynamics that they obey. Do those dynamics allow software activities to relate to the other activities of players who use them? Can we identify for software one or several activities endowed with specific economic features which subject them to a specific industrial logic? Do the dynamics of software represent a structuring factor for the computer industry?

Features of software

Indispensable to define functions of equipment and computer systems, and thereby ubiquitous, software can take multiple forms.

What is common between a few lines of Fortran written by an engineer for his own needs, the microcode of the Pentium processor, the Windows operating system distributed by millions of copies, control software for the space shuttle, an electronic game program and the management system of a large enterprise? All those forms of software express orders by which man dictates a behavior to a machine. In other words, programming is a form of human expression intended for use by a machine. Incidentally, the many developments that have resulted in establishing the legal protection rules for software have assimilated software to a work of the mind in the same way as an artistic or literary work, extending to it the copyright and royalty law.

The programming activity has the same infinite diversity and immaterial character as the closest form of human expression, writing. Like normal writing, software development is a purely intellectual activity that does not demand other tools than pencil and paper. Present-day programmers work most often directly on a computer screen and benefit from sophisticated automated assistance in the writing of programs, but not so long ago the creative phase of programming used only paper and pencil, and the computer was only used later for translation and testing. Program writing is therefore an activity accessible to an isolated individual, without significant preliminary investments. Even with the most recent programming techniques, a simple microcomputer makes the most powerful programming tools available.

From its destination, that is to be interpreted by a machine, software derives two basic features that differentiate it from the other forms of human expression. First, it is extremely easy to reproduce. Software is indeed carried by the same media as other data processed by the computer, and can be read and written by the same devices. Therefore, any tool allowing the execution of a program also allows to reproduce it, even more easily and more accurately that for normal writing. A person able to read a text is generally capable of copying it, but that is a long operation, subject to error, and the result often differs from the original at least in form. On the contrary, a computer can reproduce millions of characters in a few minutes, without risk of error and in a form exactly identical to the original, and in particular able to be reproduced in its turn. Such reproduction can involve without difficulty a change of medium or remote transmission through telecommunications media.

Some media, like CD-ROM or the other forms of read-only memory, allow only reading and therefore do not enable complete identical reproduction, but it remains very easy to extract their content and to copy it to a traditional writeable medium. There are indeed means of protection that aim to prevent the reproduction of programs or to render it more expensive, but those devices are artificial, expensive and often of limited efficiency. Extreme ease of reproduction is a fundamental feature of software. For commercial software activity, this entails an extremely low level of variable production cost, which gives to software production the features of a concentrated sector. Furthermore, the possibility of reproduction by any user raises the difficult problem of protecting the property of software.

Secondly, because it is intended to be interpreted blindly by a machine ("mechanically" in the proper meaning of the word), software demands levels of rigor and reliability rarely met for other written documents. Before being used, all software exceeding half-a-dozen simple instructions will have to be tested in order to verify that the actual behavior of a computer executing the program is true in every respect to the intentions of its author and to the expectations of its users. One must expect those tests to reveal new errors that will again need to be corrected. Those corrections will demand a new verification of the program, and so on. The development of software is thus a cyclic operation where writing and correction operations alternate with tests on the computer. Its duration, its difficulty and its cost are in direct proportion to the size and complexity of the program involved.

The forms of software are as widely diverse as the possible forms and uses of writing. The program of a few Fortran lines that the engineer writes for his own needs is the analog of the handwritten note that he may leave to a colleague or of the sticker that he pastes on his refrigerator. The small program has a known user and a precise and limited use. It is intended for a single utilization and will be forgotten after being used. Its preparation costs its author only a few minutes, but it has no meaning or usefulness outside of the specific relational context between author and user, who are often one and the same person, or two close associates. It has no market value and no business intention is present in its preparation.

At the opposite, an operating system or a large software package is the analogue of an encyclopedia. It represents many years of work, that can only be justified by the hope for revenue resulting from marketing the end product. But that objective itself imposes quality demands on the form as well as on the content, that add to the time and cost of preparation, and require the intervention of specialized professionals which make the product the collective work of a business enterprise.

Between those two extremes, software can, just like writing, take many forms corresponding to many uses. The management system of a large enterprise is similar to a collection of procedures, forms and management information specific to the enterprise and prepared specifically for it. An electronic game program is the analogue of an illustrated book for children. A leading-edge program materializing a computer research activity is the analogue of a scientific communication. Its main goal is to prove the validity of an idea and not necessarily to be its industrial imple-mentation.

All those activities have in common to eventually translate into software, just as the writing of the sticker, of the encyclopedia, of management procedures, of the children's book and of the dissertation translate into a written text. But as for the document, the preparation and utilization contexts, motivations, modes of production and general economics of the operation introduce differences between those activities, which are far more significant than the similarities resulting from their common representation as software. In other words, the production of software is as varied an activity as writing can be, and there is not more a homogeneous software industry than a homogeneous writing industry. Software must not be considered as a product in itself, but as a material used separately or in combination with others. In the products where it is used, software can be a secondary component, in which case the product will obey its own industrial dynamics. Other industrial activities have software as their main production, but the nature of the activity varies widely depending on the nature and the utilization of that software, and can correspond to different competitive and economic logics, and therefore to different industry structures.

Finally, software is the material of complexity and of innovation *par excellence.* Contrary to hardware, software remains changeable at any time and thereby enables experimentation and gradual development of new functions. Indeed, all new ideas and any exploration of a new area or a new mode of utilization translate first into the development of programs, before possibly giving birth to circuits or specialized equipment. Only when the area has been sufficiently explored and the complexity of the processes mastered, will it become conceivable to cast functions in silicon. People sometimes lament that software is more complex and more difficult to master than equipment, forgetting that it is the very nature of software to implement functions too complex for hardware.

Complexity and cost factors

Schematically, if we except very simple programs, the preparation of a program includes three stages: overall design, writing and testing.

The design of software obviously involves algorithms, that is to say methods of processing information that will be implemented by the program, but also data structures, modes of interaction between the program and its users, connections with other programs, etc. A large part of those elements can be reused from previous productions, but others can present an original character, and even constitute real inventions that necessitate research, development and specific validation work.

Even when starting from a known base, writing a program of some importance remains a delicate operation. Every person who has approached programming even remotely has learnt at his or her expense that the computer does not tolerate the most minute error. More exactly, it interprets literally each instruction that it meets, even if they do not exactly represent the programmer's intentions. Many writing mistakes can escape the most attentive proofreading, and the only means of verifying the accuracy of a program remains to execute it on the computer for which it is intended. Unexpected results, or any abnormal behavior of the computer during execution, constitute symptoms of errors in the program. Going back from those symptoms to the causes of errors often proves as difficult as identifying the murderer in a good detective novel. When the error is finally located and hopefully corrected, the only possible verification consists in executing again the amended program, which most often reveals new errors and takes back to the start of the same cycle. Even for a relatively simple program, that iterative process can turn out to be long and expensive. One can attempt to shorten it by being particularly careful during the initial writing, but that too contributes to cost and development time.

Moreover, a piece of software of some importance is never formed a by simple sequence of instructions that execute in a fixed order. It also contains many test instructions that, according to the current value of such or such a variable or according to the state of such or such an indicator, bypass or execute such or such an instruction sequence or jump to another point of the program. There are thus a large number of possible paths in the program, that must all be executed successfully in order for the program to be considered as correct.

Now, when the size of a program increases, the average length of the sequences between two branch instructions does not increase as much as the number of branches, so that the number of possible paths increases as a power (the square?) of the size of the program. The time necessary for testing increases therefore very rapidly with the size of programs, and rapidly exceeds the initial writing time, even if that writing phase has been undertaken with all the care required to minimize the number of errors. Note in passing that there are currently no practical means to certify that a program contains no error, nor *a fortiori* to anticipate the time necessary for eliminating all errors contained in a program. Besides, experience shows that despite months of intensive testing prior to their distribution, highly complex programs like operating systems still contain errors several months after being put to extensive usage.

The effort necessary for developing a piece of software varies in very large proportions depending on the nature, the functional content and the destination of the program. One can reasonably estimate that for writing and testing activities, productivity ranges from 60 tested instructions per man-day for a simple program to less than 2 instructions per man-day for highly complex systems. A program containing several millions of instructions, as is the case for some of the large systems on the market, requires therefore a development investment of several thousand man years, which demands a genuine industrial organization.

Types of software and types of players

In addition to volume, intrinsic processing difficulty and functional richness of the program, other factors related to modes of operations add to development costs by demanding an industrial discipline. Let us mention in particular the diversity of equipment configurations on which the program must be able to execute, the diversity of users and modes of utilization, as well as the nature of the relationships between authors and users of the program. One can schematize these various development contexts by three main modes implying increasing levels of complexity, and in parallel a range of players of increasing professionalism.

A first category of players includes individuals or small groups who develop software for their own needs. At this end of the spectrum, the writing of software is an ancillary activity subordinate to another professional activity. Like all activities of the mind, it can also be undertaken for the mere satisfaction of its author, as an amateur in the original sense of the word: somebody who loves[60]. Let us recall that micro-computing started in that way. The first microcomputers of years 1975-1980 were designed by and intended for programming amateurs, who have remained numerous until our days.

In that context, the only source of difficulty is the intrinsic processing complexity. The program is meant to be executed on a single well-known machine configuration, that which happens to be available to the author/user. That individual has only modest demands concerning user-friendliness and reliability, he needs neither training nor documentation and will by definition be highly tolerant to any possible lack of quality of the software. Very often, he will use the program only a few times in a small number of particular cases, and will never worry to know whether the program works correctly in all possible cases.

A variant of this situation is that of a research organization where software is a validation and proof instrument, for example in the fields of numerical calculation, engineering techniques and applied sciences. Verifying or proving a theory can require very complex programs from an algorithmic viewpoint, but tolerate rudimentary software in terms of ease of use and robustness.

A different context is when a piece of software must be developed to address the needs of a distinct user population, to which the author generally does not belong. For those users, who often possess only limited knowledge in computing, software is meant to be a more or less critical tool, with corresponding high demands for ease of use, reliability and availability. The very number of users and their potential diversity entails a variety of usage conditions and necessitates a large range of functions, that considerably increase the complexity of the program by multiplying possible execution paths. Configurations on which the software must execute can be varied and evolutionary, which requires testing on multiple configurations. Finally, the program must be documented and must come with adequate provisions for user training and support.

All those requirements call for the involvement of professional specialists, coming either from the internal development teams of the user enterprise or from services companies. Custom development of programs for a client company is an important component of the computer services activity, to which we will return in chapter 13.

Finally, writing a piece of software can be undertaken for unidentified third-parties, that is to say for an anonymous target market. In that case, it constitutes a genuine industrial undertaking, where all the requirements mentioned above for

---

60   The French word "amateur" is derived from the latin "*amare*" (to love) and literally means "lover".

functional richness, user-friendliness, reliability, documentation, … are strengthened by the need to actually satisfy a hypothetical demand in a competitive market. Moreover, in case of commercial success, the variety of users, modes of utilization and configurations used will end up exceeding the estimates of the authors. That makes extensive testing even more mandatory, and creates a demand for improvements and extensions that constitutes in itself another field open to competition. We enter here the field of commercial software packages, whose competitive dynamics will be the subject of chapter 11.

The following diagram summarizes that analysis. The horizontal axis corresponds to increasing complexity, and therefore to the integration capability required of the organizations developing the software. The vertical axis indicates increasing target user population size, therefore increasing distribution and support capability required of the same organizations. At the lower left, simple programs developed for few users can be implemented by isolated individuals, while complex systems developed for a large market (at the upper right) demand development and marketing organizations typical of industry. In between, relatively simple programs, but aiming at a wide distribution, can come from small enterprises, while big laboratories can create complex systems, but limited in their distribution.

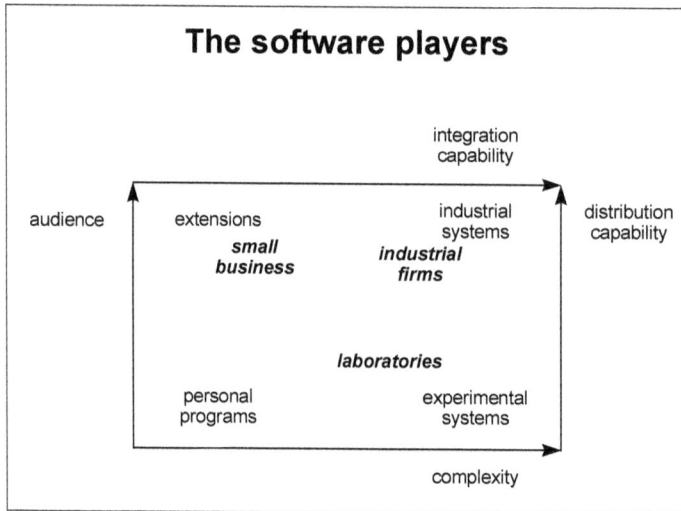

The software players

integration
capability

audience   extensions   industrial   distribution
                                 systems   capability
             small   *industrial*
             business   *firms*

                    laboratories

             personal   experimental
             programs   systems

                              complexity

Those different development contexts translate in particular into different cycles, in the meaning that we have introduced in chapter 9. It concerns here the time delay required to verify that the software produced does meet the needs of its users. In any case, that period is obviously all the more long that the software is complex and its users diverse. But when the user population is known and accessible, it is possible to put in place a development system allowing progressive validation, and thus limit risk and uncertainty. In the case of the development of software packages for the market, adequacy to user needs translates directly into revenue and can be ascertained only at the end of the cycle, whatever precautions are taken during development. That factor alone gives to the development of software packages the features of a concentrated sector: long cycles, high investments, and therefore high production scale.

In summary, the activity of software development can take many forms ranging from a non-specialist writing a few lines of code for his personal usage to an industrial large scale project. Software authors can be isolated amateurs, non-computing professionals, computing professionals in specialized teams, small enterprises, large services companies or firms specialized in software packages. Their motivations can be passion or simple curiosity, the execution of a contract or profitable introduction of a product on the market.

From an economic viewpoint, each development context possesses its own features that overshadow the common characteristics related to the nature of software. More than as a homogeneous activity, software must be considered as a material used in different activities, products and services, where it can be combined with other ingredients and where its intrinsic properties may disappear as well as dominate. Thus, writing custom software will have all the features of a service, implying transfer of property of a work product whose definition is negotiated, while software packages will have all the features of a product defined unilaterally by the supplier, even if it legally involves only a transfer of usage rights.

Service and "self - service"

Conversely, a potential user who feels a need for a piece of software can choose between several ways to satisfy that need. He can be lucky enough to find a suitable ready-made package; he can have it developed within his enterprise or sub-contract its implementation to a services company; he can also consider implementing it himself. Those alternate modes allow to satisfy a same software requirement, although the last approach does not involve a market transaction, while the first one entails the purchase of a product, and the other one uses a service transaction. Incidentally, one could imagine more complex forms of transaction still satisfying the same need, for example purchasing one or several pieces of software complemented by a purchase of services to adapt them to the particular need.

With that example, we encounter an approach to services proposed by Jonathan Gershuny and known as the theory of "self-service economy"[61]. For this author, the demand for services and therefore their place in the economy must not be analyzed separately for a family of goods on one hand, a family of services on the other hand, but according to the common needs that products and services compete to satisfy. The definition of a market segment must be widened to the demand for satisfying a need, where different forms and combinations of products and services, all aiming at the satisfaction of that need, constitute as many competitive offers between which the consumer will have to arbitrate.

---

61   Gershuny J : After Industrial Society? The Emerging Self-Service Economy [Humanities Press, 1978]

For example, the purpose of supplying computer equipment is to satisfy a need for information processing, which can be satisfied not only by purchasing products, but also by renting them on a temporary or permanent basis, or by buying services from a processing company. Similarly, a need for transportation can be satisfied by purchasing a car, but also by renting it, by using public transportation (a catalog service) or calling a taxi (a custom service). In the competitive analysis which is the subject of the present study, products and services not only form a continuum without clear borderlines, but are competing in many elementary market segments rather than constituting separate market segments. We will retain this viewpoint in chapter 13 to analyze the respective place of products and of the different forms of services in data-processing.

Conclusions

At the end of that analysis, the "software and services" nomenclature appears as a statistical hodgepodge deprived of any homogeneity and without any meaning in terms of industry structure analysis.

Within that continuous and multidimensional universe formed by products and services, we must isolate software packages, that present the typical features of a product. They are defined unilaterally by the supplier in the hope of finding a market; they are tangible, invariable and not perishable, and are subject to a definitive transfer of usage rights. Concerning the economy of their production, their cost is essentially formed by development costs incurred in totality before the program is introduced on the market, while variable unit costs are extremely low. This cost structure gives to the software package sector the dynamics of a concentrated sector, analogous to that of components, and at the opposite of most services such as custom development of specific software. Software packages belong to the industrial approach typical of products and must be analyzed as such.

Software packages are closely comparable to products for the economy of their production as well as for their modes of marketing, while services activities demand specific structures and company cultures. Speaking of a "software and services" sector makes no more sense than speaking of a "fuels and taxis" sector in transportation. No one of the leaders in software packages, or even none of the firms of any importance that have succeeded in that sector, has ever been a services company, and no services company has become a leader in software packages. In reality, there are no "software packages and services" companies to speak of, and assimilating software packages to a service borders upon mental aberration.

Even within the services family, offerings of a different nature coexist, which cannot be substituted to each other, but where each one is in a certain way competing with hardware or software products. Services constitute therefore in turn a heterogeneous group whose most significant common feature in terms of industry structure is direct contact between the market and the production facility of each supplier. That feature makes the nature of the production and the personality of each firm even more closely interdependent than in the case of products.

In the following chapters, we will therefore study separately software packages (chapters 11 and 12), and then services (chapter 13), even if this last category has no real internal coherence and must be analyzed as the juxtaposition of different sectors and trades.

Chapter 11 - The software package industry

The slow rise of packaged software. A paradoxical sector structure. Basic software and applications software, systems and extensions. Development cycles, complexity and cost of integration. The formation of prices and market shares. Concentration dynamics in multiple sectors. Software packages versus components. Prices are not related to costs. Problems and personality of the packaged software company. A kind of perpetual motion.

The present chapter concerns those programs that are defined for an anonymous market and not for a particular user, marketed ready for use, and usable independently of their author.

Among the large number of products and services of different natures that use software as their base material, such software packages have all the usual features of products in the most classical sense of the word. The main offer is defined in a catalog, and the customer makes his purchase decision on the basis of a description prepared unilaterally by the supplier. In return for a single royalty similar to a purchase price, the customer acquires an unlimited usage right, the only restriction compared to a classical product being a constraint of his right to reproduce it. One speaks commonly of "buying" a software package. From a legal viewpoint, software packages are protected by copyright, and therefore comparable to a book or a record, while being also possibly the object of patents, like other products. Many identical copies of a software package are distributed. The activities of creation and distribution are two separate functions within the producing firm, and may even be performed by distinct enterprises. All those features are at the opposite of custom software development as practiced by many services companies.

The software package activity defines therefore a product made of software. Its production presents the attributes of an industrial production activity, and more precisely of a concentrated sector where fixed costs (of development) are high and variable cost (of reproduction) virtually zero. Contrary to a preconceived idea, the production of software packages is radically different from a services activity from an economic viewpoint, and closer by its industrial logic to the production of components, that we have studied in Chapter 7. Nevertheless, the specific features of software give to the sector very particular features that we are going to examine in this chapter.

History and situation

Only in the seventies did software gradually appear as a possibly independent industrial activity capable of producing revenue and profit. Before IBM decided in 1969 to invoice separately certain types of software, computer manufacturers provided it "free" with the equipment of which that software was somehow part. That included primarily utility programs required for the utilization of equipment, for example operating systems or compilers for programming languages.

For their part, users developed themselves software that they needed, mainly application programs, or had them developed by services companies. In the scientific field, the tradition of free program exchange continued, as inaugurated in the first times of data-processing. That tradition was followed by micro-computing clubs, to the point that Bill Gates came up strongly in 1976 against the micro users of the time by opposing the piracy of fee software. This free exchange tradition survives in our days under the form of "*freeware*" and "*shareware*". That shows to what extent the concept of software as a creation of the mind that should escape commercial channels is still deeply rooted in the mind of many people.

Apart from manufacturers for general programs, the first attempts to market software are made by service companies that have developed a program for a particular customer, and think it is possible to sell that same program to other customers. Such endeavors are often undertaken in partnership with the initial customer, who hopes to recover in that way part of his investment. In most cases, it proves impossible for the new customer to use exactly the same program as his predecessors. The activity of the service firms involved remains therefore primarily to supply custom solutions, where previous developments are more or less cleverly reused in each new contract. Although such pieces of software are often dressed up under appealing names and strongly exploited in the commercial communication of services companies, they are in reality only the support of specific services that are still required not only for their initial installation, but also for their ongoing utilization. That activity is therefore different from packaged software as we have defined it, which assumes that they can be implemented without any involvement from the author.

Nevertheless, the difference of nature between that type of software and genuine software packages has long been ignored, which is probably the reason why software and services are still often considered as one and the same activity, contrary to any rational analysis. Moreover, some services companies do charge a separate royalty for the utilization of existing software modules in their custom services, which probably explains the appearance of a "*software*" item in the statistics concerning those firms, although they do not offer packaged software in the real sense of the word.

On the computer vendor side, separate billing is consistent with the increasing importance of software in terms of costs and in the organization of suppliers as well as in their competitive weaponry. Very rapidly, manufacturers implement for software packages a discipline and a professional organization derived from that already in use for hardware and radically distinct from their services organization, thus confirming that software packages are products. Moreover, under the pressure of tougher and tougher cost competition in hardware, manufacturers gradually move away from their initial policy of subsidizing software by the sale of hardware. This translates into a gradual increase of prices for software packages and a gradual disappearance of free software. For the same reasons, manufacturers that had been late in following IBM on the path of separate software pricing, hoping to obtain a competitive advantage by giving it away, now adopt the same policy of billing. General utility software is thus the first area to change into an independent sector of industrial software packages, where manufacturers who were alone in the beginning are joined by some specialized firms such as Computer Associates.

Up to the seventies, developing software assumes easy and permanent access to a large computer. Such access in virtually possible only for employees of large enterprises, whose activity is oriented towards the production of specific software for their employer, or for researchers whose natural tendency in that period is to distribute their programs free. Availability of a computer is a significant obstacle to entry into the field of fee software. That obstacle to the creation of independent enterprises is lifted at the end of the seventies by the arrival of micro-computing, which makes software development accessible to small independent enterprises and even to isolated individuals, at the same time that it creates a market for software packages thus developed.

This market becomes a mass market with the introduction of the PC in 1981. A multitude of small enterprises appears a that time, often formed by a handful of programmers, each one offering its particular package for a specific type of utilization. But the somewhat amateurish initial proliferation quickly gives way to a competition that soon places in dominant positions enterprises with an industrial character: Microsoft for operating systems, after eliminating Digital Research and a few others, Microsoft again for word processing and spreadsheets, with one or two challengers in each area (Wordperfect and Lotus for word processing, Lotus and Borland for spreadsheets), or Novell for networking software, where Microsoft is now in the role of the challenger.

This specialized sector of software packages for microcomputers develops in parallel with the more traditional software activity of hardware manufacturers for their own systems, with IBM OS/2 or Apple System/7 as examples in the area of micro-computing. Thus, among the enterprises with the 20 largest shares of the software package market, one finds in 1992 five generalists with more than 48% of total sector revenue, and 12 specialists, of which 9 in micros and 3 in large systems, for approximately 36% of total revenue. The top 20 list also includes Apple (1% of total revenue) and two services companies for about 3% of the total, but probably only because of undue use of the "software package" category. In 1994, the share of specialized software firms has increased to more than 54%, no services company shows up in the top 20 any longer, and the same five generalists now add up to only 40%.

As we have seen in chapters 4 and 5, firms specialized in packaged software present characteristic features that make them rather different from the other firms in the computer industry. In general, they are narrowly specialized, totally absent from the hardware market, and offer only a modicum of ancillary services such as maintenance or services. They devote a high share of their expenses to R&D (typically between 8 and 20%) and their commercial activity is overdeveloped, with marketing and administrative expenses higher than 30% of revenue, but their production cost is low in relative value (under 35% of revenue in most cases). Their performances, measured in terms of profit, fluctuate in a very wide range, with each year a maximum higher than 20% and even exceeding 25%, but also heavily nega- tive results for some firms. Nevertheless, the number of unprofitable firms is very low each year, and average profit for the sector is almost always above 10%. Finally, this sector has not been hit by the profitability decline that the rest of industry has experienced between 1987 and 1989.

Features of the sector

At first glance, the packaged software sector presents paradoxical features to the superficial observer. The large number of firms present and the small size of most firms give it the appearance of a fragmented sector. In the sample of 100 firms that we have examined, 53 are present in software packages in 1994, among which the first (IBM) has a market share of 31%, while the market share of the first specialist (Microsoft) is 12%. Of those 53 firms, only 20 have a market share higher than or equal to 1%, and there are in addition a large number of firms too small to appear in the top 100, with market shares lower than 0.1%.

That large number of small firms seems consistent with the fact that obsta- cles to entry seem almost non-existent. In the beginning of 1975, it did not take much more than four weeks for two young students called Bill Gates and Paul Allen to write the Basic interpreter which started the success of Microsoft. Still today, with an investment of 2000 to 4000 $ in a PC, anybody can write a program in his spare time and attempt to market it in order to become the most wealthy person in the United States.

If the production of software packages was really a fragmented sector by nature, one could not explain the persistence of very high profit levels, nor the vir- tually absolute dominance of Microsoft in such segments as operating systems for microcomputers (81% with MS-DOS), spreadsheets (73% with Excel) or to a lesser degree word processing (55 % with Word), nor the dominance of other firms in different areas such as Novell with 70% of the market for local networking soft- ware. In addition, in those market segments and in some others, the distribution of market shares is strikingly similar to that which characterizes strongly monopolistic sectors like components: three or four firms present, with the first one occupying 60 to 70% of the market, and the others sharing the rest of the market in a very unequal manner. That situation is consistent with the fact that the economics of software production obey a highly monopolistic logic, since the quasi-totality of the cost is formed by fixed costs, the marginal cost of making a new copy being virtu- ally zero.

Therefore, while the low obstacles to entry seem to characterize a fragmented sector, economies of scale are high and endow the sector with some of the attributes of a concentrated sector, in particular high profitability. The keys to this apparent paradox are the following:

First, packaged software firms must not be considered as forming a single sector, but as many sectors as there are areas of application. As we have seen in Chapter 6, relying on the study of competition to understand industry structures demands considering separately each "group of firms that offer closely substitutable products", which Porter calls an "industry" and its French translator "*secteur*". Real competition only takes place between software packages offering similar functions. A word processing package such as Word, a database management package such as Paradox and a local network manager such as Netware are not mutually substitutable products. Computing offers a large number of different application areas that create as many opportunities for developing software packages, and that define as many distinct markets. An operating system, an accounting program, a word processor, a data base manager, a statistical analysis library, a musical composition program and a video game fulfill radically different functions, and therefore satisfy different needs and can not be substituted to one another. The sector of software packages is in reality, by Porter's strict definition, the juxtaposition of a large number of sectors, each one corresponding to an application area.

As suggested in the preceding chapter, software must not be considered as a product or a sector of activity, but as a material which can be used to build a large variety of different objects. The fact that Windows and video games are both made of software does not make them competitors within a same sector of activity, not more than a kitchen table and a fishing boat, that are nevertheless both made of wood. In other words, the relevant market segments are kitchen furniture, boat construction, spreadsheets and video games, which can define related industry sectors. Woodworking or software writing are crafts that can be applied in different sectors.

Subjecting packaged software to our structural analysis method, that relies on the working of competition, requires considering that each possible area of utilization of computers defines a market segment where competing firms offer mutually substitutable products satisfying the same customer need in that area. In the first analysis, competition in each of those segments is independent from competition in the other segments. Software packages that are not mutually substitutable define as many separate sectors which structure themselves independently of the others.

Second, although reproduction costs are always low, development costs can vary in very wide proportions depending on the nature and ambitions of the software package under consideration. They are low for individual efforts, or even sometimes invisible when development is subsidized in totality or in part by another activity, for example research. At the other extreme, they can amount to tens or even hundreds of millions for complex general systems. The extreme variety of software forms that we have mentioned in the preceding chapter can be found in software products. Depending on the magnitude of development expenses, either the ease of entry will dominate by giving to the activity the features of a fragmented sector, or at the opposite the high economical production scale will submit the activity to the dynamics of concentration.

In summary, monopolistic competition resulting from the small variable unit cost takes place within each of those many sub-markets, not for the software package industry as a whole. In each sub-market, the monopolistic forces will be all the more strong that the nature of the segment considered demands complex software entailing high fixed development costs. Competitive forces that push towards concentration act separately inside each elementary sector and make each sector (operating systems, spreadsheets, word processors, compilers, accounting software, drawing software, …) evolve towards the asymmetrical concentrated structure that we have described earlier (see Chapter 7). Each elementary sector obeys the logic of concentration, which explains the observed high profit levels and dispersions.

In summary, considering the monopolistic economy of its production, the sector of software packages is actually formed of a large number of sub-sectors, each one a concentrated sector. Indeed, if one no longer examines the market shares at the overall level where their economic meaning is questionable, but for each area, one does find the characteristic distribution of concentrated sectors, with a leader exceeding a 50% market share: 81% for MS-DOS in operating systems, 73% for Excel in spreadsheets for DOS, 54% for Word in word processing for Windows, 70% for Netware in local area networks, etc.

But the number of such sub-sectors is sufficiently high, and there are enough firms specialized in only one of them, for the "macro-sector" constituted by the totality of software packages to look like a fragmented sector by the number and size of active firms. In each sub-sector, the leading enterprise can be of a modest size. Even Microsoft, which is the leader in several sectors among the largest, makes only a few thousand million dollars of revenue, approximately 12% of total software package revenue.

Moreover, the vitality of data-processing in general results in the constant appearance of new application areas which are as many emerging sectors where relative ease of entry opens the door to a multitude of small new enterprises. The different sectors are thus at very different degrees of maturity. While the concentration phenomenon has already led some sectors to the characteristic structure of asymmetrical oligopolies, other sectors are still in the emerging phase. That probably explains in part the high dispersion of results that we have observed in Chapter 5, and the difficulty that we had to interpret the apparent behavioral features of the sector.

Nevertheless, the multiple sub-sectors that constitute the software package sector are neither disconnected nor tightly separated. The development of software packages is a single trade, and those competitive advantages that allow a firm to succeed in a particular application area are also valid for the other areas, even if they must be complemented by advantages specific to each sector. Finally, we will see that borderlines between application areas are often blurred and provide multiple crossing opportunities. In total, the overall dynamics of the software package sector result from a complex interplay between segments, each governed by concentration dynamics, but covering in total a whole spectrum ranging from emerging sectors, wide open to new entrants, to stabilized sectors dominated by asymmetrical oligopolies, with those different sectors communicating and interacting with one another.

Forms of packaged software

It is usual to distinguish two major areas within software packages: base software or "system" software, and application software. The first family includes a group of programs enabling the use of equipment without being specialized for a particular task, and fulfilling general functions such as hardware management, task management, data management, communications management, etc. Those programs are linked to the hardware and surround it with a richer and more easily usable set of functions. On their part, application packages tailor the computer to a particular utilization such as accounting, word processing, simulating the birth of galaxies, musical composition or the game of Super Mario.

Base software supports basic functions like storage of files on disk, scheduling of programs and dialogue with the user. To make those functions usable, they define a certain number of general standards that will have to be adhered to by all components of the base software itself and by the application programs. The set of functions in the base software thus structures itself into a system, made consistent by those common standards and by the possibility for each component to use the others. The utilization of a particular system has lasting effects like familiarity with a certain form of dialogue, but also under the concrete form of files preserved in a certain format and conforming to certain conventions. That is the reason why the vast majority of users uses only one system and changes to another only exceptionally, while they can use a multitude of applications, some in a very ephemeral manner.

System software is necessary whatever is the utilization of the computer and can be considered as the common base for all possible applications. Each application program uses a certain number of functions of the base software, and therefore assumes the presence of a certain system on the computer. Each particular software system thus determines what set of applications the computer will be able to execute. Each system creates therefore not only a set of user habits, but also a galaxy of application programs usable with this system. The choice of an operating system is of key importance for the user, because it determines, in a virtually irreversible manner, the range of software packages that he will effectively be able to access, and even the areas of application that he will be able to approach.

For that reason, concerning operating systems, the market demands products rich in functions and capable of being extended in parallel with the evolution of hardware and of new forms of utilization. Those systems must also be reliable, robust and easy to use in a wide range of utilization areas. Indeed, while a possible flaw in an application program has only limited effects, a flaw in a system may have an effect on all users and all applications. Moreover, users demand that those systems be supported by organizations on which they can rely for resolving possible difficulties, constantly developing extensions required to support new equipment and new forms of utilization, and for satisfying requirements for improvement coming from the market. The production of operating systems therefore demands heavy developments, a permanent support activity and guarantees of supplier durability, that reserve it to enterprises with an industrial stature.

Conversely, any author of application software packages must select the operating system(s) to which he will attach his product. This choice too has profound consequences, because it determines not only certain features of the software package and the conditions of its development, and therefore its cost, but also the accessible market. The application package developer is therefore motivated to rely

on the most widespread operating systems for the target customer set (that can incidentally be different depending on application area). The most widespread systems
will also be those that come with the widest choice of application packages, which
gives them an additional competitive advantage.

Specialists tend therefore to rally behind the most popular systems, thus
forming around them constellations of independent firms offering extensions and
complements to the base system, as well as applications using it. The variety and the
quality of those offers constitute a competitive advantage for each firm in the constellation when compared to their equivalents belonging to competing constellations.

In terms of competition between systems, success thus goes to success.
Those who enjoy the strongest competitive advantages occupy a growing share of
the market, and a high market share is in itself a competitive advantage. Even disre-
garding the economics of its production and the scale effects that we have
described in chapter 7 in the case of components, the market itself induces a positive feedback by automatically reinforcing acquired advantages, leading to concentration of the sector on a small number of function-rich systems. As we will see
thereafter, market demand complements and strengthens the industrial dynamics
that also tend to extreme concentration of the operating systems sector.

A similar phenomenon concerns general applications. Before the appearance
of microcomputers, applications were almost always specific to each enterprise and
only operating systems and some utility functions like database management or program development possessed a sufficiently universal character to justify developing
general software packages. Today, application sectors related to general activities
such as document production or calculating with tables have developed, with corresponding word-processing and spreadsheet packages, but also other types of programs for other areas. Each existing software package defines its own utilization
conventions, its file formats, … and calls for complementary developments coming
from innovative independents, that must comply with those standards. Around
those "quasi-systems" formed by basic applications like word processing or spreadsheets, the same dynamics as described above between operating systems and applications organize, and contribute in the same manner to the concentration of each
such sub-sector.

Alongside with the traditional distinction between base software and application software packages, we have just sketched another distinction between "systems" and "extensions" or "add-ons". Systems, which can be found in certain
major application areas as well as in base software, attempt to address the totality of
an area by offering to the user a large array of consistent functions. To that effect,
they define standards concerning data formats, user communications, communications between system components, etc. Add-ons implement a particular function
and most often comply with existing standards concerning the area where their
function is located. Systems imply expensive and high-volume developments, and
therefore a high economic production scale that combines with market demand
into strong sector concentration dynamics. Extensions are more modest develop-

ments in volume and cost, but generally more innovative, and that can therefore better adapt to the fragmented type of competition.

Borderlines between those types of software packages and between areas of applications are fuzzy and permeable. In a sense, applications are extensions of base software. More significantly, borderlines between applications tend to blur. For example, word-processing packages like Word or Wordperfect are incorporating table processing functions that resemble spreadsheets like Excel or Quattro. At the opposite, text processing functions usable within the cells of a spreadsheet are gradually offering possibilities similar to those of word processors. The same is true for drawing functions, graph preparation, etc. Documents capable of being manipulated by such programs become composite documents which can incorporate all forms of information including sounds, photographs and animated images, which requires software able to process all those forms in a coordinated and homogeneous manner.

Packages so far separate, such as word processing, spreadsheets, drawing and presentation programs, database, messaging, ... are therefore merging into "suites" (Office from Microsoft, PerfectOffice from Novell, Smartsuite from Lotus), within which each program can use the services of others, and which include common functional module libraries. Those general modules used by all applications actually take on the status of basic software functions, thus starting a migration of application functions into base software. That same movement concerns extensions to base systems as well as application systems, which systems suppliers are gradually incorporating into their offers. We will see that this phenomenon of continual migration of functions from the periphery of applications towards the core of systems plays an essential role in the structuring of the software package industry.

The development of software packages

Let us examine, in its broad lines, the process of software package development so as to understand its economics and the structuring mechanisms of the sector.

The development of a software package of some importance is by nature a complex endeavor. To have a chance of finding a market, a software package must possess sufficient functional richness and user-friendliness, accommodate multiple combinations of user demands and be able to execute in a large variety of hardware and software environments. In practice, a software package seldom comprises less than several hundred thousands of basic instructions, and frequently several millions. The only way to build such structures in a reliable manner is to decompose them into simpler modules, that will be written and tested separately, then assembled.

In the end, any executable program is made of a sequence of elementary machine instructions. Hardware processors can only carry out simple operations very remote from the application functions offered by software packages, but which are the base for building all conceivable programs. One considers usually that the optimal size of a module, which results in the best tradeoff between its functional power and the possibility to test it efficiently, is in the order of 50 to 100 instruc-

tions, or lines of program[62]. The development of a software package must therefore begin by breaking down the contemplated program into elementary modules at
that level of detail. If that functional decomposition is correct, each module implements a simple well-defined function that can be invoked in any other program by
simply writing a line of code often called a "macro - instruction".

While respecting the empirical size constraint that enables efficient testing,
each module can therefore use the functions of other modules by calling them
through macro-instructions (or any other similar mechanism). In summary, a software package designed according to that model presents itself as a collection of
modules which make use of each other, forming a kind of pyramid whose summit
is the "master module" called by the user, which controls and summarizes all the
others.

A large software package can include thousands, and even tens of thousands
of such modules, that in their turn must be organized into homogeneous functional
sets at different levels, each one implementing a defined part of the overall functions of the package. Seen from the outside, a software package presents itself as a
hierarchical set of subsystems, themselves articulated into major functions formed
by different components, etc.

The overall development cycle for a software package is summarized in the
following diagram. At the beginning, all planned functions and objectives are
described in a specification document. The first phase consists in an analytic program design process, where each function is successively broken down into simpler
sub-functions, and where the operations to be implemented by each of those functional elements are defined precisely, as well as their relationships. If necessary,
those sub-elements are in turn broken down into simpler elements, until each element is small and simple enough to be implemented as an elementary module as
defined above.

In the next phase, each module is written in an appropriate programming language. Base modules, that do not call any other module of the program under
development, can be tested individually to verify that their real behavior is true to
their individual specifications, as they result from the above decomposition process.
When those modules work correctly in isolation, the process of integration can
begin. Integration is in a way the reverse of the decomposition process. Intermediate modules are gradually connected with the lower level modules that they use, and
the correct operations of each such sub-assembly are verified. That gradual process
of building up the system from modules continues until the whole software package has been tested in all its combinations of functions, modes of utilization and
execution environments.

---

62   In reality, a more relevant concept is "complexity" of a module, for which different
      measurements have been proposed. Imposing an upper limit on complexity implies a limit
      on size, so that we will stay with that latter concept.

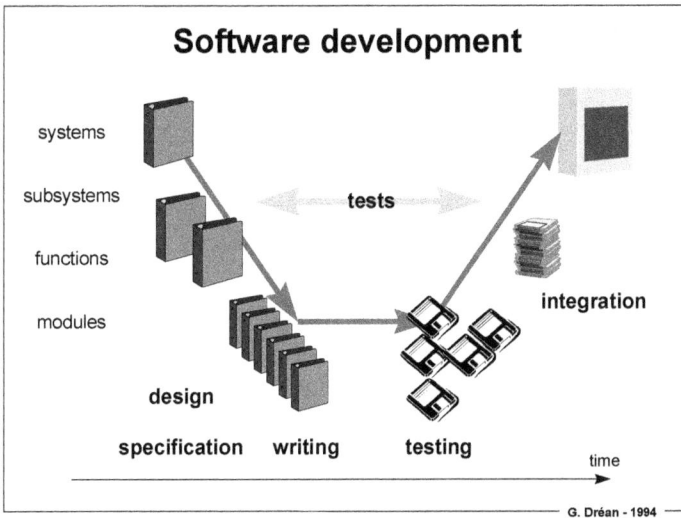

Software development

systems

subsystems   **tests**

functions

modules   **integration**

design

specification   writing   testing

time

G. Dréan - 1994

In the course of this integration process, a very large number of errors usually appear[63]. Those errors can be confined to the last modules being tested, in which case their correction has only local effects on the test level under way, but they can also be located in lower level modules which have already been tested and integrated. In that case, it will be necessary to resume testing upstream after correcting the defective modules, in order to verify that what worked correctly so far still works after the modifications (so-called "regression" testing). That requires re-executing series of tests already carried out earlier. Indeed, in the current state of programming technology, the only way to verify that a program is correct is to execute it. As long as a test run reveals at least one error and causes at least one correction, the program will have to be verified again by resuming the same test, until the test run no longer reveals any error. That, however, still does not guarantee that subsequent testing will not reveal remaining errors in those same modules.

That stage is completed when the program correctly executes the whole test library on all machine configurations available for that phase. But for a complex program, the mere fact that it has been correctly executed in its entirety in a reasonable range of utilization cases and configurations does not guarantee in any way that it will execute correctly in all foreseeable cases and configurations. There again, the only way to ensure program correctness is to proceed with real tests of sufficiently long duration, preferably conducted by representative users in real operational situations. That stage can only start after the first stage of system tests has been passed successfully, to insure that functionality and user-friendliness is sufficient to place the program into so many hands. Often designated by the term "*beta -*

---

63   Some experimental studies indicate that the number of programming errors introduced during the writing of a program, and present in the code when testing begins, can commonly be as high as 2 errors per 10 lines. For a program of 100000 lines, 20000 errors, fortunately of unequal severity, will need to be discovered and corrected.

test", it can involve thousands of users for major software packages (over 400000 for Windows 95). Trying all possible combinations is not feasible, and trying many configurations costs time and money, even when the result is positive and calls for no correction.

Without going into detailed estimates, which are the subject of a whole literature, we can use that model to see how development cost and duration may vary depending on the system, and therefore characterize the investment level and cycle duration that govern the enterprise personality of firms in the sector.

The time required for the design phase is largely unpredictable. It is obviously a function of the size and complexity of the project, but also of the methods and conventions adopted for the entire development, which define the conditions for proceeding from the analysis and design phase to the writing phase. One observes that any imperfection at the design stage entails additional integration costs far exceeding the cost of the additional design time that might have allowed to avoid it. That is the reason why most development methods tend to extend the design phase in the hope of limiting integration efforts. That first phase remains nevertheless the most difficult to estimate, all the more so that parameters such as the size of the program, the number of modules, … are not yet known with precision at this stage.

A well-conducted analysis and design phase normally ends with a fairly reliable estimate of the number of modules, of the size and the complexity of each of them, of their combinations and of the complexity of their interactions. The writing time can then be estimated with some precision. It is roughly proportional to the number of modules and to the complexity of each, assuming that modules are by definition of a similar size in number of instructions.

Like analysis time, the time required for integration and testing can hardly be estimated with any accuracy. It increases obviously with the size of the system, but it depends more precisely on the number and complexity of the possible interactions between modules. One admits generally that, all other things being equal, integration time varies like a certain power of the number of modules, the exponent of that power being somewhere between 1.5 and 2. In other words, when the number of modules of a system doubles, the time required to test it is multiplied by a factor between 3 and 4. On another scale, it takes several thousand times more time and effort to integrate and test a system of 10000 modules than a system of 100 modules! When a system reaches a certain degree of complexity, its integration time becomes much higher than the analysis and writing time, and the total time increases roughly as the square of the volume. That explains why programming productivity decreases rapidly when the scale of the project increases.

In addition, it is necessary to take into account parameters external to the system itself: the diversity of utilization conditions, the variety of target hardware and software configurations, the reliability and usability objectives, etc. In the few weeks following its availability, a new version of Windows will be installed on several million computers representing thousands of different configurations and involving thousands of independent suppliers. To be reasonably able to hope that only a few odd users will encounter difficulties obviously requires a "*beta-test*" program involving thousands of users during several months. Such "beta-testing" would not be needed if all microcomputers were configured in the same manner, supplied by a single vendor and used for the same applications following the same procedures.

In order for the total development effort to be contained within a reasonable duration, it is necessary to be able to distribute the work between several teams functioning in parallel. During the initial phase, it becomes gradually possible to conduct the analysis of several subsets in parallel, as soon as the preceding analysis has enabled to isolate those subsets and to specify them with reasonable certainty. One objective of that first phase is therefore to enable distributing the rest of the work as soon as possible between autonomous teams. In the ideal case, one thus gradually puts in place an organization that parallels the internal structure of the system under development. In reality, the organization often exists before the design of the new system, and that organization might dictate to the system a structure which is not necessarily optimal.

The highest degree of parallelism is reached in the writing phase, which contributes to limiting its duration. On the other hand, integration obviously lends itself less and less well to parallel work as the system is being reconstructed from its parts. The process of system integration simultaneously involves a process of re-integration of the organization, in a direction opposite to that which resulted from the analysis phase. Each successive level of subsets can be integrated under the responsibility of the same organization that performed the analysis of that subset, up to the highest level of the organization, where the first level of decomposition of the global system was originally defined. However, for each error found, it is necessary to search for its causes by going back to the modules that must be corrected, and to resume the integration process at the earlier stage where those modified modules were individually tested.

The very nature of the integration process makes it extremely difficult to predict the time required to reach a given degree of reliability. At the very most, one can say that the probability of detecting an existing error increases with the duration of tests, and that the probability of the existence of residual errors is all the more low that the system has functioned without incident for a longer time in a larger variety of configurations.

In practice, one addresses the issue in the opposite way, by deciding in advance on a reasonable test duration, consistent with the timetable imposed by market or competitive reasons, which can exceed one year for complex operating systems,. To meet that timetable, errors that are discovered too late in the cycle are simply flagged for correction in subsequent versions. Similarly, for some instances of non-critical problems, it will be preferable not to delay the integration process, and to postpone the correction while accepting a temporary limitation that will be indicated in the documentation.

In total, the development cycle of a program cannot reasonably exceed two or three years, and there is therefore an upper limit for the size of systems which can reasonably be tested in a single integration cycle. Particularly ambitious developments will necessarily have to be implemented in several successive versions, so that each one can be validated by intensive usage in real environments before attempting to integrate new modifications and extensions.

For those new versions, it will be necessary not only to define new modules corresponding to extensions, but also to modify existing modules. However, although the effort required for the design and writing phases depends only on the importance of modifications, the entire system will have to be integrated and tested once again to take into account those modifications of the base. One sees that although this cumulative development process renders possible, extremely complex constructions over a sufficient period, the need to test the complete system again for each version imposes new limitations on the size and complexity of software packages thus created. Moreover, there is a practical limit to what is made possible by the accumulation of modifications, and the system will therefore have to be peri-odically subjected to a major redesign and redevelopment from the ground up.

In summary, for complex systems, the testing and integration phase con-sumes the bulk of development resources and determines the total duration of the development cycle. More generally, the constraints of that third phase govern the whole process. One also sees that the production of very general software pack-ages, that is to say those which offer a large variety of functions able to operate in diversified modes of utilization on all possible configurations, demands industrial methods and therefore industrial organizations. Indeed, only industrial enterprises can invest the personnel and hardware resources necessary to efficiently manage complex projects involving the coordinated work of many teams in parallel and adherence to a strict discipline, while facing essentially unpredictable situations that call for permanent tradeoffs whose economic consequences can ominous.

Economics of production and sector structure

Variable cost, market shares and prices

We have seen that ease of reproduction is an intrinsic feature of software. Creating a new copy from an existing program is quick, unexpensive and does not require specialized equipment, since the equipment that enables to use the program also enables to reproduce it. It is as though each car was able to freely reproduce its engine, or if cameras could produce unexposed films.

For an individual, reproducing even a complex software package such as Windows costs only a few minutes and the price of a few diskettes. The profes-sional distributor who wants to produce many copies can invest in specialized equipment that will further reduce variable cost, to the point that most of the unit cost will be due to the documentation rather than to the program itself. To give an idea, one can estimate that the variable manufacturing cost of a package including 8 diskettes (over 12 million bytes) and 1500 pages of documentation is in the order of 15$. That figure must be compared to a probable development cost in the order of 10 or 20 million dollars. The ratio of fixed costs to variable cost, which as we have seen determines the economical production scale and governs the degree of con-centration of the sector, amounts therefore to millions.

Variable reproduction cost is roughly proportional to the size of the software package and of the documentation that comes with it, with a threshold effect for the program itself corresponding to the capacity of a diskette (currently 1,4 million bytes). But we have seen previously that fixed development costs increase more rapidly than the size of the program because of test and integration expenses, where productivity declines quickly when size increases. It results that the economical production scale is all the more high that the software package is bigger and more complex. A simple program can make a profit with a few thousand copies sold, while a complex system will need a distribution of several millions.

Although that relationship between fixed costs and variable cost translates into a lower ratio than that which we have estimated for components (counted in tens of millions), it confers to each competitive field defined by the functions of a given package all the attributes and dynamics of a concentrated sector, as described in Chapter 7. Variable unit reproduction costs are small relative to the fixed cost of the prototype, and therefore the average unit cost decreases strongly with volume.

Since the same causes produce the same effects, the production of software packages is an industry with monopolistic trends, much like hardware components. In each of the sub-sectors that compose it, we will find a small number of suppliers with very unequal market shares, roughly distributed on a logarithmic scale. For example, in the typical case of operating systems for PC microcomputers, the MS-DOS/Windows complex from Microsoft occupies over 80% of the market, IBM a bit more than 10% with OS/2, the different suppliers of Unix systems sharing the rest.

Let us repeat here that this inequality is neither fortuitous nor the result of unfair dominance maneuvers, but is an intrinsic feature of concentrated structures. In other words, the action of competition between firms determines which one will obtain 70% of the market or more, which one will be around 15%, and which ones will survive by sharing the scraps. But it can neither allow a large number of firms to subsist, nor tolerate an even distribution of market shares. For one firm to occupy 80% of the operating systems market is an inescapable consequence of competitive dynamics. It so happens that Microsoft has won the first prize. History might have awarded that prize to IBM or Digital Research or someone else; it could not have made five, ten or fifty suppliers share the market equally.

Concerning prices, they will settle as for electronic components, at a level low enough for the price sensitivity of the market to be virtually zero. This implies in particular that the choice of the market will be based primarily on other attributes of the product[64]. Selling prices for operating systems are now under 200$, less than one tenth of the price of the computer that they operate. At that level, differences in the prices of competing systems have only a small impact on customer choices compared with the other features of the product. Furthermore, as in the case of components, prices are much lower than the best interest of a monopolist would dictate according to classical economic theory. Indeed, doubling (for example) the price of a software package would only increase the total price of the system by 10% and would not appreciably reduce the total number of units sold, thus translating into higher revenue and profits for suppliers of software packages.

---

64   see chapter 8

The originality of the sector

Although the software package sector presents similarities with the sector of components, it also distinguishes itself by a certain number of features.

First, as we have seen, software packages do not constitute a single sector where all suppliers would be competing with each other. There are a multitude of independent market segments that form as many competitive arenas where the different suppliers elect to be present or not. Sectors thus constituted can have features sufficiently different for the modes of competition to be different, as well as the enterprise personalities adapted to each of those sectors. On the other hand, the borderlines between those elementary sectors are fuzzy and mobile. The structure of the software package industry is therefore more complex and more unstable than that of components.

We have seen earlier that software development investments are located in a lower and relatively wider range. While the stakes for components range from a few hundred million dollars to a few billions, a ratio of about 10, they seldom exceed a few tens of millions and can be as low as some tens of thousands of dollars for software packages, a ratio of one thousand. The economical production scale, which is in the order of ten millions for components, can range from a few thousands to millions for software packages, depending on the extent of the development. The concentrated character of the sector may therefore be more or less pronounced depending on the application area.

Secondly, investments only involve the development phase and are formed essentially by human work. Packaged software requires only relatively modest hardware investments and no heavy manufacturing investments. A motivated team willing to invest a lot of personal time can thus undertake the development of a software package without having to find significant capital at the outset. Obstacles to entry can easily be overcome or ignored for innovative developments or developments of moderate size. Even for more important projects, it remains possible for foolhardy characters to underestimate the real industrial problems as well as deterring prices and to embark nevertheless into the adventure. Some might even succeed.

Furthermore, development technologies and software distribution technologies do not quite know the same overwhelming pace of evolution as components. All other things being equal, the economical production scale of software remains therefore rather stable. Since the market is growing, in particular for innovative application areas, the ratio of market size to economical production scale is probably increasing in many areas, making room consequently for an increasing number of firms. The concentration process, which for components inescapably entails elimination of the competitive laggards, is related here only to the local maturation of each sub-sector and has no reason to continue when it has resulted in market shares and prices acceptable by all suppliers.

Moreover, the invasion of all human activities by computing results in the continuous emergence of new application areas, and therefore of new competitive sectors for software packages. The number of sub-sectors can thus remain indefi-

nitely increasing. Each of those sub-sectors can correspond to different development requirements and therefore to different economic scales and concentration
levels. At any point in time, sub-sectors are in different stages of evolution in their
concentration process. In particular, the most recent ones have not reached the
asymmetrical concentration state yet. Since in addition some areas can be dominated by a firm specialized in that one area only, and therefore relatively small, the
software package industry considered as a whole can have the appearance of a fragmented sector if one lumps together its many diverse areas.

The long term technological evolution also takes a different form. For microprocessors, we have seen that exploiting the technological potential demands
designing a new chip and building new production lines for each generation, making the preceding chips totally obsolete. On the contrary, the plasticity of software
and the relative stability of its development technologies enable software packages
to evolve in a cumulative manner by successive versions. As for components, a challenger must seek his competitive advantage in the qualities of the product, which
motivates all contestants to develop new versions incorporating new added functions and improvements to existing functions, required both by the leader to maintain his dominance and by the challengers to dethrone him. Existing systems can
always be improved upon, new ideas can appear even for areas already explored,
and new unsatisfied market needs are created permanently which feed those successive versions.

Finally, while microprocessors are sold by their producers only to hardware
assembly enterprises for incorporation into their machines, many software packages
are marketed directly to users. The proportion of direct sale to users versus indirect
sales through hardware firms varies depending on the nature of the software package. The great majority of initial sales of operating systems is made through equipment vendors who install the operating system of their choice on their machines.
The user can also order a standalone machine and select an operating system, but
most of the time he accepts the pre-installed system and will only obtain directly
the new versions of that system. At the opposite, the most specific application
packages are always acquired directly by their users.

Those distinctions are important in terms of modes of competition and price
sensitivity of the market. The operating systems sector works like that of components: total size of the market is feebly sensitive to prices, competition for market
shares takes on the same modes and leads to the same asymmetrical structures. The
same is true for widespread and complex application programs such as word processing or spreadsheets, that are also used on virtually all machines and increasingly
often pre-installed by hardware vendors, like operating systems.

On the other hand, for less universally used applications, the software packages market is only a fraction of the installed computer inventory, all the more low
than the application is more confidential. The total sales volumes are now sensitive
to prices, and no longer only the distribution between suppliers of an essentially
fixed total volume. That sensitivity increases when the application concerned is of
potential interest for a large number of users.

The pricing of software packages

The prices used for software packages provide a good illustration of the result of the classical mechanisms of price formation in a monopolistic sector, where variable unit costs are very low relative to fixed costs, development costs in this case.

First, prices are almost independent of the functional content of the product and therefore of its costs. The general price scale is structured into a few main families related more directly to the size of the target market and to its price sensitivity. Simple utilities, and all games whatever their complexity, are priced under 100$; base systems (DOS, Windows, OS/2) and more complex utilities cost between 100 and 300$, application systems and tools (word processors, spreadsheets, graphics, …) between 400 and 1200$. Only a few exceptional tools such as compilers for languages seldom used on microcomputers reach the 2000$ to 4000$ zone. However, it is quite clear that Windows 95 at 100$, or a Visual C++ compiler sold for 300$ are more complex and more expensive to develop than a Fortran compiler selling for 4000$.

The supplier of a new software package must choose its price from those standard price ranges that have formed on the market. In a way, selling prices exist before the package does, and are independent of its development costs. Price being essentially a given, the problem for each potential or current supplier is to manage costs and volumes so as to produce a profit if possible.

At the marketing stage, the cost of the product, which practically includes only development costs, has become irreversible and can no longer be modified by any action whatsoever. Any incremental revenue, however small, is therefore profit and is worth going after. For that purpose, the classical technique attributed to monopolies by the economic theory is called differentiated pricing or segment pricing. That approach consists in selling the same product at different prices in different market segments, provided that it is possible to identify segments isolated enough from each other to prevent the lowest price from being used everywhere. In the case of software packages, such separation is facilitated by the fact that software packages are not legally transferable between users, which eliminates in theory all possibilities of tradeoff between segments.

That is the reason why the price of the same software package varies depending on the customer, conditions, place, time, etc. For example, operating systems are sold to hardware manufacturers for pre-installation in their systems at a much lower price than the price used for direct sales to users. Those prices can be all the more low that reproduction costs are incurred by the hardware vendors rather than by the producer of the software package. For example, a microcomputer manufacturer pays Microsoft less than 35$ per copy of Windows, although the price of Windows is approximately 100$ when sold separately. Upon delivery, the contribution of the software package to the total price of the system remains notably lower than the price of the isolated software package. The objective of the package supplier is obviously to create a captive market for subsequent versions. A somewhat similar case is that of "site licenses" and all their custom variants, which authorize a large user to use a package on several machines without having to pay a corresponding multiple of the unit price, in exchange for supporting reproduction cost and possibly part of technical support costs.

The pricing of successive versions is another form of differentiated pricing, since each new version of a system includes a large number of unmodified modules from the preceding one, which are thus sold several times to the same customers. System upgrades sell for less than the price of the standalone system, even though they contain most often the complete system and not its modified parts only. Moreover, they also include additional code to verify that the previous version is indeed present on the machine at the time of installation, which is a way to isolate upgrade customers from new users. As a consequence, the upgrade package actually costs more than the system sold to new users, although it is sold for less. That is a case of "functional pricing" reminiscent of the early days of data processing[65]. A variation of this approach is to offer a reduced price to users migrating from competitive products.

For the big software packages, the struggle for market shares involves primarily agreements with hardware vendors to install the package on their machines, reduced prices for users of competitive products or promotional prices for the first purchase of a new software package. When the customer's choice has thus been determined, the new features of each version and the cost of converting to a competitive package contribute to user acceptance of the additional payments for successive releases. After many years of usage, those upgrades add up to a cost far exceeding the acquisition price of the current version of the package at that point in time.

Other forms of differentiated pricing are used for software packages for large computers. Those forms consist most often of taking advantage of the hybrid status of software to charge it as a service rather than as a product. For example, certain programs are charged in proportion with their usage or according to the power of the processor on which are executed. Others call for periodic payments similar to rentals, covering maintenance and follow-up versions in addition to usage. All such billing systems enable the supplier to register more revenue than he would through a plain one-time license. Whatever are the efforts of those suppliers, it is unlikely that those practices be someday extended to software packages for microcomputers. It is far more likely that they will gradually disappear from the world of large systems, as software vendors from the micro world invade the large systems market and disseminate their usual practices.

Note finally that the extreme ease of reproduction of software packages using a large variety of media makes it possible to copy and distribute them illegally, a practice that contractual dispositions can only partially prevent. The possibility of software "piracy" contributes to imposing an upper limit on market prices. Users will be all the more tempted to obtain a free unlawful copy that the price of the package is high, that the package is widespread and therefore easily accessible, and that they live in a permissive environment. Piracy introduces another form of price

---

65   See chapter 1

sensitivity in the market, which involves the proportion of copies invoiced among copies used, rather than the number of copies distributed.

Overall dynamics

In summary, the software package industry appears as a sector radically distinct from services (to which it is too often assimilated), made of a complex of sectors, each defined by one application where several firms offer substitutable competitive products addressing the same need. All those sectors obey the same competitive logic, consistent with the cost structure that characterizes the production of software packages, and which relates those sectors to the concentrated type, but in varying degrees of concentration.

Let us follow the evolution cycle of such a sector, considered in isolation. When the relevant application area is still unoccupied, it is easy to penetrate with relatively modest developments that will often suffice to satisfy a latent need, since the very nature of the investment includes only a small material or financial part. It is likely therefore that several suppliers will appear and begin competing for market share. This will initiate the classical process of price decrease towards standard prices and formation of a stable asymmetrical oligopoly formed of a few suppliers, one of which will be strongly dominant. At the end of that process, the respective positions will be locked by deterring prices largely independent of the content of the package.

We have seen that the concentration forces are all the more vigorous that the package is bigger and more complex. Sectors corresponding to intrinsically simple applications will therefore be able to preserve a more egalitarian and more fragmented structure for a longer period. Most often, market demands and competitive forces will cause the package to evolve naturally towards increasing functional content and growing complexity, and thus accelerate the process of concentration.

Entry into an emerging application sector can also be attempted by firms already established in other sectors. Those firms will most often adopt for the new sector a kind of preemptive strategy, by introducing from the very start high-function products at the standard rates of the market, thus discouraging the entry of small specialized firms. In that case, competition can only involve suppliers of that same type and will immediately take the form characteristic of concentrated sectors.

The same price formation logic that we have seen at work in the case of electronic components (see Chapter 7) eventually sets the market price at the level of the survival price of the smallest supplier. For software packages, where standard market prices exist, it is more accurate to say that the only suppliers to survive are those whose survival price is lower than the market price, which demands a minimal sales volume. Respective profit levels range from the neighborhood of zero for marginal suppliers to unusually high values for leaders. This phenomenon explains the large dispersion of profit levels that we have observed in Chapter 5.

Players in packaged software

The diversity of sub-sectors that compose the software packages sector implies a large diversity of players. Although all practice the same trade, in the sense that we have defined in Chapter 6, areas of application are many and in different stages of maturity. Moreover, we have seen that the demands of the integration process reserve large complex systems for important enterprises, which are the only ones capable of playing the role of professional integrator necessary for the industrial success of a system. A dichotomy thus appears between the suppliers of major systems and the secondary specialized suppliers.

The activity of software package supplier

The success of a software package depends not only on its functional content, but also and maybe even more on its ease of use, user-friendliness and reliability, and its capabilities of customization, extension, evolution and connection with other programs. The development skills required belong to three main areas and often require close cooperation between the three corresponding types of specialists. First a good knowledge of target users, of their needs, working habits, preferences, etc. Second, good specialist knowledge in the specific application technologies, to define the appropriate processing techniques. Finally, general computing skills in the implementation techniques for industrial-level software packages.

Depending on the nature of the package, those skills are required in variable proportions. If the planned functions are of a purely data-processing or sufficiently general nature, like operating systems or word processing, the application skills merge with general computing skills. For specific applications such as accounting, statistics, aerodynamics or portfolio management, a specific knowledge of application techniques is necessary. As long as the program remains reasonably simple, the application knowledge dominates, and relatively common computer skills can bring success to firms not specialized in data-processing but expert in the application area. An example is that musical software, where firms like Roland or Yamaha are actively present.

If on the other hand one moves away from simple applications towards large application systems intended for a diversified user population, knowledge of the application must be supplemented by a high expertise in the software development process, which non-data-processing enterprises only rarely enjoy, and of which they tend to underestimate the need. This is why one can no longer keep count of the failures of enterprises that have attempted to market a software package in their specialty area, without taking care to assign its development to a dedicated organization with sufficient computer skills.

As a whole, the activity of software package production is ruled by long cycles and competition of the concentrated type. The corresponding features, that we have described in Chapter 9, are all the more marked that one moves from the production of relatively simple software components or applications to complex systems. For a simple program, the development cycle can be measured in months, while it goes up to several years for the large integrated systems, as is the case for microprocessors.

As for all products, the two activities of developing and distributing a given software package are separate in time, and are assigned to two separate branches of the organization. For the development arm, the key problem is to put on the market, at the right time, products that correspond to a demand and which will be winning competitors against the still unknown products of competition. For the marketing arm, the key problem is to obtain maximum revenue from the existing products, so that the company can cover its ongoing expenses and finance the development of the next products, and show a profit if possible. That demands a strong marketing organization, combining if necessary direct sales with a network of distributors, and operating efficiently on a large territory.

Commercial activity can easily be measured. Like the distribution of standard products, it can be organized and managed according to methods adapted to short cycles. For development on the contrary, success on the market cannot be measured in the short term during the course of the activity. The only part that can be formalized is cost and schedule control, not adequacy of the product to market demand. On that latter point, the decisions of the enterprise rely exclusively on the confidence that it grants to its developers, based primarily on their past achievements. Such trust is all the more natural that executives personally participate in product design and development decisions, and remain familiar with the products of the firm and of the market.

In a software package enterprise, the basic role of the leader is therefore to make sure that products under development will indeed satisfy the future demands of the market, and in a better way than possible competitive products. That role can only be played successfully by an expert in data-processing, probably experienced in the utilization and development of software packages, who must in addition to be competent in the management of the enterprise.

Now it is more common for a data-processing professional to master management that for an administrator to become competent in software. This is why, behind most successes in software packages, one finds a particularly perceptive developer who has been capable of creating and managing his company. But the very success of his products can cause this person to be overwhelmed by administrative problems. If he is then replaced by an administrator ignorant in the technical area, one must fear that the new executive management will divorce from the development teams and thus put the whole enterprise in jeopardy. It follows that the efficient size of a software package enterprise is limited to what a data-processing professional is capable of managing without losing contact with the technical issues. That maximum size depends on the personal qualities of the manager, and big success stories are due to exceptional individuals. Successful software package firms are necessarily linked to exceptional personalities.

Those features contribute to explaining why all firms that succeed in software packages are specialized firms of a relatively small size. IBM, who pioneered software packages in the sixties for its own large systems, has never proved capable of becoming a major player in the applications area, nor of competing seriously against Microsoft in microcomputer operating systems. One can also consider that the size of Microsoft makes it an exception to the above rule, but it is likely that this situation is directly related to the personality of Bill Gates, which is also an exceptional one.

Major players

Systems suppliers are interested in attracting the largest possible number of supporters, be they application developers or hardware manufacturers who will pre-install the system on their equipment. They will therefore seek to design their products in such a way that they are open to extensions offered by others, and to facilitate the development of such extensions with information and support programs for the other firms. That form of competition, through the seduction of secondary suppliers, can translate into more or less formal forms of association with those suppliers, in particular by the formation of consortia aiming at the definition of common standards or at joint marketing actions.

Competition between the large integrators pushes them to constantly extend their products by offering successive versions. Extensions or improvements offered by secondary suppliers constitute a permanent reservoir of functions which might be candidates for integration into future versions of the system. The major system vendor can either rewrite those functions in a form competing with the secondary supplier, or acquire them from one of these suppliers. In the long term, one thus sees a migration of functions, which begin as independent minor extensions, then merge into standalone subsystems to finish their course inside large integrated systems.

To benefit from this movement, large systems integrators may acquire relevant software from secondary firms, and often acquire the firm itself to take advantage of its skills and customer base. The migration of functions comes with a continuous process of absorption of small enterprises by large industrial firms, compensated by the permanent appearance of new players in new peripheral areas.

Secondary players

The large systems in place are the result of accumulated investments amounting to tens of millions of dollars, while their market prices are most often established around 200$ or less. A potential candidate to entry should therefore first invest up to that same level during years, then sell tens of thousands of copies of his new system to simply cover his development costs. Therefore, there will probably never be any more new entrants in the operating systems sector, or into text-processing systems or spreadsheets for the same reason.

On the other hand, the infinite variety of applications and the constant emergence of new areas create permanent opportunities of entry into particular niches. Those opportunities can be seized by firms already in place, but also by new firms, most often launched by a developer starting from a personal idea, and financed by his personal effort or some risk capital. But even if barriers to entry are apparently low, and therefore temptation is strong, a new entrepreneur can succeed only if he arrives very early on the market with a perfectly adapted product, supported by an important and efficient marketing effort.

Many of those small firms will disappear if the idea that has given them birth is wrong or not original, less well implemented or less well sold than competitive products, or overtaken by a major supplier in the meantime. Others will survive in the parallel world of *"shareware"* where payment of a royalty is left to the appreciation of the user, and where packages are publicized through a variety of channels such as press advertisements or more recently CD-ROM's inserted in specialized magazines, or on the Internet computer network.

Among the firms that succeed, some will offer products original enough and of a quality good enough to be of interest for major suppliers, that will then seek to acquire the product or the firm. For those small enterprises, disappearance can be the reward of success and the objective of their creator, who can then retire or resume the same adventure all over again with another idea.

Summary and perspectives

In summary, by analyzing the software package sector with the help of tools that we have built in part two of this book, we discover a complex and diversified macro-sector, formed in reality of distinct sub-sectors according to the functions of software packages. Factors that determine the form of the competitive game and the resulting sector structure vary from sector to sector depending on the size and complexity of the products of each sector. Borderlines between sectors are fuzzy and permeable, and the whole macro-sector is crossed by continual movements.

At one end, the size and complexity of the large systems impose a high economic production scale that makes the concentrating factors of the sector predominant. The dynamics of the large systems vendors are similar to those of component manufacturers and let only survive a very small number of firms and systems, which share the market in a very unequal manner. We will examine the features and the consequences of this situation in more detail in the following chapter.

At the other end, for developments of a limited extent in new areas, the low level of obstacles to entry dominates and enables a blossoming of innovation and innovators. New areas of computer utilization appear constantly, and go through an initial phase where the structure of the corresponding sub-sector is fragmented and enables open competition between alternative solutions. This phase can give a chance to very diverse players and make room, for small enterprises, research laboratories or exceptional individuals, alongside larger established firms.

Those two worlds live in symbiosis. On one hand innovators and secondary suppliers form constellations of alliances around the market standards constituted by major systems. On the other hand the large manufacturers constantly seek to enrich their offer by incorporating new functions developed by innovators, which can imply acquisition of packages or enterprises.

The dynamism of the sector has two competitive engines. The first one is, as for components, the rivalry between the leader and his challengers within each sub-sector. The second one is the continuous widening of the field of computing, and the attending constant emergence of new application areas and therefore of virgin sectors where every new entrant can hope to have a chance of becoming a leader, provided that he is the first to offer a good solution.

Contrary to hardware, the potential evolution of software is not limited by specific independent physical limitations. The size of programs is limited only by the available storage capacities, and program execution speed is that of micropro-cessors. Progress of components makes progress of software possible, at the same time that the growing diversity of equipment, applications and users calls for the development of new software. The only specific constraint is related to develop-ment techniques and in particular software integration, whose current state makes it practically impossible to produce systems exceeding a certain level of complexity. It is in that area that we must expect the most significant progress, and to a lesser degree in areas such as data representation and processing methods, which largely condition program performance and the design of man-machine relationships. We will address those questions in the following chapter, specifically devoted to operat-ing systems.

Chapter 12 - Operating systems and standardization

Functions and structure of operating systems. What is an open system? Standards, innovation and competition. Experimental systems and industrial systems. What purpose does UNIX serve? Objects and kernels in perspective. The border between hardware and software. Perspectives.

Among products "made of software" (software packages), operating systems occupy a central position. Their functions make them a mandatory intermediary between users, applications and hardware. Users access applications and hardware through functions of the system. Symmetrically, hardware functions make themselves available to users by responding to calls from the operating system, and applications become usable by attaching themselves to the system. The operating system incorporates therefore a set of conventions that make it the main image of the computing system for each one of its users and contributors.

That intermediate situation between users, applications and hardware makes operating systems the place of standardization efforts *par excellence*, and the arena where the battle of standards is fought. We will therefore devote part of this chapter to an analysis of the competitive and economic phenomena associated with standardization.

Within the macro-sector of packaged software, operating systems cover a field wide enough to include separate sub-sectors, taking all the structural forms that we have described in the preceding chapter. At one extreme, suppliers of integrated systems of industrial quality form a strongly concentrated sector whose dynamics are similar to those of microprocessors. Smaller innovators, forming a complex of sub-sectors of the fragmented type, operate at the other end. The particular area of operating systems thus allows to take a closer look at the general structuring mechanisms of the packaged software industry.

Concerning the mid-term and long-term evolution, operating systems also play a central role. Software being the preferred material of innovation because of its plasticity, many developments concerning the future of computing are first implemented in operating systems, or at least on their fringes. Moreover, we have seen that the very dynamics of the packaged software macro-sector make the operating system the analogue of a "black hole" around which all developments gravitate and towards which they eventually converge. Finally, any evolution in hardware, applications or modes of utilization translates into an evolution of operating systems, which transmits the impact of the original development to the other areas.

Functions and structure of operating systems

To fully understand the importance of operating systems in data-processing and their evolutionary perspectives, we must examine more precisely their functions and their structure, and define some frequently used terms.

Relationship with hardware

The first role of operating systems is to carry out the relationship between the other programs and the hardware. The physical units of the computer can execute a repertoire of elementary operations, each one being activated by an elementary instruction. Many functions frequently executed in programs require execution of a more or less complex sequence of elementary instructions. Rewriting those sequences in every module where they are needed would be tedious and would in addition be a source of errors. Those functional sequences are therefore coded once and for all and made available to programmers as standard library subroutines.

In that way, a programmer can call a synthetic function like "save an area of memory to disk" by specifying only the memory area involved. The standard subroutine will measure the size of the area, locate a free site of sufficient size on disk, position the write mechanism, copy the content of the designated memory area, verify the accuracy of the copy by reading it back and comparing with the original, erase and restart the whole process using another area of the disk in case of error, and finally report to the calling program that the operation has been correctly completed, keeping track of the disk location where the information has been copied.

The operating system thus complements the elementary hardware functions with more synthetic functions closer to the thought mode of programmers and users. That mediation allows in particular to define different forms of utilization for the same physical unit, for example different file organizations on disk. Conversely, it is possible to define functions that can execute indifferently on different physical units. For example, a printing subroutine may write to a temporary disk file if the printer is not available. Such a function must be complemented by a function that constantly supervises the state of the printer, and automatically reads back and prints the file when the printer is made available.

One sees on this example that the operating system has another basic function, that of maintaining tables representing an image of the machine and of the state of its different components, and automatically reacting in an appropriate manner to changes of state. Those functions generally use an interrupt system whereby each unit of the computer can interrupt processing in order to signal an event. That internal representation of the computer, elaborated by the operating system, is used by all programs.

That approach is used in particular to manage interactions with users in systems that allow direct dialogue with the computer. User actions, that he can conduct independently of the progress of the program under way, are reflected in tables describing the state of the computer, and can be signaled to the program. Conversely, presentation of the work under way is implemented by subroutines that convert the functional commands of the program into sets of colored points displayed on the screen. Those input and output functions define the form and style of the dialogue between the machine and its users.

In summary, by creating a synthetic image of the computer and by offering a repertoire of high level functions, the operating system defines for the programmers and users an abstract or "virtual" machine, designed both to simplify the tasks of users and to isolate in a specific part of software the impact of the variety and evolution of hardware. Evolution of the periphery can thus be dissociated from evolution of the central system. Modifying the composition, the functions and the instruction repertoire of the hardware can leave the rest of the system unchanged inasmuch as the hardware-dependent software layer can easily be modified.

Program execution control

A second role of operating systems is to schedule and supervise the tasks assigned to the computer. When computers could only execute one task at a time and when their time was expensive, it was necessary to minimize the time required for moving from one job to the next, during which the computer was idle and unproductive. One of the first functions of systems was therefore to automate operations by automatically preparing and scheduling successive jobs, assembled beforehand out of the computer room. To that effect, the system had to manage the installation of removable media such as magnetic tapes or printing paper, load programs to memory and launch them, and also to be capable of automatically handling possible incidents during execution.

For the developer or the user of a program, the machine no longer appears as a simple collection of physical units that appear "bare" to each application, but as an organized set *a priori* endowed with global functions, and containing many permanent elements such as general program libraries and private files. The operating system must manage those elements, give each user access to those elements that concern him and to them alone, and protect them from involuntary or voluntary actions of the other users. Those functions extend to the management of users and of their authorizations, to usage accounting, etc.

With multiprogramming, where several programs can reside simultaneously in memory and share machine resources, the operating system receives in addition the responsibility for allocating dynamically each of those resources to the programs, while protecting them from interference by the other programs. One thus sees appearing in operating systems a whole group of functions that are by nature external to applications, and no longer by convenience like those presented in the preceding section.

Assistance to users

Every program to be executed on a computer, whether it concerns applications or utility functions, must insert itself into a predefined structure formed by the operating system. All programs somehow execute as subroutines of the operating system. They must comply with a certain number of conventions specific to the system and can use a library of subroutines that embody those conventions. For the programmer, the system presents itself as a collection of functions that he can

implement through calling conventions usually called API's for *"Application Program-*
ming Interface".

Those API's include instructions that give access to all system functions
usable for application development, organized in major families according to the
area addressed: memory management, printer management, file management, communication between programs, communications with the user, etc. Those instructions form a language with its syntax and semantics, which constitutes a natural way
to represent general functions, even when they do not belong to the classical functions of an operating system in the strict sense. That language is produced and
manipulated by the different development support programs such as translators of
high level languages (Cobol, Fortran, Pascal, C, etc.).

From the user's viewpoint, the API's define the environment of his relationship with the entire system. Indeed, all applications that use the standard API for
user dialog will implement the same constructions and conventions for presentation
(windows, dialog boxes, menus, ...) and will respond in the same way to user
actions such as mouse click, selecting an area on the screen, etc. Moreover, the
operating system directly provides to the user general functions like file management, configuration management, a variety of information transfers, usage of the
system clock, etc.

Variety and structure

Although they are broadly consistent with the preceding description, existing
operating systems are different depending on their origin. All the generalist manufacturers have developed operating systems for their own hardware, and often several systems for different families of hardware and types of utilization. Some users,
such as large laboratories and universities, have also written operating systems,
either to satisfy their own needs or as part of research projects in computing.
Finally, more recently, independent firms like Digital Research or Microsoft have
placed on the market operating systems for microcomputers.

The external boundaries of those systems, which define their functional content, vary from system to system. Each of them is distributed in the form of a
more or less rich nucleus that constitutes the operating system properly told, and a
collection of independent utility programs, some of which can be regarded as
applications. For instance, where does data management stop? Should it be limited
to managing files as opaque global entities, provide simple access to the individual
records which constitute them or go as far as managing complex database structures? Similarly, which text, image and sound management functions should be
included respectively in the system base, in system utilities or left to application programs?

Neither the borderline between operating system and utility programs nor
between utility programs and applications is defined in a precise manner. They
result only from the decision of system designers to include or exclude such or
such functions in their products. For example, the Windows system contains two
simple word-processing programs and a compiler for the Basic language, while

more complex word processing packages like Word and all the other language translators are marketed separately as applications.

Functions present in several systems may be implemented differently, and in
particular their calling conventions by user programs (API's) may be different. A
program written for one operating system cannot be executed on another one, even
if the two systems reside on the same machine, and *a fortiori* on different machines.
Moreover, the functional system content, the distribution of functions between the
different layers, and even the form of API's, evolve in time for a given system as a
result of its gradual enrichment, so that application programs must sometimes be
modified to continue to operate with the new versions of systems.

The situation is just as varied concerning the internal structure. An operating
system is a complex structure whose construction demands a rigorous internal
organization, which is mandatory to allow distributing development, integration and
testing work as well as subsequent evolution.

The traditional approach is to divide the system into major functions corresponding to the various areas of the external API's, and to further decompose each
function into layers based on relative proximity to hardware and to the user. Within
a major function, each layer can communicate only with the next lower and next
higher layer, the ones just closer to hardware and just closer to the user. Therefore,
the most external layers explicitly embody the API and the conventions for communication with the outside world, while the deepest layers are the only ones in
direct relationship with the hardware. Those low-level functions generally merge
into a nucleus of basis functions used by the lowest layers of all subsystems. Classical examples are the communication subsystems (SNA defined by IBM in 1974, and
later the standard ISO model), both including seven such layers.

But except in the rare cases where the system respects an external standard,
the definition of subsystems and of their layers is the responsibility of the producer
of the system and matches his own ideas and his own objectives. That structuring
also involves tradeoffs between performance and structural elegance. Indeed, while
rigor calls for scrupulous respect of all design constraints, performance often
requires transgressing them, for example by bypassing intermediate layers in a subsystem or by letting subsystems communicate at intermediate levels. In reality, not
only is the structure of the system specific to each supplier, but it remains complex
and tangled, by more or less allowing each functional module to use all others. Far
from being a harmonious structure, the system forms an opaque block for anybody
other that its designers, and remains difficult to integrate, to extend and to modify,
even for its authors.

The "open system" concept

It is tempting to take advantage of the central place of the operating system
between hardware and its various users to assign it a unifying role that would enable
all application programs to operate on any hardware. To do that, it would be sufficient that all operating systems writers agree upon a common definition of API's,
resulting on a standardization of the virtual machine that each system defines. The
set of programming primitives used by developers would then become independent

from the hardware, and it would be the responsibility of operating systems to implement that set of common functions in a manner appropriate to the specific hardware elements. One would thus benefit from the flexibility of software to make it absorb differences between hardware implementations.

Such is the ambition of the promoters of so-called "open" systems, whose main goal is to allow "portability" and "interoperability" between different systems. Portability concerns three areas: it means that programs can be executed indifferently by several systems, that data must be able to be written by any system and read by all others, and that user skills required must not be different for the different systems. Interoperability means that two different systems must be able to communicate by exchanging the information required to operate together harmoniously.

The API standardization approach described above would require a precise definition of the borderline between the operating system and applications. We have seen that such a definition would be largely arbitrary and constantly challenged. A solution is to apply the same standardization approach within the system itself, by defining a standard structure and standard internal interfaces for the main constituting functions. An "open" system is therefore also a modular system conforming to a standard structure. In theory, that makes it possible to replace one standard subsystem by another, either as part of the normal evolution of the system or in a competition between suppliers of different implementations of subsystems.

One may guess that the implementation of the open systems concept carries the seeds of potentially important consequences for the structure of the computer industry. Making applications and software packages independent of hardware, and allowing any piece of hardware to be supported by all systems, would complete the separation of the industry into sectors specialized by type of supply and nature of unit. It would thus accelerate the transition from a historical industry structure dominated by generalists to the typical PC structure, dominated by specialists. Making all elements compatible with all others widens the potential market for each one and favors the fragmentation of each sector. Finally, making the operating system explode into standard components developed independently can lead to the explosion of that sector and to a weakening of concentration forces.

Therefore, even though the question of standardization concentrates in the area of packaged software, its implications concern the whole computer industry. This is why we are going to devote part of this chapter to an analysis of the mechanisms and economic aspects of standardization.

Standardization, innovation and competition

Norms and standards

Let us first clarify a few definitions. Like IBM for System/360, we will retain the word "architecture" to designate a set of conventions enabling independently developed products to work together. An architecture can be internal to a firm, or it may concern the relationships between the firm and the users of its products and suppliers of related products. For example, the 360 architecture was the set of conventions enabling users to develop programs executable on hardware of that IBM family. Architectures are generally defined unilaterally by producers. Regarding third parties, they make possible the utilization of products and the connection of complementary products. Internally, they allow distributing the work between units of the enterprise and constitute internal standards for developers.

A standard is a set of architectural conventions followed by independent firms, each acting in its own interest. By defining standards, dominant players seek to favor the existence of complementary offers that will make their products more attractive. The objective of secondary players can be to benefit from the leadership of the dominant player to facilitate the marketing of their complementary offers, but they may also offer directly competitive products conforming to the architecture of the dominant player. Adherence to a common standard enables products developed independently in different areas to function together, for example peripherals and computing units, or microprocessors and operating systems. In particular, standards serve as a base for new developments, but can also serve as a common specification for the implementation of competitive products.

The existence of a standard assumes an architecture definition authority, which can simply be a dominant firm, or an organization formed for that purpose by the firms involved. The decision to adhere to a standard is taken freely by each firm according to its own interest.

A standard becomes a norm when it is supported by an authority distinct from the enterprises involved, which gives it a mandatory character by possessing some means to enforce it. Norms are generally promulgated in the name of user interest, in order to insure both his freedom of choice and the durability of his investments.

Standardization and competition

Products or services that compose each particular sector, and that can by assumption be substituted to each other within each sector, can be subject to standards or norms. Obviously, producing standards and producing products conforming to the standard are two distinct activities. Enterprises do not earn money by selling standards, but by selling products that meet standards in varying degrees, or may on the contrary become the definition of new standards if the market so decides.

Even in sectors subject to strong standardization, the different suppliers are competing and therefore seeking to differentiate from one another to obtain a competitive advantage that may earn the preference of the market. Now adherence to standards eliminates possibilities of differentiation. Since standards most often concern the external functional specifications of products, standardization displaces the field of competition towards prices and modes of implementation, and away from the functions themselves or their modes of utilization. Progress being the fruit of competition, standardization therefore tends to slow down and even to freeze progress in the definition of functions that it covers, and to orient it towards the search for improved performance and reliability at a lower cost.

One sees that the moment when standardization occurs in the life of a product is of crucial importance. Too late, it leaves room for a waste of resources by allowing useless experimentation and futile innovations, and entails a cost of incompatibility between products for suppliers as well as users.

At the opposite, premature standardization has a sterilizing effect for the sector. It can lead to non-viable products to the extent that all needs may not be correctly taken into consideration, and alternate solutions have not been sufficiently explored. For standards defined on the initiative of users or of their representatives, the implications of the different alternatives, in practical terms of cost, performances or compatibility with other areas or future developments, are often inadequately analyzed. In areas where technological evolution is rapid and market requirements are not known precisely, a period of competitive experimentation is a mandatory preliminary for the establishment of standards. The best standard is that which emerges spontaneously from the interaction between suppliers and the market at the end of that period.

The existence of a standard has several effects on the sector or sectors where it applies. First, standardization lowers the obstacles to entry by exempting entry candidates from part of the investment required for defining a new product. For customers, it facilitates change of supplier by reducing switching costs. Therefore, competition is sharpened although it may now relate only to such points as performance, price and ease of use. Those two effects combine to increase the fragmentation rate of the sector, and therefore tend to reduce the potential profitability and to increase the instability of competitive positions.

The beneficiaries are customers, candidates to entry and to a certain extent secondary suppliers who see the leader's competitive advantages eroded. The losers are the established leaders of the sector. In the favorable case where their products have been the base for the standards, the competitive advantages that they derived from owning the *de facto* standard vanish, and they must now preserve their position by seeking other advantages based on economies of scale, protected technologies or a better know-how. If the standards retained are different from the specifications of their products, they face an expensive choice in any event: either comply with standards and support additional product development for that purpose, or compete against standard products, while attempting to make standards evolve in their favor.

Let us insist on the fact that a dominant supplier has an interest in seeing his products become standards only if he has enough other competitive advantages to preserve his market share in the sector covered by that standard, despite the lower obstacles to entry. Otherwise, the effect of standardization is to breed additional and more aggressive competitors, while increasing the relative power of customers two factors that can only reduce both his margins and his market share. Within enterprises, engineers can seek recognition through the adoption of their products as standards; strategists are far more cautious and avoid soliciting that poisoned present.

The production of standards

In an industry like data-processing, standards develop naturally without demanding action from an outside authority. All suppliers implicitly adopt architectures that define at least the interface between their products and the customer. At the same time, those standards enable other suppliers to offer complementary products whose existence will make the offer more attractive for the market. Suppliers of complex and varied offerings are also led to define internal architectures that subdivide their offer into distinct products, so as to be able to develop and manage them independently of each other. Those products can be separate software components within a system as well as separate hardware units within a machine.

If the elements, between which the architecture defines standardized interfaces, can be not only produced but also marketed separately, the definition of an architecture enables specialists to compete with the main vendor for each such component, while being sure that those components will integrate themselves efficiently with the overall offer. For such suppliers of "compatibles", the potential market is all the more large that the architecture to which they refer is more widespread. By solving the development problem raised by the complexity of his offer, the vendor of complex products therefore creates the conditions that will cause the explosion of his sector into specialized sub-sectors. The architecture defined by the major supplier becomes a standard for all those resulting sub-sectors. This is what happened for example in the beginning of the seventies, after IBM introduced the 360 architecture on the market.

We have seen that market shares in concentrated sectors are highly unequal. In a structurally concentrated sector – one that is not liable to explode into sub-sectors – the product of the dominant supplier constitutes a *de facto* standard by its dominant presence on the market, and also by the existence of compatible products or "clones". In such a sector, it is very unlikely that the dominant firm, with 60 to 80% of the market, would accept to negotiate with its challengers to establish a common standard that would not comply in every respect with the specifications of his own products. Standardization by consensus is therefore practically excluded.

On the other hand, *de facto* standards defined unilaterally by the dominant supplier of each concentrated sector also apply to the related sectors that use those products. Firms belonging to different sectors, and therefore not in direct competition, could benefit from getting together to establish common standards. But Porter taught us (see Chapter 6) that fragmented sectors have little influence on concentrated sectors. It is therefore likely that the dominant suppliers of concentrated sectors will impose their standards to related sectors if they are fragmented, and that the dialogue about establishing common standards will be limited to the respective leaders of related concentrated sectors. Intel imposes its standards on hardware assemblers, but negotiates common standards with Microsoft.

The preferential position of the dominant supplier in each concentrated sector imposes on him certain responsibilities concerning the standards that he has created. On one hand, the existence of a standard facilitates competition from imitators. The leader might therefore sometimes be tempted to use his development resources to part from the standard and thus acquire competitive advantages making the clones obsolete. But the dominant supplier would then alienate his users and complementary suppliers, and would thus offer another competitive advantage to clone vendors, that of continuity. The dominant supplier is therefore condemned to comply with the standard that he has created, and to seek his competitive advantage in the implementation of products derived from that standard. In the past, this phenomenon has led IBM to abandon its FS project in 1975 (see Chapter 2). Today, it still forces IBM to maintain the 360/370 and even MVS architectures in its future multiprocessor systems based on the PowerPC, and also forces Intel to preserve the 80x86 architecture in the Pentium and its successors.

Fragmented sectors are submitted to the relevant standards of related concentrated sectors. A possible need for other standards, either internal to the sector or concerning the interconnection between products of different fragmented sectors, can only be satisfied through an explicit dialogue between firms. That demand will come mainly from secondary suppliers and candidates to entry into the sector.

The definition of standards by consensus results from a negotiation ending in an agreement between independent partners, who preserve their independence after the standard has been defined. No committee can constrain one of its members to act against its interests. Each participant can leave the discussion at any time, and retains the freedom not to conform to the resulting standards anyway. Each participant arrives at the negotiation table with his own view of his interests. If the discussion aims at a consensus, it will progress too slowly for impatient participants, and forced compromises may end in a mediocre result that will disappoint the most demanding ones. If on the other hand the objective is reach a quick result, the discussion will have to ignore a certain number of objections and experiments, which will probably lead the most serious firms to withdraw their support. In both cases, the process can lead to the formation of competing groups supporting different standards. The road to consensus is strewn with pitfalls and its issue is uncertain. Even unanimous agreement does not guarantee the quality of the resulting standard, whose adoption remains subject to the ultimate decision of the market.

An authority external to the supplier community can intervene to force the adoption of a standard. The existence of standards and compliance with them, even independently of their quality, is obviously in the best interest of customers. Competition between suppliers is intensified, which pushes towards product improvements and a reduction of their costs, the choice of product and suppliers is widened, and investments are better protected. Customers can form pressure groups to accelerate the standardization process or to orient it in a direction that they consider as favorable, but it seems that their action has never resulted in a hasty standardization, and that they implicitly understand the need for a preliminary period of competitive experimentation.

On the other hand, standards are sometimes promulgated by an authority acting in the name of user interests, or for others motives like industrial policies. If the standardization organism only accelerates or facilitates the natural standardization process and underwrites its results, its action may be beneficial. It can become disastrous if it results in premature standardization or if its objective is to oppose the *de facto* standards.

An example of the first case is Cobol, where the first available language has been promulgated as a standard and adopted in a general manner for lack of an alternative, drying up research and development in commercial programming and condemning programmers to eternally use a rigid and inconvenient tool. In the second case, one finds cases where standardization is used as a weapon of industrial policy to oppose a natural "de facto" standard in order to fight against the firms representing that standard. A classical example is the OSI model for network architecture, conceived from the start as a replacement for the SNA model from IBM, but that has never been able to win support from the industry and is being superseded by other architectures, more effective and more consistent with current needs. The standardization efforts around Unix, which we are going to discuss below, largely belong to that "fighting" standardization approach.

Fortunately, while a *de facto* standard is by definition respected by a majority, an artificial norm may not to be respected or remain a minority. If an official norm is not satisfactory, suppliers will continue to seek alternative solutions which the market may designate as standards independently of the norm.

The formation of standards is an evolutionary process. Premature or unsatisfactory standards will always be challenged by competitive developments that will be as many candidates to standardization. Even widely followed standards will someday be obsoleted by the evolution of technologies and requirements, and therefore challenged in their turn. Some suppliers will adopt differentiation strategies by parting from the majority standards, and if their products receive a sufficiently favorable welcome, they may in turn become candidates to standardization. In short, as long as we do not live in a normalized totalitarian world, standards will not cease to evolve and there will always exist competitive standards.

Systems evolution and the place of Unix

An experimental system

Since their origin until the mid-sixties, separate operating systems have been associated with each variety of hardware. Some types of computers have even been supported by several operating systems, either for different modes of utilization such as conventional processing, timesharing or real time processing, or for different families of configurations. In the context of integrated offerings until the eighties, operating systems were produced by the generalist manufacturers and marketed as part of hardware. Independent operating system suppliers did not exist, and the mere idea of a universal system common to different hardware lines had not even emerged.

A few universities or laboratories nevertheless developed their own systems in support of teaching and computer research. One such system is Unix, originated in the Bell Laboratories, which spread to several American universities where it became a ground for studies and experimentation, and at the same time a basis for computer training. Initially, Unix is only a minicomputer implementation of the Multics system from General Electric. It owes its success partly to its functions and architecture, well adapted to the needs of universities, and also to its availability in source form in a high level language (the C language), starting in 1973. Unix is therefore well adapted to teaching the concepts and design of operating systems and to experimenting with new functions and implementation approaches.

To operate efficiently as a common laboratory system in a typical academic cooperative environment, Unix must comply with a set of conventions which enable developing and experimenting with new modules, as well as exchanging them between the different laboratories. Communications must also be facilitated thanks to a common language and common references. Those conventions form a solid standard base on which many extensions or alternative implementations can be grafted, gradually giving birth to alternate competing versions of the system.

The base for a standard system?

Simultaneously, the beginning of the eighties saw the emergence of scientific workstations. Some young enterprises saw in Unix a system that was at the same time available and not protected by a manufacturer, already familiar to users in this market, designed to allow easy evolution and actively supported by the most active and creative research centers. In a way, adopting Unix enabled manufacturers to rely on an independent source of base software and to concentrate their efforts and investments on hardware. Unix became therefore the operating system for the most innovative workstations, and most large manufacturers followed suit by introducing derivatives of Unix into their catalog, alongside their own systems.

So started the dual conflict that dominates the whole history of Unix and still persists today, and which makes technical considerations inseparable from industrial policy considerations. First, each industrial supplier must reach in his systems the best possible balance between compliance with standards and competitive differentiation. Second, at the global level, the demands of an industrial standard are often quite different from those of a research and development platform. Finally, the standardization process aims openly at defining not only a Unix standard that would be applicable to implementations of that system, but a norm that would apply to all systems and would elevate Unix to the status of standard operating system. This *a priori* will to establish an independent norm appeared as early as 1981 with the creation of Posix.

Those ambiguities, as well as the number and variety of the players involved, hinder the progression towards standards. Moreover, those major players who enjoy some competitive advantage concerning Unix hesitate between exploiting it in proprietary versions and renouncing it by fully associating themselves with standardization. For instance, in 1983, ATT, that had so far allowed a liberal distribution of Unix, tried to take advantage of its sudden popularity by demanding increased royalties. The other interested manufacturers reacted by creating in 1984 the Xopen organization in order to promote a really open and easily accessible system. Similar reactions happened again in 1988 with the creation of the OSF to counter an alliance between Sun and ATT announced in 1987, and in 1994 with the creation of the Cose consortium when Microsoft announced its Windows NT system, which includes many features of Unix and competes with it on its traditional market. Every time one player takes an initiative that might make him the dominant player, the other concerned parties use standardization as an explicit instrument of competitive struggle by creating organizations for competitive standardization.

Pushed simultaneously by the absence of a consensus on standards, by the competitive need for differentiation and by the uneven quality of implementations coming out of university laboratories, all manufacturers end up developing their own version of Unix, made of a particular assemblage of standard elements and original proprietary elements. Adding together university implementations, systems proposed by manufacturers and those proposed by specialized firms such as the Santa Cruz Operation, one witnesses a blossoming of systems, all claiming to be Unix but all different in varying degrees. The number of such implementations of Unix is estimated at approximately a hundred. Incidentally, such diversity is encouraged by the fact that the name Unix was until recently the property of ATT and could not be used by other firms. Since the developers of Unix systems had to call them by some other name anyway, they could as well make them something else.

For those reasons, the Unix world is just the opposite of a standardized world. On the contrary, it is the marketplace where competition specifically concerning operating systems is the most intense. In the traditional world, the very idea of an operating system common to hardware from different suppliers is alien, and competition concerning systems is eclipsed behind competition concerning hardware. In the PC world, the whole industry has rallied behind MS-DOS and now Windows, and the remaining competition in the operating systems sector has taken the asymmetrical form characteristic of concentrated sectors. The process of Unix standardization leads at best to a hope, not to a state of fact. It is precisely because the Unix world has a crying need of standards that it devotes so much effort to standardization.

At the same time, innovation being the other face of competition, the Unix world is the favored hotbed for innovation in the area of operating systems, where not only specialized or non-specialized manufacturers are contributing, but also universities and other research laboratories. Moreover, the power range of most Unix systems encroaches both on the high range of personal computers and on the low part of the large systems range. Being at the hinge of traditional data-processing and micro-computing, the Unix laboratory is ideally suited to experimenting with the technologies that will enable those two worlds to come together in a symbiotic fashion, as well as to transfer existing technologies from one to the other.

For example, Unix did not originally shine by its user-friendliness, nor by its performance, nor by its business computing capabilities, nor by the variety of hardware supported. In other words, the choice of Unix did not rely in the least upon an advantage in terms of user satisfaction, other that for academic users. On the other hand, its position as an experimental platform has resulted in a huge array of extensions and improvements developed in those areas and others. Today, there exist in the Unix world all necessary ingredients to build on that base a system both more user-friendly than Apple (for example NextStep) and richer in business data-processing and systems management capabilities than the large IBM systems.

The Unix world is the place where *avant-garde* products are being born, that will enable replacing large systems by complexes of systems or microprocessors from the micro world, and therefore the merger of the three worlds of traditional systems, micros and Unix into a single industry with the price-performance features of micro-computing.

The proliferation of alternate solutions characteristic of the Unix world comes with an intense and stubborn standardization effort, which supplements the competitive confrontation and the spontaneous choices of the market, with a rational comparison between the various solutions proposed for each technical problem. The conjunction of the innovation effort and of that will to standardize contributes to making the Unix movement the crucible where standards are formed that will apply tomorrow to the whole software industry.

Different interests

The proliferating world of systems is located at the confluence of the interests of users, application developers, hardware producers and research, and of primary importance to the producers of packaged software. One can therefore expect that the will to standardize will raise conflicts of interest between players.

Users, and firms specialized in application development, wish to have a durable and robust basis for application development. To that effect, they ask for standards covering all aspects of systems, and embodied in products of industrial quality. At the same time, they want those standards to be capable of evolving by incorporating all new developments, especially those that are stemming from Unix-based research, without jeopardizing robustness, generality, reliability or ease of use of the underlying system.

Now, as we have seen in the previous chapter, systems of industrial quality can only be produced by industrial organizations, which are the only ones able to afford the required investments in the hope of profit. A software package of industrial quality can therefore only be offered for a fee. Moreover, the prevailing rule for industrial firms is that of competition, which forces them to seek to differentiate. In a sector as dynamic as that of operating systems, it is highly unlikely that all competing firms would cease to differentiate by the functions of their products and limit competition to performance, prices and quality.

An industrial firm cannot blindly trust an external standard. As long as several firms continue to compete in operating systems, they will retain their critical attitude towards external standards, complying with them when it matches their self-interest and avoid them in the opposite case. They will at least always seek to offer a better product than what standards prescribe. One can predict that there will never exist a system combining absolute conformity to an external standard with industrial quality, including the support of all configurations, high reliability, good documentation, guaranteed maintenance and evolution, etc.

On their side, the research community and the other innovators need a common base for development and exchange independent of "commercial" systems proposed by manufacturers. Among the qualities of products that could form that base, they favor modularity and clarity of the internal structure over performance and reliability. Every innovator wants at the same time general standards for what is outside of his field of research, and total freedom within that field. Since the *raison d'être* of those teams is to extend the base system, there will always exist several versions of the Unix reference system, each one being more advanced than any industrial system in certain areas, and including functions absent from industrial systems. Researchers will always prefer not being linked to a manufacturer, and therefore using a separate reference system. If one manufacturer happened to select a version of Unix as its commercial offering, the research community would probably turn away from it and adopt another independent reference.

Unix and industrial systems thus play definitely different roles and will continue to coexist. Unix serves as a framework for an independent or academic research and development activity that will always remain a basic factor of progress. Industrial systems aim at satisfying concrete needs of the market while benefiting in a selective and differentiated manner from progress realized in the Unix world. Between the Unix world on one hand, both a reference system for innovation and an unreachable ideal for standardization, and on the other hand the prosaic world of competitive industrial systems, a dynamic equilibrium of conflict and cooperation establishes itself. That situation will most probably last as long as there remains a potential for progress in software, which is as far as one can see.

On the side of the industrial supply, we must distinguish between the utilization of the Unix label as a promotional banner and Unix as a real system. Manufacturers that currently advertise themselves as Unix suppliers do so because it is a way to differentiate, precisely because Unix is not the *de facto* standard. Should Unix eventually become a genuine standard adhered to by the majority of suppliers, it will like all standards contribute to fragmentation of the sector and to limiting profitability, and manufacturers will have to seek other ways to differentiate. In other words and in an apparently paradoxical manner, pushing the standardization of Unix is consistent with the interests of established suppliers only as long as Unix is in a minority position on the market and remains thereby a differentiating factor.

The immediate future

So far, the Unix world has remained separated from the rest of data-processing because it uses mostly different families of processors implementing the Risc philosophy. This separation is being challenged by the merger of the Intel and Risc worlds inaugurated by the Pentium and the PowerPC, that will lead to the gradual elimination of most current Risc architectures (see Chapter 7).

Several versions of Unix for the Intel processors characteristic of the PC world are already available, like Xenix from Microsoft and Solaris from Sun, but their distribution is confidential when compared to the distribution of MS-DOS and Windows. At the opposite, Digital Equipment has recently brought Risc processors into the PC competitive arena by offering a PC using MS-DOS and Windows equipped with its Alpha microprocessor.

The event that started the merger of the PC and Unix worlds in the operating systems area was the introduction of Windows NT by Microsoft in the beginning of 1993. This system will eventually work on Risc processors as well as on Intel processors, since all the coding dependent on a particular processor is consolidated in an easily interchangeable layer of software. By implementing appropriate application interfaces (API), Windows NT can support application programs written for Unix as well as for MS-DOS and Windows. It can cooperate with Unix systems in a network, by respecting interoperability standards defined by Xopen and the OSF. Finally, it incorporates many functions which previously were only available in Unix, in particular symmetric multiprocessing.

Windows NT, and its present and future derivatives, is not only a successor of Windows, but becomes a reasonable alternative to Unix systems, including Risc-based systems, multiprocessor systems and high-end configurations used in client-server architectures. As is the case for components, the sector of Unix systems and that of PC operating systems, essentially separate up to now, are in the process of merging.

The merger of those two sectors implies that, as for processors, the competitive concentration dynamics are now going to work in a single market segment covering both PC's and Unix systems. For such software packages, the optimal production scale is expressed in millions, and is therefore significantly lower than the size of the market. That leaves room for a certain number of competitive offerings. One can therefore expect typical industrial enterprises such as Microsoft, Novell or IBM, to offer competitive operating systems at a level of quality which will leave only little room to those that might be developed by brilliant amateurs, or by committees with even the best intentions.

Like Windows NT or Unixware, those different systems will seek to differentiate by their functional repertoire, their user-friendliness, their performance, reliability, etc. At the same time they will target the largest possible market by implementing the most general application interface and data exchange standards, as well as by being able to execute on all processors available on the market.

To reach those objectives, all will draw upon the source of ideas constituted by the Unix laboratory and will implement the standards that are stemming from it, but without depriving themselves of their own original developments. In this sector of operating systems, now becoming autonomous relative to that of components as well as compared to hardware, the focus of competition will not be Unix versus the others. All major competing systems will use pieces of Unix to some extent and all will incorporate a variable share of original, so-called "proprietary" modules.

Most firms that currently offer operating systems of the Unix variety follow the model of traditional data-processing as opposed to the PC model, in that they also offer their own hardware, either built from their own Risc microprocessors like Sun, Silicon Graphics, Digital Equipment or Hewlett-Packard, or from off-the-shelf microprocessors for the new converts like Unisys. On the operating systems segment, those firms are increasingly going to be challenged by specialists in software packages (not necessarily Unix) like Microsoft, Novell, the Santa Cruz Operation, or future specialized offsprings of IBM or Apple.

The "Unix generalists" will then be faced with the following alternative: either to continue to develop their own operating systems, or to give them up and concentrate on hardware. The first term of the alternative —to continue — assumes that they enjoy some competitive advantage in this sector, although it will be difficult for them to offer the same quality and prices as Microsoft or its immediate follower because of the scale effect. The advantage of this option can be to use the system as a differentiating factor, but that strategy runs against compliance with standards.

The growing competition from specialized firms, for which specialization is precisely the source of competitive advantages, will acutely reveal the problems of coexistence between activities. The development of software systems implies a pro-duction scale much higher than hardware and operates according to long cycles. That forces to recognize different enterprise personalities and works towards the explosion of mixed firms. Generalists operating today under the Unix banner will be forced, like their older predecessors, to separate their hardware and packaged software activities from each other and to offer their operating systems separately, or quit.

We will return to those issues in Chapter 14. Our conclusion will be that, as is already the case in the PC world, operating systems will gradually become the domain of specialized enterprises forming a distinct autonomous sector with a con-centrated structure, in particular with highly unequal market shares. Through that evolution, the price levels and the marketing practices for operating systems will converge towards those practices that are today characteristic of the PC world.

Perspectives

The industrial structure of the operating systems sector is still hybrid. It includes players from three different origins: traditional generalists still offering their own hardware-specific systems, specialized firms of the PC world taking advantage of the increasing power of microcomputers to compete with generalists, and a complex of suppliers of different sizes and natures grouped around the Unix banner and the open systems ideal.

We have seen that generalists will probably be forced to dissociate their hard-ware and software activities from each other. Thereby, that heterogeneous set of actors will gradually organize, in the few years ahead, into an independent macro-sector of operating systems, separated from that of hardware and dominated by specialists of packaged software as is already the case in the PC world.

As for packaged software in general, the operating systems macro-sector will be made of a continuum of communicating sub-sectors. At one extreme, the sector of complete industrial systems will have all the features of a highly concentrated sector, where a small number of firms, counted on the fingers of one hand, will share the market in a very unequal manner, similar to the microprocessor sector. At the other extreme, new ideas and new enterprises will constantly be born and will produce new functions or alternative implementations of existing functions. This proliferation of innovations will be facilitated by the existence of standards and of a conceptual reference system called Unix, even if the idea of a world where every-thing would be governed by standards respected by all will forever remain in the realm of utopia.

Between those two extreme limits of the sector, intermediate firms will be able to act as integration relays in areas such as systems utilities or general applications close to operating systems, a role that is played today for example by Syman-tec or Computer Associates. Through the whole sector, ideas and products will migrate continuously from the innovative fragmented fringe to the poles of attrac-tion constituted by industrial integrated systems. That migration will result in widening the functional perimeter considered as separating operating systems from application packages. As part of that movement, firms belonging to fragmented sectors will be acquired by enterprises of more concentrated sectors.

What about the general equilibrium of the sector? Between the competitive forces that push to concentration and those which favor the birth of new enter-prises, which are the stronger? Is it realistic to believe that the regeneration of inno-vative enterprises almost exactly compensates for the disappearances or acquisi-tions, giving thus to the overall sector the appearance of a kind of stationary flow where the proportions of the different types of populations remain the same, while their composition changes continuously? Or can one fear that the rate of new cre-ations is lower than that of disappearances, so that the whole industry would tend to collapse into a handful of suppliers? On the contrary, are there reasons to believe that the dynamics of concentration might slow down, so that the sector would evolve towards an explosion analogous to that of hardware in the years 1975 - 1990?

Software engineering and sector structure

The preceding questions are related to the likely evolution of software devel-opment technologies. The economic engine of concentration dynamics is the cost and complexity of systems integration. The most complex systems are built by assembling modules or subsets, that could as well be marketed separately if inte-grating them did not present difficulties or risks. It is only the problem of integra-tion that requires distributing them together and supporting enormous fixed costs.

The root of the problem is that, with current development techniques, con-formity of an element to its specifications does not guarantee that it will be inte-grated without effort or errors into the system of which it is intended to be part. If it were possible to specify and implement all components of a system in such a way that the conformity of each element to its specifications would guarantee its smooth integration, and that the correct functioning of the system in one configu-ration would assure that it works correctly in all others, then it would become possi-ble to develop and to market systems as independent pieces. The production scale applicable to each of those components would be significantly lower than for inte-grated systems, and the production cycle would be much shorter. As we have seen in the preceding chapter, this would favor the fragmentation of industry, and sys-tems integration would become a specialty among others, similar to that of hard-ware assembly.

"Software engineering" technologies determine both the intensity of concen-tration forces for the integrators and the level of barriers to entry for the smallest enterprises. There is already a wide choice of toolboxes enabling to develop easily software of professional quality and appearance, and such assistance to develop-ment can only become richer and better. Obstacles to entry will remain low for innovators, and opportunities will remain unlimited as long as the utilization of data-processing continues to diversify.

Whatever is the power of the writing and integration assistance tools made available to programmers, the program can in the end only be executed in machine language form, where all references to information or to other points of the program are converted to binary addresses. At this stage, that of testing and integration, the modular architecture that has served to build the program has disappeared and the system is now a compact indissoluble block. Modifying or adding any part of the system requires a complete reassembly whatever is the importance of the modification.

For the same reason, grafting a program onto another, which is necessary for instance for executing an application program in the framework of an operating system, must have been explicitly anticipated and takes place according to rigorous and constraining conventions. Various techniques have been developed to defer the resolution of inter-program references, which lead to the "mass freezing" described above, and to allow independent programs to establish links with each other at execution stage. Examples of such conventions are the DDE (*Direct Data Exchange*) or OLE (*Object Linking and Embedding*) mechanism from Microsoft, but the most significant and most promising developments are the so-called "object programming technologies", which we will now briefly describe.

Objects

In traditional programming, code, formed by executable instructions, is separated from the data on which it operates. Data is organized in structures, tables or files, which are used and manipulated by many modules of the program. That structure introduces an implicit interdependence between every module and the data structures, as well as between modules through their common data. Such hidden dependencies create risks of unexpected program behavior called "side effects" and contributes strongly to the difficulty of testing. Moreover, if one wants to change the format of a table, either to correct an error, to introduce new functions or to improve performance, all the program modules that use the table must be modified.

In programming jargon, an "object" is formed by data and associated program modules (usually called "methods"). A possible utilization the object programming technology is to package into an object a set of data and the subroutines giving access to those data, and to forbid access to that data except by using those methods. Inasmuch as access methods have been defined in a sufficiently general manner, any modification of the data structure requires only modifying the methods of the object, but not the many external program modules that happen to use the data.

Execution of the methods of an object is triggered, directly or indirectly, by the reception of messages in a repertoire that the object can recognize. For example, in a system capable of handling a variety of different data structures, each such structure can be implemented as an object recognizing the four standard messages "print", "display full", display summary" (for example as an icon) and "save to disk". Every object will include four corresponding methods to react to the four messages, the exact working of which obviously depends on the structure and the meaning of the object. For example, the "display" method for an object "rectangle" will be different from that of an object "circle", but the two objects will react appropriately to the same "display" message.

Grouping in that way the specifics of an object into a consistent self-contained construction brings many advantages. Each method of each object, for instance the way it displays itself, can evolve while leaving all the rest unchanged. One can also add new objects to those that the system already knows how to process, by simply endowing them with the appropriate methods to react to system messages. The system will thus be able to manipulate them without any further change. In the jargon of objects, one speaks of "polymorphism" to designate the possibility of different objects to react appropriately and differently to the same set of incoming messages. For example to display a list of geometrical patterns, the global display management program is independent of the nature of the displayed objects. Introducing a new pattern simply requires incorporating the appropriate display method in the object that represents it. The object-oriented approach appears as an essential concept for the implementation of graphic interfaces and more generally of multimedia applications.

In most object-based development systems, defining new objects is facilitated by the mechanism called "inheritance" that consists in defining a new object by referring to an existing object, retaining some of its methods, redefining some or defining new ones, without having to access the source code of the base object. That mechanism reduces the required coding and minimizes risks of error by allowing to use already proven methods in new objects. It also allows replacing each individual object in a system by another object presenting the same external interfaces, but which may differ from the original object in a variety of ways ranging from simple implementation details to a complete rewrite.

Message-based communication implies that all communications between objects, for example calling a method of an object from another object, takes place indirectly through a basic function of the operating system. That system function can in particular be responsible for resolving cross-references between objects, thus allowing to maintain a modular structure until the execution stage. Among other possibilities, such a structure can serve as a basis for the implementation of distributed systems where component objects can reside on different execution units. The message management function is responsible for locating the objects and routing messages accordingly without requiring the different objects to be aware of their respective locations. The object concept thus also appears related to the client-server concept and to multiprocessing.

From this summarized introduction, one may guess that object-based programming is not only the source of new paradigms for application development, but also a potential basis for achieving real modularity of software. For those hopes to materialize still requires considerable experimentation and probably more invention. Appropriate standards will also need to be agreed upon at the proper time, without untimely haste that would prematurely freeze immature norms. Packaged software companies will also have to invent and implement new design and programming disciplines, including for example an object administration system with built-in motivation for reuse.

An emergent technology related to objects is that of "micro-kernels". At every point in time, a modern system can contain several execution programs under way, that are isolated from each other by hardware protection devices in order to prevent the propagation of execution errors, or any other incident. For example, each program will only be able to access those areas of memory that have been allocated to it. Among other functions, it is the responsibility of the operating system to allocate available memory to the different jobs and to ensure switching from one program to another. When doing that, the operating system must temporarily disable those protections, by leaving the normal mode of operations, or "problem mode", and entering a "system" mode that authorizes access to the whole memory and the execution of certain "privileged" instructions.

Clearly, any program that uses the system mode directly must be protected and submitted to drastic restrictions, and cannot easily be developed and distributed separately. In a system that would be composed of objects developed independently, none of those objects should be authorized to use the system mode otherwise that by sending request messages to a special system object (the "nucleus") having the monopoly of that mode.

A "micro-kernel" is defined as the smallest part of the operating system that is dependent of the machine and must execute in system mode. The exact definition of micro-kernels is currently a subject for debate and experimentation. All proposals include in the micro-kernel memory management, task management and communication between processes, but they differ by the exact distribution of tasks between problem mode and system mode, in particular for the management of peripheral devices. As is always the case in programming, those decisions about the distribution of functions correspond to different tradeoffs between conceptual purity and flexibility on one hand, performance on the other hand.

The two best-known implementations of the micro-kernel concept are coming from the Unix world: Mach, born from a cooperation between the Carnegie-Mellon University and IBM, and Chorus, developed by the French company Chorus Systems. The Mach micro-kernel has been adopted as a standard by the OSF and is used in the new systems under development by IBM, Apple, Sun and others, while Novell has chosen Chorus. Microsoft, on its side, is basing its most recent systems like Windows NT on a proprietary micro-kernel.

Although the technology of micro-kernels is at the heart of object-based systems, none of the above systems is really an object system. In currently available systems, the code that implements functions external to the micro-kernel is still developed and structured according to traditional methods. It will be necessary to wait for the next system generation expected by the end of the century in order to see most functions implemented as collections of independent objects communicating through the micro-kernel.

At that time, it may become possible for independent suppliers to specialize on specific objects and to enter in competition with the market leaders, in much the same way as compatible hardware suppliers have started competing with IBM in the seventies. If those technologies fulfill their promises, they can result in the explosion of the packaged software industry, just as System/360 and later unbundling have caused the explosion of the traditional computing industry.

Software and hardware

Another related major issue is the location of the dividing line between software and hardware. The power of microprocessors is increasing inexorably. It is a safe prediction that they will contain a hundred million transistors by the year 2000 versus 3 to 5 millions at present, although half a million transistors is largely sufficient to implement a complete computing unit. Can we then believe that the microprocessors of the XXIst century will be formed of hundreds of computing units functioning in parallel, or should we think to expect their functions to be considerably richer?

If microprocessor manufacturers do choose the second route, the first functions to be candidates for residence on the chip as some form of microcode[66], and even for direct implementation by active circuits, are those parts of the operating system that are closest to hardware, beginning with the micro-kernel. Given sufficient physical capacity, all systems software could reside in a memory included on the microprocessor, and more radically everything that is implemented by software could conceivably be implemented by circuits and vice-versa. Incidentally, there are many intermediate forms between hardware and conventional software, such as microcode, code residing in read-only memory, drivers for peripherals, that can reside in the central system or in the input/output unit, etc.

The history of computing offers several examples of function migrating between hardware and software, and in both directions. Taking functions out of hardware to transfer them to software generally follows theoretical motivations. The famous "Türing machine" represents the simplest machine capable of carrying out any calculation, but it is only a purely abstract model used in information theory. Its physical implementation would have ridiculously low performance and would be unusable precisely because of its rudimentary instruction set. The same approach of systematic simplification of hardware, by accepting to delegate more complex functions to software, has presided over the developments that led to the Risc concept.

The reverse migration from software to hardware is more frequent in the real world. It is always motivated by practical reasons of performance or reliability, and is only constrained by the hardware technology limitations on one hand, stability and generality of the functions involved on the other hand. Indeed, functions "etched in silicon" can no longer be modified except with great difficulty, and only those parts of software that are perfectly tested and stabilized can really be candidates. Throughout the life of System/360 and its derivatives, the hardware instruction set has been periodically extended with new privileged instructions replacing

---

66 See chapter 1

sequences of instructions in the operating system. The FS project[67] planned to incorporate into hardware many functions including a major part of database management. In the micro world, each successive processor from Intel incorporates new functions such as energy management, which would normally have been implemented in software. Even the Risc concept has evolved from a set of about ten machine instructions in its original pure form to some 200 instructions in its recent implementations, which is as much as for classical Cisc processors.

In spite of occasional and temporary backwards steps, the constant long term trend is the migration of functions from system software into hardware and especially into the microprocessor, as well as into peripheral hardware which includes increasingly powerful "driver" software. If the industry eventually comes to an agreement on a set of API's to define a standard virtual machine, it is likely that hardware manufacturers will offer diverse implementations of that machine, some of which will include part of the system software objects required for its operations. Such migration will start with operating systems, but can spread to certain functions of application programs. In any case, it will force to reconsider the relationship between producers of hardware components and of software systems, as well as the borderline between those two sectors.

Conclusions

Operating systems form an original sector because of the specific economic and technical features of the activity of packaged software development, as well as by the extent of the area covered, which makes room for sub-sectors ranging from extreme concentration to extreme fragmentation.

For major industrial operating systems, the currently dominant trend is concentration, which should normally, by the end of the decade, end in a structure analogous to that of components. To the leader and challenger pair formed probably by Intel and PowerOpen for microprocessors would correspond a pair formed by Microsoft and IBM (or the fruit of its alliances with Apple and others), followed in both cases by a small handful of more marginal firms. For software, the leaders would be surrounded by a fluctuating parade of innovators, more or less associated under the Unix banner, some of which would gravitate around one of leaders to the point to being absorbed.

But technologies carry the seeds of a potential complete overhaul of this picture, by enabling in the medium term an explosion of the system and therefore an explosion of the sector. If it happens, this move would work in favor of a multiplication of small enterprises and to added emphasis of the fragmented character of the sector. One would then see for packaged software a new version of the "*unbundling*" scenario. What would then happen to present leaders? Who would then take responsibility for integrating objects from different sources into a consistent robust system? The user himself? Specialized services companies? Those are some of the profound structural and industrial implications of "object systems".

---

67 See Chapter 2

That possible restructuring would still be more complicated if the evolution of components entailed in parallel a reshuffling of functions between system software and microprocessors. At the same time as the packaged software industry would explode, part of it would more or less merge with the hardware industry to give birth to hybrid integrated products. More than ever, software remains a particularly diverse and moving area, whose evolution is at the center of the whole computer industry.

Chapter 13 - The world of services

A multi-dimensional world. Support services, replacement services and computerized services. Processing services and their evolution. The rise and fall of Service Bureau. Technical assistance, development and integration. The pitfalls of fixed prices. Different structures and cultures for different activities. Specialization and dead-ends. Do products need services? How about facilities management?

In the preceding chapters, we have often mentioned the field of services without entering into its detailed analysis. When reviewing the computer industry in part one, then when preparing our instruments for analysis of industry structure in chapter 6 and seeking to organize our thinking in chapter 10, we have noted that services are an area with blurred outlines and a heterogeneous content.

Incidentally, such heterogeneity is consistent with the traditional definitions, that most often boil down to calling "service" everything that is not a product. But we have seen in chapter 10 that the usual differentiation between products and services actually refers to several independent criteria. Far from being reduced to a bipolar situation, that differentiation gives birth to a multidimensional classification, where every criterion can take intermediate values between the pure "service" and "product" modes. Those considerations have already led us to treat separately packaged software, which has all the features of a product and whose assimilation to services, although usual, is absolutely not justified.

Even after eliminating packaged software, services cannot be distinguished from products as radically as generally accepted in the literature, and are too diverse for one to be able to make many relevant general statements. On the contrary, the analysis of service activities must bring to bear the complete set of tools that we have built and validated by applying them to products, and leads to conclusions as varied as the forms of services themselves.

Despite this large diversity, services are the subject of many comments where the more or less organized confusion of situations gives birth to the most incorrect generalizations and approximations. It is in this area that approximations and wrong ideas are most abundant, spread mainly by the self-serving statements of suppliers seeking to promote their services offerings, and relayed by the analyses of professional gurus. In total, the dominant speeches and preconceived ideas concerning services do generally little but add to the confusion. The goal of the present chapter is to analyze the area of services in an objective manner, distinguishing its parts according to the old Cartesian precept, and to analyze the relationships and the mechanisms of symbiosis and competition with products in order to uncover perspectives for each of the main types of offer. In so doing, we will not hesitate to challenge a few popular ideas.

According to the dominant opinion, the area of services carries many hopes, to such a point that some predict that services will eventually supersede products. Such interest in services is sustained by two frequent statements: first, that services revenue is increasing more rapidly than hardware revenue, and second that services are more profitable than hardware. One sees a proof of the above in the fact that almost all large traditional suppliers are showing ambitions in services, and even take pride in the relative share of services in their revenue. Superficial commentators see this rush to services as the consequence of higher intrinsic profitability and present it as a major trend leading to a definitive supremacy of services over hardware.

Statistics do show that services are developing more rapidly than hardware in general, and especially faster than traditional equipment (other than microcomputers). But that finding must be tempered by the fact that most figures quoted in the press concern the sum of packaged software and services, with the first clearly growing more rapidly than the second.

On the other hand, as we have seen in chapter 5, it is inaccurate to say that services are more profitable than products. Over the period 1985-1993, the average and median net profit ratio of specialized services firms fluctuate around 5%, just like those of firms specialized in PC's, workstations or peripherals. Moreover, variances around those averages are large enough to include, since 1989, services companies with negative results along with hardware companies showing a profitability more than 10 percentage points higher to that of the most effective services companies. In other words, not only are the averages of the different sectors very close, but the differences between companies of the same sector are far larger that the tiny differences between sector averages. Average and median profits in services are clearly superior only to those of generalists or large systems specialists until 1993, but the situation changes in 1994 with generalists, mixed firms and large systems specialists all improving and approaching the same profitability level as service companies. Anyway, even those three categories include firms with profitability exceeding that of many services companies.

Similarly, as we have seen in chapter 5, one does not observe for non-specialized firms any correlation between their profitability and the share of services in their revenue. The most clearly observable difference of behavior between products and services is the narrowness of variation ranges for services, and their higher stability over time. The crisis that precipitated many hardware manufacturers into the red from 1991 on has had no visible effect on the overall profitability of services, where relative difficulties started in 1989. For manufacturers in trouble, developing their services activity has enabled them to limit the impact of losses due to hardware, mainly by charging for their excess personnel, even at moderately profitable rates.

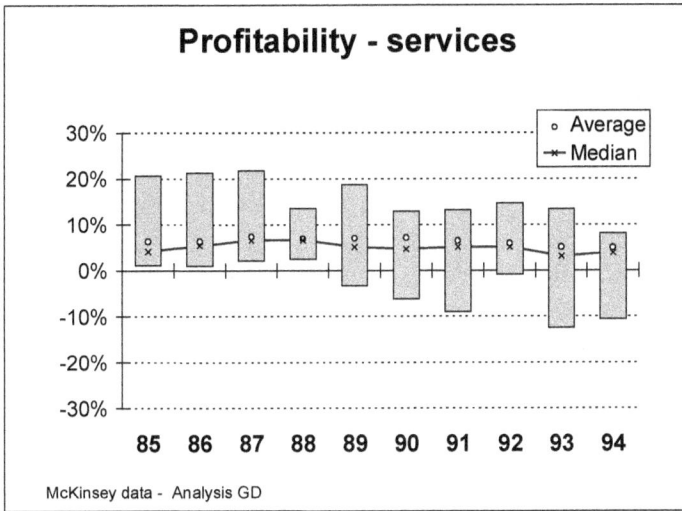

The reason for the unwarranted profitability reputation of services is probably that relative insensitivity to the crisis of standard hardware. This illusion is
upheld by commentators who include services in the same artificial "sector" as
packaged software, the profitability of which is indeed better, with averages often
higher than 15%. But this simple difference of level is a clear indication that services and packaged software are different activities submitted to radically different
competitive dynamics.

Computer services and computerized services

Even when restricted to the area of computing, services do not form a sector
in the sense of Porter, that is to say, transposing the classical definition, "a group of
firms producing services that are close substitutes of each other". Technical assistance, software development, maintenance, application processing, systems integration, backup, etc. represent a wide variety of services, each one satisfying a particular need. Those services form as many offerings which cannot be substituted to
each other and therefore define separate sectors.

In each such sector, the production mechanisms and the competitive forces
can take a specific form, leading to different sector logic. The degree of concentration and the potential level of profitability vary depending on the nature of services. Success factors and appropriate strategies differ from one sector to the next
and call for different enterprise personalities, organizations and cultures. Those
variations are even so significant that services cannot be considered as a homogeneous activity (a trade) in the sense that we have introduced in chapter 6, that is to
say a group of sectors obeying the same form of competitive dynamics, like for
example hardware assembly or the production of packaged software.

Heterogeneous by the nature of services offered and by the competitive
dynamics that structure each sector, the area of services is also heterogeneous by
the diversity of players present, who implement diversified strategies. Specialized

players are numerous: in the sample of 100 large enterprises that we have studied in chapter 4, one counts 25 firms specialized in services. In addition, there are also, in the USA as in Europe, a multitude of service enterprises too small to appear in this sample. Moreover, many firms are present in services without being specialized. It is the case for virtually all the generalists and close to 40% of the other specialists.

Besides, it is likely that this picture is itself an imperfect representation of reality. Many forms of service have traditionally been offered by product suppliers as complements of their main production, without necessarily being charged separately. The literature still often presents services as attributes of products, meant to provide them with some competitive advantage, but not to produce profitable revenue by themselves. Separate billing of services, introduced by IBM in 1969, is far from constituting an absolute rule for all manufacturers. The same type of service can be offered free by one firm and carry a fee when offered by another one, specialized or not.

Those divergent motivations and modes contribute to blur even more the contours of the services field, already uncertain by nature. We have seen that the usual view of a services world opposed a world of products is an artificial dichotomy when compared to reality. The range of services is too heterogeneous to enable attaching them a set of common characteristics that would differentiate them globally from products. Quite on the contrary, some services can more easily substituted to products than to other services, for example the service bureau that we will study later in this chapter.

In summary, the diversity of services is similar to that of the entire range of products. In order to understand them, we will need to call upon the whole set of conceptual analysis tools that we have presented so far: competitive analysis of concentration and fragmentation factors, inventory of available strategies, chronology of decisions, enterprise personalities and compatibility between organizations. The world of services will then appear as a varied and unstable world, parallel to that of products and linked to it by complex relationships of complementarity and competition.

To undertake this analysis, we must first structure the area of services into competitive sectors in the sense of Porter, each sector including only "closely substitutable" services intended to satisfy the same need. At the highest level, we can already classify computer services according to three main typical destinations.

Most services traditionally offered by computer service companies are intended to facilitate or otherwise support the implementation of computer systems. This category includes for example the activities of advice, assistance, program development, system integration, etc. for which the customers are most often computer professionals and managers. The market for such services is created by the sale of computer products, and is in the first analysis increasing together with that the product market itself. The different services of this type can be competing with each other, but form globally a specific group which cannot be replaced by services external to the computer industry. We will call this category "support services".

A slightly different case is services that are an alternative to the acquisition of computer products, such as the service bureau and certain forms of "facilities management" based on sharing hardware or software resources between customers. From the viewpoint of the market, such services are in direct competition with computer products. Even if, in the end, the service provider is a customer of the suppliers of hardware and packaged software, his intervention reduces their market by definition. We will call this category "replacement services".

A third category is formed by services whose usefulness is external to computing, but that rely on computers for their implementation, in order to obtain a competitive advantage. For example, accounting and personnel management, even computerized, retain a utility external to data-processing and are actually competing with other forms of accounting or personnel management, not with other computer services. Their market is that of accountants and personnel managers. We will call this category "computerized services" or "application services".

Computerized services result from the introduction of computer technology into the implementation of other services, which most often already exist, and whose market is defined by the users of those existing services, whatever is their degree of computerization. Even if the use of computing technology may enable the creation of new services or bring profound changes to the activity and the respective competitive advantages of suppliers, the competitive game is played in an arena separate from that of computer products. For that reason, we will consider that computerized application services do not properly belong to the computer industry. The problematic of computerized services is a particular case of computing technology spreading across all human activities and will be addressed in the last chapter concerning the borderlines of the computing industry.

On the contrary, the competitive dynamics of support services and replacement services is directly linked to that of the other sectors of the computer industry. In this sense, those services are an integral part of the computer industry and are addressed in the present chapter. Let us keep in mind, however, that many services of a general nature are used in support of the computing activity without taking a significantly different character in this context. It is for instance the case of financial services, transportation services, electricity, etc. Trucks are used to deliver computers, banks to finance them and electricity to power them, but that is no reason for including road transportation, banking and power utilities in the computer industry. We will limit accordingly the discussion in this chapter to support services that are specific to computing. This excludes, among others, distributors, brokers or leasers, whose activity is not fundamentally different whether it relates to computer products or to other products.

Furthermore, the distinction that we have just introduced between support services, replacement services and application services has not always been as clear. In the first times of computing, a computerized accounting service was considered first a computer service; it was offered by firms specialized in computing and not by accounting firms. Now that all accountants use computers, computerized accounting has become commonplace and no longer belongs to the computer industry. We will see that this migration phenomenon is characteristic of the evolution of processing services. Moreover, the same support services can come with products and replacement services, or be an integral part of the latter.

Finally, support services that are not specifically computer-oriented can become computerized systems and thus invite to confusion in two ways. The most significant example is telecommunications services, which many commentators describe as merging with computing. For this author, the relationships between those two industries pertain essentially to the growing utilization of computing in communications, in the same way as in banking, transportation, entertainment or all the other industries, a phenomenon which we will examine in chapter 16. On the other side, it is true that telecommunications services form an increasingly vital component of computing systems, but this does not imply that telecommunications enterprises provide services of a type significantly different from their usual activity, which remains the transmission of information unmodified between distant points. The utilization of its services by computing does not lead the telecommunications industry to structure itself differently or to obey a different economic logic. We will return to this subject in the last chapter of this book.

Replacement services and the history of the Service Bureau

In its first years, the computer industry provided along with hardware, without separate billing, customer training, hardware maintenance and technical assistance, including an important share of custom software development. But the cost of the first computers and the scarcity of skills required for their implementation reserved them to a small number of large enterprises. Computer manufacturers, in particular, saw an important market for shared computer centers that would serve the needs of the majority of users, too small to afford acquisition of their own processing resources. Thus was created the "Service Bureau", which is in essence a service offering designed as an alternative to the acquisition of computer products.

Note in passing that the same reasoning had led previously to the opening of "service bureau" centers on unit-record punched cards equipment. The first computer services resulted simply from the installation of computers in the classical unit-record Service Bureau, that already existed since several decades before the appearance of computers. Originally, this service was the only one to be subject to a commercial offering and separate billing, whether offered by equipment manufacturers or by the first independent services companies.

The initial service bureau offering was a global alternative to the utilization of dedicated resources. In the same way as equipment vendors provided ancillary services at no separate charge, service bureau suppliers included program development, operating personnel and possible user assistance in the price of processing. In both cases, the expensive and scarce resource was hardware, while the cost of personnel was relatively secondary.

The service bureau thus appears as another mode of accessing computer equipment and associated services, addressing mainly the small and average customers, as well as occasional projects or projects requiring special skills. Conceptually, the service bureau competed with the acquisition of dedicated computers, but in reality such competition was initially limited due to the high cost of equipment and the novelty of applications. In 1957, IBM believed that the market for scientific computing in Europe would be satisfied by a handful of computers acquired for their own needs by a few large organizations such as nuclear agencies, the rest being served by a computing center managed by IBM in a service bureau mode. Even for equipment manufacturers, potential competition between the two offerings remained theoretical.

The service bureau thus formed a relatively well-delimited sector isolated from equipment, especially since the largest supplier, IBM, had assigned that activity to a specialized subsidiary as a result of the 1956 Consent Decree. Even if that decision only applied to activities in the USA, a tradition of separate management spread to the IBM Service Bureau activities in the whole world.

To offer good service quality, processing centers had to be physically close to customers, which separated the market (and the sector) into geographical competitive zones, two distant centers not being really competitors. Each sub-sector thus constituted was initially concentrated, like besides the whole industry , as predicted by the theory for emerging industries. Indeed, the acquisition costs of a computer and the scarcity of skills required to exploit it constituted sufficient obstacles to entry to discourage candidates, on a market still perceived as narrow. For the same reasons, the most natural offer was an integrated supply associating the products (or pseudo-products) with the new services enabling their utilization. The charge for the bundle was based on the products, which formed the expensive and scarce part, and therefore the support of the value.

Fragmentation of the Service Bureau

Starting from that initial situation, the cost of equipment did not stop decreasing, and with it the price of entry computers. This consequence of technological progress has entailed two series of consequences for service bureau, which contributed to modeling the area of computer services.

First, the share of hardware in the overall service package decreased, forcing suppliers to restructure their rates by dissociating the different services, which was a prelude to the explosion of the sector into specialized sub-sectors. Second, the part of the market where service bureau and hardware are really competing expanded constantly and the economic advantages of acquiring equipment increased. This led first to the decline, then to the virtual disappearance of the market for shared facilities, and therefore of the corresponding industry sector.

From the beginning of the sixties, and especially after the introduction of the 360 generation of equipment, the share of personnel and packaged software became an increasing part of the costs of service bureau and of the invoice of its users. At the same time, the spreading of skills and the growing availability of packaged software enabled customers to write their programs or to use existing programs, and only buy from services companies access to the machine and minimal assistance in its operations. To adjust their supply and their invoice to that diversifying demand, service companies were led to distinguish and to price services such as technical assistance, program development, etc. separately from the use of equipment or software. Even within processing, the variety of utilizations led to distinguish units of work such as processing time, usage of the different levels of memory, manual interventions or the use of particular units.

In the second half of the sixties and in the beginning of the seventies, two additional phenomena occurred, working in two opposite directions. On one hand, some large users with their own computer equipment appeared on the processing services market in order to resell their unused machine time, sometimes creating specialized subsidiaries for that purpose. This additional supply of raw computing time, often at marginal rates, accelerated the price decline of pure computing time

At the same time, technical developments in multiprogramming and in the utilization of telecommunications and time-sharing gave birth, by the end of the sixties, to the concept of the "computer utility". At that time, the economics of computer processing still obeyed the so-called "Grosch's law", which stated that it is less expensive to execute a job on a large shared computer than on a small dedicated computer. Many observers concluded that computing would evolve to a worldwide network where a few very large computers would supply "computing energy" to users through a global telecommunications network. Anticipating such evolution, existing service suppliers accelerated their conversion towards "teleprocessing", at the same time as new entrants specialized in "time-sharing" (Tymshare, General Electric, McDonnell, …).

Those technical mutations changed the competitive dynamics of processing services. On one hand, use of teleprocessing erased physical distances and made the market a worldwide one. Some suppliers even believed that they could derive a competitive advantage from the time differences by selling off-hours processing on one continent to customers on another continent. On the widened market created by the utilization of telecommunications, Grosch's law and the economies of scale that it implied gave a competitive advantage to the largest suppliers and favored the boom of worldwide enterprises.

All those events pushed to increasing separation of computer processing services from the so-called "professional" services like development and assistance. At the same time, in the early seventies, a similar separation occurred on the product side, on the initiative of IBM (see chapter 2). We have seen that the strategic ambition of IBM on that occasion was not to dominate the new market of services that it had just created, but rather to offload the bulk of customer support tasks by transferring them to service enterprises. A new sector of "professional" services, concerning mostly the development of application programs and the installation of complete systems, was thus put in place as a natural evolution of the service bureau companies as well as by the appearance of new specialized firms.

For that last type of services, the physical proximity of the service provider with the customer remained desirable and the optimal production scale was quickly reached even on a local market. This sector retained therefore a fragmented structure, from a geographical standpoint as well as within each local market.

The seventies saw the boom and the diversification of computing services companies. New players, often coming from other industrial sectors like banks, industry or telecommunications, adopted specialization strategies along two main directions: technical assistance and application development on one hand, distribution of "computing energy" and access to libraries of application programs on the other hand. On their side, most of the large traditional service bureau enterprises tried to preserve their generalist status by offering the full range of services, while often structuring themselves into specialized units for each one of the above main types of services.

Decline and disappearance

In the late seventies, the market for shared processing, which had been at the origin of the whole services sector, began to decline gradually until vanishing in the mid-eighties. This gradual erosion is the direct consequence of the continuous improvement of the price-performance ratio of equipment and especially of the increasing power of entry-level equipment such as minicomputers, and later micro-computers. Moreover, sharing a large computer between independent users implies coordination and protection costs in addition to transmission costs inherent to teleprocessing, so that the famous "Grosch's law" was now reversed: it became more economical to execute a program on the smallest machine that can accommodate it than on a large shared computer. As a growing number of users acquired their own computing resources adapted to their needs, the market for timesharing diminished to the point of vanishing by the end of the eighties.

Enterprises operating in that sector were condemned to reconvert or disappear. Those that had been able to anticipate by separating their rates and their services at the right time were able to purely and simply leave the sector without too much damage, especially if processing represented only a marginal share of their revenue. The other enterprises, whose profitability rested on the sale of processing services, had to face recession of their revenue while redeploying their operating personnel to new activities. To that effect, they had to choose between several paths depending on their situation, their vision of the future, and to take advantage of at least one of their processing-related assets:
- possession of powerful computing and storage resources,
- command of a data transmission network,
- skills in implementation and operation of large systems,
- skills and software concerning specific applications or markets.

For a small number of enterprises, computer processing on a shared basis was only the support of an application know-how concerning the needs of a particular clientele such as accountants (CCMC) or insurance agents (Policy Management). It could also perform operations that are by nature common to several enterprises like credit card processing (Sligos in France, First Data in the USA). As long as their particular market could survive the democratization of computing, those enterprises were able continue their timesharing activity, but their competitive advantage was increasingly related to their application knowledge, and less and less to their computer skills. Thereby, even if the use of shared means remained a viable alternative, those enterprises were increasingly threatened by competition from firms in their client industry, while their evolution possibilities were increasingly limited to that customer sector. In summary, their behavior became dictated by their interactions with the client industry more than by the evolution of other computer services. Regarding their competitive behavior and the resulting industrial dynamics, those firms actually left the computer industry to become increasingly close to the client industry.

Some companies tried to postpone the fatal outcome by concentrating on supercomputers, but even the high end of the range finally succumbed to the democratization of equipment. Others thought that they could exploit their network and centralized resources to offer access to shared databases. But they quickly found out that the value of the service, as well as its cost, essentially resides in the creation and updating of information, which transferred the relative power to the information producers. Computer services companies that engaged into this path were rapidly reduced to a role of facility designers and operators for the benefit of information producers.

Still others like General Electric, Tymshare or IBM tried to fall back on offerings directly related to telecommunications management, such as messaging or file transfer. Just as in the case of computerized services, they then left the competitive arena of computing to enter that of telecommunications by becoming competitors of the large traditional operators.

It is in this context that the debate on "value added services" started in the USA on the occasion of new regulation projects for telecommunications (wrongly called "deregulation"). One question was to what extent the utilization of leased lines should be restricted to the leasing party, or whether he can be authorized to offer access to these lines to third parties, and if yes under which conditions. Telecommunications operators viewed that possibility as a serious threat to their rate structure and financial balance. Therefore, they were seeking to limit it, while users of telecommunications, and primarily the large enterprises of all branches, wished to be granted maximum freedom.

In that debate, computing services companies played an unexpected role. The telecommunications operators interpreted the concentration of some processing companies on services closely linked to their existing network as the prelude to a competitive attack of their own sector. The maneuvers by IBM in that same area even revived the old fantasy of the worldwide computer network. Concerning usage of leased lines, services companies naturally adopted a liberal position reflecting their desire not to complicate further their move away from processing, or their community of interest with their customers in the case of systems engineering firms. But that position reinforced the belief of the telecommunications vendors that computing services companies (and IBM) were only waiting for the liberalization of communications to engage into an aggressive strategy of installing "value added networks". It is not even certain that the surrealist controversy that followed will not be revived someday about the "information highways"...

The above summary of some thirty years in the history of computer processing services shows, over a relatively short period, the complete life and death cycle of an industrial sector, as in an accelerated movie sequence. In accordance with theory, the sector started integrated and concentrated, then firms became specialized and the sector became fragmented as the market grew. The maturity phase, and then the recession of the market took the industry back to a concentrated structure as the number of firms active in the sector decreased. At the same time, some enterprises operating in particular niches survived by integrating themselves into the industry sectors with which they maintained privileged relationships. By bursting into pieces as a result of competition from hardware, the extinct sector of processing left fragments behind, that aggregated somehow with other industries.

Current statistics still show slightly more than 15% processing within computer services, gradually declining at a rate of 1 to 2 percentage points per year. Considering the identity of the firms involved, a majority of those services are actually computerized application services such as credit card transaction management, or services to accountants or insurance agents. Those services figure in the computer industry statistics because they are provided by enterprises labeled computer services companies, while other similar application services, just as much computerized, do not appear because they are provided by other enterprises, not categorized as such. One could quote many examples in the area of messaging, databases, electronic trade, or companies like Prodigy or Compuserve. In other words, the presence of a "processing" category in computer services is essentially a statistic archaism.

The example of processing services also illustrates the close interdependence relationships between the sector of services and that of products. On one hand the market for services is created by products, and on the other hand competition between products and services for the satisfaction of the same needs leads some services to regress and disappear. Note that in this competition, contrary to the "post-industrial" thesis that we have mentioned in chapter 10, the "product" mode has prevailed upon the "services" mode.

Can one then conclude that technological progress, by bringing computer products into the reach of all potential users and by eliminating economies of scale for users, has definitively made replacement services such as the service bureau obsolete? It is one way to approach the issue of the new forms of service which have appeared —or reappeared — recently under the generic name of "facilities management". Those services are related to replacement services to the extent that the service provider, not the user, owns the computing resources and assumes permanent operations responsibility on behalf of his customers. Like timesharing, this service is for the customer an alternative to the acquisition of products, and the services firm has (within certain limits) the possibility to share some resources between several customers.

Seen from that viewpoint alone, facilities management services could have a difficult time finding a durable economic justification. The same reasons that led to the disappearance of the service bureau should limit the market to extremely narrow niches. But facilities management can also be seen as an attempt to reintegrate into an overall service not only computer operations, but also services of a different nature such as software development, maintenance, operation assistance, etc.. For this reason, we will defer the discussion on those forms of service, which are the subject of lively controversy, and return to them after looking at support services.

Support services

After the virtual disappearance of processing services, computer services are now essentially so-called "professional" services: advice, assistance, training, systems engineering, software development, systems integration. Let us keep in mind that the present chapter is limited to services used for the implementation of computer systems, excluding computerized application services.

The large enterprises specialized in services, like besides the equipment manufacturers present in this sector, have sought to offer all the above services or to evolve from one to the other in response to market demand. But even the "professional" forms of services present sufficient differences between one another to demand different structures, management systems and company cultures. Moreover, the very nature of services activities puts the whole enterprise in direct contact with the market and renders its performance closely dependent upon the adequacy of its enterprise personality to the expectations of the market.

Cultural differences take therefore a higher importance here than in classical production activities where the production machinery is isolated from the market. They explain the difficulties that enterprises come across in seeking to make activities of different natures coexist, or to undertake new activities foreign to their basic personality. They contribute to structuring the area of services into separate sectors between which moving is difficult, and to sketch the likely evolution of the sector.

We have presented in chapter 9 the roots of these compatibility problems. Let us examine them in more detail, using the typical examples of technical assistance on one hand, systems development on the other hand.

Characteristics and economics

For development as for assistance, production costs are constituted almost exclusively by personnel costs or costs directly related to personnel (premises, individual equipment, supplies, …). Investments are low and can practically be reduced to zero by leasing premises and equipment. Obstacles to entry are limited to individual acquisition of the required skills. A small enterprise can be competitive, and potential economies of scale are limited. Both sectors are therefore fragmented and modest profit margins can be expected.

Consulting activities can be assimilated to assistance in terms of production structures. The basic difference between assistance and consulting on one hand, systems engineering, software development, and systems integration on the other hand resides in the nature of contractual commitments made by the service provider: commitment to provide means in the first case, commitment to produce results in the second.

Systems engineering differs from software development by the fact that it results in the supply of a complete system including hardware. It is commonly called "systems integration" if that hardware includes heterogeneous elements from different manufacturers. We will see that those activities are not fundamentally different in terms of matching enterprise personalities.

Technical assistance boils down to making available to the customer people possessing skills that he requires. Those persons are integrated into the customer teams and their work is actually managed by the customer. The service is billed proportionally to the time spent, based on an hourly or daily rate related to the skill level. In other words, the revenue of the service provider is directly proportional to the time spent by each individual, whatever the nature, the quality and the results of their work. For development, on the contrary, billing is based on the achievement of results specified in the contract, most often independently of the effort really spent to obtain those results.

It follows that the tactics and strategies that must be adopted to succeed in the face of competition are radically different for the two categories of services, as well as the organizations and company cultures that must be implemented to support those strategies.

The assistance activity can operate on a very small scale, even that of isolated individuals. The structure of this sector is therefore extremely fragmented and the working of competition approaches the "pure and perfect" model. In particular, market prices result from matching global supply and global demand and are imposed on each supplier. Moreover, the very nature of the activity imposes physical proximity between suppliers and their customers. All firms competing in a given market operate therefore in the same region and support identical personnel costs. Competitive firms, living by the same stringent management practices, are led to use virtually identical rates and can therefore differentiate only through the individual skills of their employees. Exploiting such differentiation can imply that the enterprise chooses a particular specialized niche in order to benefit from learning effects. In any case, even efficient firms will only realize low margins, but can limit profit variations to a narrow band by suitably managing their personnel resources.

In the case of technical assistance, the only workable tactic consists in maximizing the time invoiced for each person and to reduce to a minimum "unproductive" staffs such as management and administration. At the strategic level, it is necessary to correctly anticipate future demand and to adjust staff in number, skills and quality. Such forecasts can be facilitated if the enterprise limits itself to a particular niche. In any event, a possible mistake can be corrected rapidly enough if the enterprise preserves sufficient flexibility in the management of its work-force. The cycle of the assistance activity is therefore short.

In the development activity, it is necessary first to close business by proposing a more attractive offer than competitors, then to satisfy contractual commitments without exceeding anticipated costs. In general, the customer presents a problem for which the supplier must propose a technical solution with an estimate of its operating costs and performance, and an implementation plan also with its estimated costs and schedule. Through this proposal, the supplier commits himself to reach certain explicitly specified results, for a price and according to a schedule that can be either indicative and subject to revision according to contractual procedures, or fixed by the contract. The customer chooses supplier by comparing competitive proposals, which will often push the service providers to propose maximum service for a minimum price, especially if the customer is an administration where the contract is awarded to the lowest bidder.

After the contract is signed, revenue depends on meeting commitments and achieving results, while costs depend on resources actually expended to reach those results. Making a net positive profit eventually emerge from the balance demands significant skills in the design of computer systems, in project estimating and in project management.

All those skills are normally the fruit of experience, but specific investments are often needed to acquire and maintain them. Those investments can imply the acquisition of equipment or the development of software that will embody the skills and will enable presenting more attractive and more believable proposals than competition. Obstacles to entry are therefore more serious than for simple assistance.

The preparation of proposals itself demands significant work, that can become very important in the case of complex problems. The related expenses must of course be committed by the enterprise before knowing whether the proposal is accepted, and constitute therefore an investment in the full meaning of the word, which must be financed by the profits realized on ongoing contracts.

Finally, the numerous uncertainty factors place significant risk on the profitability of each project, which can only be supported by enterprises of a sufficient size to absorb possible failures by spreading those risks over their entire activity. In summary, the development sector, and *a fortiori* systems integration, are more concentrated sectors where size provides a real competitive advantage. On the other hand, the statistical probability of failure of each project keeps the average profitability of the sector at the same modest level as for assistance, with nevertheless a wider range of variation going from quick bankruptcy for the least successful to the hope of comfortable margins for the most competent or the luckiest.

The customer-supplier relationship

We have seen in chapter 11 that the characteristics of the customer-supplier relationship are one dimension along which services can be distinguished from products, and the various types of services between one another. Assistance services represent a typical service to the extent that they consist simply in making a productive resource available to the customer without commitment to a specific result, and for a charge proportional to the time the resource is made available.

On the contrary, a development or integration contract relies on the definition of the target result, and calls for the definitive transfer to the customer of a good, defined through negotiation between the customer and the service provider. That definition could in principle serve as a base for agreeing in advance on a fixed price and thus transferring to the service provider the positive and negative risks associated with the completion of the project. Competition between suppliers would then be based on one hand on the proposed price, at the time of the struggle for closing contracts, and on the other hand on the management of actual projects, to ensure their profitability and therefore the survival of the enterprise.

Reality is less simple, and this type of fixed-price contract is far from being the common practice of the sector.

Implementation of a computer development project of some scale, and *a fortiori* of a system integration project, can last several years, in the course of which a multitude of issues must be resolved in a concrete manner that had not been foreseen, let alone resolved, at the time of the overall design. Each of those practical decisions can have important consequences in terms of usefulness, ease of use, reliability, performance or operational cost for the customer, but also for the implementation cost and schedule. Moreover, the detailed design and implementation of the system require the intervention of a growing number of people that were left out of the initial general design phase. Those individuals do not always consider themselves committed by the original specifications and contract, and their wishes can nevertheless not be ignored since they include in particular the real users of the system.

Many people have believed, and some still do, that the solution is to extend the initial study sufficiently far, so that all implementation decisions with a possible impact on the costs or schedules will be taken before closing the contract. This approach is twice deceptive: first, it would result in a prohibitive duration and costs for the preliminary study and would thereby lead to elimination of the most honest bidders. In addition, the conclusions of such a study would end up being challenged anyway. On one hand the environment evolves during the project, and so do the functional needs, the available means and technologies and the ideas for solutions. On the other hand, users often cannot state clearly their requirements at the necessary level of detail before seeing a first implementation which will (quite rightfully) trigger new requirements or modifications of their previously expressed needs. For real-world computer applications, the complexity of the final product forbids any reliable and exhaustive *a priori* specification. The real needs can only appear gradually in the course of development.

In that situation, putting in place dispositions aiming to prevent any deviation from the initial specifications, whatever their quality, can only end in a final product unsuitable for the real needs and preferences of its users and therefore doomed to certain failure. One must accept the idea that the system can only be defined gradually and that there is no way to determine in advance its costs, performance and schedule with anything approaching certainty. The initial proposal can only be indicative and the contract must be viewed and designed essentially as a framework for the gradual establishment of actual specifications and corresponding contract amendments.

For service companies, it is no longer sufficient to adjust resources correctly to the expected demand by cutting down "non-productive" staff to the minimum level and by containing personnel costs. They must also develop reasonable project cost estimates, not only at the time of the initial proposal, but also throughout their life, recognizing the changing expectations of customers. They also need the ability to negotiate the reciprocal adjustment of contractual costs and specifications, while meeting commitments made to the customer concerning results as well as commitments made to the enterprise concerning costs. They must not be brought to provide additional service without additional billing. The final profitability of a project will therefore depend on a large number of factors: the skills of the enterprise in estimating and managing projects, the good allocation of people to the project, their technological know-how and their productivity.

Such a situation creates conflicts between customer and supplier, but also between different motivations within the client organization. All modifications of demand that intervene in the life of the project must be subject to a tradeoff analysis between their cost and their interest, so as to decide on their implementation. Only the customer can validly make such decisions, since he is the one who eventually benefits and must therefore support the possible additional cost and delay. The customer thus retains an important responsibility whatever the terms of the contract. But he is not always prepared to discharge that responsibility, which he may think has been offloaded onto the supplier. If the conflict of interest within his own organization is too acute, there is a big temptation to avoid it by rejecting full responsibility on the supplier.

In general, neither customers nor service providers truly know how to reconcile reality, where the real project is defined during implementation, with contractual frameworks applicable to other, more stable forms of implementation. Services companies that seriously engage into that direction are quick to find out that an evolutionary management of both specification and contract is the only realistic approach, but they encounter great difficulty in presenting competitive bids on that basis. To avoid systematically losing business, they must in practice align themselves with their less experienced or less scrupulous competitors. In summary, the market is not mature for fixed-price development contracts and continues to seek ways to resolve that issue.

Structure and management system

In the technical assistance activity, each individual is billed independently of the others and constitutes therefore the basic unit of management (the "business unit"). There are in this sector a large number of independent workers, and very small enterprises which actually operate as associations of a small number of independent workers. In enterprises large enough to justify a real hierarchical organization, only limited administrative and commercial tasks are centralized at the level of the management of each team or of the whole enterprise. Every individual essentially manages his or her own activities, and management intervenes only in case of problems, for example insufficient workload.

Each basic team groups together a certain array of skills, generally adapted to the needs of a specified group of customers. The basis for differentiation is therefore both the specialization of skills and the structure of the market. Within each team, each individual sells himself at the same time as he or she produces. The commercial activity is not separate from the production activity, even if it is a more important part of the team leaders' activity. But the specific part of the managers' role is essentially administrative and they have virtually no share in the definition or allocation of tasks to the people who report to them. In the same way, the central staff of the enterprise is reduced to a minimum. Everyone including the managers reject central structures as "unproductive", and each unit feels that it would work better alone.

Operational management is reduced to verifying that all employees are engaged in activities billed at the normal rate, and that the firm as a whole produces a positive margin. A profit and loss statement consistent with that of an enterprise can validly be associated with each unit, whatever its level, and even to each individual. The most efficient management system consists in maximum decentralization of all current management actions, coupled with daily follow-up of the profit and loss statement of each unit. In summary, the enterprise works as a conglomerate of small autonomous units, each one managing its own profit and loss account similar to that of an independent enterprise and to that of the whole enterprise.

In an enterprise entirely devoted to assistance, the role of top management is not fundamentally different from that of middle and first-line management. The structure of the enterprise is stable and executives are not faced with difficult organizational issues. Adjustment of resources to market trends can be largely decentralized to the level of basic units, that are highly motivated to remain in sync with the foreseeable needs of their customers. Because of the ambiguity of the organization, executive management may have to resolve potential conflicts between units, for instance when one seeks to sell its skills to traditional customers of another one, or on the contrary when one unit must call upon another to satisfy the demands of its customers. In summary, using the concepts that we have presented in chapter 9, the assistance firm is characterized by a homogeneous organization at all levels, with very little differentiation and therefore little need for integration mechanisms.

Development or integration activities are quite different. For one, the basic management unit is the project and no longer the individual. This imposes a far more complex structure than for assistance.

First, the commercial activity and the implementation activity are far more distinct. While implementation can involve a large number of persons with very different skills over a long period, preparation of a proposal and the actual selling activity involve a limited number of persons, generally people with unusually high skills and experience, during a relatively short time. Moreover, proposals are not all followed by an order and the start of an implementation project, so that the commercial activity must be conducted in a structure different from the project implementation structure.

When a proposal is accepted and implementation begins, the implementation team must be composed according to the specific needs of the project and can vary in the course of time. It must be possible to draw the necessary persons from a reservoir of skills and to return them there when their involvement in the project is over. Certain resources can be shared between several projects and therefore belong to separate project support units. The structure of the enterprise must therefore provide for the coexistence of a project structure, varying in time according to the projects under way and their degree of advancement, and of a resource center structure that constitutes the permanent framework of the enterprise and the basis for personnel management. Moreover, projects in the implementation phase and projects in the proposal phase are most often handled in two different structures.

Finally, the need for critical skills or for shared general-purpose facilities can justify the existence of centralized support services.

Operational management must simultaneously pursue several objectives. For each project being implemented, commitments made to the customer, concerning functions and performance of the system, implementation schedule or induced costs for the user must be met, and resource usage must be maintained within the estimates used for quoting the price. At the level of the entire enterprise, the objective is to ensure the full utilization of resources by allocating them judiciously to accepted projects and by maintaining a backlog of current proposals consistent with the present and anticipated availability of resources. The information system must therefore concern itself with the status of projects and the probability of meeting schedules and technical objectives, as well as with resource usage accounting, identification of available resources and follow up of open proposals.

Contrary to the assistance enterprise, where the role of management is similar in all positions and at all levels, the different units and therefore their managers play here differentiated roles that require integration mechanisms and efforts at the higher levels. At the lowest levels, local managers are assigned defined tasks, resources and schedules and must ensure that assigned tasks are executed on schedule with the allocated means. At the project level, the manager's main responsibility is to correctly allocate tasks and resources in order to reach the contractual results on schedule at the lowest cost, in a dynamic manner according to the actual situation of the project. The role of those execution managers is therefore mainly technical. The administrative and commercial roles that they play in their relationships with the customer and the rest of the enterprise are based on that technical role.

In the assistance enterprise, no first-level employee is normally led to make important commitments on behalf of the enterprise. In development on the contrary, each individual can commit heavily the whole enterprise, for example by designing a system architecture or by estimating the cost and the duration of a project. Because of their potential consequences, some of those decisions must be reserved for the appropriate level of responsibility. This requires an explicit system of limitation and delegation of power, complemented by a formalized control and approval system. Each level of the hierarchy is no longer free to make its own decisions, but has to solicit approvals and to abide by external controls that often call for direct executive intervention in the detail of business.

Direct involvement of higher levels, including executive management, is also necessary to appreciate and controm the technical and commercial risks taken in proposals, to arbitrate conflicts between units in the allocation of resources, and to manage disagreements with customers. For top management of the enterprise, those operational responsibilities are added to their strategic responsibilities.

In summary, the development or integration firm possesses a differentiated organization in the sense of Lawrence and Lorsch[68], that requires correspondingly strong integration mechanisms.

---

68   See chapter 9

Values and culture

In services enterprises with a strong human component, each employee inter-venes in the relationship with the customer and thereby contributes to building the image of the enterprise. Moreover, each employee, even at modest levels, may be the origin of decisions vital for the success of the enterprise, for which he or she alone holds the information or the necessary skills. Finally, he or she often operates far from the framework of the enterprise, without close supervision nor easy access to management in case of difficulty. Each employee must therefore model his or her personal behavior on a certain number of norms, principles and values that are part of the culture of the enterprise.

For technical assistance, the objective of each employee must be to possess skills sufficiently recognized to be the subject of a strong market demand, and therefore to be sold at a high price and in high quantity. Success is directly mea-sured by the percentage of time billed, which summarizes the judgment of cus-tomers on the adequacy of skills, the usefulness and the quality of the work pro-vided. But those last criteria are not independent objectives or values *per se*. In a way, it matters little that the work may be useless, of poor quality or unproductive as long as the customer is happy to pay for it. It is recommended to stay as long as possible with each customer, which suffices to prove the usefulness of the work and the satisfaction of the customer, and minimizes both idle time not invoiced and commercial expenses for obtaining new contracts. Each employee will therefore attempt to arouse new requirements that justify extending his or her assignment. Time spent on the job has a positive value and must be maximized.

In technical assistance, each employee is seconded to a customer and inte-grated into one of its teams. Relative to the enterprise to which he or she belongs, the employee works individually and has only few professional relationships with his or her colleagues, with whom he does not feel strongly interdependent. The dominant culture of the firm is individualistic. At the very most each individual feels close to the small team where he or she belongs, but in its turn this team and its manager feel and want to be independent, and regard the enterprise more as a source of constraints and obligations than as a favorable environment. On the other hand, the concept of the profit and loss account and the objective of balanc-ing it are common to all. Although identification with the enterprise is low, culture is homogeneous in the whole enterprise.

It may happen that the employee of a technical assistance enterprise identi-fies with the customer rather than with the enterprise that employs him, which can create a potential risk for time management and billing. This very loose bond between the firm and its employees entails a low fidelity and an important mobility of personnel. Conversely, no single individual is critical for the enterprise and their fidelity is not vital. The enterprise can, without much risk, implement restrictive social and personnel management policies so as to preserve moderate costs and the necessary flexibility in management of its workforce.

In development, the tasks of each employee are allocated and controlled by a line manager belonging to the enterprise, and the work often takes place on the premises of the enterprise. Each individual is judged by his or her managers and not by the customer, on his or her results and not only on skills. Contrary to the case of assistance, membership in the enterprise is operational and unequivocal. The activity is conducted with lower autonomy than technical assistance, but in counterpart individual decisions are more complex and of a broader reach.

The implementation activity occupies the majority of employees of the enterprise and determines its basic culture. Even the commercial activity relies on strong implementation skills, and the people involved are coming from the implementation side and remain involved in implementation most of the time. The objective of each employee is to accomplish his or her assigned tasks as rapidly as possible and at the least expense while meeting functionality and quality objectives. Contrary to the case of assistance, the time spent on a task must be minimized and constitutes therefore a negative value. When an extension seems desirable or is requested by the customer, one must be able to refrain from any commitment until a corresponding extension of the contract is proposed and accepted.

Development is the work of a team where the individual roles are differentiated, requiring team spirit in proportion. The team culture must also accept external constraints, controls and judgments which we have seen are necessary and key to success. Finally, commitment to the project must go with sufficiently strong identification with the enterprise to accept changes in assignments and reporting, that may call for a certain level of physical mobility.

Among the conflicts of interest inherent in the development activity, one of the most crucial concerns the commercial activity. To win a contract in a competitive situation, it is necessary to promise a lot for the lowest possible price, and therefore often to take the risk that the actual cost of implementation might exceed the contractual cost and leave no profit margin to the enterprise. At the opposite, not taking that risk can lead to loss of the contract and therefore an even more negative effect on profit. The commercial activity related to development requires therefore uncommon business acumen and a high maturity. In a way, the qualities required to succeed in the execution of a project (lucidity, prudence, honesty,...) are as many potential reasons to lose contracts.

At the same time, original solutions in systems design or in implementation methods can constitute a decisive competitive advantage. In addition to realism in estimates and rigor in management, creativity in the definition of solutions must also be encouraged.

An overview in the nineties

The pitfalls of evolution

With the decline of service bureau, technical assistance has become the main mode of computer services. Until the nineties, this sector developed rapidly by benefiting in particular from the shortage of skilled personnel.

A certain number of enterprises moved towards packaged software by trying to reuse programs written earlier for other customers, and by building part of their promotion and of their reputation on those previous developments, presented as packaged software. In reality, those programs or pieces of programs were implemented in a specific manner for particular customers and were most often not directly usable for other customers without significant adaptation work. They demonstrated real skills and knowledge in the application area concerned, they could result in development savings on and therefore more attractive proposals to customers. But as a rule, such existing software was only a way to sell specific development and its main role was to provide a competitive advantage in the sale of assistance services.

To go further, the enterprise would need to implement an organization adapted to the radically different trade of packaged software, that demands investments, operates according to a long cycle and must market products. Even if it is of limited size at the beginning, that organization would have to be adapted to long cycles, which means being differentiated on a functional basis and endowed with appropriate integration mechanisms. Moreover, the dominant culture in this organization would have to be radically different from the rest of the enterprise: it should value long term vision rather than immediate profitability, perseverance rather than rapidity of reaction, and especially set as its objective to minimize the requirement for assistance in the implementation of products, instead of relying on a high level of custom work to produce a profit.

Another path for many services firms is that of "turnkey" systems, also called "solutions engineering". This service consists in proposing, for a given application, a complete solution including hardware, software and the necessary assistance as a single package. Concerning software and assistance, this form of service raises the same problems as the pseudo-packaged software that we have just mentioned, but including hardware adds a subtle trap. Equipment manufacturers are rightfully interested in such contracts, and offer preferential conditions to service firms that become thus their retailers. The manufacturer's rebate on the purchase of hardware is generally higher than the profit margin realized on the service part, so that the supplier of "turnkey systems" is tempted to give priority to the resale of hardware, forgetting to earn his living on the services part. At worst, the services company risks changing into a hardware retailer and providing its own services at a loss, often neglecting hardware-related activities such as supply logistics, maintenance, etc. Such a policy becomes catastrophic when hardware vendors cut down on the hardware margin or when customers prefer to buy hardware separately.

Similarly, some enterprises attempt to address the demand of customers that wish to subcontract complete projects on the basis of committed results. But there again, as we have seen earlier in this chapter, succeeding in that activity demands very different skills, organization and culture from those that suit assistance. Not only is it mandatory to have competent project managers, but an important share of internal power must be taken away from traditional team managers and transferred to project managers. A brand new culture of cooperation must be introduced into the enterprise, the motivations of employees must be transformed and a totally new balance must be found between centralization and delegation. Executives must be able to involve themselves personally in the technical and commercial control of projects, an area of responsibility for which they are not prepared and of which they are often incapable.

Those examples illustrate the importance of cultural and organizational factors for success or failure in the services business. For the assistance enterprise, succeeding in packaged software or in development demands putting in place, somewhere in the enterprise, a foreign organization and a foreign culture that the rest of the enterprise and in particular its executives will have a hard time tolerating, since the structure and the culture are otherwise homogeneous.

To undertake this transplant would demand exceptional management acumen concerning the conditions of success, and to allow it to survive for the time required would demand stubbornness. Now, when a leader has succeeded in a certain type of activities, it is quite unusual for him to admit that new activities demand a different organization and management approach from what has brought him success so far. Every successful manager believes that he or she has found the key to good management, without understanding that that key only opens certain locks, and without imagining that attempting to use their usual key in other locks can only end in fracturing one or the other.

For all those reasons, and despite their promotional talk, services companies are generally reluctant to move out of their traditional assistance activities and to truly commit to activities demanding a higher level of responsibility. Most often, they misunderstand or underestimate the conditions for success, and therefore fail, or they content themselves to disguise their conventional services under the vocabulary of the new activity. Such is the reason why no services company has ever played an important role in the packaged software sector, and why enterprises that actually work on the basis of fixed contractual commitments are few.

The demand for support services

A persistent and widespread belief is that the need for support services increases inescapably. This idea relies on the implicit assumption that services required for the implementation of a given computer capacity would remain virtually constant in time. The need for services would then be proportional to the installed computing power and would therefore increase far more rapidly than hardware expenses, at the same time as new products and new uses create new support requirements. Similarly, the capacity of users to carry out the corresponding tasks by themselves in "self-service" mode would become increasingly insufficient, which would result an explosion of the services market.

Although that reasoning is as old as computing itself, its announced consequences have never been observed. In 1972, when IBM was starting its "Future Systems" project, the computing costs of enterprises were split 40% for hardware, 40% for personnel and 20% for the various other items, which was not appreciably different from the distribution in the sixties. Based on its hardware projects, IBM anticipated that, barring radical changes in methods and tools for development and operations, the share of total market expenses devoted to hardware would decrease dramatically and the share of personnel would become preponderant. This would have induced a strong demand for services but also a severe revenue restriction for equipment suppliers.

IBM, and following it all manufacturers, undertook developments aiming to automate or to alleviate the tasks of computing personnel by partially transferring such tasks to hardware, mainly through appropriate software: assistance to programming, assistance to installation, assistance to operations, etc. Even if the FS project never saw the light of day, this policy has borne its fruit. More than twenty years later, the breakdown of computing expenses is still virtually the same, even though the installed power is considerably higher. The needs for personnel (or service) required to support a given processing power have therefore decreased in practically the same proportions.

Schematically, one is witnessing a permanent migration of support functions from *ad hoc* services into specific software or products, and then often to functions incorporated in the very product that requires support. For example, all the major software packages for microcomputers incorporate means of training and user assistance that make it useless to attend courses, and even to read the documentation before use. Only users raised in the tradition of large data-processing are still expecting to attend courses or to read the documentation; the true personal computer users would consider it as a deterring obligation. On the contrary, they correctly judge the quality of a product by the ease of using it without preliminary training. Besides, the explosion of the personal computer has not entailed a parallel explosion of the demand for services. The non-professional user needs no assistance with operations, cannot afford specific developments and expects therefore the products that he or she buys to be directly and immediately usable. It is probable that this attitude will generalize to all computing at the same time that the micro-computing culture will invade society at large.

The same process is under way in other areas. It is well advanced for program development, with the vast array of software engineering tools improving and extending practically from day to day. It is also under way for systems maintenance and management, including the most complex networks. In a first stage, computer aids appear for the execution of certain tasks by the user, or in the form of service offerings, most often using innovative software packages implemented by university laboratories or small software firms. Those exploratory developments are followed by industrial products or computerized services providing similar service. Their functions are eventually adopted by the large integrators and incorporated into their major products. Alternatively, those products can be modified to eliminate or reduce the need for services, for example concerning training or maintenance.

This "productization" of services has been and still is a constant concern of product manufacturers. The original goal was to eliminate obstacles to the distribution of products by making them more user-friendly and more intuitive, and by simplifying implementation tasks. It is accelerated by the explosion of the industry and its favorable effects on innovation, and by the very dynamics of the packaged software sector, which encourage both local innovations and the accumulation of experience without raising the price of the end product, provided volumes are sufficiently high. Moreover, it satisfies the dominant demand of the micro-computing market, where users manage themselves by tradition, an attitude that will gradually generalize to the entire computing field, together with the structures and practices of the PC world.

Since the origins of computing, this phenomenon has maintained the need for personnel and services at an almost constant level compared to total computing expenditures, and has prevented the explosion of services, endlessly forecast by the augurs. We have seen that there is no reason to believe that this phenomenon will stop in the next years, quite the contrary.

The new requirements

Starting in 1990, the demand for support services has been impacted negatively by the general slowdown of growth and by the democratization of computer skills. In most skill areas, available personnel has become sufficient, so that the situation of scarcity on which service companies have prospered has given way to a state of abundance favorable to buyers, entailing a stagnation of demand and a decline of market prices. This situation has been aggravated by arrival on the services market of the traditional manufacturers and of the many employees that they have dismissed.

The dominant technical assistance activity, that represents approximately half of the revenue of computer services (not counting packaged software and maintenance), is a short cycle activity. Enterprises can therefore adjust quickly their staffs and expenses to demand, inasmuch as they are authorized to terminate those employees whose skills have become obsolete, or to find ways of redeploying them. The impact on profits can therefore be limited. Moreover, the market continues to require specific scarce skills, and enterprises that have such skills available can maintain higher activity and profit rates.

The market requirement for integration services increases regularly with the explosion of the hardware and packaged software industry. But we have seen how difficult it is for this latent need to transform into a solvent demand, and for supply to respond to that demand in an efficient and profitable manner. Despite that, one can expect many attempts and therefore many failures in this sector. The number of firms effectively and durably present in systems integration, low at the outset, should not increase very rapidly as long as the market does not reach sufficient maturity to evaluate soundly the quality of a proposal and to accept to compensate the responsibility taken by suppliers at its just value.

In terms of industry structure, assistance and integration remain two different sectors, even if some large firms are present in both. Assistance can accommodate a very low production scale and forms therefore a highly fragmented sector, populated by a multitude of small enterprises. As we have seen, integration demands a higher enterprise size and presents more serious obstacles to entry. It is therefore a more concentrated sector, but where profit margins, that should in theory be higher, are limited in practice by the immaturity of the market. It is probably the explanation for the evolution of profit ranges that we have presented at the beginning of this chapter. Under the effect of the recession, the minima fall below zero, but the maxima and averages remain roughly at the same level, the maximum range remaining relatively narrow.

Even if it is gradual, the rise of systems integration has an influence on the assistance sector. Every integration project uses a combination of different skills, varying from project to project, that the integrator cannot possess permanently. To satisfy those changing needs, he must call upon suppliers of specialized skills, namely assistance firms. His integrator responsibilities will make him very demanding in terms of skill level and quality. Moreover, he may tend to prefer small highly specialized enterprises, in order to avoid the risk of having to share his leadership with too powerful subcontractors.

Having to coexist with the system integration sector tends therefore to preserve or to increase the fragmentation of the assistance sector into firms specialized by skill or applications area, operating in relatively narrow niches. On the other hand, if their skills become obsolete, those specialized firms will not always be capable of converting to other skills. One can therefore expect the evolution of the sector to take mostly the form of disappearance of enterprises and birth of new ones, rather than in-place evolution of an essentially fixed population.

Along the major traditional services – assistance, software development and systems integration – and services in the process of disappearance – timesharing and turnkey systems –, one has seen recently the appearance and rise of new "facilities management" offerings where the service provider takes responsibility for systems operations.

The original offering, introduced by the American firm EDS, consists for the service provider to take control of the totality of the customer's computing resources for an undetermined duration. The services company repurchases installed equipment from the customer, hires his personnel and commits to providing a contractually specified level of service in return for an all-inclusive periodic royalty. Presented as a natural evolutionary path, beneficial for the customer and inescapable in the long run, this global form of facilities management has so far been limited to a small number of spectacular and strongly publicized cases, but has not met with the announced success.

In its place, a range of less radical services and more limited have appeared, like the so-called "transitional" facilities management, of limited duration, or partial facilities management limited to central site or network operations, or specific operations support services such as hotline management, inventory management or application maintenance. Originally conceived as an attempt to reintegrate fragmented services into a single offering, facilities management is already following the explosion and specialization dynamics that dominate the entire computer industry.

The definition of facilities management thus becomes increasingly blurred, as it disintegrates into separate services, some of which are not new by any measure. The increasingly frequent use of the term "outsourcing", that can stand for all forms of subcontracting, makes it increasingly a fashionable term used to dress up old services as well as services built upon existing skills, in the hope of extending their commercial life.

As always when a fashionable term is defined in such a loose manner, it becomes the occasion of heated discussions where marketing motives are obviously not absent. Are the advocates of facilities management right in claiming that it is a globally preferable economic alternative to owning a computer system, as supported by some arguments usually advanced in its favor: "concentrate on the main business", "transform fixed costs into variable costs", "place computing management in the hands of true specialists", ...? If yes, computing would evolve towards a pre-eminence of services enterprises, contrary to the trend observed all along its 40 years of history. For services themselves, does the future lie in a global service as stated by the advocates of the "global FM", in a direction opposite to the general movement of the industry? We will return to those questions in chapter 15.

Conclusions

Even after extracting packaged software, services form a complex of activities, highly heterogeneous by their nature and by their relationship with the other sectors of computing. It is not always obvious to separate computer services properly told, that belong unequivocally to the computer industry, from those services where the only link with the computer industry is to use some of its products, as do practically all the other industrial activities. For computing services properly told, the interaction between the demand for services and the evolution of products is complex: *a priori*, the widespread usage of products should increase the demand for services, but on one hand products evolve is a manner which reduces the need for support services, and on the other hand some forms of service could have a negative effect on the demand for products.

Services are also heterogeneous by the economy of their production. Most are feebly capitalistic and can accommodate a very modest production scale, while others, like processing or certain forms of facilities management, demand investments high enough to resemble industrial production activities. The result is a range of sector configurations going from extreme fragmentation to a certain level of concentration, and in particular the need for enterprise personalities adapted to each type of activity. The latter point is especially significant. To the extent that services activities have anything in common, it is their extreme sensitivity to adequacy of the organization and company culture to the specifics of the activity.

The macro-sector of services contains therefore a large part of the diversity and problematics of the entire computer industry. One encounters service generalists along with firms specialized in a particular form of service. In chapter 14, we will address the conflict between generalists and specialists, and we will conclude that the latter will inescapably dominate the industry. We believe that that conclusion is also valid within the area of services. But the demand for services is particularly mobile and volatile, so that firms too narrowly specialized run the risk of disappearing with the demand that has given them birth.

One of the keys of the evolution of the services sector is this permanent search for adaptation of firms to demand, whether by converting from one specialty to another, for the more modest, or by trying to maintain a generalist position for the more ambitious. To consider that all services enterprises look alike, operate in the same manner and obey the same competitive mechanisms, or that all services enterprises are equally capable of addressing all forms of service, would be to condemn oneself not to understand the very dynamics to this sector. The history and the future of services companies are made of their efforts to find their identity and to follow demand in that diversified changing world, with their many failures and occasional successes.

Part Four - Towards a new industrial order

To unify, is to better tie together particular diversities,
no to ignore them for a vain order.
Antoine de Saint-Exupéry

Up to this point, our approach has been essentially analytic. Starting with a first rough breakdown of the industry according to the main economic criteria for structuring industrial sectors, we have been able to analyze each of the four areas of components, hardware, packaged software and services, and to break them down further into separate sectors whose structure is characterized by their level of concentration.

The production of components is subject to very powerful concentration dynamics which allow the survival of only a small number of producers of very unequal sizes, including both full-function and "fabless" producers. The hardware area is formed of a large number of sectors, specialized by nature of unit, all dominated by fragmentation dynamics of variable strength depending on the assembly level where the firm operates (cards, units, etc.) and on its chosen strategy (original hardware versus standard equipment). For packaged software, one finds a general concentration logic analogous to that prevailing for components, but which operates in a large number of specialized sectors, as for hardware. The specifics of packaged software production introduce considerable differences in production scale between those sectors, and induce a global movement where the more concentrated sectors absorb peripheral sectors, compensated by the permanent birth of new sectors for new areas of application. Services also include several specialized sectors ranging from extreme fragmentation for specialized assistance to a certain level of concentration for integration services.

We have also seen that, in order to succeed in a given sector, an enterprise must possess a structure and a culture adapted to the particular rules of competition in this sector. With each sector can therefore be associated a specific enterprise personality, in such a way that it is practically impossible for one enterprise to succeed simultaneously in two sectors requiring different personalities and belonging therefore to two distinct trades. This incompatibility phenomenon is particularly critical for services, and works anyway all the more strongly that the competitive environment is more intense. It contributes to perpetuating the acquired specializations and sector structure, and cause the explosion of firms that are not specialized in a single trade.

The analyses in the preceding chapters concern enterprises specialized in each sector. They concentrate therefore mainly on the PC world, dominated by specialists, while generalists still dominate the traditional world and the open world. In the last part, we are going to examine the computer industry in its totality and combine the conclusions of the preceding chapters to propose a global view of the industry, of its future and of its place in the whole economy. We will address two main questions: how each enterprise determines its activities and how enterprises organize between each other to satisfy the market. Our guiding thread will be the competitive analysis approach presented all along this book.

In Chapter 14, we will see how competitive forces push enterprises to separate their activities according to the borderlines of those same sectors, and the difficult problems that this explosion poses to generalists. It is therefore the whole computer industry that is exploding in specialized sectors, inside which representatives of the three worlds are competing. In each of those specialized sectors, competition erases the borderlines between the three worlds of the PC, of traditional computers and of open systems, and results in globally unifying the data-processing industry.

But in this exploded industry, the products of the different specialists must eventually be integrated into systems to satisfy the needs of users. Chapter 15 examines this problem of integration and the opportunities that it presents for suppliers, in particular in the area of services. It also shows how players can palliate their specialization by weaving more or less formal alliances, with objectives going from the definition of standards to industrial partnerships, and which can turn out to be more or less efficient.

Finally, chapter 16 will return to the theme of the borderlines of data-processing, that we have mentioned many times, only to defer its examination. Starting with the forces that structure the computer industry, and that also rule the related industries, we will examine the interactions between data-processing and other industries, in particular telecommunications. This analysis will complete our global evolution scenario for the computer industry.

Chapter 14 - The exploding computing industry

Generalists and specialists. Dis-integration and specialization versus integration and diversification. The explosion of generalists. The three worlds of computing merge and become homogeneous. Microprocessors, client-server and multiprocessors. The mechanisms of dis-integration. The agonies of transition and the future of generalists.

Analysis of the different forms of production, that we have developed in the two preceding parts, relies on the specializations that have appeared in the PC world since 1981. But such specialization has not always been the rule. As we have seen in the first part (chapters 1 and 2), the first half of the 45 years of the computer industry has seen the undisputed dominance of integrated generalists. Still now, those generalists or their successors continue to dominate a certain number of market segments such as large and midrange systems, or maintenance. They are also actively present in the other segments, including micro-computing where they coexist and compete with specialized firms.

The integrated generalist model underwent its firsts attacks by the end of the sixties with the separation of charges decided by IBM, and then a bit later with the appearance of compatible devices. But those events, although they enabled the boom of a large number of specialized firms, had only a minor impact on the structure and operating mode of the large firms, whose range of services remained as broad as before. Similarly, at the very moment when micro-computing was creating a new PC world, fragmented by birth and that has remained so, Apple was taking the leadership in personal computers by adopting a generalist strategy and by offering integrated hardware and software. Soon after, IBM attempted to revive that same model with the PS/2 for hardware and the OS/2 operating system. Later again, it is still by adopting the integrated model that workstation pioneers like Sun or Silicon Graphics developed, by offering not only specific equipment and operating systems, but by manufacturing their own microprocessors and offering their own application software. Contrary to the large traditional generalists, all those enterprises have chosen a specific market segment, but like the generalists, they offer to customers of this segment a system incorporating the full range of products and necessary services.

Does that mean that specialized firms and generalist firms will durably coexist in a large number of sectors, and if yes how do they compete with each other? What happens when specialists and generalists are competing in the same segment, for closely substitutable products? More precisely, what competitive advantages and disadvantages result respectively from a generalist strategy and a specialization strategy? Can that comparison allow to anticipate the gradual demise generalists, their fragmentation or on the contrary the regrouping of specialists?

A first indication can be found in the trends and performance indicators that we have examined in chapters 4 and 5. Since 1989, generalists experience a slow-down of their growth and a decline of their profitability that push them to restructure, to cut back staff and for some of them to withdraw from certain businesses. We have also seen that the few mixed firms that are positioned somewhere between generalists and specialists succeed generally less well than firms specialized in the individual services supplied by those mixed firms. It seems that simply offering an extended range of products and services, different either by their nature or by the market that they aim to cover, has become a handicap. If such is the case, competition between diversified firms and specialized firms works in favor of the latter and leads inescapably to complete specialization.

That being told, we now need to take a closer look at the mechanisms and respective advantages of disintegration and integration, in order to account for the current evolution of the large generalists and to identify the basic trends that will shape the future of the industry.

Integration and dis-integration of enterprises

For an enterprise, specialization is opposed to both integration and diversification. A diversified enterprise produces several different goods that can be unrelated to each other, or that can be related either by the market or by the production process. We will only mention for the sake of completeness the case of totally independent goods, or goods related by the production process but independent on the market (for example sheep meat and wool), which are not significant in computing. In data-processing, diversified firms produce related goods, in the sense that they are used jointly and that a variation of the quantity sold for one product entails a variation of demand for the other, generally in the same direction. One then talks of complementary productions (of products or services).

For a given product, the firm is more or less integrated vertically according to whether it executes all the successive production stages that lead to the finished product. For example, for most of its computers, IBM manufactures memory components and microprocessors, integrates them on cards and in boxes and assembles complete units, while many microcomputer vendors only implement the final assembly from elements acquired on the market.

A firm producing related goods can integrate its supply horizontally, by proposing composite products grouping several related products. This practice is called "bundling". The firm can also introduce more subtle forms of interdependence between its products, for example using different rates and conditions for a product depending on whether the customer buys another product. It can also set the selling price of each product in such a way as to maximize its overall profit rather than maximizing profit for each separate product, thus introducing internal cross-subsidies between products.

In general, the economic and management literature, as well as the dominant practice of enterprises, favors diversification and integration by considering them as the most normal behavior of the firm. Like all decisions of the firm, diversification and integration present disadvantages as well as advantages, but the latter are generally better known and better accepted that the former. It is accepted that all enterprises seek to grow and to extend their field of influence, and therefore to diversify horizontally and to integrate vertically.

Through diversification, companies hope to obtain competitive advantages by offering compatible complementary products, by exploiting more completely their marketing organization and by presenting customers with a complete range allowing "one stop shopping" and inviting higher loyalty. Concerning costs, diversification can result in economies of scale or economies of scope through consolidation of activities at the stage of production, marketing or logistics. Those advantages can be the basis for a differentiation strategy and create obstacles to the entry of competitors into the composite sector corresponding to the complete range of products offered by the firm. Well-planned diversification is also considered as a protection against risks and seasonal variations. Finally, it is a prerequisite for combined sales, bundling and cross subsidies.

Vertical integration has been studied by several economists, in particular in the framework of theories of the firm. Those theories seek to explain why production activities give birth to structured organizations where relationships are governed by a more or less hierarchical internal discipline, rather than by the rules of the market that form the very basis of the economy. A key idea, proposed by Coase[69] and Williamson, is that all transactions, whether between two independent economic agents or between two parts of the same firm, have a cost that depends in particular on the nature of the relationship between the parties[70]. Relying on the market implies exploration and selection costs, costs for negotiating, establishing and managing the contract as well as for resolving possible conflicts. Those costs can be reduced or eliminated by replacing market transactions by the use of an internal production unit submitted to the same management authority.

In Williamson's view, the trend to internalize (or integrate) an activity increases with three factors: the specificity and cost of assets required for the subject activity, the degree of uncertainty concerning the market and the correct execution of the transaction, and finally the frequency of the transaction. This analysis explains the formation of firms and other hierarchical organizations, which enable replacing reliance on external markets by direct management coordination of the different activities. It also constitutes an implicit conceptual justification of mergers and acquisitions, which we will discuss later. But it also forms the basis for a critical examination of integration. Just as integration is justified when internal transaction costs are lower than costs of equivalent market transactions, it must be avoided in the opposite case.

---

69   R. Coase, The nature of the firm, Economica, 1937

70   O. Williamson, Markets and Hierarchies; The Free Press, 1975

The drawbacks of integration

What are therefore the costs and disadvantages of integration and why are they so often overlooked, when the reality of the computer industry proves that they are sufficiently high for the predominant overall movement to be in the direction of fragmentation?

A rather complete inventory of potential disadvantages appears in Porter[71], much in the form of a checklist for correctly weighing the pros and cons of integration in a preliminary examination of opportunities. He presents the risks as so many issues to be addressed to ensure efficient integration, but he does not go as far as presenting them as potential reasons to "dis-integrate" an already integrated firm. Those negative factors, that partly build upon transaction cost analysis, can be summarized by three main considerations.

First, economies of scale or scope expected from the sharing of activities can only be significant if those precise activities are subject to economies of scale, and if they form an important share of product cost. If such is not the case, the advantages are of little importance. Secondly, an interconnection between activities does not necessarily result in a competitive advantage. Exploiting potential interconnections demands implementing an explicit strategy and particular efforts in the firm, which implies a cost of coordination. Moreover, activities to be brought together can have different management requirements, so that combining them may entail costs of compromise and costs of rigidity due to the loss of flexibility. Finally, efficient management of integration goes against decentralization principles and can weaken profitability incentives. This last type of considerations takes us back to the discussion of chapter 9 where we showed that productions of different natures require different enterprise personalities, which often cannot coexist in the same firm.

Recent trends in strategic analysis and enterprise management challenge the established dogmas of diversification, integration and growth. The so-called "excellence" school of thought[72] invites the enterprise to concentrate on what it is able to do better that the others, even if it means doing fewer things. It emphasizes reactivity and adaptability, and challenges growth as an overriding objective by proposing the motto "small is beautiful".

For the so-called "value" school[73], the objective of the enterprise is to increase its economic value, defined as its actualized net cash flow, more than its profit margins or its revenue. In the modern economic world, size is no longer a decisive advantage, since small structures can now access the sources of capital, talent and information as easily as the large ones. Increasingly frequent changes in life cycle, factor costs, global competition, interest rates, etc. jeopardize economies of scale and synergies. More active shareholders and even raiders force chief execu-

---

71   M.Porter, The Competitive Advantage; The Free Press, New York, 1985

72   Peters TJ, Waterman RH : In Search of Excellence (Harper & Row, 1982)

73   Alfred Rappaport : Creating Shareholder Value (The Free Press, 1986)

tives to submit every one of their activities to constant critical examination. In that logic, a reduction of activity can increase the value of the enterprise if the discontinued activity is destroying value by being a net cash consumer. Divestments and transfers of activities become normal management actions, facilitated by the development of the market for enterprise control.

Therefore, integration does not present only advantages. It is possible to describe cases where dis-integration is on the contrary the optimal behavior of the enterprise, as the study of the computer industry seems to provide many examples.

Dis-integration versus integration

The bias of management literature and of many executives in favor of integration strategies can be explained by different factors.

On one hand, it turns out that arguments in favor of integration translate rather easily into market shares or economies of scale or of scope, whereas opposite arguments can less easily be quantified and often relate to cultural considerations or to more recent less popular theories. In many real cases, the relative weight of positive quantifiable factors can be much lower than that of negative non-quantifiable factors, but the economic literature tends to favor the easily quantifiable, and therefore to overestimate factors that tend to favor integration. One thus gives credit to the idea that the natural movement of economy is towards higher integration, contrary to what we observe for computing. This is an example of a distortion due to abuse of mathematics in economics, that can lead to conclusions opposed to the observable reality.

One must also recognize temporary fads, which themselves are related to the overall economic conditions. A period of growth places revenue objectives in the forefront and reinforces all factors in favor of integration, while in difficult periods, the profit objective becomes paramount and reinforces factors favorable to specialization. Since growing is far more rewarding that struggling to remain profitable, company executives are prompt to endorse arguments in favor of integration, and do not readily accept those that push towards dis-integration, except by pretending that they are only valid by exception.

More generally, several economists have proposed the idea that the integration or disintegration phenomenon is related to the cycle of each industry or sector. In a model proposed by Stigler[74] and made popular by Porter, a new industry always starts integrated, and remains so as long as the size of the market is not sufficient to support firms specialized in the different product components or in the different stages of production. Moreover, in those early stages, market requirements are not yet diversified and production processes are still unstable, which makes horizontal specialization as well as vertical dis-integration difficult. The growth and maturity stages favor specialization by niche, by nature of product or by stage of production, in agreement with the early remark of Adam Smith that "the division of work is limited by the size of the market". Eventually, the decline of the industry and the withdrawal of many players will start a gradual process of re- integration.

---

74   George J. Stigler : The Organization of Industry (Richard Irwin, 1968)

Dis-integration and homogenization of the industry

The evolution of generalists

The above mechanisms are those that we have seen at work for data-process-ing in the first part of this book. The integrated product called "computer", appeared on the market in 1951, then gradually broke down along three dimen-sions, starting in the second half of the sixties: by nature of service (equipment, software, different types of services), by type of equipment and by market niche. This separation occurred both through the appearance of new specialized enter-prises and by the more or less clear separation of services within generalist firms, both of those developments calling for and facilitating the other.

Traditional generalists designed and priced their offer globally. Some services were free, for example product support services, and the prices of those that were invoiced separately were set to produce the highest possible total revenue consider-ing product complementarity, drag-along effects and possible substitutions. At the cost level, each invoiced product or service supported a share of the cost of other free services and products, and the individual profitability of each element could vary in large proportions from negative values to highly positive values.

Each customer contract, considered separately, used the different elements in different proportions that can result in different profit levels. The global profitabil-ity of the generalist firm thus involved compensation phenomena between con-tracts and between products. Marketing actions tried to avoid too unfavorable cases, for example providing a lot of free assistance for an isolated and marginally prof-itable piece of software, even if the customer's demand was legitimate. Part of mar-ket demand was therefore not satisfied. Conversely, there were also cases favorable to the supplier, where demand was satisfied in an unusually profitable manner.

The widening of the market and the diversification of needs multiplied those particular cases, where the foreseeable composition of demand was atypical com-pared to the average demand on which the supply of generalists was based. An enterprise could then acquire a competitive advantage by specializing on those mar-ket niches and adapting its supply and its pricing, which implied most often keeping its selling prices close to actual costs for that niche. For example, as soon as the market included an important share of renewals and multiple installations of identi-cal systems, demand for "bare" hardware became sufficient to open a market for suppliers who were able to offer attractive prices by doing without an assistance work force.

Similarly, existing enterprises (mainly services) were able to extend their ser-vices to data-processing. Let us use hardware financing as an example. In the begin-ning, financial organizations stayed away from data-processing, and the correspond-ing service was provided by the generalist manufacturers who offered the possibility of renting or leasing their equipment. With the passing of time, financial organiza-tions became interested in this new market, first through specialized affiliates, and eventually integrated computer financing in their mainline financing activity. Since financial firms are likely to enjoy the strongest competitive advantage for that ser-vice, the computer financing activity ended up moving entirely out of the computer sector into the financial sector. Although, in the beginning, the originality of the object overshadowed the nature of the activity, in the end the nature of the activity dominated and its object became commonplace. One could say the same for many services such as distribution, installation, maintenance or the provision of personnel.

To face such competition, specialized in segments where they are vulnerable, generalists had to follow this movement of prices, or even precede it as IBM did with unbundling. But maintaining their overall profitability required increasing the gap between costs and selling price for those services which were specific of segments where they remained dominant. That made them more vulnerable in those segments and tended to facilitate the entry of new competitors. The more segments were attacked by specialists, the fewer and more vulnerable the relatively protected segments became. On the whole, on the long term, all selling prices had to align themselves with costs plus standard profit, including services so far provided free that now carry a separate charge.

Through this breakdown of their offer, generalists actually gave up certain synergies and competitive advantages resulting from the very breadth of their supply, which tended to facilitate even more the development of a specialized competition. The breakdown of the generalists' supply and the proliferation of specialists fed therefore on each other and gradually extended to the whole range of products and services. Sooner or later, increasingly tough competition between generalists and specialists on each market segment acutely raised the issue of the organizational and cultural adequacy of the firm to its productions, and prompted generalists to challenge their own structure. Should they keep all their services within an integrated organization or segment their organization into more or less independent enterprises so as to leave each piece free to adopt the organization and culture that will give it the best chances of succeeding in its sector?

A basic condition for that explosion process to take place is that the niches where opportunities for specialization exist be visible enough and large enough to justify investments by specialists. Now the computer industry was originally dominated by a few generalists that differentiated from each other by the architecture of their systems and in particular the conventions enabling interconnection of their elements. Those generalists formed a concentrated sector where market shares were unequal by nature. The specialists' obvious interest was to attack first the supplier who commanded the largest potential market, namely IBM. The erosion and explosion process described above affected the generalists in the order of decreasing market share. It was particularly quick for sectors where the required investments were lowest and the cycle shortest, which means the sectors most dispersed by nature.

Thus, in the seventies, a constellation of firms developed around IBM, offering specific products and services, individually substitutable to the corresponding offers of IBM while remaining compatible within a multiple-vendor system. While complying with *de facto* standards defined by IBM, those firms and IBM were competing in many sectors. The overall effect was a price decline, elimination of cross subsidies between products, improvements in quality and diversity in all their forms, and introduction of new products and services.

For customers, this internal competition provided the IBM world with many advantages compared to the other manufacturers: more competitive prices, additional contributions of complementary suppliers, increased quality and diversity of products. The other generalists had trouble to remain competitive when faced with such vitality and were protected mostly by the importance of switching costs between their products and those of the IBM world. In total, even if IBM as a firm was hurt by this new type of competition, the IBM world in its totality remained increasingly dominant and the other generalists became more and more marginal. As a consequence, specialists found little interest in attacking other generalists, and the explosion process was practically limited to IBM.

On the other hand, for the leader IBM, competition with specialists of each of its offerings entailed an erosion of its own market share, as well as of its privileged relationship with customers, of the influence that it can exert on the market, and in the end of its profit margins. But, if it can remain competitive for a sufficient range of products and services, the overall advantages of the world to which it belongs over the other generalists may compensate for its own relative regression within that world.

This process of explosion of the offer tends to gradually separate all elements for which the requirement can be expressed and satisfied independently: services from products, among products those that can be physically separated from each other and provide distinct functions, among services those that satisfy specific needs, and more generally all elements whose production process can be isolated.

On the other hand, one does not observe much vertical disintegration until 1981, except if one considers systems integration as the ultimate stage of production. Computer manufacturers continued to produce their own components and to carry out all levels of assembly themselves. But as technological evolution increasingly concentrates value added into the components and renders the production of components increasingly capitalistic and therefore concentrated, processing unit manufacturers are forced to draw closer to the large semiconductor producers. That process only leaves in this sector firms like Fujitsu (and its affiliate Amdahl), Hitachi or NEC. One thus observes a certain trend to the re-concentration for computers (and operating systems), along with continuing fragmentation for peripherals, services and application software packages.

The merger of the three worlds

The structural evolution of the traditional data-processing world resulted mainly from increasing size of the market and rising average customer skills. The appearance of the micro-computing world was the direct consequence of crossing a critical technology stage: the appearance of microprocessors on the market in the beginning of the seventies. The micro-computing industry built itself, from the outset, according a vertically dis-integrated model involving independent suppliers of microprocessors (Motorola and Intel), equipment manufacturers, software producers and distributors. Firms like Atari, Commodore and especially Apple partially conformed to the traditional model by combining hardware and software, while IBM inaugurated with the PC, beginning in 1981, a totally fragmented structure, even for the operating system with Microsoft.

As we have seen in chapter 3, the explosion of the PC world did not have an immediate direct impact on the structure of the traditional world, because the two markets remained separate for a long time. micro-computing deprived traditional data-processing of a large part of its growth potential. But as long as it was not practically possible to massively replace traditional systems by microprocessor-based systems, the two worlds did not really enter in competition and their structures did neither confront each other nor come together.

Similarly, the Risc/Unix world appeared in the eighties remained separated from the traditional world as well as from the PC world for a long time. It offers two main types of systems. On one hand "workstations", that is to say personal computers adapted to scientific usage and to high-quality data presentation, which requires powerful processors, large screens, advanced graphic capabilities, long without equivalent in PC's or traditional computers. The other main type of Risc/Unix machines is "servers", which are midsize computers destined to be shared between different users in a network of stations or microcomputers. Those servers are competing directly with traditional computers, but can only be exploited in the framework of a new systems architecture called "client-server". As long as this architecture has not reached a certain maturity, real competition from servers is limited to minicomputers.

But, as we have seen in chapter 7, progress in microprocessors is going to continue at a high pace during at least 10 more years, and they are going to catch up and eventually exceed in performance the current large computers. Thanks to the specific competitive dynamics of this sector, one will always find on the market a choice of microprocessors of the latest technological level at a price of a few hundred dollars per unit. Even if this choice is limited and gradually restricted to 2 or 3 architectures per generation, it will enable assemblers using those "off the shelf" chips to offer equipment featuring a better price/performance ratio than integrated firms, for a growing share of the total computer market.

This phenomenon alone would suffice to constantly increase the compound market share of specialists and to decrease that of generalists. But other technological developments under way will accelerate the invasion of all data-processing by both the technologies and the industry structures originating from the micro-computing world. One is systems interconnection and networking techniques and the "client-server" architecture, which enable replacing a large system by a complex of interconnected systems working in harmony. Another key area is multiprocessing techniques, that enable building a powerful machine by assembling microprocessors working in parallel.

The developments required for implementing the client-server concept translate solely into software to handle communication between systems, distributed database management, distributed systems management, etc. In each concerned area, there exist already many competing offers, generally incorporated into standard operating systems or compatible with them, and new developments as well as improvements to existing software are going on at a hectic pace. The market offers or will soon offer all the ingredients necessary for the implementation of complete systems using the client-server architecture. But adoption of this approach by users assumes a redesign of existing applications, and indeed of their entire computer organization. Consequently, replacement of the large integrated systems by networks of smaller systems is paced by the capability of users to evolve more than by the availability of technologies.

Multiprocessing technologies raise both hardware issues for interconnection and communication devices between processors and memory, and software issues for overall systems management. Those problems increase in severity with the number of processors. For a small number of processors (2 to 4), they are already sufficiently well mastered in order for many SMP ("symmetric multiprocessing") machines to be available on the market, and for the necessary software functions to be included in standard systems such as Windows NT or many Unix derivatives. The same technologies are present in upper-range Unix servers, which can commonly include up to 64 processors. Such "moderate" parallelism will undoubtedly soon become a standard possibility offered by many vendors of microcomputers and industrial level packaged software.

In the case of so-called "massively parallel" machines, where one seeks to make several hundreds and even thousands of processors work together, those same problems are still only partially resolved. Those machines currently enjoy a competitive advantage only for particular problems with a high degree of intrinsic parallelism, and provided that they are programmed specifically for this architecture. Such systems are still only offered by large systems specialists like Cray or Convex, or large generalists like IBM or Fujitsu. But in this area maybe more than others, it is necessary to count with the proliferation of innovation coming out of the Unix world and from university laboratories, that will someday result in incorporating massive parallelism into standard industrial level systems, according to the mechanism described in chapter 12.

In summary, at the same time as standard "off the shelf" microprocessors reach the power levels of the largest systems while retaining their modest price, hardware assemblers will put on the market multiprocessors multiplying those performances. Similarly, software packages coming from the micro world and offered by specialists like Microsoft will gradually incorporate the functions required for building complete systems based on that hardware. Equipment assemblers and packaged software specialists, relying on components specialists, will thus gradually enter in competition at all levels with generalists or less narrowly specialized firms.

In such competition, the most fragmented worlds enjoy the maximum competitive advantage, as we have seen previously when looking at the IBM world. One can identify currently different levels of price/performance ratios within data-processing. For example, the price of a Mips[75] for a PC is approximately one thousandth of what it is for large traditional computers. The cost of the same job is 10 times higher on a large traditional computer than on a workstation, and a PC is

---

75   million instructions per second

roughly 3 times less expensive than a workstation of equivalent configuration and power. Similarly, prices for packaged software in the PC area bear little resemblance with those of similar packages for large systems. Those differences were of little competitive consequence as long as the substitution possibilities remained limited by the differences in power ranges or supported functions, but they are going to become decisive as the areas of actual competition extend.

The overall movement will naturally happen from the low range upwards, and will therefore concern first the Unix/Risc world and what is left of conventional minicomputers, before propagating upwards into the world of large systems.

An important part of the Unix world has been built on the traditional integrated model where each manufacturer produces his microprocessor, his hardware and his software, every element being dependent on the others. Until now, this world has been individualized by the utilization of Risc processors and of Unix-based systems. But specialized software package vendors of the PC world, such as Microsoft, Santa Cruz Operation, Novell or the IBM/Apple/Taligent complex, will most certainly offer competitive operating systems to that user population. Similarly, among the many hardware assemblers of the PC world, some will offer cheaper equivalents of current workstations and servers.

Integrated Unix-based vendors like Sun or Silicon Graphics, will thus be competed against, for each element, by specialists that will enjoy competitive advantages in prices, diversity, quality, etc. Staying with an integrated offer would be suicidal for them, because any relative disadvantage in a single sector could condemn the totality. They will therefore be led to separate their offerings and to fight competition separately for each one. Their future in each sector will depend on their capacity to preserve or acquire specific competitive advantages in each of the sectors where they remain present. In any case, they will have to face the issues of vertical dis-integration that we are going to address later.

Through this merger of the micro world and of the Risc/Unix world, servers will be aligned with the price/performance standards of the micro world and will become all the more competitive with traditional data-processing, thus reinforcing the competitive advantage of client/server systems. An analogous movement, although probably somewhat later, will increase the advantages of large massively parallel systems over conventional systems. Eventually, the technologies, performance standards and fragmented industry structure of the PC world will extend to the whole computer industry, forcing generalists to re-examine their offerings, their prices and their organization. Such are the real industrial implications of the technological developments under way in client/server architectures and multiprocessors.

Sector structure and innovation

Among other competitive advantages, a fragmented industry structure is globally more favorable to innovation and therefore brings to users more rapidly and more completely all the potential progress enabled by the evolution of technologies.

New products that potentially result from technological progress relate to existing products in different ways. They may address new requirements and therefore not be in competition with any existing product, or on the contrary they can constitute a possible replacement for existing products and therefore compete with them on the market.

In an integrated or diversified firm, such conflicts are generally resolved by executive management. On one hand, the different development projects are competing with each other, and resources are allocated to them according to the general policy of the enterprise. On the other hand, research feeds a reservoir of potential products whose possible introduction on the market is planned globally over the long term by taking into account their mutual impact.

Such a planning approach is all the more necessary that the firm occupies a large part of the overall market, and all the more easy to implement that the firm exerts leadership. Thus, IBM traditionally maintained an impressive portfolio of leading technologies and innovative products, but generally introduced them on the market only under the pressure of competition, giving thus the image of a technical laggard. Although that mode of management probably improves the quality and coherence of products, it entails a delay of marketed products relative to the possibilities of technology, and renders the firm vulnerable to attack from focused competitors that would exploit the latest possibilities.

On the contrary, in a fragmented industry, each player acts according only to the interest of his own products. The more specialized a firm is, the less room for choice it has in the allocation of its development resources, and the fewer constraints to introduction of its new products. In a way, the selection of products to be introduced on the market, which is largely made by the management of firms in an integrated world, is now externalized and results from the verdict of the market. Consequently, everything happens as if progress had become an autonomous force: each firm must assume that there will always be someone to exploit the latest technological possibilities. No player can control the process, and all must organize in order to react to progress and no longer to attempt to control it.

Let us add that the advent of micro-computing enables the explosion of many projects of very variable scope, and creates the possibility to pursue in parallel several research directions at acceptable cost and risks. The fragmented world of micro-computing and workstations is therefore twice the preferred place of innovation. One should therefore expect a global acceleration of innovation in computing as the structure of the micro world conquers the whole industry.

The process of vertical dis-integration

Supply fragmentation creates particularly difficult problems for suppliers who offer products in different sectors obeying different competitive dynamics. They may be involved in capital-intensive activities belonging to a monopolistic concentrated sector such as components and packaged software, along with activities with a low production scale belonging to a dispersed sector, such as hardware assembly or most services. Such is the case for traditional generalists, but also for firms specialized in one market segment and whose strategy is to offer on this segment the full set of products and services.

In the traditional model, each one of the firm's activities operates on the same scale, determined by the market share of the entire firm. Depending on activities, that production scale can be close to or above the specific economic scale of the activity, or on the contrary it can be lower. In this latter case, the unit cost of the product is higher than what a higher production volume could allow.

As long as no specialists exist in sectors corresponding to the firm's activities, it is competing only with generalists like itself, for an integrated offer whose total selling price covers total costs. The rules of the competitive game in that sector and the resulting industry structure are those of the most capital-intensive activity, and therefore take the monopolistic concentrated form. To succeed, firms must adopt the structure and culture which is adapted to long-cycle activities.

On the other hand, if there are specialists in certain sectors and if they occupy a non-trivial share of the market, the generalist firm operates actually in distinct competitive sectors where the rules of the game and success criteria are different, and in each sector it must fight against specifically adapted enterprises. Since it is unlikely that a generalist could be as efficient as specialists in all sectors, generalists will probably lose market share in some areas to specialists of those areas. In particular, possible excessive costs for components and software, due to limited volumes, translate into high prices for the equipment that constitute the main source of revenue. Moreover, the organization and culture adapted to long cycles become a competitive handicap in the short-cycle hardware and services sectors.

Can the integrated character of the offer provide enough competitive advantages to compensate for those handicaps? That might be the case as long as the advantages of specialists are modest, or if some important needs are not addressed by specialists, or if customers are not competent enough to buy from different suppliers. But those potential advantages cannot be durable, especially when competition results from technological evolution of the products of an already fragmented strongly competitive world, which brings them in competition with products of the integrated firm, as in the case of micro-computing. The competitive fragmented world is then already constituted, and only the time required for customer adaptation can delay horizontal fragmentation of the sector and the decline of generalists.

We are left with the problem of hardware, for which producing proprietary components in limited volumes results in excessive unit cost and therefore in a competitive handicap relative to hardware based on off-the-shelf components. That handicap is all the more high that volumes are low and that a high proportion of equipment cost is found in components. If it entails a loss of market share for equipment, such a handicap increases markedly as the level of production drifts away from the economic scale, and can trap the firm in a fatal declining spiral.

The firm has two solutions available to reduce the cost of components: either to cease its own production activity and use off-the-shelf components available on the market, or to increase its production volumes towards the vicinity of the economic scale, which it can only achieve by selling its components to other equipment assemblers. In choosing the second approach, the firm would become a competitor to the other suppliers present in the component sector, and would thereby enter the characteristic concentration dynamics that we have studied in chapter 7. This sector is already strongly constituted, and therefore entry is extremely difficult and survival is highly problematic.

If nevertheless the firm continues to manufacture components, it can only reach a sufficient scale by selling them to assemblers that will use them in their own products, in competition with the products of the firm itself. The possible competitive advantages of those components can no longer provide a sufficient advantage to the products where they are used. The downstream activity of the firm, namely the assembly of equipment, can only remain competitive by differentiating from the other vendors through specific features of the hardware assembly itself.

Moreover, the production of equipment, now isolated from that of components, is a short-cycle activity where agility and freedom of action are decisive competitive advantages. Constraining the downstream sector to use only components made by the mother company would limit its options and could have the same effect as staying with an integrated offer. Authorizing the upstream firm to sell to others than the downstream firm has for natural counterpart authorizing the downstream firm to buy from others that the upstream company. Furthermore, cultural and organizational factors become increasingly critical in the competition between specialized firms, and each segment of the firm must be able to adapt its personality to the sector where it operates. Under penalty of failure, the upstream activity and the downstream activity must become autonomous not only in their competitive behavior outside of the firm, but also within the fragmented firm, that tends to break down into independent enterprises.

An analogous reasoning applies for operating systems, which constitute a highly concentrated sector, as we have seen in chapters 11 and 12. If their development cost can no longer be partly subsidized by the price of hardware, the generalist firm has no other way to face competition from the major specialists but to extend the market of its software packages to the customers of the other manufacturers. It thus makes its operating system development activity as independent as that of component production, depriving at the same time its other activities of the specific competitive advantages of those systems. And in the same way as for components, the monopolistic dynamics of the large software packages can lead the firm to withdraw from this sector more or less rapidly.

The mutation of large manufacturers

The preceding considerations allow to explain the recent well-publicized difficulties of the large generalist enterprises, that invented and dominated data-processing during the first thirty years of its history. Those firms are now confronted with serious problems, which can only become worse in the next coming years. As just described, they have already seen their market shares shrink and their profits change into losses for several of them. They had to cut down accordingly on their resources and lifestyle, at the price of painful internal restructuring and discontinuance of some activities. Not only are they faced with a difficult transition, which not all of them have completed, especially those that have not been too severely hurt yet, but the environment in which those firms find themselves after the transition is tougher than the old one.

Some generalists have pulled out of component production, as did Unisys, NCR, Bull and more recently Hewlett-Packard. To that effect, they have decided to rely on suppliers like Intel, PowerOpen or NEC. Hewlett-Packard has even managed to present its withdrawal positively as an alliance between peers with Intel. Many of those who continue in the component sector have given this activity virtually complete independence relative to their other productions, like the Japanese Toshiba or Hitachi that are now mostly focusing on memory and custom chips, while NEC and Fujitsu continue to produce also specific microprocessors for their large systems. IBM is associated with Motorola in the PowerOpen consortium, which operates autonomously relative to IBM.

On the contrary, Sun, Silicon Graphics, and to a lesser degree Digital Equipment, are still basing their entire hardware strategy on the possession of a proprietary microprocessor. Therefore, they cannot give to that activity the independence that it would require to reach the economic production scale and reduce their unit costs to fight efficiently against the other suppliers. In any case, we have seen in chapter 7 that the coming years will see firms leave the microprocessor sector one by one, with more or less serious consequences for the rest of their activities and for their survival. The three above mentioned firms are the top (involuntary) candidates for that renunciation.

The picture is more blurred in operating systems, the other area where the economic production scale is high. The intrinsically monopolistic character of the sector, which submits it to concentration dynamics similar in every respect to that of the components sector, seems clearly less well understood by players and by observers alike. The specific demands of the production of industrial quality software, and their strategic and economic implications that we have presented in chapter 12, are still imperfectly recognized.

Most suppliers of traditional equipment, including workstations manufacturers, continue to offer their own specific operating systems for their equipment. The oldest firms offer proprietary systems designed for their large or midsize computers; the more recent offer proprietary implementations of Unix. The product ranges of the largest manufacturers, like IBM or Digital Equipment, include both Unix systems and proprietary systems. One has still hardly seen, beginning with Windows NT, the announced movement by which systems coming from the micro world will gradually implement all the functions needed to replace systems coming from the traditional world or that of workstations, at prices consistent with prices of current microcomputer operating systems such as Windows.

Nevertheless, several generalist firms are slowly moving towards making their operating system development activities autonomous. For example, Sun has ported its system to processors other than its Sparc chip. IBM is engaged in a vast operation of redesigning all its existing systems to use the PowerPC base and to make them comply with the Posix standard, while announcing the development of new systems in cooperation with Apple. But at the time of this writing, those agreements seem in jeopardy, their objectives uncertain and the strategy unclear. Apple speaks of making its future system (Copland or System/8) available independently of hardware, but it is not obvious that they are willing to dissociate it from the PowerPC base. The strategy of Apple is thus linked to that of IBM and suffers from the same haziness. In any case, even if many firms decide to remain in the now autonomous sector of operating systems, the monopolistic competition and the dynamics of concentration will gradually reduce their number.

In the end, most generalists will have to limit themselves to activities with a lower production scale such as the assembly of equipment. Those that will survive in components or operating systems will have to specialize accordingly different branches of their internal organization. As a consequence, their hardware assembly activities will be isolated and will need to be able to withstand specialist competition by their own means.

Now those activities belong to fragmented sectors, where maximum market shares are in the order of 15% and where profitability is lower than in the concentrated sector which traditional data-processing used to be. By itself, this difference raises difficult problems for the generalist manufacturers who prospered in a concentrated structure where the reward for the most efficient was a market share higher than 60%. In the new environment, the reward for the best player is only a maximum 15% of the market, which does not imply in the least a loss of competitiveness, but only a different sector structure. If the leader had really lost its competitiveness, his share would have gone down to less than 5%, not a respectable (in such sectors) 15%!

When the reward for success drops from 70% market share and 15% net profit to 15% market share and 5% net profit, and even if the market is expanding, even firms present in many sectors will inevitably be forced to reduce their resources, their staffs and more generally their lifestyle. But this mutation also challenges the management system and the integrity of the enterprise, its generalist strategy, its personnel policies, etc. It eventually demands profound modifications of organization and methods, and a radical change of culture and lifestyle.

The sum of those difficulties is the background for the crisis of the large traditional generalists, at the forefront of which is IBM, and not such or such specific mistake as suggested by superficial commentators. One often reads that the reason for the misfortunes of IBM is that this firm would have "missed the micro-computing revolution". Now, on one hand, IBM was the first of the large manufacturers to enter this market forcefully, by establishing durable standards, and rapidly conquered enviable positions among the leaders of that market, which it still retains today. On the other hand, it was absolutely unrealistic to expect that the microcomputer activity would quickly replace a major part of the traditional activity, because it concerned and still concerns largely separate markets. Finally, except for the minority sectors of components and software packages, microcomputer activities are less profitable than traditional activities anyway. In reality, IBM quickly became one of the pioneers of micro-computing and succeeded rapidly and durably in that field, but that success did not shield it from the crisis of conventional data-processing, and could no more protect the company from alignment on different market share and profitability standards.

Life in a fragmented world

In a fragmented sector, established situations are constantly challenged. In a very dynamic environment where quick reactions are necessary, firms have neither the time nor the resources for long preliminary studies before launching their products. They must try their luck earlier than the others if possible, and leave the decision to the judgment of the market. In doing so, they must take into account the possibility of failure, contain *a priori* its potential effects through a partitioned organization, be quick and ruthless in terminating projects with no future, and accept without undue fuss the consequences of failures, now considered a normal possibility.

To succeed, it is no longer sufficient to correctly address the general requirements of the market. One must in addition offer a better answer than competitors to the specific needs of the particular target segment or segments. The traditional marketing approach of analyzing demand thoroughly must be complemented by a clear understanding of the distinctive advantages of the firm, and even make room for a strategy resting first on those advantages rather than on expressed demand. The firm must concentrate on what it knows to do better that others, hoping that a market will appear, and not simply produce what the market wants without worrying to know if it has an advantage in that activity. Before all, it must exploit its specific advantages, and leave the sector in the absence of such advantages.

Finally, at the marketing stage, each supplier must know that it will confront competitors whose strategies, and therefore organizations and marketing approaches, are very varied. Every one of them, in the areas where it operates, encounters a multifaceted competition and must consequently adapt its own marketing behavior to face all kinds of competitors.

The convergence of the three worlds thus confronts the large traditional vendors to multiple challenges: organizing themselves to operate in sectors where the rules of the game are fundamentally different, maybe abandon some of their activities, reducing the size of the enterprise and its lifestyle to match the reduction in market share and margins. It also imposes on them a complete upheaval of their culture.

The ambitions displayed by many traditional manufacturers concerning services must be placed in that context. Notice that this attitude is the opposite of the strategy that they adopted through the seventies and the eighties. After having provided free services as an integral part of their supply, manufacturers used separate billing to limit their involvement in services and to favor the creation of specialized enterprises. The seventies and the eighties actually saw a relative movement of hardware manufacturers away from services and the gradual rise of an autonomous services sector.

The about-face that one observes since a few years, particularly visible for the large traditional manufacturers, is partly aimed at preserving or acquiring a competitive advantage for products (that would be even bigger if service was provided free), and to respond to a growing customer demand for increased responsibility of overall results. But its first motivation is probably to derive revenue from personnel resources that are now in excess. For that purpose, there is no need for services to be particularly profitable. As long as one does not accept to dismiss that staff, it is always better to charge them at the market rate, whatever the profit level, rather than to pay those people for being idle or to give away their services for free. In addition, that supply meets a demand increased by the explosion and the growing complexity of the computer supply, which pushes many customers to rely on a professional integrator, and even to demand that their main equipment supplier accept some contractual responsibility for its implementation.

It is nonetheless true than succeeding in services demands very different forms of organization, management systems and company culture from those that suit the hardware sector in general, and the traditional sector in particular. The future will tell whether manufacturers know how to manage their services activities to create a competitive advantage relative to specialized services suppliers, and to organize in such a way that their presence in such markedly different sectors provides more advantages than disadvantages.

In summary, life is harder for equipment vendors in a fragmented or "open" world. One understands why most traditional manufacturers have sought to extend as long as possible the previous models that presided over their success, if only to buy time for achieving their transformation. This attitude contributes to explaining why even those manufacturers that were present in the three worlds actually did little to favor their merger, and why the somehow marginal world of Unix is the favored birthplace of the innovative techniques that will enable the convergence of large and small systems.

The new industrial order

The preceding discussion describes the general movement towards fragmentation of the industry as resulting from the combination of two mechanisms. On one hand, at firm level, there are motivations pushing enterprises to act in the direction of fragmentation. On the other hand, at the global level, there are competitive or economic mechanisms that favor and amplify those actions of fragmentation, and transmit their consequences to the whole industry.

Within the generalist firms, the dividing lines run between activities whose competitive dynamics are very different, as well as their organizational and cultural demands. Each piece separated from the rest joins the corresponding specialized sector. The overall structure of the computer industry, which was initially a single sector of the concentrated type, populated by generalists, transforms itself into a complex of autonomous specialized sectors, each obeying its own dynamics and developing its own structure, ranging from extreme concentration to extreme fragmentation.

Each of those sectors includes firms coming from the traditional world as well as firms from the PC world. Internal competition within each sector tends to invite all firms to emulate the most efficient and to render the organizations, cultures and behaviors more homogeneous, whatever the origin of the enterprise. The explosion into sectors thus comes with a homogenization of firms within each sector.

The firms better adapted to the dominant form of competition in each sector are those that have been operating there the longest and have thus demonstrated their competitiveness under the locally prevailing rules of the game. Generally, they are those that originated in the PC world, except for services where the micro world has not really produced a new breed of services companies different from those that already existed in the traditional world. The submersion of all data-processing by the micro-computing technologies is accompanied by a submersion of the whole industry by the business practices and industrial cultures of the PC world.

Of course, it remains possible that some large generalists will continue to operate in several sectors, and even that some other firms succeed in setting foot and staying in sectors other than their original one. For that purpose, those firms will probably adopt an internal model closer to the conglomerate than to the integrated firm, with autonomous entities implementing independent strategies and adopting structures and cultures adapted to their particular sector. Enterprises present in different sectors with similar competitive dynamics, for example the assembly of different varieties of equipment, will be able to keep those activities within a common structure and to benefit from possible economies of scope. On the other hand, operating in radically opposed sectors such as components and hardware assembly, or packaged software on one hand, hardware or services on the other hand, will demand separating those activities more clearly by assigning them to distinct legal entities.

Conclusion

By observing the structure of the computer industry and by analyzing its history and the current developments in the light of competitive dynamics, we have been able to isolate and characterize the sectors that compose it, to understand the phenomena that happen in each sector and the interactions between sectors. The apparent current chaos is actually the visible manifestation of a profound transition movement of the industry from a homogeneous concentrated structure to a structure of specialized sectors obeying different competitive and economic laws.

This transition is going to take the whole computer industry to a structure and an operating mode which currently characterize the world of microcomputers and more specifically of the PC, that has been growing since 1981 alongside the world of traditional data-processing. The forces in favor of convergence between these worlds, long not strong enough to counterbalance the forces that kept them separate, are clearly beginning to take over. Their effects are going to accelerate, partly due to the preferential role of Unix, which is both on the borderline between the two main worlds and a unifying innovation laboratory.

This "big unification" points towards a world where, like in the PC world, specialized suppliers will exist for each element of a computer system, whether it concerns equipment, packaged software or services. To be capable of being combined with each other, those elements will comply with standards, but as a rule the choice of a supplier for any one element will leave a large number of possible choices open for every other element. This independence in supplier choice, com bined with the possibility of assembling products from independent suppliers, is characteristic what one calls an open world.

Those upheavals of the industry have already started, but they are far from being over yet. So far, competition between traditional data-processing and micros has been largely overstated. In reality, such competition is only beginning, because theoretical competitive advantages take effect only within market segments where the two offers are really substitutable, which has been exceptional so far. But one should not conclude that the current coexistence is going to continue in the same relatively peaceful mode. Actual competitive arenas are multiplying and widening, and gradually extending to all application areas and all performance levels. In each one, the micro world enjoys the strongest competitive advantages, due precisely to its fragmented specialized structure. This world, with its industry structure and its technologies, is going to gradually submerge all data-processing, upsetting all play-ers, and providing customers with new standards of price, performances and usability.

In total, for industry players, life is tougher in an open world. Some of them, operating in monopolistic sectors such as components and packaged software, will be able to exploit dominant positions, but at the price of an increasingly expensive succession of technological bets where they will put their leadership at stake every time. Others will operate in sectors where risks are more reasonable, but where market positions are volatile and where nothing is ever acquired for sure. It is pre-cisely this dangerous world that guarantees the best possible offer to customers.

Transition to the new industrial order is particularly painful for those players who were the most prosperous in the old environment. Their dramatic adaptation difficulties, coming on top of the normal ups and downs of players in the new open world, cause many observers to wonder about the health of the computer industry.

To make an overall diagnosis, one must use the right criteria. The health of an industry is measured first by its vitality, that is to say its capacity to satisfy the needs of its customers, and to improve their satisfaction in all respects: functions, performance, costs, reliability, usability, wealth of choice, etc. By this measure, the computer industry is in splendid health. Of course, some players have disappeared and more are going to disappear. But one should not confuse the health of an industry with that of every single one of the firms that compose it. Elimination of the least efficient enterprises is precisely the main mechanism by which an industry keeps itself in good shape. Of course, many enterprises are downsizing, but only to be better armed for continuing the competitive battle. We tend too often to judge enterprises according to their ability to create jobs, and to forget that their real pri-mary mission is to provide products.

Chapter 15 - The integrating mechanisms

Users facing the exploded world. New roles for DP executives. The integration issue and vendor strategies. Integration services and integrated products. Is facilities management economically viable? Partnerships, alliances, participations and industrial agreements. The banker, the predator and the entrepreneur. What is a good agreement? Why acquisitions fail. Interpreting alliances. Mergers, acquisitions and sector structure. Forecasts by sector.

The preceding analyses conclude that the industry is exploding into specialized differentiated sectors. They rely essentially on the examination of the motivations, opportunities, actions and dynamics which characterize the players on the supply side. The market is considered as an external organism which, by its purchase decisions, approves or disapproves the actions of each supplier and thus prompts them to behave in an appropriate manner. Since the needs and the purchasing capacity are limited, suppliers are competing for each segment of that demand. Each one of them will therefore seek to elicit from the market more favorable reactions than the other competing firms, especially a more favorable purchasing behavior. Those reactions of the market eventually select, for each product segment, the best adapted products, supplier behaviors, firms and enterprise models.

Through this natural evolution process, the market selects the production structures best adapted to its satisfaction. As Alfred Marshall already stated: "a method of industrial organization replaces another when it offers a better service at a lower price". But, even though the fragmented structure towards which the computer industry is evolving carries net global advantages for users, it nevertheless presents a certain number of disadvantages that some players can perceive as market opportunities. It is therefore likely that some players will undertake corrective actions that will tend to slow fragmentation down or cause local consolidation of players, although they will not be sufficient to reverse the general movement.

Like all reaction forces, such antagonistic forces operate all the more visibly that industry fragmentation becomes more complete. In addition to the legitimate objectives of proposing solutions to the user problems created by the explosion of supply, and of building a profitable activity sector on that market demand, less rational motivations stemming from visceral trends towards integration can also come into play. Moves towards cooperation or alliance between suppliers can materialize by participations, acquisition or merger of enterprises, potentially leading to new combinations, different from those that existed previously in the industry and are being destroyed. Those movements, in reaction to fragmentation of the industry, are the subject of the present chapter.

Systems and the integration issue

The abundance and diversity of a fragmented supply require that users be capable of finding their way through the many competitive or complementary products, of choosing intelligently between them, and of effectively assembling products into systems. Users can develop the necessary skills and information mechanisms by themselves for their own use, but those new requirements also create a latent demand and therefore an opportunity for service enterprises. As long as this fragmented structure concerned only micro-computing, and especially the general public, those orientation and integration requirements have been easily satisfied by distributors and users themselves, assisted by an abundant specialized press and occasionally by vendors. Personal systems are indeed simpler, and their configurations present fewer variations, at least initially. Their range of applications is more limited and largely covered by software packages which dictate configuration standards. More significantly, it seems that users of personal computers have developed their selection and integration capabilities in synchronism with their application needs, and therefore generally did not have to confront integration problems that they could not solve. That assumption is consistent with the absence in that area of a demand for services in the traditional sense, which would have only a small chance of being solvent anyway.

The attitude of microcomputer users in enterprises has always been notably different. They expect the enterprise to provide them withsupport services which non-professional users can happily do without for identical types of usage, even including maintenance services. Those expectations translate into a demand, which is solvent since it emanates from enterprises, that ranges from training, installation, assistance or inventory management to the design, development and deployment of complex microcomputer-based systems specific to the enterprise. That demand becomes general when the fragmented structure of the micro world gradually extends to the whole computer supply.

The remainder of this discussion concerns essentially "conventional" users like the enterprises, that have developed the habit and the means to acquire specific systems, by calling upon specialized companies if necessary. It leaves aside the general public, whose integration needs are limited and most often satisfied by the users themselves.

New roles for DP managers

For users, an open world presents many advantages, especially that of choice and independence from suppliers. Indirectly, because of its underlying competitive dynamics, it also enables the best possible exploitation of the available technological potential, through introduction on the market of a large variety of products competing in quality at the lowest possible price.

But the very abundance of products can create problems for many users, who are now increasingly faced with the responsibilities for choosing and assembling the elements available on the market.

Data-processing is an invasive technology by nature, capable of being applied to countless uses by very different users. That infinite variety of uses is matched by an infinite variety of hardware and software configurations, assembled in a tailored manner into systems adapted to each particular utilization. Conversely, each component proposed by the different specialized suppliers, whether it is hardware, software or services, only takes on a real utility and therefore value after that integration operation[76].

In a fragmented or open world, the vast majority of suppliers proposes only a single element or a few of the elements required for building the system. The only ones who offer complete integrated systems are firms specialized in narrow application areas where the number of configurations needed to satisfy their market is limited. Outside of those particular cases, each user must select and assemble the elements of the system that will satisfy his needs.

Moreover, in the disintegrated open world towards which data-processing is evolving, the choices relative to each component of a system are independent from the choices relative to the other components. Contrary to the situation that still prevails today, all major operating systems will eventually work on all major microprocessors, and therefore selecting an operating system will not automatically entail the selection of a microprocessor nor that of a specific line of hardware. Conversely, a growing number of large hardware assemblers, like IBM, Digital Equipment or Hewlett-Packard today, will offer a choice between several microprocessors. Choosing a manufacturer for hardware will not impose the choice of a microprocessor or, indirectly, of an operating system. Similarly, for each functional hardware or software element designed to provide a given service (storage, printing, communication, data entry or display, sound production, etc.), one will find on the market several competitive products compatible with the rest of the system.

Note in passing that the existence of norms or standard tends to complicate that problem of choice rather than to simplify it. Indeed, standards allow to homogenize the most visible features of similar products, and therefore to widen the choice by increasing the number of directly substitutable products. At the same time, they push suppliers to differentiate on more subtle criteria, and therefore more difficult to evaluate correctly. In the absence of standards, the choice is often reduced to a small number of rather different products; in a world governed by standards, the choice is between many similar products with more subtle differences.

Once the choice is made, standards can alleviate the integration problem, but certainly not make it totally disappear. Moreover, standards will never be final, nor universal, nor perfect, and will continue to evolve. As long as competition exists and keeps technical progress ahead of standardization (hopefully forever!), competing standards will exist, and the choice of a manufacturer for one element will not be entirely neutral relative to the other elements.

---

76   This is the usual definition of a "system" as "a collection of complementary products that must be used together to produce value"

In the traditional world of the seventies, a customer had an opportunity to forgo those problems by opting once for all for a generalist manufacturer. In an open world, he must assume those choices by himself, or hand them over to a services company.

In an integrated industry, each generalist manufacturer manages a complementary and compatible product catalog, where each new product is introduced on the market only when the rest of the product line has been adjusted to accept it. By relying on one preferred supplier, the user can therefore offload part of the selection and integration work for products composing his system. Moreover, the marketing message of this supplier puts forwards the coherence of his product line and its adequacy to the specific needs of each user, of which a preferential relationship gives him a certain knowledge. In such a relationship, the generalist supplier is therefore led to play a training and orientation role for his customers.

On the contrary, in a fragmented industry, each player only seeks to develop and to promote his own products. He introduces them on the market as soon as he considers them ready, and is neither desirous nor capable of ensuring that the products of the other manufacturers are made compatible. Marketing arguments are limited to presenting each product as the best possible in its category, although only the features of the integrated global system make sense for the user, and the relationships of products with each other often have as much importance as their individual features.

A small number of competitive actions, all concerning the overall system level and its concrete advantages for the user, gives way to multiple arguments, most often inconsistent with each other when they concern different products, and contradictory by definition when they concern substitutable products. The user himself must now interpret that communication in the context of his own needs and determine the respective potential contributions of competing products to the value of his application system.

When his choice is fixed and his decisions made, he will no longer be able to count on the same assistance that a preferred generalist supplier could provide at the integration stage. No specialized supplier will be capable or desirous to bring more assistance than strictly necessary for the installation of his products. Moreover, hardware suppliers, operating in a highly competitive, fragmented and poorly profitable sector, will seek to limit their free interventions.

Fragmentation of the supply thus confronts users with more severe problems in two areas: systems design and the choice of components on one hand, systems integration on the other hand. Most customers used to rely more or less deliberately on a preferential supplier for that form of assistance, and this reassuring role has significantly contributed to the success of IBM and of its most important followers. A customer could always break loose from that tutelage, but he would then discover the cost and problems of independence, so that only the largest users could afford it in a systematic manner.

To resolve those problems by themselves, users now require skills that they do not necessarily possess, and must accept responsibilities for which they are not always prepared. Many are now looking for tutors able to help them bear the burden of selection and integration. Such demand lies behind the current vogue of systems integration offerings of all kinds including facilities management, and of much marketing talk on the theme of "solutions selling". It represents a hope and a sales argument for the surviving generalists like IBM, Digital Equipment, Unisys or Bull.

Formerly, the computer department of each enterprise was the sole holder of computer knowledge. Management of the enterprise as well as users trusted it and had no real means to challenge its decisions, even when they criticized them. The computer department was also the mandatory entry point for all computer suppliers. If one of them managed to win its confidence, it could then establish a preferential relationship where the supplier played an advice and guiding role, which was challenged only in case of disaster.

Now, computer knowledge is becoming trivial. Many users are able and willing to satisfy their needs by themselves or by dealing directly with suppliers. Competition is ubiquitous and solicits directly top management and users, often to challenge or suggest reconsidering decisions made by the computer department. In this new context, if the computer executive wants to continue to exert a leadership over users and to preserve the confidence of his management, he must deserve his position every day by proving to all those counterparts that every one of his decisions is well-founded and in the best interest of the enterprise, although many people are constantly trying to prove the contrary. He must also remain a preferential source of information and support, although everybody is submitted to an avalanche of more or less accurate, more or less relevant and more or less biased information. He must finally anticipate needs and not be seen as a retarding force, while respecting his basic objectives of continuity and security of the enterprise information system.

Certain of his responsibilities, including development and integration activities, can be managed as separate projects with a defined duration and objectives, and therefore can in particular be subcontracted to specialized third parties. Such is not the case for orientation and follow-up of the data-processing policies. In any case, the computer executive remains responsible for choosing the method (make or buy), selecting the possible subcontractor and for the overall control of operations.

This change of context and mode of work calls for a difficult mutation, of which all are not immediately capable. The difficulty of that transition probably explains in part the hesitation and slowdown in computer evolution that one currently observes in many enterprises, as well as the increasing technological lag of enterprise data-processing behind personal computing and even family usage. It often results in challenging the position and role of the computer executive, and even the place of data-processing in the enterprise, and leads executive management to lend an attentive ear to the sirens of "facilities management".

The organization of supply

Faced with those new problems of users, at least part of the suppliers seek to organize either to reduce the needs for orientation and integration through alliances or cooperation between suppliers, or to address those needs by offering appropriate services, that we will designate in a general manner by "integration services". Even though such alliances are a secondary phenomenon compared to the general trend to the dis-integration of industry, and even though integration services are only one form of services among others, the responses of the different players to integration problems are not without effect on the overall industry structures and on the strategies of players.

Providing integration services is generally considered as a source of global competitive advantages. The integrator has an opportunity to intervene upstream in the selection of components to be integrated, and therefore to favor his own productions or take advantage of his power to recommend in his relationships with the other suppliers. The integrator thus places himself in a preferential position not only relative to the customer, but relative to the rest of the industry.

In a fragmented industry, the role of integrator can be held in multiple ways and by multiple players. One can schematically distinguish two approaches: the integrator starts by identifying a need and associated market, and integrating in advance the system or systems required to satisfy it. Such an approach is of the "product" type, because the supplier defines unilaterally the functional features and the commercial and financial conditions of his offer, and must invest to develop his product before proposing it and discovering the reactions of the market. In a second approach, the "services" type, the integrator starts from the specific needs of each customer and builds a unique custom system for each case.

Only the "services" type of approach allows charging for the integration activity as such, and can therefore be adopted by specialized integrators who do not produce the elements of the systems that they integrate. On the contrary, a "product" approach requires that integration costs be recovered through the billing of system elements. When all or part of those elements are available separately on the market, the integrator is confronted with the problem of selecting those elements that will support the additional price and justifying that supplement compared with the acquisition price of separate elements. That position will be easier if the integrator produces certain key elements of the system.

The "products" type integration is reminiscent of the now obsolescent "turnkey systems" offering, and constitutes one avatar of the now fashionable "solutions marketing". For the above reasons, it can only succeed if offered by vendors of specialized products such as application software packages or specific peripherals, who enjoy a good knowledge of specific applications requirements and a preferential access to the corresponding market. It is probably what explains the failure of virtually all services companies that have approached this area without having a proprietary product offering on which to base the billing of their activity. It can call for permanent cooperation between suppliers if the integrator does not produce all elements of the system and must acquire some from other suppliers.

On the contrary, the "services" type integration activity can be invoiced separately, and will generally be in an exploded world. It can therefore be undertaken by many players, ranging from the generalist manufacturers to specialized service companies. But the only ones to succeed are those who enjoy sufficient competitive advantages for that activity considered in isolation, one of which the ability to deal freely with all hardware and software suppliers. That last consideration works in favor of independent specialized integrators and forces manufacturers offering integration services to separate them clearly from their product sales activities, in accordance with the considerations in the preceding chapter. In other words, the answer to the integration problem is not so much a kind of reintegration of the exploded supply, but the emergence of integration services forming a distinct competitive sector and following the general movement of explosion and specialization of the computing industry.

Substitution services

The integration issues related to the emergence of an open fragmented world restore new life to the concept of the preeminence of services over products. As we have seen in chapter 13, old variations of that concept such as service bureau, and later teleprocessing, have not survived, because their economic justification relied on sharing hardware resources, the price of which has collapsed. Today, the costs and disadvantages of such sharing far exceed its advantages, and all forms of service bureau, other than services of a dominantly application nature, have practically fallen into disuse.

The new variant of that thesis is that customers want results, that is to say a service to users, and are not concerned with the details of computer technology. They would therefore prefer buying an all-inclusive service produced under the responsibility of a single supplier, rather than obtaining the required individual products and retaining the responsibility for producing the service.

That logic can imply various forms of customer-supplier relationship. In the most complete, the customer would subcontract the totality of system design, development and installation tasks as well as day-to-day operations management. The service provider would thus be entirely responsible for the results and for their conformity with the specifications prepared by the customer. In more limited variants, the customer may subcontract the development of the system and all or part of the selection of its elements. That is known as the activity of system integration, where the service provider builds and hands over to the customer an operational system that the customer will operate. At the opposite, the service provider can take over operational management of an existing system, of which it can acquire the property and ensure subsequent evolution. One then speaks of "facilities management".

The economic justification of those forms of service relies on the sharing of professional resources required for design, integration and production of the service. , Sharing of hardware resources remains possible, but is no longer the essential part of the service. Many services firms and some generalists are pinning big hopes on a dramatic growth of the systems integration or facilities management markets, and some commentators predict that the future of the computer industry will be dominated by those two services.

Is it only the comeback of an old classical myth, or is it on the contrary a reasonable forecast this time around, or more simply commercial statements for the purpose of creating a market attitude profitable to some suppliers? Let us try to see clearly by going back to the analysis of relationships between products and services that we have started in chapter 13.

Observe first of all that systems integration and facilities management have quite different potential impacts on industry structure. Systems integration is a support service, to the extent that it consists in a temporary intervention of a specialized service provider. The system and all its components become the property of the user at the end of this intervention, even if they have passed through the service provider during the integration operation. It does not really affect the structure of the industry since the final customer remains in relationship with suppliers and often play a decisive role in the competitive choices, even if the integrator occupies a privileged place. We have seen previously that such service follows the normal dynamics of the services sector. Its development is favored by the explosion of the industry, and firms or organizations that specialize in those activities enjoy in the sector a competitive advantage over generalists.

In facilities management on the contrary, the customer buys a service from a single service provider instead of buying products from the different specialized suppliers. It is this service provider who will bear the main responsibility for the selection of products required for producing the service and for relationships with the other suppliers on behalf of users. We have called this type of service a "substitution" service because it replaces the normal relationship of the customer with suppliers of products, hardware and software. If, as predicted by some augurs, this type of services takes a dominant place on the market, its providers could play a key role in the evolution of industry structure.

The economics of facilities management

In order for a service to exist in a permanent manner, at least one firm must supply it at a durable profit. That assumes on the one hand that there are customers for whom that service presents advantages compared to other ways to satisfy the same need. In that precise case, the cost of the contract must be lower than the cost of internal resources required to produce the same result in level and quality of service. Simultaneously, for the supplier to make a profit, the amount of the contract must be higher than its cost for the service provider. In total, the cost for the service provider must be much lower than the cost that the customer supports or would have to support for the same result. If that cost advantage results from investments made by the service provider, the market must moreover be of a sufficient size to justify those investments, in other words in order for at least one firm to reach the economical production scale.

In comparing the amount of the contract to internal costs, the customer should obviously include only the cost of those resources that the contract allows to save. Therefore, contrary to a certain accounting orthodoxy, the valuation of internal resources should be limited to direct costs. Using the complete costs would indeed imply that, in the case where the enterprise chooses the facilities management solution, it would actually save those resources that correspond to the overhead share of the complete cost, that is to say executive management, functional services, etc. – which is extremely unlikely.

For a facilities management contract to be really interesting financially, its amount must be less than the direct cost of computer resources to which it is substituted. That rule is obviously unfavorable to facilities management, but represents the only realistic base for comparison.

At the opposite, in order for the contract to be profitable for the service provider, its amount must cover the complete cost of production resources that are assigned to it, plus commercial expenses for preparing the proposal and the contract, as well as for the commercial activity in general including unsuccessful proposals. It must finally leave a sufficient profit margin to the enterprise. Now the unit costs of basic resources are practically the same for the services enterprise and for its customers. The service provider must therefore be able to implement savings of at least 20% on the real resources devoted to the contract, compared to what the customer uses or would use. Those mandatory savings increase to 40% if the service provider wants to make the customer benefit from a 20% reduction of his computer expenses, as some do not hesitate to promise.

It is difficult to imagine what real savings of that order of magnitude a service provider could implement without impacting the level and quality of service, and that the customer himself could not implement if he had the will to do it. Sharing hardware resources between customers can no longer be a source of substantial savings and can raise issues of security, performance and management. The potentially most promising source of savings is straightforward reduction of operating staffs, but such reductions could most of the time be achieved by the customer as well as by a service provider.

We are left with a limited potential for sharing critical skills. But if there are activities where sharing with others can result in a substantial economy, that can justify a service offering limited to that activity, but is not sufficient to justify an all-inclusive service. In a competition between a global offer where most activities are not profitable and specialized offers limited to profitable activities, the latter will necessarily win, forcing integrated suppliers to dissociate their services, as we have seen in the preceding chapter.

In summary, in the vast majority of situations, there is no economic reason why the price of a complete facilities management service could be significantly lower than the internal cost of the same services. We must therefore expect many failures and desertions in the suppliers camp, much disillusion in the customer side.

In a vast increasingly diverse market, there can nevertheless exist a sufficient number of cases, although always a minority, where such a complete service is justified even if its financial advantages for the customer are very tenuous. Can the usual slogans allow to characterize such cases? Certainly not "concentrating on the mainline activities", when data-processing can be efficient only if tightly integrated in all activities of the enterprise. Not more "transforming fixed costs into variable costs", because most facilities management contracts include long-term commitments that any competent accountant will quickly reintegrate into the firm's liabilities. Neither "placing DP management in the hands of real specialists", because if the enterprise does lack that competence, it would be well advised to acquire it, if only on a part-time or consulting basis.

Can the discussion of internalization versus externalization proposed by Williamson and presented in chapter 14 be applied to the choice between making and buying, or in Gershuny's terminology, to the choice between service and "self-service"? In the absence of decisive cost advantages, resorting to the organization rather than to the market has the effect of avoiding transaction costs, that are all the more high that the assets involved are specific to the activity involved, that the transaction is frequent and its implementation is subject to more uncertainty.

Most computing systems are specific to the user enterprise, especially when data-processing is integrated into the current life of the enterprise, includes a large number of specific programs and transactions, and must abide by local confidentiality, security and reliability constraints. Moreover, a well-integrated computer system lives with the enterprise. If its definition must be the subject of contractual transactions, such transactions will be very frequent and will entail a certain level of risk. In summary, for well-conceived and efficient data-processing systems, all factors work in favor of internalization rather than recourse to an external service provider. Exceptions could be situations where the computer system is loosely integrated in the enterprise, where transactions between data-processing and its users are rare and can easily be formalized, stable systems or slowly evolving systems, in other words mediocre and antiquated systems.

In such cases, priority should be given to a total recasting of the system, which can be facilitated by subcontracting operations of the existing system in order to devote the resources of the enterprise to developing the new one, or on the contrary by relying on a service provider for development and operations of the new system. But in this latter case, if the new system is really a modern well-adapted system, it will be too tightly integrated into the life of the enterprise for its operations to be subcontracted. Anyway, operating a modern well-designed system is inexpensive enough not to warrant it. In both cases, facilities management could only be a temporary arrangement, generally called "transition FM".

In its most complete form, which would nevertheless be the best way to address the assumed needs of the market, the service provider would be responsible for both integration of the system and ongoing production of the service. That form of facilities management is actually extremely rare. Most often, the service provider takes over an existing system already operational at the customer site, often including the personnel, and promises savings in operations costs. That approach eliminates the risks related to design and development, but at the same time place an upper limit on potential savings. Its most obvious effect is to transfer to the service provider the burden of social problems associated with the reduction of operations staff, which can be a sufficient argument for some customers.

Beyond current fashions, that only involve a limited number of accounts, a global long term operations contract can only satisfy a market of exceptional situations, or of firms abdicating their responsibilities. The current trend is towards the fragmentation of the offer into specific operations support services, limited in duration and addressing the specific needs of a particular stage, or differentiated in nature and defined by the subcontracting of specific tasks. A currently popular example is network management, which concerns only the infrastructure and not the application superstructure. The corresponding tasks are generic, relatively easy to specify and to quantify, and can be covered by a standard contract, which makes that service a quasi-product.

In contrast with the variety of services and opportunities related to operations, complete facilities management is therefore a narrow niche addressing exceptional and highly specific cases. Its ephemeral vogue in the media can be interpreted as a promotional attempt by the large computer services companies, relayed by sympathetic commentators, aiming more or less consciously to reinstate into the services sector an integrated total service approach and the dynamics of a concentrated sector, where size and diversification would become the source of competitive advantages. But facilities management is actually being overtaken by the dominant dynamics of fragmentation and specialization before having been able to take hold of the market that many gurus have predicted and that some suppliers have hoped for.

Partnerships and alliances

Faced with the market issues resulting from the explosion of the computer supply, suppliers can find competitive advantages in tying alliances, that can be directed towards various objectives and take a variety of contractual and legal forms. But just as it is vital for a firm to have a personality consistent with its activities, it is important for an alliance to select a form consistent with its objectives. Otherwise, the sanction is the same: an alliance poorly adjusted to its objective will fail like a firm poorly adjusted to its sector.

Let us therefore review the different modes of alliances between enterprises and compare them to the different possible motivations, to better understand how enterprises can organize their relations to satisfy the market, and also to better interpret the real industrial significance of alliances, which the press is reporting almost every day.

Ownership and industrial cooperation

Agreements between companies can involve capital participation ranging from symbolic levels to full control, but can also be limited to contractual or even purely verbal agreements. Let us review separately the industrial or operational aspects and the ownership aspects involved in shareholding, to determine in particular to what extent the two are related.

Let us first remember a few obvious facts, easily forgotten in the excitement of capitalistic speculation. First, the power given by stock ownership is proportional to the level of that participation. As a rule, owning 5% of the capital of an enterprise entitles to 5% of the profits or losses and to 5% of voting rights in the general stockholders meeting. In terms of power, the owner of 5% of the capital has hardly more than an opportunity to voice his opinion once a year on the general orientations of the enterprise. If by luck those 5% buy him a seat on the board of

directors, he can also participate in its deliberations, with a weight again proportional to his share of the capital. One must cross certain magical thresholds (for
instance the 33% "blocking minority" under French law) to benefit from the purely
negative right to oppose certain decisions, and one must own as much as 50% to be
certain of having the power to orient the actions of the enterprise.

Beyond that simple arithmetic begins the subtle game of coalitions and struggles of influence most enjoyed by investment bankers and professional board members, and which gives to a given participation a different weight according to how
the rest of the capital is distributed, and depending on the passive or active, friendly
or hostile attitude of the other shareholders. Taking a minority stake can be a foot
in the door, a waiting position or a reinforcement of an existing coalition. But most
of the time, when an investor decides to buy into the capital of an enterprise, he
can generally do little more than ignore the possible future coalitions and act
according to what he acquires at the moment. That is the viewpoint that we will
adopt in the continuation of this analysis.

By themselves, stock ownership can be motivated by very different considerations, normally matched by similarly different behaviors, which we can summarize
as follows:

The first possible motivation is to invest available cash. The buyer will look
for a healthy profitable enterprise where he can trust the management in place. He
will avoid interfering with the management of the firm and will be therefore be satisfied by a minority interest, which can easily be disposed of if needed. It is the
motivation of the passive investor.

The motivations of "turnaround" and "takeover" investors have much in
common. Both will look for cheap enterprises, therefore probably in difficulty,
where they believe that their personal intervention can restore a satisfactory situation. To achieve that, they must hold the majority, remove most of the managers in
place, and personally take the reins of the enterprise. But while the takeover
investor aims for the long term and intends to remain at the head of the enterprise
for a long time, the objective of the turnaround investor to sell it quickly after
restoring its financial health, and to realize a capital gain.

A variant of the turnaround strategy is that of the "predator", where the
buyer has determined that certain activities of the target enterprise, taken separately, have a total value higher than the price at which he hopes to be able to buy
the entire enterprise. His objective is therefore to break up the enterprise into its
different activities and to sell them one by one, eliminating the activities with no
value. At the end of such an intervention, the enterprise in its original perimeter no
longer exists.

Of the above motivations, only that of the takeover investor corresponds to
a real industrial or entrepreneurial motivation, where the buyer involves himself in
order to contribute to the long-term prosperity of the enterprise. However, such
action, like the actions of turnaround investors, entails no structural modification
of the sector. The actions of the predator result in breaking up diversified firms in
difficulty, and therefore contribute to the fragmentation of the industry and to the
specialization of firms.

Minority interests do not give the power to orient unilaterally the actions of the firm, and cannot, by themselves, enable to reach genuine industrial objectives. They are nevertheless often used to symbolize a cooperation between firms. In that case, the only part that really matters from an industrial viewpoint are the underlying industrial agreements or those that will result from the dialogue initiated through the participation. In general, such agreements could as well exist and work without any participation in the capital. In any case, the possibilities of positive cooperation between independent firms are limited, and raise enough operational problems to require being spelled out in detail.

Not only is a participation in capital not sufficient to institute operational cooperation, but even when such cooperation is covered by explicit and specific agreements, it can only translate into action at the expense of profound changes in the organization and management of the enterprise.

Within an enterprise, the will of management is not executed without an appropriate organization, or if it is in contradiction with the culture of the enterprise, as we have seen in chapter 9. In the same manner, it is not sufficient to sign an executive-level agreement between two enterprises for that agreement to be automatically followed by effects. People concerned in the enterprise must now act in accordance with the terms and objectives of the agreement, which calls for specific management provisions, and even modifications of the structure and management systems. Even after such management actions, the objectives will be reached only if the expected behavior is not in contradiction with the own objectives and personality of the enterprise. This implies a certain kinship between the two enterprises, or at least between those parts of the enterprises which are involved in implementing the agreements.

Faced with those issues, the best interest of the parties is therefore that agreements have a limited and clear object, that risks of failure be recognized and taken into account, and that each enterprise preserve its full independence in the areas not concerned by the agreement. One will therefore prefer forms of agreement requiring the lowest possible level of commitment that is nevertheless compatible with the common objective. For the same reason, agreements will have to be of limited duration and to anticipate actions in case of failure.

In other words, in the vast majority of cases where contractual agreements are sufficient to define the target cooperation, it will be better to avoid participations in capital. Similarly, if parties to the contract can live up to their commitments by remaining in full control of their respective resources, it will be preferable to stick to that type of agreement and to avoid the creation of joint subsidiaries.

If the objective is simply to agree on common standards, the most appropriate arrangement is the informal club. If it is to establish privileged customer-supplier relationships involving preferential treatment, or to exploit complementary market positions, the contractual form will have to be retained. The same applies if the objective is to acquire or exchange technologies, which is akin to a customer-supplier relationship, or to combine complementary skills such as those of integrator and that of experts in each of the products or areas of activity. Only when putting resources to work together in an integrated structure will it become appropriate to create a common subsidiary and therefore to resort to capital actions.

Contractual agreements without capital participation are far more efficient that participations without specific precise industrial agreements. Outside of their role as pure financial placement, minority participations do not play by themselves any role other than symbolic, and when they are matched by a seat on the Board, that of an observatory allowing to identify opportunities for operational cooperation and to facilitate their implementation. But in and of themselves, they have no operational importance.

Contrary to a widespread opinion, the same goes for relationships within a group. For an enterprise, taking into account the interests of another enterprise, even if it belongs to the same group, can be a competitive handicap that the advantages of group membership may not compensate. If membership in a group is the pretext for excessive integration, it is a source of weakness rather than strength.

Majority holdings and acquisitions

The most frequent properly industrial motivation of acquisitions is to subordinate the acquired firm to its buyer, in order to build, from two independent enterprises, a new entity with competitive advantages that neither one possessed before. It is analogous to the takeover motivation and has nothing to do with the motivations of the passive investor, the turnaround investor or the predator. In any case, it implies changes of strategy that necessitate the control of a firm by the other, and in some case changes of management and significant restructuring.

The uninformed public believes that capital transactions that come with a takeover constitute the important event. In reality, like simple participation, control takeover is not sufficient by itself to change the strategies of the firms involved. Implementing the potential synergy that motivated the acquisition demands a follow-on effort whose cost and duration are most often underestimated. If this effort is not undertaken early after acquisition, the synergy and therefore the expected benefits will not materialize. If it is indeed undertaken, it may cost enough in money and other resources to discourage the buyer to carry out all the required actions, which can fail anyway.

In short, acquiring an enterprise, or entering into its capital at some level, is to an industrial project what buying a plane ticket to Katmandu is to climbing the Himalayas. One has spent part of the budget, but the adventure has not started yet and all failures are still possible.

A typical case would be for a packaged software firm occupying for example 40% of the market for its product, to acquire another enterprise holding some 25% of the same market. Commentators would be quick to celebrate the fact that the buyer now holds 65% of the market. But they are misled by an arithmetical illusion, forgetting that the two products are still different at that stage, and that economies of scale can only materialize when all users use the same product. In order to achieve that, the firm must heavily invest in development and marketing. It is also likely that many customers will take the opportunity of that forced conversion to shop around and maybe turn to another supplier. At the end of the day, the buyer will have spent significantly more than the acquisition price to acquire a lower market share than the acquired company originally enjoyed.

Generally, the magnitude and difficulty of efforts required obviously increase as the two firms were initially more remote in their activities, their cycle of operations, their organization and especially their culture. The buyer often underestimates the cultural incompatibilities, and by attempting to precipitate the merger in order to reap quickly the expected benefits, it only frustrates the employees of the acquired enterprise, and possibly causes the departure of the best, voiding the acquisition of its substance.

In the case where both enterprises belong to the same sector, other difficulties must be expected, due to the fact that they were competitors prior to the acquisition. It will be necessary to consolidate and rationalize productions, therefore to discontinue some products by creating dissatisfaction for those who created them, those who sold them and customers who used them. It will be necessary to devote time and efforts to pacify internal struggles and to make adversaries of yesterday cooperate. That whole process will take time, because those same people who were committed to compete against your products do not become overnight their most active advocates, nor the most believable.

Some factual studies that have attempted to evaluate the real results of acquisitions conclude that most fail, to the extent that the hopes that had initially motivated the operation do not materialize thereafter. The percentage of failure is estimated at 60% if the two firms operated in the same sector, 80% if they operated in different sectors. Incidentally, the stock market is not fooled easily. As a rule, when rumor says that a firm is going to be purchased, the value of its stock goes up. On the other hand, when the transaction is disclosed, the stock of the buyer most often declines. In other words, the immediate effect of an acquisition is to weaken the buyer. The long term effect depends on the actions undertaken after the acquisition, and on their success. The only sure winners are the shareholders of the acquired firm, who have pocketed the appreciation created by the buyer's hopes even he fails to realize them.

In summary, for the neutral observer, cases where acquiring another enterprise really results in strengthening the firm should be considered as exceptions rather than the rule. At the time of announcement of an acquisition, and in the absence of any specific information that would allow to predict a success, the most likely forecast is one of the following. Either the two firms will continue to coexist and to implement largely independent strategies consistent with the logic of their sector, whatever are their capital ties, and nothing will have really changed. Or the acquired firm will be eliminated, the buyer will be weakened in the short term by his efforts and internal problems, as well as by the acquisition expenses, and the long term effect will at best be negligible. In a very dynamic, fragmented, quickly evolving sector, one can even fear that the temporary weakness following acquisition might translate into a handicap in the long run, if it makes the firm temporarily unable to seize available market opportunities. This forecast can obviously suffer exceptions, but it would be a mistake to consider them as the norm.

One obvious exception is acquisition of a foreign company to serve as a foothold in another country, as part of an internationalization strategy. In that case, a local subsidiary is required anyhow, and buying an existing company is generally more efficient than creating one from scratch. In addition, it provides local image and connections, as well as knowledge of local laws and customs. However, those benefits can materialize only if most of the existing local management remains in place, and reaching the proper balance between recognition of local specificity and efficient contribution to the strategy of the mother company remains no simple task.

Putting aside the cases of simple construction of conglomerates, one can wonder why so many enterprises use mergers and acquisitions as instruments of their industrial projects, often very aggressively by the number and size of acquired companies. Several factors probably come into play: ignoring or underestimating the actual problems of compatibility between cultures, believing to be in the particular case that will succeed, the congenital optimism of entrepreneurs, etc. The most important may be that many executives feel more at ease in capitalistic construction games, where they find a reserved powers area, a space of freedom and a feeling of superiority, rather than in the fastidious chores of managing production and marketing operations that form the real life of the enterprise, but where they are often less competent than their subordinates. One often gets the impression of a separation between two types of executives: those who attend to efficient management of the enterprise and for whom capital transactions belong to a foreign universe, and those who regard business as a game of participations in the capital of "black boxes" that they would most often be unable to manage.

Those differences of attitudes and skills are entirely legitimate. Being a shareholder and being an operational manager are two different activities, just as useful as each other, but that rely on different motivations, different views of the enterprise and different repertories of possible actions. It is a very widespread error to mistake one for the other, whether as an observer or, which is far more serious, in action.

Partnerships and "coopetition"

The fragmented world of contemporary computing contrasts with the old world not only by the specialization of its players, but also by the abundance and the diversity of alliances between them. Some observers are puzzled by that situation of "coopetition" (a mixture of cooperation and competition) where one no longer knows who is friend and who is foe. The following considerations may help to unravel this maze and to understand the real meaning and importance of the partnership announcements reported daily by the press.

A first rule is to always look for the real substance of the agreement, that is to say its motivations and its financial or industrial provisions, behind the commercial or image motivations which explain its presentation. One will verify in particular whether such dramatic "partnership" announcements are not simple window-dressing for an ordinary customer-supplier relationship, as it is often the case. A big headline like "Company X allies with manufacturer Y for the computerization of..." most often announces that X has ordered hardware from Y. In the same vein, "microcomputer manufacturer Z becomes a partner of Intel" means that Z has decided to use Intel microprocessors, like hundreds of others.

A real partnership is defined by a sharing of risks and implies that the parties will operate under different rules than their normal contractual practices. For example, if an enterprise subcontracts to another all or part of the development or manufacturing of a product, it will be necessary to find out who defines the specifications, who sets the selling price and who takes what risk on the revenue. If the product is defined unilaterally by the subcontracting firm and if the revenue of the subcontractor depends only on conformity to specifications, that is only a trivial case of subcontracting. A real partnership requires that the subcontractor participates in the definition of the product and that his revenue depends on the revenue of the subcontractor.

A second rule is to separate participations and industrial agreements, and to always search for the agreements behind participations. In the absence of explicit agreements, minority participations may be ignored as being of no operational importance, until specific agreements are announced.

For control takeovers, one will similarly look for underlying industrial projects, relate them to general structural trends, and ask the question of the cultural compatibility of the firms involved. In the absence of specific information about the transaction, the most realistic attitude is to assume as a matter of principle that acquisitions have strong odds of being management mistakes, or of becoming mistakes in the medium term. Starting from that postulate, one must then search for reasons to believe that this particular acquisition can exceptionally turn out to be a good deal for the buyer, given a sound estimate of its cost, in time and efforts over and above the acquisition price. Once this real cost is estimated, one should compare the results of the acquisition with the other actions that would have been possible for the same cost.

Third, one must remember that there are good and bad alliances, that all alliances do not necessarily strengthen the firms involved, and that an alliance, even if it is a good one in theory, can succeed or fail depending on how it is managed. Whether in the framework of an alliance or not, each enterprise is only pursuing its own interests. An alliance must enable every one of its members to earn more, to spend less or both. In addition, one cannot receive without giving, so that a good alliance imposes constraints on each partner, that must be more than compensated by its advantages.

It will therefore be necessary to always look at the negative side of the agreement, that is to say what each partner refrains from doing, either contractually or in fact by accepting a constraint on his resources or by giving up their control. It will be necessary to compare the gains and sacrifices made by each enterprise and to estimate how their motivations meet and agree. Finally, it will be necessary to remember that a good alliance has a limited and precise object, that too ambitious or too vague alliances have all odds of failing, and finally that environment changes can make a good alliance obsolete.

Towards a recomposition?

We have shown that the major visible movement in data-processing tends to make the industry explode into specialized sectors, and we have been able to describe the logic of that movement. It is nevertheless legitimate to wonder if this movement is irreversible. Are there reasons to believe that a movement of recombination is going to emerge from the phenomenon of alliances that we have just analyzed? If yes, who will be involved and where will it lead? In other words, are there motivations pushing enterprises to undertake actions going in the direction of integration? Moreover, are there global competitive or economic mechanisms of such a nature to amplify those integration actions and to transmit them to the whole computing industry?

One can easily admit that such motivations are powerful and widespread, even if they are not always very rational. Almost all enterprises seek to grow, and are not always satisfied to make better and more of what they are already making. Managing a large enterprise has more prestige than managing a small one. Industry classifications are generally ranked in order of absolute revenue or profits, which makes bigger look like better. Successful executives want to extend their actions to other sectors, sure to know the secrets of good management and convinced that their past successes guarantee their future success. Those who encounter difficulties are most often blaming them on a bad choice of sector, and believe that changing activity will solve their problems. By going into a new activity, a successful firm can hope to exploit more completely its real or assumed competitive advantages, or simply invest the profits accumulated thanks to its past successes. Finally, an abundant literature presents diversification and acquisition actions as the normal behavior of the enterprise, encouraged by business consultants and merchant banks who make their living from such transactions.

We will not enter the debate on the goals of the enterprise. It will be sufficient for us to observe that many enterprises will engage into actions of "diversification", justified or not, some implying various forms of alliances. Our purpose is to examine which ones of those actions may succeed frequently enough to change the basic structure of the industry.

The recombining process

In order to grow, an enterprise can use two methods: either rely on simple endogenous growth, or acquire other enterprises. In both cases, the new activities, whether they are undertaken within the firm or are the object of the acquisition, can be more or less similar to current activities. An acquisition can even concern a direct competitor and therefore activities belonging to the same sector as that of the buyer.

By and large, entry into a new sector through internal development raises the same issues as entry from scratch through creation of a new enterprise. Whatever are the qualities of the original firm and the sector where it operates, entry into a fragmented sector will be easy and entry into a concentrated sector will be difficult and risky. The existing activities of the enterprise indicate competitive advantages in the sector of origin, which may or may not prove relevant in the new sector and will seldom be sufficient there. More deeply, the organization and culture that have enabled the success of the enterprise in its sector are more or less adapted to the new one. The odds of success will be maximal if the new activities can be accommodated within the same organization and the same culture, therefore if the cycles of major activities are similar in duration and if sectors have similar levels of concentration.

We have also seen that firms adapted to long cycles, and therefore to concentrated sectors, can rather easily tolerate within themselves organizations adapted to short cycles, while the opposite is far more difficult. Moreover, firms operating in fragmented sectors generally have moderate profitability and capital, so that they will only exceptionally have resources available for entry into a concentrated sector. It is therefore practically impossible for a firm in a fragmented sector to enter a concentrated sector through endogenous growth. At the opposite, firms in concentrated sectors can rather easily attempt to penetrate fragmented sectors, but they only will succeed durably if they create and preserve for those activities an organization and a culture opposed to their original personality, which can hardly be guaranteed except by a clearly separated organization.

For a firm initially operating in a fragmented sector, undertaking different activities, but also belonging to a fragmented sector, is a relatively easy operation and can succeed. But in this type of sectors, the potential economies of scale are small. Merging such activities into a single firm presents therefore only limited advantages, that must be seriously compared to the possible loss of autonomy, agility and specificity. In the majority of cases, two activities of the fragmented type would succeed as well separately. Merging them creates a competitive advantage only if there are many possibilities of synergy between their value chains[77], and specifically for activities where the optimal scale is high enough to exceed the scale of each enterprise.

Evolution within sectors

How can the combination of the explosion process and of the process of recombining change the internal structure of each sector? In particular, if the forces of dis-integration are as powerful as the preceding discussion leads to assume, should we expect further explosion of current sectors? Or on the contrary, since acquisitions and extensions within a sector have almost a 50% chance of succeeding, can the movement of re-concentration nevertheless prevail?

In sectors already fragmented, increasing market share or extending the product range is of limited interest for the firm. But as we have seen in Chapter 8, those sectors have room for varied strategies, where specialization strategies can coexist with volume or range strategies, provided that the production cycles are close enough to accommodate the same organization and the same culture. Those sectors, where obstacles to entry are low and profits are moderate, are the place of many ephemeral successes that enterprises will seek to extend, but also the place of

---

77 see Porter (The Competitive Advantage) for a description of the concept of "value chain" and connections between value chains

as many failures that may become targets for takeovers. Note nevertheless that if the real asset of an enterprise in trouble is its personnel, as is most often the case in services, there are more straightforward and more economical ways to obtain it than to buy the firm. Similarly, it is often better to create a new enterprise than to purchase an existing one fraught with problems. In summary, it is likely that fragmented sectors, that is to say most of equipment and services, will know an important internal restructuring activity, but without effect on their global concentration level.

In concentrated sectors, acquisition is the most normal mechanism in the concentration process. Indeed, the total number of firms is bound to decrease, but on the other hand, as we have seen in Chapter 7, a high market share constitutes by itself a decisive competitive advantage. A dominant firm and a firm willing to leave the sector will therefore rather naturally find a common ground, the first one buying market share and perhaps rare skills, the other recovering a part of its past investments and offering an evolutionary path to its customers. It is for example what happened between Intel and Hewlett-Packard.

But enterprises in concentrated sectors, especially in the components sector, are also submitted to strong tensions driving towards vertical dis-integration. To share colossal investments and to dissociate different economical production scales and cycles, some enterprises specialize in one of the three main stages of chip production: production of silicon wafers, engraving of circuits and packaging of chips. The activity of "silicon foundry" can be made available to third parties for producing circuits of their own design, which further divides the investments between production firms, the "foundries", and firms that design chips and subcontract their production, called "fabless" component firms.

Such an explosion of the components sector of is under way. Firms specialized in one or several stages of foundry are being created in the Far East, most often on the initiative and with the financial support of local public authorities, and engage into the production of memories. At the same time, western enterprises abandon the foundry activity to concentrate on the design of microprocessors. Only a handful of companies such as Intel and IBM still master the totality of operations of the sector including the design and the manufacture of standard microprocessors, while a few other founders such as Texas Instruments continue to design special microprocessors for their own needs. That evolution will probably slow down the concentration of the sector.

We have seen that the sector of packaged software, where the same logic of concentration prevails, is actually formed by a multitude of sub-sectors whose capital-intensity, economical production scale and cycles cover a very large range. This sector is therefore already fragmented in fact, but the movement of absorption of the small firms by the large ones may currently be stronger than the compensatory movement of firm creation in new sectors. The sector may therefore be globally evolving towards a growing concentration. As we have seen in Chapter 11, that movement may slow down or even reverse if the new development technologies such as object-oriented programming reduce the costs required for systems integration, and even displace activities of packaged software integration towards the users.

Possible mergers between sectors

We will consider that two sectors merge if a significant number of enterprises of one penetrate into the other, either by extension of activities or by acquisition. Moreover, activities must really merge into a single enterprise. If they only belong to a conglomerate, they remain specialized enterprises if having a common share-holder does not prevent them from implementing independent strategies and does not lead them to agree on abnormally favorable mutual provisions. In any case, should one company take too much account in its actions of the interests of a company of a different sector, under the pretext that it belongs to the same con-glomerate, it is likely that it would degrade its competitive advantages in its own sec-tor.

We will seek therefore to identify cases where the merging of two sectors of activity provides the firm with competitive advantages higher than the costs of compromises that it creates. If that is the case, it is probable that the operation will be attractive for an important proportion of firms in that situation, and also that the odds of success are reasonable; actual merging of sectors will therefore take place. Otherwise, even if some firms attempt the operation, it has strong odds of failure, and in case of success to remain an exception; sectors will then remain sepa-rate. We do not want to prejudge the totality of approaches that will be attempted, but to identify among them those actions that have the most chances to succeed and to influence the general structure of the industry.

We have seen in Chapter 9 how incompatible productions with long cycles and productions with short cycles are within an enterprise. More precisely, a short cycles enterprise cannot practically tolerate long cycles enclaves, while the opposite is possible. Especially, as we have seen above, it is practically impossible for a short cycles enterprise to penetrate a long cycles sector other than by acquisition, but the merger will encounter serious problems of coexistence. Moreover, short cycle enterprises are not capital-intensive. In favorable periods, they are not motivated to diversify, and in difficult periods they cannot afford it. It is therefore extremely unlikely that fragmented sectors like hardware or services will absorb components or packaged software.

For analogous reasons, a global merger between fragmented sectors would not truly make sense. Whether the idea is for a hardware firm to be present in ser-vices or for a services firm of to offer some hardware, the operation is relatively easy in both directions. But because of the fundamentally fragmented character of the two sectors, the market shares of firms will be low, and probably limited to spe-cific niches of the new sector which have privileged relationship with activities of the old sector.

On the other hand, it is foreseeable *a priori* that components or packaged software companies will want to be present in equipment or services. But when an enterprise of a concentrated sector sets foot in a fragmented sector, that does not change the fragmented sector into a concentrated one. The market share that the firm can hope for is of the magnitude that a fragmented sector allows. In other words, if Intel penetrates into equipment or Microsoft in services, the probability that they reach in those sectors as dominant a position as in components or operating systems is minimal.

Concerning services, there are many reasons why firms from concentrated sectors should not penetrate there on a large scale. We have seen that success in services activities is extremely sensitive to the personality of the firm, and that personalities required for the different forms of services are all remote from that of components or packaged software firms. Moreover, profitability levels in fragmented sectors are low compared to those enjoyed by suppliers in concentrated sectors. For those reasons, it is probable that the presence of components and packaged software firms in services will be limited to services that are in direct support of their products. For packaged software, that means essentially technical assistance to users, possibly going as far as systems integration where products of the firm are involved. For components, opportunities are reduced since producers are not in direct contact with users, and it is therefore likely that the components vendors will remain completely outside of services.

The temptation and the motivations for components firms to be present in hardware are more obvious. It is already the case of Intel with motherboards, extension cards and massively parallel machines, and of Motorola for communication equipment. It is also in a certain way the case for many generalists like IBM, Digital Equipment, Sun, Silicon Graphics, Hitachi, NEC, Fujitsu or Toshiba, who produce both hardware and components, even if many of those are condemned to abandon components in the future, or at least to separate them from their hardware activities.

A new possibility would be a threat of downstream expansion of Intel, taking advantage of its financial power, or of PowerOpen that would reconstitute a dominant IBM now including all or part of Apple. One imagines what motivates component producers to be present on the markets for final products, and furthermore this movement of downstream expansion is easily feasible. But what could be the motivations and the odds of success of a large-scale invasion?

It would be necessary to assume that component manufacturers have decisive competitive advantages in the assembly of hardware, which is unlikely, or that they obtain such an advantage by giving preferential treatment to their own assembly activity through special prices or conditions. Under that assumption, they would have to engage into discrimination in the supply of chips and would be exposed to legal counterattacks, as well as to losses of market shares as long as there is another viable supplier of microprocessors. Now, as long as the hardware sector remains fragmented, profits in that sector are limited. In total, it is likely that the additional profit realized in equipment would be significantly lower than the profit lost on components.

One can therefore expect that component specialists will remain marginally present in the equipment sector, but without attempting to take a dominant share. Sectors will remain separated, and those generalists that will survive in the components sector will therefore have to implement autonomous strategies in that sector, which applies in particular to the relationship between PowerOpen and IBM as a manufacturer of hardware. An interesting possibility would be that component firms absorb a part of the packaged software sector. This movement would be consistent with the deep technological trends in components, which will integrate increasingly complex functions, starting with central functions of operating systems. It would be facilitated if base software would explode into independent objects resting on a suitable micro-kernel, the functions of which it would be tempting to integrate into silicon as soon as they are reasonably stabilized. One can then think that the continuous movement of software functions migrating from peripheral innovative firms, towards the nucleus and integrating firms, that we have described in Chapter 12, would end up crossing the borderline that still separates hardware from software.

Such a merger is all the more likely that it concerns two concentrated sectors with similar cultures, and that profits in packaged software are attractive even for a components firm. The part of the packaged software sector that concerns operating systems may therefore become gradually integrated in the component sector, which would displace the center of gravity of the rest of the packaged software industry towards applications and would contribute to fragment it further. In that movement, the component producers would absorb the producers of packaged software rather that the opposite. But some large producers of packaged software could want to write part of their products into silicon and would thus become designers of specialized chips (ASIC for "application-specific integrated circuit"), of which they would subcontract the production to foundries.

Sector Movements

origin \ target	Components	Hardware	Programs	Services
Components	normal concentration	marginal	absorbtion of functions	unlikely
Hardware	unlikely	random movements	unlikely	customer support
Programs	ASIC	computerized objects	absorbtion of functions	customer support
Services	unlikely	computerized objects	unlikely	random movements

Those conclusions are summarized in the above table, which shows for the sectors on each line the most likely significance of entry by a firm of that sector into each of the sectors appearing in the columns. To the cases presented above, we have added the possibility for some packaged software or service firms specialized in particular application areas to translate their specific skills into a "computerized object", thus penetrating the hardware sector.

Conclusions

In spite of some forces favorable to a re-integration of the computer indus-try, which come mainly from the difficulties of traditional users and the disappear-ance of functions traditionally assumed by generalists, the explosion of the industry is a lasting trend. Large scale re-integration is not foreseen, apart from continuation of the concentration in sectors already most concentrated: components and base software packages. But that concentration may come with an explosion of the two sectors themselves and a merger between some of their components such as micro-processor design and packaged software development. That perspective, which remains an open question, can influence the evolution of Microsoft and Intel on one hand, of the IBM/Motorola/Apple galaxy on the other hand, and conse-quently of a large part of the industry.

At the user level, integration requirements will be satisfied by networks of alliances between independent firms rather than by merger of enterprises, by the emergence of specialized integrators rather than by the return of generalists. Con-cerning operations, multiple assistance services will be proposed by the services sector. Some will disappear quickly, made obsolete by the evolution of products, but other needs will appear that will give birth to other services. But "self-service" will remain the most widespread practice, and demand will not be sufficient to pro-voke the often announced dramatic explosion of the services sector. In particular, total facilities management will remain a niche market with no global strategic importance.

In all sectors, and especially in the most fragmented and the most dynamic ones such as hardware and services, one must expect to see, among many possible strategies, attempts at partial re-integration most of which will remain isolated and with no major effect on sector structure. The dynamism of these sectors will con-tinue to give birth to a multitude of alliances addressing a variety of motivations and taking widely different forms. Most have no importance other than in the media and their duration will often be ephemeral. They must therefore be consid-ered with a cold critical eye.

Be that as it may, one will continue to see many mergers and acquisitions, most of which will fail, especially if they involve enterprises operating in different sectors. Their global effect on the evolution of industry structures will anyway be limited to mergers or breakups of enterprises within each sector, without notable effect on borderlines between sectors.

Chapter 16 - The frontiers of the computer industry

Where are the frontiers? Computerization, production scale and cycles. Computerized products and services. What is a computer? Competitive arenas revisited. The computer and the electric motor. Data-processing and communications. Causes and consequences of opening up competition. What convergence? Multimedia and information highways. Business cycles and computing. 1950, 1975, 2000, 2025... The end of data-processing?

In this last chapter, we will return to the question of the limits of the computer industry, that we have deliberately left pending on several occasions. In chapter 6, we have seen that the economic theory does not provide rigorous criteria allowing to isolate any part of the economic system to study it independently of the rest. Let us recall Chamberlin: "The economic world can be considered as a network of interdependent markets and sectors, whose borderlines are chosen to render the representation convenient, but that are essentially arbitrary". The concept of "industry" that has served us all along this book, and that we have defined as a set of interdependent sectors, is just as arbitrary if not more.

We have stumbled on that imprecision on several occasions. In chapter 1, we have seen data-processing separate from the electronic industry and from unit-record, from which it was born, in order to become an autonomous industry. In the analysis of industry statistics that we have undertaken in chapter 4, we have seen that neither Datamation nor McKinsey include the production of electronic components in the computer industry, although that sector plays a central role in it. At the opposite, there are many firms where data-processing, defined in the strict sense that we have used, is only one activity among others. Do we have to accept that those firms operate in several different industries or on the contrary should we consider that all the activities of ATT, Hewlett-Packard, Canon, NEC, Hitachi, Siemens, Olivetti, Toshiba or Xerox belong to data-processing by definition?

Those questions would be relatively academic if the term "industry" was not frequently used and if common usage did not give it an intuitive meaning. What should we think for example of a frequent statement such as "the computer industry and the communications industry are converging", which is meaningful only if one is able to tell on one hand why they should be considered as separate so far, and on the other hand to describe what would constitute their convergence?

We have provisionally defined the computer industry as "the set of organizations that produce goods or services entering in the composition of computer systems or used in their implementation"[78]. But we have immediately stumbled on the same inadequacy of the definition of a computer system: data-processing is now everywhere, including in "computerized objects" produced by unquestionably different industries like cars, airspace, domestic appliances or musical instruments. Conversely, computer systems use products and services from other industries: communications, finance, etc.

Whether a good or service is part of data-processing has been variously appreciated in time. We have seen in particular that certain services for data-processing, such as financing, have been offered first by computer firms as an integral part of their overall supply, then have been taken over by firms specialized in that type of service, but not specialized in computing. Similarly, data-processing firms have offered services which were useful primarily outside of data-processing, such as banking or messaging services. Those services are now dominated by enterprises having that type of services as their main activity, and for which data-processing has become a trivial tool. In both cases, activities that initially belonged to the computer industry have migrated to user industries.

The very dynamics of the central sectors of data-processing—components, equipment, packaged software and services— entails moving borderlines and movements through borderlines. The economic logic that dominates the sector of components compels manufacturers to distribute them as widely as possible by promoting the utilization of microprocessors in all objects and all industries. The diversity and dynamics of the fragmented sector of equipment motivate players to seek a return on innovation in original niches. They can thus propose atypical variations of the computer concept, specialized by type of utilization or by function, such as personal assistants, or hybrid machines like those that combine the functions of printer, scanner, copier, fax and telephone. Do such products still belong in data-processing, or are their market niches so exotic that they must be considered as colonies in foreign territory?

Finally, as we have seen in chapter 11, software, the basic ingredient of data-processing, is a material like handwriting, that can enter into the construction of anything. Like information of which it codes processing, software can be present everywhere, taking multiple forms ranging from the simplest programs to cathedrals of complexity. But software writing, like writing in general, is a basic skill that will increasingly be present in all organizations, thus extending well beyond the borderlines of the computer industry where it originates.

At the risk of disappointing the devotees of clear-cut classifications, we will accept that attempting to draw rigorous borderlines within the economy is a futile exercise. We will start from the definitions, recognized as arbitrary but nevertheless reasonable, that have served us until this point in this book, and we will examine the interactions which take place on the border areas. That will help us to understand what influence the evolution of data-processing exerts on other industries, and mostly on the information industries. We will develop in more detail the exam-

---

78   see Chapter 6

ple of telecommunications whose convergence with data-processing is a currently fashionable theme, but which is also an occasion for many questionable variations.

The analysis of the relationships of the different sectors of data-processing with other industries will help us to address some questions relative to the place of data-processing in the whole economy. Finally, we will be able to take into account those interactions and the borderlines phenomena to sketch a general evolution of the industry in the longer term.

Data-processing and the other industries

It is a trivial observation that data-processing is an invasive technology which penetrates all the other sectors. Virtually all human activities, and in any case all production activities, contain some information processing component, for which computers are an efficient and universal tool. Enterprises spend an important share of their resources processing information to know and serve their market better, or to satisfy their obligations to third parties. Many products and services contain more or less complex information processing functions. Some products are even nothing more than information supports, like books, disks, films or newspapers, while many services boil down to providing or manipulating information, for example financial services, publications of all kinds, news, reservations, communications, etc.

Many writers explore the possible consequences of the growing utilization of data-processing for all human activities, behaviors and individual values, social structures, etc. The issues that we will address here are limited to industry structures, that constitute the subject of this book. Does the dissemination of data-processing in the whole economy entail substantial modifications of some market segments or of some industry sectors, in their very definition or in the dynamics that they obey? In particular, does the penetration of data-processing in an industry translate into drawing together the structure and dynamics of that industry with those of data processing, as is often stated in the case of telecommunications?

Let us distinguish two main levels of intervention of data-processing in an existing industry: first a purely internal utilization that does not modify directly the products and services offered by the firm, and secondly the incorporation of computing functions within the products or services marketed by the firm. In the first case, the competitive fields and the structure of the market are unchanged and sectors remain the same; the utilization of data-processing can provide a competitive advantage to certain firms and therefore modify their position in the sector, but without modifying the basic structure of the sector. On the contrary, the second situation raises the issue of a kind of vertical integration between that industry and some sectors of the computer industry, and therefore the question of borderlines between industries. When Microsoft offers an electronic game, one says that data-processing invades the toy industry; when The Times publishes a newspaper on Internet, should one say that the press invades data-processing?

Data-processing for internal usage

When using data-processing for their own needs, firms are trying to improve their efficiency in a certain number of areas such as management, production, marketing, research and development, etc. The, benefits that they actually obtain are the occasion of many controversies that are not within the scope of this book. One can admit *a priori* that the judicious and efficient utilization of the computer tool is a new differentiation dimension for enterprises, which can result in new competitive advantages or disadvantages depending on its impact on the overall value chain[79].

As long as those advantages only concern indirect activities such as management, their only potential effect is to help the firms using data-processing most effectively to develop at the expense of others, the competitive rules of the game remaining unchanged. The real impact of those potential advantages must in addition be weighted by the importance of the activity to which they apply relative to all the activities of the firm. Improving a marginal activity, even significantly, can only bring a marginal advantage.

On the contrary, if introduction of data-processing enables profound changes in manufacturing processes, production methods or development cycle, the economics of production can be upset enough to change the economical production scale and therefore to influence the concentration level of some sectors. We have been able to relate the main differences between sectors, especially the possible portfolio of available strategies, the local modes of competition, the distribution of market shares and the personality of enterprises, to two characteristics of production: the economic scale, that depends on the relationship between permanent costs and variable cost, and the production cycle, that summarizes the timing relationship between expenses and revenues. How are those two basic factors affected by the invasion of computer technologies?

In the past, data-processing was expensive and reserved to large organizations. Inasmuch as its utilization is the source of competitive advantages, it could have been a concentration factor working in favor of large enterprises. But it seems that organizations are more inert than computer technologies. Existing structures have determined the penetration of data-processing more than data-processing has transformed structures, except for a few exceptional cases.

Today, data-processing has become inexpensive and offers very low entry points. Tailored effective computerization is now possible whatever the size of the enterprise. Moreover, data-processing brings into the reach of small enterprises the advanced management, production, research and development techniques that were previously reserved to large enterprises. Used correctly, it can also shorten operating cycles, which tends to reduce the economical production scale and to favor enterprises with a personality adapted to short cycles. In summary therefore, computerization tends to favor fragmentation, especially in sectors where the primary concentration factors are related to information and management techniques.

---

79   see Porter, "The Competitive Advantage"

Of course, the relative strength of this pressure towards fragmentation is limited to those elements of the value chain where data-processing can bring substantial gains. There are sectors where concentration remains the rule for more fundamental reasons independent of data-processing. The electronic components industry is an extreme example: although production is highly automated, the nature of fixed costs and variable cost makes them largely insensitive to data-processing, and the economical production scale remains gigantic in any case.

Packaged software represents an interesting intermediate case. The basic cause for concentration of the sector is the complexity of the product. That problem might possibly be resolved in the long run through proper usage of data-processing, if the product itself, and the nature of its complexity, were not made of the same material, software. This is another form of the issue that we have mentioned at the end of chapter 12. If technologies allowing to master software complexity, such as object programming, progress more rapidly than systems complexity, the packaged software industry may evolve towards a fragmented structure. In the opposite case, it will preserve and even reinforce its concentrated structure.

Data-processing can also influence the sector structure of other industries by being used in the relations between enterprises. One generally believes that data-processing, by facilitating communications, works in favor of enterprise specialization and sector explosion. But that effect is due mainly to progress in telecommunications, and therefore data-processing plays here only an indirect role. Moreover, when used correctly, data-processing can also reduce internal transaction costs, and therefore work on the contrary in favor of integration. Historically, internal data-processing has progressed far more rapidly that intercompany data-processing or telecommunications. Only in the few last years did telecommunications take full benefit of advances in data-processing, and especially did direct data communications between enterprises start a real boom. In this area, data-processing has probably first been a concentration factor, and has become an additional fragmentation factor only recently.

Computerized products and services

The technologies and components of data-processing are already present in many products: vehicles of all kinds, television sets, tape recorders, cameras, telephones, musical instruments, machine-tools, to quote only a few. Data-processing is also an integral part of many services such as banking, information and reservation services, electronic trade or telecommunications. Potentially, all products which may include information processing functions, as well as all services using or providing information, may sooner or later integrate computer components.

Furthermore, the industry is rich in mechanisms insuring that those possibilities will be exploited: on the computer side, the search for volume by players in the concentrated sectors (components, packaged software) and the quest for new niches by players of fragmented sectors (equipment, software, services); in the other industries, the search for new competitive advantages and new markets by all players. In summary, one can be sure that virtually all industries will gradually incorporate data-processing into their productions, as miniaturization and decline of costs will permit it.

Does that form of invasion of the other industries by data-processing challenge the borderlines of those industries? In particular, can one talk of a reasonably well delimited computer industry in the presence of a wide array of objects and services containing data-processing in variable quantities, sometimes more than most computers, as is the case for example in airplanes and telephone switchboards? When looking at a PC, an automated camera and a flight simulator, is it possible to tell which can be called a computer and which must be called by some other word?

What is a computer?

In our analysis of the competitive mechanisms of industry structuring, we have relied on the concept of "substitutable goods", that is to say goods that satisfy the same need or provide the same service. In order to assign products and services to categories that have a meaning for our purpose, we will consider the need that they aim to satisfy, therefore their functions and not the technologies that they use. In this spirit, a camera remains a camera and a flight simulator remains a flight simulator, whatever their degree of computerization. In economic terms, that means that a computerized camera competes primarily with other cameras and not with computers. In other words, the firm that offers such a camera operates in the sector of photographic equipment whatever its activity so far, and its success in this new sector will depend on its capacity to exploit the local rules of the game and to obtain valid competitive advantages in the camera sector. In a general manner, computerized objects belong to the same sector as non-computerized objects providing the same functions. In that sense, introducing data-processing into the productions of a sector does not modify its definition nor in general its borderlines.

Therefore, if computerized objects belong to the sector defined by their function, the unique feature of a computer, that distinguishes it from all the other objects containing data-processing, is precisely its universality. We will therefore define a computer as "a machine to execute programs which process information". This definition implies the capacity to execute programs that did not exist when the computer was built. It assumes therefore the existence of means for entering and storing new programs to be executed. It also implies that the area of application of the computer is not limited *a priori* by the nature of input and output devices, and therefore that those are general enough to accept and present information of a general nature in a reasonably convenient manner. This excludes machines whose program is fixed or must be selected from a given finite set, or those where the nature of input and output mechanisms restricts the possible applications to a narrowly defined class.

Thus, a computer is by definition capable of providing services that had not been explicitly anticipated during its construction. Note in passing that this definition does not restrict the computer to electronic technologies. As long as it retains its general character, it can be mechanical, hydraulic, pneumatic, optical, etc.

A machine that does not satisfy those conditions of universality, whatever are its information processing capabilities, fulfills limited and specific functions aiming to satisfy a particular need. Its price and the market share of the firms that offer it result from the working of competition between objects satisfying that particular need and not of competition with universal computers, even if that machine uses some computing technologies or components. From an economic viewpoint, that object targets a market segment external to the computer market and its producers form a particular sector external to the computer industry.

Let us immediately recognize that this definition is imperfect and leaves many uncertain cases. For example, the famous "Türing machine", if it were implemented physically, would have particularly rudimentary input and output devices, and is nevertheless capable of executing any information processing operation. More specifically, what minimum size makes a display capable to "present information of a general nature in a reasonably convenient manner"? Tradition answers "24 lines of 80 characters each", and conversely one easily admits that a single line of 5 characters is not sufficient, but is it possible to set a precise threshold? Depending on the answer, "personal digital assistants", or PDA's in short, will for example be classified among computers or not.

To look for a definitive and general reply to this sort of questions is probably a useless exercise. It is more efficient to use them as a method for understanding particular cases. To that effect, one will consider such specific cases as defining a particular market segment and a particular industry sector, of which we will explicitly examine the links with the different sectors of the computer industry and other related industries.

Offerings and sectors

When a new product or service appears, it is natural to associate it to the sector of the enterprise that has taken the initiative. But if this product is substitutable to existing products, it enters a competitive arena (a segment) that can be different from the segments where that supplier operated so far. The supplier can also be joined on that new segment by suppliers from other sectors. Very rapidly therefore, this new product can become integrated into an existing sector, that may not be that of its first supplier, or on the contrary give birth to a new sector. In any case, it is the particular competitive dynamics of that sector that will determine the respective positions of the different suppliers.

In an existing sector, introduction of data-processing can entail the entry of new players and the appearance of new competitive advantages, leading to a new distribution of market shares, and even to the possible exit of existing players. It can also entail a modification of competitive forces, and therefore lead to a new sector structure.

That evolution depends primarily on the dominant source of competitive advantages in the segment considered. If it is knowledge of the application, of the segment and of the particular sector, then specialized firms will quickly take the lead over computer firms and the sector will become integrated into the user industry. This was the case for management application services such as accounting, it is now the case for example for musical instruments, graphic arts or the movies. One must also take into account the importance of the change and the capacity of assimilation of data-processing by existing players. If this assimilation is fast, play-ers in the sector will quickly acquire the same competitive advantages as players from the computer industry and will thus retain their superiority. There will be therefore relatively few changes in the structure of the sector.

If on the other hand the dominant competitive advantages of the new prod-ucts are mainly related to the proximity of computer technologies or to general skills in information processing, then computer firms may be the most competitive. The sector will then remain in the computer industry, even if the product does not necessarily satisfy the definition of the computer proposed earlier. Perhaps this will be the case of "personal assistants".

If products are so new that they cannot be directly substituted to existing products, they correspond to a new market segment. In that case, acquisition of decisive competitive advantages will most often require a combination of computer skills properly told and specific skills in the segment considered. It is then possible that the most effective players are new firms, for example mixed players created as joint ventures between companies of the sector and computer companies. The introduction of data-processing will then give birth to a new sector obeying its own logic, where data-processing is nothing more than a primary technology and not a product. It is for example the case of electronic games.

Computer and non-computer growth

Many diverse players can take the initiative of offering a new computerized object or service. A traditional supplier in the specialized sector can discover the potential of data-processing and think of using it to provide its productions with a competitive advantage. At the opposite, a supplier of computer equipment or ser-vices can seek an advantage in a particular application niche by offering a computer dedicated for that usage, or more exactly a machine specialized in a function that one usually implements in a universal computer. Or a supplier of a particular sector of the computer industry can seek to expand the market for his products by incor-porating them into other products, probably in cooperation with a specialist of the target sector. We have seen that the very dynamics of data-processing favor all those processes, and therefore even if a large number of those attempts fail, the number and variety of computerized objects and services are bound to grow inescapably.

It is likely that this invasion of all industries by computer technologies will result in putting an upper limit on the demand for general-purpose computing equipment and services. The more objects and services will incorporate their own information processing functions, the less need there will be for universal informa-tion processing machines. In other words, the more computerized objects there will be, the fewer computers will be relatively needed.

This evolution is similar to what happened in the area of energy. The first steam engines were voluminous, complex and expensive objects. Each of them had therefore to feed a maximum number of energy-consuming machines, that one gathered in large workshops so that they could be served by a single source of energy. Engines were universal and shared, and their utilization demanded complex transmission mechanisms.

Introduction of the electrical engine first enabled replacing the steam engine within the same centralized organization. But most importantly, the electrical engine rapidly evolved into a wide range of power levels and physical sizes, and it became possible to produce simple engines through mass manufacturing processes that allowed them to reach modest price levels when produced in large quantities. The most common machine now contains many motors of various sizes and models, and the large shared central motor has disappeared. This does not prevent machines from communicating with each other within automated workshops where transfers between machines exploit again specialized electrical motors.

In information processing, the analogue of the engine is the microprocessor. Originally, a single information processing machine served all the needs of the enterprise at the cost of a universal character and devices for communications and sharing. The same universal machines have first spread to more specialized workshops, then microcomputers have served individual needs, but generally by remaining general-purpose so that a single machine could satisfy all the needs of each individual.

We are currently witnessing the gradual increase of the number of computers per individual, that will someday reach or exceed one per person and place of use (for example one at the workplace, one at home and a portable for traveling). That number is unlikely to increase much beyond, but on the other hand each individual may have access to many information processing machines, each specialized for a particular utilization for which it will be better adapted than other machines including general-purpose computers. Those machines will probably be able to communicate between themselves and to form collectively a real information processing system, or more exactly several systems whose configuration will vary according to the need of the moment. All those machines will contain one or several microprocessors and a variable quantity of software, and nevertheless very few will be "computers" as defined above.

The development of computerized products will entail a divergent evolution of the four main sectors of data-processing, at the same time that their borderlines with the other industries will become more blurred. Well defined hardware and services sectors of a specifically computing nature will coexist with computerized equipment and services in other industries, but the transition between computer products and computerized products will probably be continuous, and many enterprises will offer a range located across the borderline. As for the components and packaged software sectors, they will remain clearly individualized because of their concentrated character, but they will increasingly serve other industries. The relative share of computer equipment and services in their output will decrease, and therefore the relative weight of data-processing in the competitive game that models them.

The dynamics of the component sector is dominated today by their use in microcomputers, and large traditional data-processing no longer determines the behavior of the sector. In the same way, data-processing in its strict meaning will no longer determine the behavior of the components sector, nor probably of packaged software. The competitive evolution of those two sectors will be gradually dominated by the utilization of their products in computerized objects and services rather than in general-purpose computers.

In summary, by invading all industries, data-processing will lose its visibility and its originality. For the observer, that will emphasize again the need to consider separately the different sectors and to recognize clearly their differences.

Telecommunications

Let us spend some time on the particular case of the telecommunications industry, whose relationships with the computer industry are the subject of many comments and of many predictions.

Telecommunications existed before data-processing. In essence, they consist in transmitting information from one point to another in a reliable manner, in the sense that the information received must be identical to the information sent. It takes the form of a service by necessity, since the sending customer and the receiving customer both participate in the production. It is nevertheless a strongly capitalistic activity because it relies on very expensive infrastructures and therefore of high investments, while the marginal cost of a communication is almost negligible. It is therefore a highly concentrated sector, all the more that the value of the service to the user increases with the number of destinations that he can reach, and therefore with the size of the network and of the enterprise.

Monopoly and competition

In the fifties, when the computer industry was born, the communications industry was characterized almost everywhere by a situation of protected state monopoly functioning according to the rules of "public service". It produced a rather simple service with very few options (for example a limited choice of transmission speeds). Modes of supply of the service, especially rates, were not governed by competitive logic but by administrative decisions resting more or less on an economic reasoning aiming at "public welfare". Industry was in general totally integrated, the same organization providing the service and building all the machines required by users (terminals) as well as the infrastructure of the service.

Very soon, data-processing applications used telecommunications services. As soon as the end of the fifties, computer manufacturers offered, among input-output units connectable to computers, units specialized in the management of connections to transmission lines, and such facilities were used to acquire data and to distribute results to distant sites. The marriage of data-processing and communications within teleprocessing systems is almost as old as data-processing itself, and is in no way a feature of the nineties. But in the majority of computer applications, communication is only one ingredient among others, that enters in enterprise management applications, process automation, scientific calculations, etc. It is excessive to claim that data-processing is a branch of communications, although examples of applications oriented mainly towards communication have appeared in the sixties, such as message switching or electronic mail.

But telecommunications services have not known the same technological evolution as data-processing. While in the latter area, performances improved on the average by 20 to 25% per year at constant price, nothing similar happened in telecommunications, hence a growing divergence between the capabilities of data-processing, and therefore its telecommunications requirements, and the possibilities offered by operators. This resistance to change in telecommunications is largely due to their monopoly situation, that, among others misdeeds, encourages managers to despise the mechanisms of the market and to believe that they know the needs better that the market itself. At any rate, the protected monopoly eliminates the competitive mechanisms that alone can guarantee the implementation of the potential for technological progress.

Simultaneously, communications internal to enterprises, that are not subject to monopoly and constitute a market ruled by competition, underwent dramatic improvements in transmission speed, reliability and functions. Since technologies are essentially the same, users became increasingly aware of the potential of applications combining data-processing and telecommunications, but which could not be implemented because of the inertia of traditional monopolies. That created a strong demand for opening the field of telecommunications to competition, where the whole computer profession and especially manufacturers played a driving role at the side of users.

On that occasion, some computer players tried to penetrate the sector, more to compensate for the shortcomings of operators or to prod them than to actually compete with them, and most quit rather quickly. Telecommunications players nevertheless interpreted the attitude of the large manufacturers as aggression on a large scale, an illustration of the rule according to which players in a sector have difficulties to understand the motivations and mechanisms of different industrial sectors. Despite the defensive somewhat paranoiac attitude of the telecommunications operators, that pressure eventually caused the opening of telecommunications to competition, most improperly called "deregulation". That word indeed implies the suppression of the existing rules, while opening to competition requires on the contrary the definition of an entirely new set of rules, that were useless in a situation of state monopoly where public authorities decided unilaterally and sovereignly.

Opening of telecommunications to competition is a worldwide movement that follows very different calendars according to countries. Economies with an Anglo-Saxon liberal tradition are generally ahead of countries with a more "centralized" tradition like France, the European Community being an interesting area of confrontation between those two traditions.

The new industry structure

Whatever the calendar and implementation details, opening telecommunications to competition causes a breakup of the integrated monopolies and fragmentation of the industry into sectors whose structure evolves according to the particular competitive dynamics of each. Schematically, one finds:

- sectors of equipment manufacturing, rather fragmented for equipment using widespread technologies and of low unit value such as terminals or local communication equipment, more concentrated for major network equipment;
- "basic" telecommunication services which own and exploit the transmission infrastructures, and obey a logic of high concentration;
- "value-added" communication services, which use the base services to offer a range of more elaborate services to users, and form a more fragmented sector by avoiding heavy investments.

In 1995, competition is the rule almost everywhere for terminal equipment. More generally, hardware manufacturing is separated from network operations. The distinction between basic services and "value-added" services is still subject to debate, as well as the advisability to open them to competition. A commonly accepted theory is that "value-added" services should be opened to competition to favor creativity, diversity and price reduction, while basic services should remain protected monopolies.

Opening telecommunications to competition brings to bear the normal mechanisms of the market economy. It enables the industry to structure itself into sectors, and sectors to organize through natural evolution according to their own economic dynamics. One can therefore think that a complete opening to competition would result in natural economic forces having the same effects on telecommunications as on data-processing, *mutatis mutandis*. In particular, the sector of basic services should remain highly concentrated, and might even remain a *de facto* monopoly because of its natural structure.

But in reality, the evolution of that monopoly would be very different. Telecommunications start from a situation where national monopolies devoid of economic sense coexist side by side, while data-processing started from a natural asymmetrical oligopoly already formed on the worldwide market. Left to the laws of nature, geographical telecommunication markets would certainly not develop according to national borderlines, but would cover much larger areas. In each of those new markets, which enterprises would take the leadership? It is certain that most of the present national operators would disappear. Concerning those who would emerge as winners, what efforts and what internal mutations would they have to accomplish? To preserve their relative position, traditional suppliers would encounter difficulties analogous to those that the historical leaders of data-processing have experienced, and they would have to consent similar and probably even more severe sacrifices. Those perspectives explain, but do not excuse, that many are attempting to hang on to the *status quo* as long as they can.

What convergence?

Be that as it may, can one speak, as many commentators do, of a convergence between the computer industry and the telecommunications industry? First of all, since the dominant dynamics in both industries is a growing fragmentation into diversified sectors, what would their convergence translate into? Would a majority of players of one industry become also players of the other ? Or would one see the emergence of many new players operating in both industries, with either existing offers or with new offers materializing the convergence?

It is clearly impossible to formulate a general answer for the totality of the two industries, without reasoning sector by sector. One should first apply to telecommunications the sectoral analysis step that we have used in this book, to identify the different sectors, the competitive dynamics that apply to each one, and the corresponding adapted enterprise personalities. One should then take into consideration, for each possible combination of a sector of one industry with a sector of the other, the compatibility of enterprise personalities and the competitive advantages that firms can enjoy in a sector because of their presence in the other.

We will not go into the detail of that reasoning, which would show areas where a local convergence is possible between sectors, according to different modes. The component sector, because of its extreme concentration, serves and will continue to serve both industries, and the same microprocessors will increasingly be used in computers and in computerized objects like telephones, fax machines, telephone exchanges, concentrators, routers, etc. Concerning specifically those objects, which define a large number of sectors in the sense of Porter ("groups of firms that manufacture closely substitutable products"), there exists and will continue to exist firms offering both computer equipment properly told and equipment pertaining more to telecommunications. At the level of the macro-sector of hardware, there is therefore a continuity between the computer industry and the communications industry, and it will be increasingly difficult to locate a borderline, as both will call upon the same components. Integration services will naturally be used, as it is already the case, to combine communications products and services with computer products and services. Finally, in the same way that it is difficult to trace a borderline between computer equipment and computerized products, one will see "value added" services from communications come together with computerized services from other industries.

In all the preceding areas, it is vain to try and define a precise borderline between computing and telecommunications, although some sectors could be unequivocally included in one or the other industry. That takes us back to the basic idea expressed by Chamberlin: "The economic world can be considered as a network of interdependent markets and sectors, whose borderlines are chosen to make the representation convenient, but that are essentially arbitrary". Conversely, since the question of the borderlines of an industry does not accept an exact answer, deciding whether two industries are converging is also meaningless at that level of generality. Only for each elementary sector is it possible to identify a preferential relationship with one or the other industry, or for some of them an intermediate or mixed position. Among the sectors into which the telecommunications industry is in the process of organizing, that of "basic services" remains typical of telecom-munications and has no counterpart in the computer industry. Those services are partly substitutable to certain "value-added" services belonging to the telecommu-nications industry, but no part of what composes data-processing is substitutable to them: neither products of course, nor services which are restricted to services of assistance, development and integration since the disappearance of processing ser-vices. Moreover, the "basic services" sector is highly capitalistic, its operating cycles are long and the economical production scale is very high, all features that are the opposite of those of the computer services sector.

One concludes that the core of the telecommunications industry, formed by what remains of the traditional monopolistic operators after competition breaks them apart, constitutes a separate sector that can not converge with any sector of computer industry. Indeed, basic telecommunications services benefit from progress in data-processing, as all other sectors of all other industries, and they enter into the composition of most information systems along with computer products and services. But firms that produce them must possess a personality that is incompatible with success in other sectors.

Telecommunications and computer services

Nevertheless, everywhere in the world, telecommunications operators (such as ATT and MCI in the USA, France Telecom, British Telecom and Telefonica in Europe) implement and advertise a strategy of being actively present in computer services, most often by taking control of enterprises in that sector. The proclaimed reasons have varied in time, but they can be summarized under two main headings: first, as architects or administrators of total solution, computer services companies have the power to influence the choice of customers concerning telecommunica-tions, and secondly the software skills of those enterprises are necessary to satisfy the needs of operators.

Neither of those reasons stands up to examination and justifies that telecom-munications operators must integrate or control computer services companies. First of all, their prescription power concerning communications is largely overesti-mated, and we have seen in chapter 13 that the base trend is towards separation of the roles of integrator on one hand, supplier of elements to be integrated on the other hand. By seeking to play the integrator role in order to better sell their ser-vices, telecommunications operators actually weaken their integration activities by making them less competitive.

As for the development of software that they require, the best interest of operators is to subcontract them in a normally competitive manner, and if that is prevented by industrial property problems that can not be solved by appropriate contractual clauses, to develop them in-house with their own resources. How then to explain this infatuation of telecommunication operators for computer services? Probably mainly by negative factors: ignorance of industrial structuring mecha-nisms and of compatibility problems between enterprises, confusion between financial participation and industrial synergism, search of power and personal ambi-tions not tamed by a considered and strong enterprise strategy, widespread illusion over the profitability of services, ignorance of their diversity and the persistent belief that services companies are highly desirous to offer communications services.

On the positive side, one finds the desire to remain close to users at a time when "value-added" services are threatening to interpose between basic services operators and the market. But however valid that objective, trying to satisfy it in that way is illusory. It is indeed not sufficient for one company of a group to be in contact with the market to make the whole group benefit from that contact. What formal mechanisms make the information move up from the battle lines where the computer services company operates to the decision makers and other involved persons of the telecommunications operator? And if those mechanisms do exist, what costs and what constraints do they impose on the services firm? Do those costs and constraints translate into a competitive handicap which at best distorts its vision of the market, and at the worse condemns it?

Materializing a real advantage would demand a close coordination of activities. Now the difference of enterprise personalities is such that a telecommunications operator would prevent its service activities from succeeding if it did not cautiously confine its role to that of shareholder[80], thus forbidding most of the hoped-for strategic and operational benefits.

In summary, the so-called "convergence" between data-processing and telecommunications is meaningful only for users external to both industries. By associating productions of data-processing and telecommunications, they can offer new products and services whose economic impact can be dramatic and profound, but that does not constitute in the least a new phenomenon. Such "convergence" is a lot less real and has much less industrial and economic meaning when it applies to the structure of those two industries. Fertile by its implementation in other industries, the "marriage of data-processing and telecommunications" has no reality other that in the media for these industries themselves.

Multimedia and the "information highways"

One often mentions multimedia and the "information highways" as current examples of successful marriage of data-processing and telecommunications. Let us look more closely to sketch a few implications in terms of industry structure.

The word "multimedia" evokes combining information of different natures (at least text, images and sound) and presenting it in various forms and on various supports. Data-processing enables to represent all forms of information in a common digital form. It provides the means to encode all that information from its current material form into its digital form, or to create it from scratch. Conversely, it enables restoring it under forms accessible to human senses or to other acquisition or utilization devices. It also enables storing and transmitting information of different natures on the same support, to create dynamic or static links between them, to submit them to all kinds of transformations and selections. It finally enables making all those operations dependent on information received from the outside, thus introducing the possibility of interactive control through a dialogue with the user.

---

80   see Chapter 15

To those same multimedia applications, telecommunications bring the possibility of transmitting remotely numerical data that represents information, and in particular enable numerous dispersed users to simultaneously access one common copy, possibly in an interactive manner. But while the contribution of data-processing is essential, that of telecommunications is secondary. One cannot conceive multimedia applications that do not call upon data-processing, while many exist that do not use telecommunications. In their limited function of information transport, telecommunications are competing with other channels such as the distribution of discrete media like diskettes and especially CD-ROM, that are more convenient and cheaper in a large number of cases, that will increase with media capacity. Using telecommunications is only mandatory when information changes frequently, if interaction between users is essential or if one wants to retrieve specific information from collections too bulky to be distributed in totality.

At any rate, in the development of multimedia, both the computer industry and that of telecommunications remain in their usual roles. The nature of their respective productions is unchanged, and so is the economics of production in the different sectors that compose them. As a consequence, their industry structure will probably be unchanged. Concerning data-processing, one can nevertheless anticipate that, in that area of application as in others, specialized computerized objects, possibly derived from television sets, from current game machines, or from new objects similar to personal assistants, will take an increasing place.

The telecommunications side is currently the most publicized part, and it is also the most immediately visible because it provides access to all the rest. It is no less a limited and specialized part of the total system, for which the term "information highway" is besides particularly deceptive. Indeed, if the development of multimedia requires, among other things, a wider range of transmission capacities, those "highways" must complement the existing network and not replace it. To remain with the road analogy, one has not waited for highways for traveling, and even in the "wired society" of tomorrow, local roads and country paths will still be used.

If multimedia entails modifications of industry structures, it will be in the communication industry in a broader sense. A detailed study of that industry and of the likely impact of data-processing would obviously go beyond the scope of this book, but it could probably make profitable use of the concept and analysis tools that we have presented. One would thus identify a large variety of players and of more or less interdependent sectors, operating in different competitive arenas and requiring enterprises even more diversified and mutually incompatible than for data-processing.

In the same manner, one would identify a natural trend towards fragmentation and specialization, as in all complex industries subject to competition and in phase of growth. This conclusion seems contrary to current events, where one only speaks of mergers and consolidation. Economic logic leads to believe that these attempts are as poorly justified as those that we have examined in more detail in the framework of data-processing, and that they will not be of much consequence for the long-term structure of the industry. The actions of enterprise leaders are far from being always rational, but their effects remain submitted to the impersonal laws of competition and the sanction is unavoidable.

The long term evolution

At this point of our study, can we attempt to bring together all the trends that we have identified, including those relative to interactions of data-processing with other industries, and to sketch a global evolution scenario for the computer industry?

One of the least hazardous ways to anticipate the future is to look for regularities in the past, to identify their mechanisms, to determine if those mechanisms are active in the present and, if such is the case, to extrapolate their past effects. In the field of economics, it is the theory of development and more precisely of business cycles that can provide us with the basis of that reasoning.

At first glance, that path is encouraging. Several economists have observed that the western economy develops according to cycles of approximately 50 to 60 years, consisting of a growth period of about 25 years followed by a regression period of about 25 years, that have been called "Kondratiev cycles". The Austrian economist Joseph Schumpeter has proposed an explanation of this phenomenon[81], based on the theory of economic development that he had formulated earlier[82].

We have seen that traditional data-processing, born in 1951, has first known a period of expansion until encountering difficulties starting in the mid-seventies. Around 1980, a new computer industry was born, which is still in full growth today, but which might enter a declining phase in the beginning of the XXIst century due to a stop of the progress of components, as we have seen in chapter 7. Those movements are sufficiently similar to the cycles analyzed by Schumpeter to warrant recalling some of their theory and to examine its possible application to data-processing.

Business cycles

Schumpeter attributes business cycles to the effects of innovation. To take apart their mechanisms, he first considers an assumed stable economy, where each sector produces exactly what the other sectors require and where all flows are stationary. Such a hypothetical economy is in agreement with the theory of the general equilibrium: the prices of all goods and services are equal to their marginal costs, the remuneration of production factors is equal to their marginal utility and there are no profits outside of the normal remuneration of factors of production.

The introduction of an innovation, defined as a new arrangement of production factors, can give birth to new products or to new methods of production that will gradually supersede the old ones. The entrepreneurs who have introduced this innovation will realize exceptional profits as long as the prices of the production

---

81   J. Schumpeter, Business Cycles, McGraw-Hill, 1939

82   J. Schumpeter, The theory of economic development, Oxford University Press, 1934 - original title *Theorie der wirtschaftlichen Entwicklung* (1911)

factors that they use correspond to their utility in the old production processes. But their very success will start a phenomenon of imitation by other producers and, in the absence of more innovation, a movement back towards the general equilibrium, translating into the progressive saturation of supply and demand and the decline of profits in the second part of the cycle.

Thus, the economy reaches a new situation of equilibrium, that differs from the preceding one by many aspects. The prices of consumer goods and production factors concerned by the innovation have changed, which may have caused adjustments in sectors not directly touched. Products, enterprises and even whole sectors may have been born and others may have disappeared, in what Schumpeter calls "creative destruction". Some parts of the productive machine may thus enter into a recession.

To introduce an innovation, the entrepreneur must be able to obtain the required means of production, which are also needed by the existing stationary cycle, although the revenues that he hopes to obtain from his innovative action are not yet available. That demands an artificial creation of purchasing power in the form of capital, that has no counterpart yet in the form of real goods and has therefore an inflationary effect. Conversely, bringing to market the resulting goods, with no creation of new purchasing power, will have a deflationary effect. Those monetary phenomena, that come with the realization of innovation, contribute to explain its chronology: in the early part of the cycle, the investment capacity is saturated, the inflationary trend tends to limit credit and the resulting instability causes uncertainty, all circumstances unfavorable to new innovation. Towards the end of the cycle, the investment capacities are recreated, credit becomes easier in order to fight deflation and the stagnation of technologies invites innovation. Those factors explain the cyclical character of the innovation process.

The mechanisms just described are sufficient to explain the impact of innovation in a limited part of the economy. But Schumpeter was interested in the economy as a whole, and therefore had to explain also why, at the overall level, innovations do not happen evenly in time but in clusters separated by intervals of approximately 25 years. We will not enter into that discussion, which calls on one hand on the above monetary mechanisms, and on the other hand on the idea that profound changes in consumption and production habits are paced by the rhythm of generation renewal, which explains the figure of 25 years.

While limiting ourselves to the impact of isolated innovations, without looking at the economy in its totality, let us introduce into the theory the industry structure considerations that we have developed all along this book. We can then say that an innovation releases three parallel processes:
-   first, the diffusion of the new product, ending sooner or later with the saturation of its market. This process probably follows a S curve, with a moderate start, a rapid growth phase and then a gradual slowdown.
-   second, a process of imitation by others suppliers and development of competition, that tends to return the economy to the stationary equilibrium, in particular by reducing profits in the innovating sector.

 – third, a structural adaptation process of the industry through the breakup, the fusion and the disappearance of sectors, with a new distribution of market shares and changes in relative positions, that takes highest importance in concentrated sectors.

Those three process are obviously linked. The development of competition accelerates the diffusion of the product and contributes to industrial restructuring. The elimination of exceptional profits can be very quick in fragmented sectors, whether they were fragmented before introduction of the innovation or have become so because of it; it never will be complete in concentrated sectors.

The initial innovation can radiate from the sector where it originates, and modify a variable number of sectors, either by competing with products of neighboring sectors, or because the new products create opportunities for innovation in other sectors, or still through the modification of the price of production factors, which can be used in other sectors and force them to adapt. Those effects can in turn start similar indirect effects in still other sectors. The impacts of the original innovation thus spread in circles, more or less rapidly and reaching more or less distant sectors with various intensities.

In a general manner, the more a sector is affected at a given time, the less likely it is that new innovations will happen in that sector. Moreover, the competitive dynamics of fragmented sectors rapidly erodes their capacity for endogenous innovation, while concentrated sectors preserve a certain innovation capacity. Therefore, at any given time, the most likely sources of innovation are those sectors that have not been touched by innovation in the recent past, directly or indirectly, concentrated sectors or completely new players.

A long-term view of data-processing

The above conceptual view applies only imperfectly to the birth of traditional data-processing, that happened in the concentrated but existing sector of unit-record machinery. One must probably take into account the exogenous factor constituted by the political will of the Government of the United States, which initially helped the large firms—IBM and Sperry — to build up skills in the computer area. Thereafter, rapid growth on a virtually untapped market has been matched by an extraordinary rate of innovation coming from the same firms, so that the industrial restructuring process did not really start, and the industry remained essentially integrated and with a concentrated structure.

The emergence of the personal computer marks a crucial turning point by limiting *de facto* to large enterprises the potential market of conventional computers. The corresponding industry must inescapably engage into a process of gradual saturation that condemns it sooner or later to slower growth, thus sharpening competition and accelerating restructuring. In other words, the new data-processing locks up the old one in the framework of a finite growth that necessarily includes a maturity phase and a declining phase.

In terms of impact on the rest of the economy, traditional data-processing born in 1951 has eliminated unit-record from which it came, but apparently had relatively little general influence on the production processes of other industries. A major exception is precisely telecommunications, where the indirect influence of computers has gone as far as contributing to opening that sector to competition and to start a profound competitive restructuring of that industry. The rest of the economy has been touched almost uniformly through the automation of adminis-trative processes, but traditional data-processing has generated very few opportuni-ties for innovative products in other industries.

The second major cycle of data-processing, started at the end of the seven-ties with the personal computer, fits the theory nicely since the innovators were located outside the then existent industry. It brings not only new products for new markets, but also radical innovations in industry structure, which is born frag-mented and not integrated. We have mentioned its negative impact on traditional data-processing whose markets become limited. In addition, the traditional sectors are restructuring through modified price levels for critical elements such as compo-nents and software packages. Furthermore, through the evolution of components and partially of equipment and software, micro-computing sows seeds of innova-tion throughout the economy, and creates in many other industries opportunities for innovation, currently in different stages of implementation.

It is precisely the implementation of this innovation potential that will char-acterize the third major cycle, that of computerized objects. The event that starts this cycle is the possibility to lodge on a small chip a microprocessor with the mem-ory, input, output and operating system required for an application. Many industries will then be able to appropriate computer technologies by incorporating them into computerized objects and services substitutable to the other products and services produced by those industries. According to a mechanism similar to what we have seen previously, those developments will limit the market of the universal computer and will in turn make inescapable the phases of maturity and then decline for the personal computer sectors. After its ascension, from 1975 to 2000 or 2005, it would then enter into a recession phase from 2005 to 2030, which is consistent with our previous forecasts on the exhaustion of component technologies.

That second slowdown of growth will sustain the restructuring movement of the computer industry, by favoring its fragmentation in the maturity phase and per-haps some local mergers in the declining period. The components sector, or the sectors into which it will break, will increasingly serve the other industries, and its evolution will become independent of that of computer equipment. In particular, it is on the demand of the other industries that the pursuit of the technological progress in the first years of the XXIst century will mainly depend. The area of hardware will increasingly break down into specialized sectors, some of which will hardly be discernible from related sectors in other industries. The entry of data-processing in the maturity phase will probably be favorable to the explosion of the macro-sector of packaged software thanks to object technologies, a possibility that we have mentioned in chapter 12. That likely fragmentation will come with by the increasing availability of software skills in other industries, strengthening again their local innovation capacity.

In summary, at the same time as its technologies will spread, the computer industry will lose its borderlines and with them most of its individuality. It is sure that its players at that time will make the same efforts as the generalists of today to remain present in the new sectors, but their odds and their percentage of success will probably be similar.

By boldly extrapolating the preceding cycles, one would thus anticipate a rise of computerized objects from 2000 to 2025 approximately, and then a recession of those sectors between 2025 and 2050. What other innovations could then limit their market and start that slowdown, as the personal computer first and then computerized objects limited the market of their predecessors? In the third cycle of data-processing, innovations enabled by data-processing will be diffuse in many industries, as soon as the basic sector of components is sufficiently stabilized. It will be born and will develop with new players and new rules of the game, alongside with data-processing that will have become a relatively minor sector from which one will no longer be able to expect dramatic innovations.

The history of data-processing as such would be then be finished. It will have fertilized the whole economy, but in doing so it will have become a secondary element, barring a radically new innovation, and therefore unpredictable by definition, that would restart its dynamics. But like the future of computerized objects, this is another story...

APPENDIX - Tables for chapters 4 and 5

Categories by specialization

Tables I to XII give for each firm the percentage of its 1992 revenue obtained in each market segment shown in the columns.

Table I - Generalists

Name	Lg	Mi	PC	Sta	Sof	Per	Co	Ma	Ser	Oth
IBM	13	9	12	3	18	12	3	12	10	9
Digital Equipment	0	18	3	8	6	21	2	31	11	0
Hewlett-Packard	1	10	6	12	3	36	5	2	5	20
AT&T/NCR	1	5	10	0	3	22	32	16	11	0
Unisys	25	0	6	8	9	0	0	22	17	13
Wang	0	16	15	0	4	13	3	42	7	0
Data General	0	30	6	7	2	15	0	31	9	0
Texas	20	10	20	0	4	20	0	0	20	6
Control Data	21	0	0	25	19	0	0	26	13	0
Wyse	0	0	19	19	0	63	0	0	0	0

Table II - Large Systems Specialists

Name	Lg	Mi	PC	Sta	Sof	Per	Co	Ma	Ser	Oth
Convex	77	0	0	0	0	0	0	23	0	0
Cray	69	0	0	0	2	4	0	25	0	0
Amdahl	59	0	0	0	0	13	0	0	18	0

Table III - Midrange Systems Specialists

Name	Lg	Mi	PC	Sta	Sof	Per	Co	Ma	Ser	Oth
Stratus	0	10	0	0	0	0	0	0	0	0
Sequent	0	74	0	0	2	7	0	0	18	0
Tandem	0	41	0	6	0	27	10	15	1	0

Table IV - Personal Systems Specialists

Name	Lg	Mi	PC	Sta	Sof	Per	Co	Ma	Ser	Oth
Commodore	0	0	10	0	0	0	0	0	0	0
AST Research	0	0	10	0	0	0	0	0	0	0
Compaq	0	0	10	0	0	0	0	0	0	0
Gateway 2000	0	0	10	0	0	0	0	0	0	0
Packard Bell	0	0	95	0	0	5	0	0	0	0
Dell	0	0	90	0	5	5	0	0	0	0

Tandy	0	0	84	0	2	12	0	0	2	0
Apple	0	0	75	0	4	21	0	0	0	0
CompuAdd	0	0	65	0	5	30	0	0	0	0

Table V - Workstations Specialists

Name	Lg	Mi	PC	Sta	Sof	Per	Co	Ma	Ser	Oth
Silicon Graphics	0	0	0	79	9	0	0	12	0	0
Sun	0	5	0	62	7	13	0	12	0	0
Intergraph	0	0	0	51	19	0	0	0	29	0

Table VI - Peripherals Specialists

Name	Lg	Mi	PC	Sta	Sof	Per	Co	Ma	Ser	Oth
Tektronix	0	0	0	0	0	10	0	0	0	0
Micropolis	0	0	0	0	0	10	0	0	0	0
Conner Periphs	0	0	0	0	0	10	0	0	0	0
Quantum	0	0	0	0	0	10	0	0	0	0
Maxtor	0	0	0	0	0	10	0	0	0	0
Seagate	0	0	0	0	0	10	0	0	0	0
Western Digital	0	0	0	0	0	10	0	0	0	0
Lexmark	0	0	2	0	0	98	0	0	0	0
EMC	0	0	0	0	0	96	0	4	0	0
Xerox	0	0	5	4	1	90	0	0	0	0
Kodak	0	0	0	0	0	70	0	0	0	30
Storage Tech	0	0	0	0	0	69	0	0	31	0
Diebold	0	0	0	0	0	54	0	46	0	0

Table VII - Communications Specialists

Name	Lg	Mi	PC	Sta	Sof	Per	Co	Ma	Ser	Oth
Northern Telecom	0	0	0	0	0	0	10	0	0	0
Synoptics	0	0	0	0	0	0	10	0	0	0
3COM	0	0	0	0	0	0	10	0	0	0
Cabletron	0	0	0	0	0	0	93	7	0	0
Digital Comms	0	0	0	0	20	0	80	0	0	0

Table VIII - Software Specialists

Name	Lg	Mi	PC	Sta	Sof	Per	Co	Ma	Ser	Oth
SAS	0	0	0	0	10	0	0	0	0	0
Autodesk	0	0	0	0	10	0	0	0	0	0
Borland/Asht-	0	0	0	0	10	0	0	0	0	0
Novell	0	0	0	0	10	0	0	0	0	0
Adobe	0	0	0	0	10	0	0	0	0	0
Computer Assoc	0	0	0	0	10	0	0	0	0	0
Wordperfect	0	0	0	0	10	0	0	0	0	0
Legent	0	0	0	0	10	0	0	0	0	0
Microsoft	0	0	0	0	91	1	0	0	8	0
Lotus	0	0	0	0	90	0	0	0	10	0
Informix	0	0	0	0	84	0	0	0	16	0

Cadence	0	0	0	0	77	0	0	0	23	0
Mentor Graphics	0	0	0	26	74	0	0	0	0	0
Sybase	0	0	0	0	70	0	0	0	30	0
Oracle	0	0	0	0	60	0	0	19	21	0

Table IX - Maintenance Specialists

Name	Lg	Mi	PC	Sta	Sof	Per	Co	Ma	Ser	Oth
Bell Atlantic	0	0	0	0	20	0	0	78	3	0

Table X - Services Specialists

Name	Lg	Mi	PC	Sta	Sof	Per	Co	Ma	Ser	Oth
Comp Task	0	0	0	0	0	0	0	0	10	0
Shared Medical	0	0	0	0	0	0	0	0	10	0
SHL	0	0	0	0	0	0	0	0	10	0
ADP	0	0	0	0	0	0	0	0	10	0
First Data	0	0	0	0	0	0	0	0	10	0
Price Waterhouse	0	0	0	0	0	0	0	0	10	0
Coopers/ Lybrand	0	0	0	0	0	0	0	0	10	0
Martin Marietta	0	0	0	0	0	0	0	0	10	0
Boeing	0	0	0	0	0	0	0	0	10	0
Litton	0	0	0	0	0	0	0	0	10	0
Comp Sciences	0	0	0	0	0	0	0	0	10	0
Ernst and Young	0	0	0	0	0	0	0	0	10	0
PRC	0	0	0	0	0	0	0	0	10	0
Ceridian	0	0	0	0	2	0	0	0	98	0
TRW	0	0	0	0	0	0	0	3	97	0
Fiserv	0	0	0	0	7	0	0	0	94	0
Grumman	0	0	0	0	0	0	0	8	92	0
Andersen	0	0	0	0	10	0	0	0	90	0
Systematics	0	0	0	0	11	0	0	0	89	0
American Managt	0	0	0	0	12	0	0	0	88	0
EDS	0	0	0	0	12	0	0	0	88	0
Policy Managt	0	0	0	0	15	0	0	0	85	0
GE	0	0	0	0	15	0	0	0	85	0
Science Apps	0	0	0	0	0	0	0	15	85	0

Table XI - Specialists other

Name	Lg	Mi	PC	Sta	Sof	Per	Co	Ma	Ser	Oth
3M	0	0	0	0	0	0	0	0	0	100
Gerber	0	0	0	0	0	0	0	17	0	83

Table XII- Mixed firms

Name	Lg	Mi	PC	Sta	Sof	Per	Co	Ma	Ser	Oth
Compvision/Prim	0	0	0	22	21	0	0	51	6	0
Lockheed	0	0	0	0	0	64	0	0	36	0
Nynex	0	0	0	0	40	0	0	0	60	0
Dun & Bradstreet	0	0	0	0	25	0	0	50	25	0

Ask Computer	0	14	0	0	48	0	0	0	38	0
MAI Systems	0	0	0	0	0	0	0	43	57	0
Reynolds/Reynol	0	13	0	1	8	8	0	28	42	0
Sterling Software	0	0	0	0	52	0	0	0	48	0
Datapoint	0	0	8	20	7	8	12	0	45	0

Market shares

For each segment (in columns), this table gives the percentages of revenue realized by the 10 generalists, the specialists of that segment and the other firms, with the number of firms in each of those three categories. The figures are based on 1992 results.

Table XIII - Market share and population by segment

	large	mid	PC	stat	soft	peri	comm	maint	serv
generalists	82%	84%	40%	56%	49%	47%	58%	83%	30%
	(7)	(7)	(9)	(7)	(9)	(8)	(5)	(8)	(9)
specialists	17%	12%	59%	40%	38%	43%	40%	3%	60%
	(3)	(3)	(9)	(3)	(15)	(13)	(5)	(1)	(25)
autres	<1%	4%	<1%	4%	13%	10%	12%	13%	10%
	(1)	(4)	(3)	(6)	(28)	(16)	(3)	(17)	(23)

Analysis by market segment

Tables XIV to XXII contain for each segment the list of firms in the sample which are present with non-zero revenue. They give for each firm its category or specialization in column 2, the share of that segment in its overall DP revenue (indicating its level of specialization relative to that segment) in column 3, its share of that market in column 4. The firms are sorted in decreasing order of their market share in that segment. Only firms with a market share of 1% and higher are listed. Years 1992 and 1994 are shown, except for maintenance and services which are separated in the 1992 statistics and lumped together in the 1994 report.

Table XIV - Large systems

1992				1994			
Nom	Cat	Spec	Share	Nom	Cat	Spec	Share
IBM	GEN	12.69%	63.14%	IBM	GEN	9.30%	64.32%
Unisys	GEN	25.10%	15.16%	Unisys	GEN	20.00%	13.42%
Amdahl	LARGE	59.02%	11.49%	Amdahl	LARGE	50.00%	8.85%
Cray	LARGE	69.08%	4.25%	Cray	LARGE	62.00%	6.17%
Convex	LARGE	76.79%	1.37%	Intel	COMP	20.00%	4.98%
Texas	GEN	20.00%	1.23%	Sil Graph	STAT	10.00%	1.76%
ATT/NCR	GEN	1.37%	1.10%				

Table XV – Midrange systems

1992					1994			
Nom	Cat	Spec	Share		Nom	Cat	Spec	Share
IBM	GEN	8.92%	44.96%		IBM	GEN	9.00%	28.32%
DEC	GEN	17.65%	19.54%		ATT/NCR	GEN	44.00%	24.77%
HP	GEN	10.48%	10.39%		HP	GEN	14.00%	13.20%
Tandem	MID	40.89%	6.60%		DEC	GEN	11.70%	7.76%
ATT/NCR	GEN	4.92%	4.02%		Tandem	MID	73.00%	7.56%
Stratus	MID	99.94%	3.80%		Motorola	COMP	26.00%	3.03%
Dat Gen	GEN	29.52%	2.54%		Dat Gen	GEN	47.00%	2.64%
Wang	GEN	16.11%	1.88%		Sun	STAT	10.00%	2.63%
Sequent	MID	73.54%	1.77%		Unisys	GEN	8.00%	2.44%
Sun	STAT	5.43%	1.63%		Apple	PC	5.00%	2.35%
Motorola	COMP	20.32%	1.48%		Stratus	MID	64.00%	1.81%
					Sequent	MID	76.00%	1.68%
					Dell	PC	6.00%	1.03%

Table XVI PC

1992					1994			
Nom	Cat	Spec	Share		Nom	Cat	Spec	Share
IBM	GEN	11.86%	28.17%		Compaq	PC	83.00%	21.98%
					IBM	GEN	13.70%	21.38%
Apple	PC	75.44%	19.92%		Apple	PC	75.00%	17.45%
Compaq	PC	100.00%	15.09%		Dell	PC	82.00%	6.99%
					Gateway	PC	100.00%	6.58%
Dell	PC	90.02%	6.67%		Pack Bell	PC	100.00%	6.34%
AST	PC	100.04%	4.20%		AST	PC	100.00%	5.63%
					ATT/NCR	GEN	15.00%	4.19%
Gateway	PC	99.99%	4.07%		DEC	GEN	10.00%	3.29%
					HP	GEN	6.00%	2.81%
ATT/NCR	GEN	9.56%	3.68%					
Pack Bell	PC	95.03%	3.23%					
Comm	PC	100.05%	2.69%					
HP	GEN	5.71%	2.67%					
Tandy	PC	84.42%	2.39%					
DEC	GEN	3.18%	1.66%					
Unisys	GEN	5.54%	1.60%					
ComAdd	PC	65.03%	1.25%					

Table XVII Workstations

1992				1994			
Nom	Cat	Spec	Share	Nom	Cat	Spec	Share
Sun	STAT	62.47%	24.34%	Sun	STAT	61.00%	24.02%
IBM	GEN	2.93%	19.21%	IBM	GEN	5.00%	23.58%
HP	GEN	12.06%	15.55%	HP	GEN	15.00%	21.20%
DEC	GEN	7.91%	11.39%	Sil Graph	STAT	75.00%	9.01%
Sil Graph	STAT	79.09%	7.42%	DEC	GEN	8.00%	7.95%
Unisys	GEN	8.30%	6.61%	Int'graph	STAT	80.00%	6.13%
Int'graph	STAT	51.50%	6.16%	Motorola	COMP	25.00%	4.37%
C'vision	MIXED	22.05%	2.39%	Unisys	GEN	7.00%	3.20%
CDC	GEN	25.34%	1.33%				
Xerox	PERI	4.05%	1.24%				
Tandem	MID	5.71%	1.20%				

Table XVIII - Peripherals

1992				1994			
Nom	Cat	Spec	Share	Nom	Cat	Spec	Share
IBM	GEN	12.32%	20.04%	IBM	GEN	9.30%	64.32%
HP	GEN	36.18%	11.57%	Unisys	GEN	20.00%	13.42%
Seagate	PERI	99.99%	7.76%	Amdahl	LARGE	50.00%	8.85%
DEC	GEN	21.18%	7.56%	Cray	LARGE	62.00%	6.17%
Xerox	PERI	89.79%	6.83%	Intel	COMP	20.00%	4.98%
ATT/NCR	GEN	21.85%	5.76%	Sil Graph	STAT	10.00%	1.76%
Conner	PERI	100.00%	5.65%	DEC	GEN	0.30%	0.44%
Quantum	PERI	100.00%	3.87%	CDC	GEN	1.00%	0.06%
Apple	PC	20.71%	3.75%				
Maxtor	PERI	100.00%	3.52%				
Lexmark	PERI	97.78%	3.33%				
Intel	COMP	95.12%	2.95%				
StorTech	PERI	69.01%	2.65%				
West Dig	PERI	99.96%	2.38%				
Tandem	MID	27.05%	1.41%				
Lockheed	MIXED	64.10%	1.26%				
Sun	STAT	13.05%	1.26%				
Micropolis	PERI	100.10%	1.00%				

Table XIX - Software

1992				1994			
Nom	Cat	Spec	Share	Nom	Cat	Spec	Share
IBM	GEN	17.62%	40.56%	IBM	GEN	18.00%	30.78%
Microsoft	SOFT	90.99%	10.56%	Microsoft	SOFT	96.00%	11.92%
Comp Ass	SOFT	100.01%	6.32%	Comp Ass	SOFT	100.00%	6.55%
Novell	SOFT	100.04%	3.53%	Novell	SOFT	96.00%	5.12%
Lotus	SOFT	89.99%	2.89%	Oracle	SOFT	80.00%	5.08%
DEC	GEN	5.65%	2.86%	Lockheed	MIXED	60.00%	3.32%
Oracle	SOFT	59.69%	2.79%	DEC	GEN	9.00%	3.24%
Unisys	GEN	9.09%	2.54%	ATT/NCR	GEN	8.00%	2.45%
EDS	SERV	12.26%	2.13%	Lotus	SOFT	90.00%	2.33%
Wordperf	SOFT	100.00%	1.96%	Unisys	GEN	11.00%	1.83%
Borland	SOFT	100.06%	1.66%	Adobe	SOFT	100.00%	1.60%
Legent	SOFT	100.00%	1.59%	Sybase	SOFT	70.00%	1.54%
HP	GEN	3.26%	1.47%	HP	GEN	3.00%	1.54%
Autodesk	SOFT	100.08%	1.31%	Legent	SOFT	95.00%	1.29%
SAS	SOFT	100.14%	1.31%	SAS	SOFT	98.00%	1.26%
Cadence	SOFT	76.87%	1.19%	Informix	SOFT	100.00%	1.25%
				Autodesk	SOFT	100.00%	1.24%
				Intel	COMP	20.00%	1.23%
				Cadence	SOFT	100.00%	1.15%
				Apple	PC	4.00%	1.02%

Table XX - Communications

1992				1994			
Nom	Cat	Spec	Share	Nom	Cat	Spec	Share
ATT/NCR	GEN	31.72%	29.71%	IBM	GEN	5.60%	21.80%
North Tel	COMM	100.00%	20.62%	ATT/NCR	GEN	26.00%	18.11%
IBM	GEN	3.41%	19.72%	Cisco	COMM	100.00%	9.12%
Motorola	COMP	79.68%	6.68%	Motorola	COMP	49.00%	7.06%
HP	GEN	4.97%	5.65%	Bay n'w'ks	COMM	90.00%	6.56%
3COM	COMM	99.96%	4.50%	HP	GEN	5.00%	5.83%
Synoptics	COMM	100.05%	3.49%	3COM	COMM	90.00%	5.55%
Cabletron	COMM	92.82%	3.25%	Cabletron	COMM	90.00%	4.44%
DEC	GEN	1.77%	2.24%	Newbridge	COMM	92.00%	4.12%
Tandem	MID	9.87%	1.83%	Memorex	PERI	49.00%	2.78%
Dig Comm	COMM	80.10%	1.67%	Dynatech	COMM	100.00%	2.35%
				US Robs	COMM	100.00%	2.30%
				DEC	GEN	2.00%	1.64%
				N'work eqt	COMM	100.00%	1.63%
				Chipcom	COMM	97.00%	1.58%
				Std Micro	COMM	100.00%	1.57%
				Hayes	COMM	70.00%	1.15%
				Gen Com	COMM	84.00%	1.13%

Table XXI- Maintenance

1992

Nom	Cat	Spec	Share
IBM	GEN	11.79%	37.45%
DEC	GEN	31.22%	21.76%
ATT/NCR	GEN	16.38%	8.43%
Unisys	GEN	21.53%	8.30%
Wang	GEN	42.28%	3.10%
Bell Atl	MAINT	77.50%	3.05%
Comp'vis	MIXED	51.24%	2.69%
Sun	STAT	12.27%	2.31%
Dat Gen	GEN	30.89%	1.67%
Tandem	MID	15.00%	1.53%
HP	GEN	2.21%	1.38%
Dun/Brad	MIXED	50.05%	1.31%
Oracle	SOFT	19.16%	1.24%
Diebold	PERI	46.17%	1.11%

Table XXII- Services

1992

Nom	Cat	Spec	Share
IBM	GEN	9.93%	16.60%
EDS	SERV	87.74%	11.07%
Comp Sc	SERV	99.98%	6.41%
Andersen	SERV	89.89%	6.33%
ADP	SERV	100.00%	5.37%
TRW	SERV	97.04%	4.66%
DEC	GEN	11.09%	4.07%
Unisys	GEN	17.06%	3.46%
First Data	SERV	100.00%	3.12%
ATT/NCR	GEN	11.47%	3.11%
Price	SERV	100.00%	1.91%
Ceridian	SERV	98.47%	1.66%
PRC	SERV	99.95%	1.65%
SHL	SERV	100.02%	1.63%
HP	GEN	4.73%	1.55%
Ernst/Yng	SERV	99.98%	1.53%
Coopers	SERV	100.00%	1.53%
Syst'ics	SERV	88.95%	1.33%
GE	SERV	85.00%	1.32%
Martin	SERV	100.00%	1.29%
Stor' Tech	PERI	31.02%	1.22%
Boeing	SERV	100.00%	1.22%
Sh'd Med	SERV	100.09%	1.22%
Amdahl	LARGE	18.02%	1.18%
Sci Apps	SERV	84.99%	1.17%
Pol Mgmt	SERV	85.29%	1.10%
Litton	SERV	100.00%	1.04%

Expense structure

Table XXIII - Expense structure 1993

Name	Categorie	RetD	Coût	Gen
Science Applications	Services	0.31%	92.62%	7.08%
Quantum	Periph	3.88%	90.25%	5.87%
Seagate	Periph	5.47%	87.60%	6.94%
Conner Peripherals	Periph	5.30%	87.49%	7.21%
AST Research	PC	1.86%	86.56%	11.58%
Maxtor	Periph	8.17%	85.91%	5.92%
Compaq	PC	2.56%	85.04%	12.40%
Acer	PC	2.66%	84.47%	12.88%
Dell	PC	1.68%	83.82%	14.50%
Sun	Stations	10.44%	83.82%	5.74%
Micropolis	Periph	8.94%	80.70%	10.36%
Computervision/Prime	Mixed	5.32%	77.40%	17.27%
Exabyte	Periph	10.76%	76.58%	12.66%
Policy Management	Services	4.89%	75.89%	19.22%
Diebold	Periph	6.07%	75.50%	18.43%
Apple	PC	7.77%	73.41%	18.82%
UNISYS	General	7.23%	69.79%	22.98%
Amdahl	Large	14.79%	69.52%	15.69%
National Computer Systems	Services	3.07%	68.76%	28.17%
Hewlett-Packard	General	9.04%	68.09%	22.87%
Groupe Bull	General	7.63%	67.78%	24.59%
QMS	Periph	3.05%	67.37%	29.58%
Storage Technology	Periph	10.99%	67.12%	21.89%
Cray	Large	17.49%	66.63%	15.88%
IBM	General	7.88%	66.28%	25.84%
Ultimate	Software	3.21%	66.03%	30.75%
MAI Systems	Mixed	3.31%	65.85%	30.84%
EMC	Periph	9.79%	65.38%	24.83%
Cisco	Comm	9.45%	63.94%	26.61%
Control Data	General	5.41%	63.06%	31.54%
Cabletron	Comm	12.61%	63.03%	24.35%
Datapoint	Mixed	3.59%	62.80%	33.60%
Digital Equipment	General	9.95%	61.50%	28.55%
Data General	General	8.53%	61.05%	30.41%
ADP	Services	7.16%	60.97%	31.87%
Convex	Large	12.93%	60.24%	26.83%
3COM	Comm	10.58%	59.69%	29.73%
Pyramid	Midrange	11.84%	58.99%	29.18%
Synoptics	Comm	13.34%	58.76%	27.91%
Sequent	Midrange	8.03%	58.09%	33.88%
Digital Comms	Comm	10.31%	58.05%	31.64%

Intergraph	Stations	13.78%	56.86%	29.36%
Silicon Graphics	Stations	13.62%	56.48%	29.90%
Novell	Software	15.46%	55.07%	29.47%
Tandem	Midrange	12.34%	54.30%	33.36%
Stratus	Midrange	23.97%	43.66%	32.37%
Norsk Data	Midrange	0.43%	41.10%	58.47%
Mentor Graphics	Software	20.83%	39.79%	39.38%
Wang	General	8.41%	39.03%	52.56%
Ask Computer	Mixed	10.48%	39.02%	50.50%
Microsoft	Software	17.52%	36.35%	46.13%
Oracle	Software	11.79%	32.59%	55.62%
Adobe	Software	25.30%	30.82%	43.88%
Cadence	Software	18.36%	28.62%	53.02%
Autodesk	Software	15.87%	28.58%	55.55%
Borland/Ashton-Tate	Software	13.63%	27.00%	59.37%
Lotus	Software	15.90%	26.55%	57.56%
Sybase	Software	17.29%	26.28%	56.43%
Legent	Software	14.23%	22.72%	63.05%
Informix	Software	14.74%	16.53%	68.73%

Revenue growth

The yearly revenue growth as a percentage of previous year revenue. Blank when figures are not available

Table XXIV - Revenue growth by category

Cat	Name	86	87	88	89	90	91	92	93
co	3COM	99.4	90.4	57.0	33.6	5.7	-	35.9	38.6
co	Cabletron		>10	>10			58.3	42.2	43.7
co	Cisco		>10	>10			>10	94.1	96.0
co	Motorola	2.2	6.9	1.3	31.1	-7.9	-1.2	0.5	9.3
co	Racal	2.4	-	3.4	4.6	14.3	7.7	-6.3	2.5
co	Synoptics		-	>10			41.1	56.6	81.2
ge	AT&T/NCR	-	14.7	6.8	9.8	-5.9	-4.1	-2.9	0.2
ge	Control Data	-				-	-9.8	-	-
ge	Data General	7.4	1.3	2.0	-2.6	-4.6	-2.1	-9.2	-3.8
ge	Digital Equipment	22.9	51.8	15.4	-	3.9	5.9	-0.5	-3.7
ge	Fujitsu/ICL	64.2	27.8	25.0	-4.7	10.5	8.0	12.4	3.4
ge	Groupe Bull	26.7	21.8	9.0	-2.4	-2.2	-6.7	-3.7	-
ge	Hewlett-Packard	18.5	17.6	23.8	23.1	14.1	10.6	14.9	31.0
ge	Hitachi	63.9	25.1	40.2	12.1	2.7	7.8	10.3	3.1
ge	IBM	6.1	6.7	9.0	-0.1	14.7	-7.1	-1.4	-3.1
ge	NEC	63.9	36.6	29.2	7.5	-	28.5	1.5	9.2
ge	Olivetti	56.4	12.4	20.5	0.6	30.7	-5.7	-4.8	-
ge	Siemens Nixdorf	60.2	27.9	6.1	-2.3	3.6	-6.2	14.6	-

ge	Texas Instruments	-8.4	-2.6	10.8	5.7	21.0	7.1	6.7	-5.0
ge	UNISYS	3.4	-9.0	0.9	11.7	0.1	-	-	-8.4
ge	Wang	9.9	9.0	0.3	-7.6	-	-	-	-
lge	Amdahl	12.1	55.8	19.7	16.6	2.7	-	48.3	-
lge	Convex	>10	73.1	51.7	50.1	32.1	-5.4	17.0	-
lge	Cray	56.9	15.2	10	3.8	2.5	7.2	-7.5	12.2
mi	Norsk Data	58.5	21.3	6.5	-	5.6	-	-	-
mi	Philips	29.1	-	56.2	>10	-6.8	-7.0	-	-
mi	Pyramid	13.6	34.8	45.5	28.5	80	10.5	-	21.1
mi	Sequent	>10	92.5	97.7	91.3	70.9	-	44.1	15.1
mi	Stratus	55.4	47.8	44.0	28.6	18.3	11.1	8.4	10.7
mi	Tandem	34.0	30.3	15.5	17.7	11.7	3.2	6.9	-2.1
mix	Ask Computer	30.2	48.5	51.3	20.5	9.1	9.7	12.3	-7.7
mix	Comp/Prime	11.1	13.3	6.5	-6.5	4.7	-	-	-
mix	Datapoint	-	1.1	4.3	-	-5.2	-3.6	-3.1	-
mix	Dun & Bradstreet	24.3	27.8	4.4	4.9	-	1.9	0.9	-
mix	Finsiel	28.0	15.0	20.6	27.9	32.0	24.5	9.9	-
mix	MAI Systems	10.7	16.1	32.6	-	0.2	-	-	-
mix	Sterling Software								
PC	Acer	26.4	>10	29.5	17.4	19.0	8.0	25.0	58.0
PC	Amstrad	>10	55.1	6.0	2.5	-	-	-	-
PC	Apple	15.8	49.8	45.8	21.2	6.9	13.2	11.2	16.9
PC	AST Research	-1.2	71.6	59.0	4.6	21.7	41.1	37.9	97.8
PC	Atari	81.6	41.0	35.9	8.6	1.0	-	-	-
PC	Commodore	4.9	-2.7	18.3	-	14.9	4.3	-	-
PC	Compaq	24.1	95.8	68.7	39.2	25.1	-9.1	25.3	75.4
PC	Dell	>10	>10	62.1	50.7	40.6	62.9	>10	42.7
PC	Everex	>10	97.5			6.4	15.2	-	
PC	Nihon Unisys	56.3	30.4	66.3	8.4	3.0	27.0	28.5	-
PC	Packard Bell		>10	>10			31.6	16.8	33.2
PC	Seiko Epson	34.3	38.3	18.3	-6.3	5.6	-3.3	32.3	-
PC	Tandy	13.3	10.6	19.0	14.8	-	-4.2	-	-
PC	Tulip			101.				-	8.8
per	Archive						3.8		
per	Canon	91.3	55.2	67.0	29.4	15.3	35.1	22.5	28.0
per	Comparex			21.0	-	19.0	14.0	-	4.7
per	Conner			85.6	81.3	89.8	19.5	62.0	-
per	Diebold	1.3	5.2	2.6	4.0	1.5	7.7	9.8	22.2
per	EMC			-3.0				50.2	>10
per	Evans & Suth	37.3	23.0	-3.6	6.9	13.7	-8.1	2.6	-4.2
per	Exabyte			>10				22.8	8.0

per	INTEL	5.4	28.2	56.0	66.6	50.9	12.2	11.8	13.0
per	Mannesmann	-	43.4	15.9	85.0	-	9.3	-	-10
per	Maxtor		80.2	44.8			7.7	45.4	-
per	Memorex Telex	10.1	20.9	3.2	-1.1	-8.9	-	-9.2	-
per	Micropolis	>10	35.3	22.5	>10	-	-7.8	13.0	-3.5
per	OKI Electric	39.7	20.8	27.6	4.2	17.4	7.1	-2.0	9.3
per	QMS	47.6	48.6	30.1	15.4	24.5	2.5	-6.1	5.4
per	Quantum		53.0	-3.3			49.9	43.1	30.4
per	Seagate	11.6	16.8	21.8	12.1	-4.1	-0.5	15.4	1.1
per	Storage Tech	19.6	12.1	22.4	-	57.3	2.6	-4.0	-7.7
per	Syquest								18.0
per	Tandon	35.7	>10	7.0	22.2	11.6	9.4	-	-
per	Teradata	>10				35.8	24.9		
per	Western Digital			41.0				48.0	15.3
per	Xerox	16.5	15.0	21.9	-	>10	-2.5	7.0	2.0
ser	ADP	17.8	13.0	10.2	4.5	2.8	4.3	14.6	12.7
ser	American Mgmnt	-	28.6	22.4	>10	-	8.9	16.6	9.5
ser	Andersen Cons'g	34.6	31.9	32.4	30.2	18.4	20.3	14.5	9.7
ser	BSO/Origin			22.0				18.0	9.3
ser	Cap Gemini	71.3	>10	38.3	-	34.8	-4.6	64.9	-
ser	Ceridian								-
ser	Comp Sciences	22.1	16.0	10.5	15.1	16.4	15.8	27.2	1.1
ser	Comp Task Gp	23.9	18.6	28.6	6.5	4.7	16.9	6.2	-2.4
ser	CSK Group	60.9	23.5	29.7	9.2	6.4	16.5	1.2	-4.9
ser	EDS	21.6	26.8	33.7	13.3	40.7	24.4	20.3	7.8
ser	First Data		7.9	12.4			21.4	-6.2	25.8
ser	Fiserv			46.2				18.1	57.1
ser	GSI	34.3	23.3	13.9	5.5	35.4	12.6	15.1	-6.0
ser	Hoskyns	33.6	34.4			20.8	-	0.4	
ser	Logica	45.7	36.7	27.2	10.7	15.1	3.6	2.8	-9.3
ser	National Comp		5.9	15.6			-4.1	-0.8	1.8
ser	Policy Mgmt		19.5	20.5			20	19.7	-8.9
ser	Programmator	169.				41.2	10		
ser	Science Apps		15.7	24.7			10.5	17.0	11.1
ser	Sema Group	64.0	30.3	18.7	1.0	42.2	10.2	6.8	17.6
ser	Shared Medical	20.1	4.2	-3.1	3.0	3.4	8.8	7.0	6.8
ser	Sligos	54.6	42.9	45.3	14.8	35.3	7.4	18.2	-2.2
ser	Systematics			20.7				21.4	24.3
ser	TRW	6.7	22.5	0.5	8.0	0	4.5	-0.5	1.9
ser	VOLMAC	81.6	44.7			33.3	-6.4	52.2	
sof	Adobe	>10	>10	>10	45.4	39.0	36.2	15.8	17.9
sof	Autodesk	77.6	51.3	47.9	52.3	33.2	19.8	29.1	13.9
sof	Boole+Babbage								6.2
sof	Borland/AshtTate	>10	37.0	16.0	-	58.8	15.2	-4.5	-0.9

sof	Cadence		16.6	61.3			0.6	10.8	-
sof	Computer Ass	43.7	42.7	34.4	-3.4	20.6	17.6	-3.9	16.0
sof	Corel								56.0
sof	Informix	91.5	89.2	51.1	40.1	0.8	23.1	57.7	24.4
sof	Legent	77.7	>10	32.4	1.2	4.5	15.1	>10	-1.3
sof	Lotus	25.5	39.8	18.4	18.7	23.1	21.1	8.6	9.0
sof	Mentor Graphics	26.9	27.8	35.6	26.3	14.5	-8.1	-	-3.1
sof	Microsoft	60	75.5	57.3	32.6	55.1	54.0	42.9	26.4
sof	Novell	>10	77.6	47.3	15.2	22.7	35.0	39.2	18.8
sof	Oracle	>10	>10	>10	94.8	37.6	2.5	20.7	29.2
sof	SAP			64.6				25.0	25.1
sof	SAS								
sof	Software AG	84.8	34.4	31.8	15.5	29.0	18.7	16.5	2.0
sof	Sybase			>10				64.8	61.3
sof	Ultimate	27.6	24.1	1.6	1.3	-4.7	-1.3	-	-
sta	Intergraph	15.1	5.8	24.8	7.5	21.5	14.4	-1.6	-
sta	Silicon Graphics	88.3	>10	79.4	50.4	40.6	32.3	45.0	32.8
sta	Sun	>10	>10	93.4	41.1	34.0	25.0	10.9	17.3

Profitability by category

Tables XXV to XXXIV give the net after tax profit of each firm for the corresponding year, as a percentage of revenue. Blank when figures are not available.

Table XXV - Generalists

Name	85	86	87	88	89	90	91	92	93	94
AT&T/NCR	4.5				4.9					6.3
Control	-	-			-0.5	0.2	-0.6	-	2.0	1.9
Data	0.2	-2.1	-8.9	-3.3	-9.3	-8.6	6.4	-5.4	-7.8	-3.7
Digital	5.7	10.	12.	7.6	6.8	-0.7	-6.1	-	-0.5	-
Fujitsu/ICL	2.4	2.3	2.9	3.4	2.5	2.5	1.9	0.1	-0.4	
Groupe Bull	0.7	1.1	0.9	0.8	-0.6	-	-9.9	-	-	2.2
HP	6.9	6.9	7.3	7.5	6.4	5.7	5.7	4.9	6.0	6.4
IBM	13.	9.2	9.5	9.7	6.0	8.7	-4.4	-7.7	-	4.7
Olivetti	8.2	7.7	5.5	4.2	2.2	0.7	-5.3	-8.1	-5.4	
UNISYS	5.6	1.2	5.5	6.6	-6.3	-4.3	-	4.3	7.3	1.4
Wang	-2.6	-3.2	3.2	1.3	-	-	-	-	38.	

Table XXVI - Large systems

Name	85	86	87	88	89	90	91	92	93	94
Amdahl	3.3	4.3	9.7	12.	7.3	8.5	0.6	-0.3	-	4.6
Convex	-	10	12.	5.8	7.4	8.8	-3.5	1.2	-	
Cray	19.	20.	21.	20.	11.	14.	13.	-1.9	6.8	6.1

Table XXVII - Midrange systems

Name	85	86	87	88	89	90	91	92	93	94
Norsk Data	16.	15.	7.0	-	-	-7.1	-	-	7.0	
Pyramid	11.	-8.1	31.	10.	8.2	9.2	-5.0	-	3.7	
Sequent	ns	-4.5	10.	8.5	11.	7.6	-	4.7	-2.1	7.3
Stratus	10.	10.	10.	11.	10.	9.2	11.	11.	9.5	10.6
Tandem	5.1	8.4	8.8	7.2	7.0	5.2	-3.4	3.4	-	8.1

Table XXVIII - PC

Name	85	86	87	88	89	90	91	92	93	94
Acer	6.9	12.	6.3	5.1	-0.3	0.3	-2.3	0.2	2.2	6.4
Apple	4.1	7.7	9.2	9.5	8.2	8.7	5.0	7.3	-0.4	4.8
AST	17.	10.	2.9	0.9	2.4	9.0	8.5	5.1	-1.9	-1.5
Atari	-				1.0					
Commodor	-	-1.2	4.5	7.2	1.0	4.0	4.8	-	-	
Compaq	5.3	6.9	11.	12.	11.	12.	4.0	5.2	6.4	8.0
Dell	2.4	3.2	5.9	5.6	1.3	5.0	5.7	5.0	-1.4	4.3
Everex	5.4	5.6	4.9		5.6	-0.2	-6.4	-		
Gateway									5.8	3.6
Nihon	2.0	1.8	1.8	1.7	1.7	1.7	0.6	1.5	0.7	
Packard		2.0				1.4	0			

| Tulip | | | 9.2 | 7.9 | | | 4.0 | -4.5 | 1.3 | |

Table XXIX - Stations

Name	85	86	87	88	89	90	91	92	93	94
Intergraph	12.	11.	10.	11.	9.2	6.0	5.9	0.7	-	-0.7
Silic Graph	-4.8	9.6	1.1	3.2	5.9	8.3	5.7	-7.5	9.7	9.4
Sun	5.4	7.1	6.4	6.1	1.8	5.5	5.8	3.3	4.2	4.8

Table XXX - Peripherals

Name	85	86	87	88	89	90	91	92	93	94
Archive		2.1				2.6	-			
Comparex			5.0	5.0	3.3	5.1	3.0	1.9	0.9	3.5
Conner			9.2	8.0	5.9	9.7	5.8	6.1	-	4.6
Diebold	7.4	8.4	8.1	8.0	7.7	5.7	7.1	4.3	7.8	8.4
EMC			22.	-6.3			5.6	8.2	16.	18.2
Evans+Sut	7.8	10	10.	1.5	0.7	10.	7.4	5.1	2.9	
Exabyte			ns	8.7			13.	7.1	5.2	8.4
Iomega								3.4		
Maxtor		13.	3.5	-		0.3	-6.8	6.4	-	-9.9
Memorex	8.3	3.2	2.3	-3.3	-3.2	-3.7	-	11.	-	23.4
Micropolis	3.0	8.6	9.4	-5.5	-5.5	2.1	1.2	4.9	-5.2	
QMS	7.6	7.0	2.9	-1.6	4.8	5.3	4.9	-0.7	-1.8	1.0
Quantum		10.	4.5	-1.4		9.3	4.6	5.5	-0.5	4.0
Seagate	2.5	12.	10.	-0.4	5.8	3.4	2.7	7.2	4.9	6.4
Storage	-8.9	4.6	-	4.3	4.9	6.0	5.9	1.0	-5.5	2.6
Syquest								7.8	7.4	
Tandon	-1.4	-2.0	5.9		-1.1	6.1	-	-		
Teradata	ns	-2.5			10.	2.8	3.3			
West Digital			8.6	5.0			-	-0.2	-2.3	7.5

Table XXXI - Communications

Name	85	86	87	88	89	90	91	92	93	94
3COM	10	10.	9.1	9.5	6.1	5.5	-8.9	2.4	10.	8.2
Cabletron		7.4	16.	21.		20.	19.	23.	19.	20
Cisco		0	5.7	4.0		23.	24.	25.	26.	21.7
Dig Comms				11.					-	
Synoptics		-0.8	-4.9	14.		16.	10.	10.	10.	

Table XXXII - Software

Name	85	86	87	88	89	90	91	92	93	94
Adobe	10.	22.	22.	25.	27.	23.	22.	16.	18.	1.1
Autodesk	22.	22.	25.	27.	26.	23.	20.	11.	15.	1.7
Boole+Bab								6.5	7.4	
Borland/As	13.	12.	12.	12.	-	0.4	-	-	-3.2	-4.8
Cadence		-8.6	-	9.7		-1.6	-5.5	12.	-1.8	8.6
Comp Ass	10.	6.5	6.1	10.	12.	9.4	8.4	11.	16.	16.6
Corel								12.	19.	19.8

	85	86	87	88	89	90	91	92	93	94
Informix	23.	12.	13.	1.4	4.4	-	7.0	16.	15.	14.1
Legent	18.	19.	16.	16.	14.	19.	17.	7.7	13.	10.8
Lotus	16.	17.	18.	12.	12.	3.4	5.2	8.9	5.7	-2.1
Mentor	5.9	6.3	9.2	12.	11.	5.4	-	-	-9.4	8.0
Microsoft	19.	22.	20.	21.	21.	26.	25.	25.	25.	24.7
Novell	11.	11.	10.	10.	12.	20.	25.	27.	-2.8	10.4
Oracle	8.9	9.4	12.	14.	12.	5.4	0.1	3.5	12.	14.3
SAP			18.	18.			17.	15.	13.	15.4
Software	19.	15.	7.9		3.7	0.6		1.1		
Sybase			ns	0.4			6.2	9.0	10.	10.8
Ultimate	10.	8.6	8.7	-8.1	1.1	-	-	-20	-2.8	

Table XXXIII - Services

Name	85	86	87	88	89	90	91	92	93	94
ADP	8.6	8.9	10.	11.	11.	12.	13.	13.	13.	
Am Mgmt		3.8	4.4	2.5		4.6	4.6	5.7	4.7	5.0
BSO/Origin			8.1	8.9			2.6	2.5	-1.4	
Cap Gemini	5.9	6.6	6.7	6.9	7.4	8.2	8.0	-0.9	-4.6	-
Comp Sc	2.8	3.1	3.6	3.9	3.8	4.0	3.4	3.1	3.6	0
Comp Task	3.5	3.6	3.0	2.9	-3.3	3.0	0.3	1.9	-9.4	1.7
CSK Group	7.0	6.3	6.0	5.7	5.9	5.9	5.7	2.5	2.7	
EDS	5.5	5.9	7.4	7.9	8.0	8.9	7.6	7.8	8.5	8.2
First Data		13.	15.	13.		12.	11.	14.	11.	
Fiserv			8.4	7.4			6.5	6.9	5.9	
GSI	1.2	1.0	2.1	4.0	4.5	4.5	4.4	3.3	1.7	
Hoskyns	4.1	4.1	5.2		5.0	4.4	4.8	2.8		
Logica	4.0	5.4	6.4	7.1	5.9	1.7	-3.3	2.5	2.3	
Nat Comp		8.0	8.6	6.4		4.1	5.1	5.5	-0.8	3.9
Policy		9.2	9.5	9.5		10.	11.	11.	-	
Progr'tor	1.9	1.6			0.5	-6.2	-8.9			
Sci Apps		2.7	2.6	3.0		2.9	2.6	2.5	2.5	
Sema	2.9	3.4	5.9	2.8	3.5	2.8	2.6	7.0	4.4	5.4
Shared	13.	8.5	11.	7.8	5.9	5.6	5.8	6.0	6.2	
Sligos	2.2	2.7	5.2	4.8	5.2	9.6	5.3	4.7	4.5	
VOLMAC	20.	21.	21.		18.	13.	12.	8.7		

Table XXXIV - Mixed firms

Name	85	86	87	88	89	90	91	92	93	94
Ask	8.1	7.6	6.5	7.5	3.4	1.3	-	1.4	-4.0	
Comp'visio	-2.4	3.1	5.5	1.2	-	-8.5	-	-	-	1.7
Datapoint	-	-	4.8	1.9	-	-	3.5	-2.9	-8.6	
Finsiel		2.0	3.2	3.2		2.5	2.2	2.5	3.4	3.5
MAI	-0.8	3.6	7.4	5.5	-	-	-	ns	24.	
Sterling									13.	12.3
Wang										1.7

Bibliography

BAIN J. .S — *Industrial Organizations,* Wiley (1959)

DE BANDT J. — *Les Services,* Economica (1991)

BASHE C., JOHNSON L., PALMER J., PUGH E. — *IBM's Early Computers,* The MIT Press (1986)

BAUMOL W.J., PANZAR J.C., WILLIG R.D. — *Contestable Markets and the Theory of Industry Structure,* Harcourt Brace Jovanovitch (1982)

BELL D. — *The Coming of Post-Industrial Society,* Basic Books (1973)

BIENAYMÉ A. — *Le capitalisme adulte,* Presses Universitaires de France (1992)

BROCK G.W. — *The US Computer Industry,* Ballenger (1975)

CHAMBERLIN E.H. — *The Theory of Monopolistic Competition,* Harvard University Press (1933)

CHANDLER A.D. — *Strategy and Structure - Chapters in the History of the Industrial Enterprise,* MIT Press (1962, 1989)

CYERT R.M., MARCH J.G. — *A Behavioral Theory of the Firm,* Prentice Hall (1963)

DELAMARTER R.T. — *Big Blue, IBM's use and abuse of power,* Donald Mead (1986)

DESAINTQUENTIN J.M., SAUTEUR B. — *L'Informatique éclatée,* Masson (1991)

DESAINTQUENTIN J.M., SAUTEUR B. — *Une Nouvelle Donne pour l'Informatique,* Editions Synthèse Informatique (1993)

FISHER, MANCKE, MCKIE— *IBM and the Data Processing Industry - An Economic History,* Praeger (1983)

FISHER F.M., MCGOWAN J.J., GREENWOOD J.E.— *Folded, Spindled and Mutilated - Economic Analysis of US vs IBM,* MIT Press (1983)

GERSHUNY J. — *After Industrial Society? The Emerging Self-Service Economies,* Oxford University Press (1978)

HAX A.C., MAJLUF N.S. — *Strategic Management, An Integrative Perspective,* Prentice hall (1984)

KOTLER P. — *Principles of Marketing,* Prentice Hall (1980)

LAWRENCE P.R., LORSCH J.W. — *Organization and Environment,* Harvard School Business Press (1986)

MCKINSEY & COMPANY, INC — *Report on the Computer Industry,* (1991, 1992, 1993 et 1994)

MARCH, SIMON — *Organizations,* Wiley (1958)

MOREAU R. — *Ainsi naquit l'informatique,* Dunod (1981)

PETERS T.J., WATERMAN R.H — *In Search of Excellence,* Harper & Row (1982)

PORTER M.E. — *Competitive Strategy,* The Free Press (1980)

PORTER M.E. — *The Competitive Advantage,* The Free Press (1985)

PUGH E., JOHNSON L., PALMER J. — *IBM's 360 and Early 370 Systems,* The MIT Press (1991)

RAPPAPORT A. — *Creating Shareholder Value,* The Free Press (1986)

RAINELLI M. — *Economie Industrielle,* Dalloz (1993)

SAMUELSON P.A. — *Economics,* McGraw Hill (1948 etc...)

SCHERER F.M. — *Industrial Market Structure and Economic Performance,* Rand McNally (1980)

SCHERER F. M. ET AL — *The Economics of Multi-Plant Operation, an international comparison study,* Harvard University Press (1975)

SCHUMPETER J. — *Business Cycles,* McGraw-Hill (1939)

SCHUMPETER J. — *The Theory of economic development,* Oxford University Press (1934)

SIMON H. A.— *Behavioral Economics and Business Organizations,* 1982)

SIMON H.A. — *Administrative Behaviour,* The Free Press (1945,1976)

STIGLER — *The Organization of Industry,* Richard Irwin (1968)

WILLIAMSON O.E. — *The Economics of Discretionary Behavior,* Prentice Hall (1964)

WILLIAMSON O. E. — *Markets and Hierarchies,* The Free Press (1975) author's email : gdrean@sfr.fr

www.ingramcontent.com/pod-product-compliance
Lightning Source LLC
Chambersburg PA
CBHW051203200326
41519CB00025B/6989